Developing e-Commerce Sites

An Integrated Approach

Developing e-Commerce Sites
An Integrated Approach

Vivek Sharma
Rajiv Sharma

ADDISON-WESLEY

Boston • San Francisco • New York • Toronto • Montreal
London • Munich • Paris • Madrid
Capetown • Sydney • Tokyo • Singapore • Mexico City

The publisher offers discounts on this book when ordered in quantity for special sales. For more information, please contact:

Pearson Education Corporate Sales Division
One Lake Street
Upper Saddle River, NJ 07458
(800) 382-3419
corpsales@pearsontechgroup.com

Visit us on the Web at www.awl.com/cseng/

Library of Congress Cataloging-in-Publication Data

Sharma, Vivek.
    Developing e-commerce sites : an integrated approach / Vivek Sharma, Rajiv Sharma.
       p. cm.
    Includes bibliographical references amd index.
    ISBN 0-201-65764-3
    1. Electronic commerce.   2. Web site development.   I. Sharma, Rajiv.   II. Title.

HF5429.12.S53 2000
658.8'4—dc21

00-035573

Text printed on recycled paper
1 2 3 4 5 6 7 8 9—CRS—03 02 01 00
First printing, June 2000

To my lovely wife, Anu, without whose cooperation
this book wouldn't be possible

—V.S.

Contents

Introduction

I still remember those days in school when we spent endless hours writing a small program in C that would allow two computers to communicate. There is no doubt that C is an excellent and very flexible language. However, in today's world of breakneck speed, when everything needs to be developed by "next Tuesday," doing things in C alone can be a bit challenging. It's the day and age of specialized languages and technologies. In this book we discuss a number of languages specifically geared for Web development. And we discuss these within an even more focused environment—that of developing tools that can help in conducting commerce over the Internet.

The book not only introduces you to different languages that can be used for developing effective e-commerce applications, it also presents a large number of practical examples. In addition it deals with issues such as performance and security, which are of importance to any e-commerce site. The last section of the book presents a complete example: five systems that can be leveraged by any e-commerce site.

Rationale

There are a number of books on the market that talk about individual technologies for Web development. While these books excel in the topics they're dealing with, practical Web development requires the use of more than one language and technology. A book on databases would teach you SQL and everything related to databases. Another book would make you a master of Java. However, if you're asked to develop e-commerce systems for a company, you would need to know not only these two but a lot more, such as Javascript, JDBC, Servlets, Web servers, etc. More important, you would need to understand which language and technology are best suited for what and how they can be integrated.

This book is an attempt to fill that void. Different pieces required to solve the puzzle are presented in a logical and easy-to-follow manner. Every chapter builds on knowledge gained in previous chapters. Carefully crafted examples show you how to develop practical solutions using a combination of appropriate technologies. In short, the book was written to get you up to speed by next Tuesday, if not Monday!

Target Audience

The primary target audience for this book is technical people who want learn how to develop applications for e-commerce. These include both technical developers who want to learn the technologies and technical managers who want to see how developers can apply them.

Even though the book uses e-commerce as a backdrop, it covers everything required for building any kind of Internet application. It is thus intended to be useful even for technical people interested in generic Web development.

Here are some categories of people who can benefit from this book:

1. Software professionals who want to design and develop e-commerce applications.
2. Semitechnical managers and business school students who want to understand what e-commerce systems are, what technologies they require, and how they can be developed and deployed.
3. Consultants, developers, and computer science students who just want to learn different Web technologies and understand how they can be integrated to build powerfult Internet applications.

Highlights of the Book

The book has a number of useful features:

- It brings readers up to speed on different technologies used for building powerful Web-based systems.
- It contains a large number of practical examples.
- It teaches gradually and progressively how to build a sophisticated e-commerce system.
- It provides Java, Javascript, JDBC, Servlet, and SQL code segments that can be used to save product development time.
- It gives the "inside" view of an e-commerce system so that users have a better understanding of the whole concept.
- It provides an introduction to XML and how it can be used in e-commerce.

Organization

The book comprises four parts, followed by two appendices:

Part I contains the introductory chapter, which outlines everything that follows. This chapter also shows you how you can get your computer on the Internet and establish a Web presence. Terms applicable to the Internet are described briefly.

Part II begins with a chapter on HTML. Other chapters in this section discuss Java, Servlets, Javascript, SQL, JDBC, and XML. Everything is taught by example. All chapters except the HTML chapter end with a section called Practical Examples where we present a number of programs that solve some complex, practical problems. By making use of knowledge from previous chapters, these examples also illustrate an integration of different languages.

Part III takes a look at some practical considerations for anyone planning on building Web systems and/or e-commerce systems. Chapter 8, "Credit Card Verification," discusses several ways in which you can start accepting credit cards over the Net. Chapter 9, "Security and Performance," talks about steps you can take to make your site faster and more secure.

Part IV which completes the book, contains a complete e-commerce solution. It begins with Chapter 10, "System Design," which introduces five systems developed in the following chapters using technologies covered in Parts II and III. This chapter also presents the design of a database that is used by the e-commerce systems, which should work as a good tutorial for designing a normalized database. Chapter 11, "Functionality," talks about the user interface of the systems. Chapter 12, "Utilities," presents a number of utility classes that can be leveraged by any Web application. The remaining five chapters in Part IV discuss the actual implementation of the five systems.

Appendix A contains instructions for installing and configuring different pieces of required software such as JDBC drivers, Apache Web server, databases, etc.

Appendix B provides a complete listing of code for the systems designed in Part IV.

Acknowledgments

I would like to thank the excellent team at Addison-Wesley that helped shape this book in its current form. In particular, Mary O'Brien and Mariann Kourafas provided enormous guidance and help all along the way.

I would also like to thank all the reviewers, whose constructive comments were immensely helpful.

I am grateful to my parents for making sure I went to engineering school.

And last, but not least, thanks to my lovely wife, Anu, for bearing with me during the countless hours I spent on the computer writing this book.

Part I

Chapter 1

The Basics of Internet Technology

I've been conducting electronic commerce for years—
I sell Casios on the streets of New York!

A few years ago the only way of trading stocks was to go through a broker. To buy this book you would have had to go to a bookstore. Purchasing clothes would have meant a trip to the mall. Not anymore! Today businesses are coming to your doorstep. A number of companies have successfully managed to give a new outlet to traditional businesses—an electronic outlet. It's the day and age of electronic commerce. Thanks to dot-coms like Amazon.com and etrade.com, you can now order books and trade stocks while sitting at your computer.

There are several reasons businesses are jumping on the Internet bandwagon. An Internet store is open twenty-four hours a day, is available to customers worldwide, and can provide personalized service to customers.

But to achieve all this, complex software systems are required. This book teaches a number of languages and technologies that can be used for building e-commerce systems. It discusses practical aspects of these technologies and shows how they can be integrated to build complete systems. Each language and technology is described in its own separate chapter. A good number of examples, ranging from easy to complex, have been presented to give you an understanding of different features that can be leveraged.

Languages covered include HTML, Java, Javascript, Jdbc, SQL, and XML. A number of technologies, including databases, Web servers, and Servlets, are discussed in detail.

In addition to discussing topics of importance to any critical business application, such as performance issues and credit card verification, we also address technologies required for making sites secure. Topics discussed here include SSL and the use of Java for message digests and signing.

The book also shows how a company can get its computers on the Internet and start running Web applications.

Skill Level Required

While we do not expect you to know a whole lot about the Internet and related technologies, we do assume that you've used some Web browser like Netscape or Internet Explorer. If that's not the case, put this book away and get yourself an Internet connection—the world has come a long way since you went into the bomb shelter!

The book also assumes some programming knowledge. You will find it much easier to follow this book if you are familiar with a high-level language like C, C++, or Java.

As noted earlier, the book is divided into four parts. This first part, which contains only one chapter, introduces you to electronic commerce and some terms and concepts related to the Internet. It also gives a brief introduction to everything that is covered in the following sections.

Part II discusses six languages and technologies, with one chapter dedicated to each. Part III covers different methods of conducting credit card verification and also examines security and performance issues.

Part IV, the final part, sets out a complete example built using the technologies covered in Part II, presenting actual code and design principles. You can use the code directly or modify it according to your needs. You can also use the basic principles discussed to build more complex systems.

Let's take a quick tour of technologies, terms, and concepts that are particularly relevant to the Internet, especially for those wishing to develop applications for the Web. The "tour" consists of a few paragraphs about each of the technologies and how they relate to one another. It should prepare you for the following chapters, where we cover some of these issues in more detail.

Web Sites and Browsers

A Web site is an information portal that has been exposed to the whole world or to a selected set of people. Web sites can contain any kind of information—data sheets of a company, the resume of an individual, pictures of Yosemite National Park, video clips of *Star Wars,* and so on. The idea is to make information readily and easily available to customers or other people interested in the data.

These days it is almost impossible not to be familiar with the terms *browser, Netscape Navigator,* and *Internet Explorer.* These client applications have made the Internet a much more user-friendly place. Browsers allow you to surf the Internet and look at Web sites. Graphical browsers like those from Netscape and from Microsoft allow you to see and hear complex Web sites that contain dynamic information, sound, and video.

Web Pages and HTML

A Web site begins with a Web page. A Web page is a representation of the information that you want to put on your site; this representation is such that it is understood by browsers. Since there can be several different browsers running on several different systems with different operating systems, it doesn't make sense to put the relevant data in a platform-specific format. Instead, the data is written in a universal, ASCII text format called HTML (*Hyper-Text Markup Language*). This language allows you to format your data so that it can be visually appealing when viewed through a browser.

HTML is a pretty straightforward language with a specific set of tags, which can be used to specify how different elements in a Web page should look. Thus, if you want a section to appear in boldface type, you begin that section with a bold tag, <B>. If you want your text centered, you put the <CENTER> and </CENTER> tags around it. Similarly, HTML allows you to insert images and sound in Web pages. When a browser reads the web page, it looks for these tags before displaying the page. Then, depending on the tags it encounters, the browser displays the document according to the tags' instructions. Any text in the document between the <B> and the </B> tags will thus be displayed in bold in the browser window.

HTML files end with the extension ".html" or ".htm." Following is an HTML file that contains tags for making text bold, italic, and underlined.

Each HTML page starts with an <HTML> tag and ends with a </HTML> tag. The <BODY> portion is for the main body of the page goes. The tags are discussed in more detail in Chapter 2.

```
<HTML>
  <HEAD></HEAD>
   <BODY>
      <B>Bold Text</B>
      <I>Italicized Text</I>
      <U>Underlined Text
   </BODY>
</HTML>
```

If you view this file through a browser, the words "bold text" will appear in boldface, "italicized text" will be in italics, and "underlined text" will be underlined.

Figure 1.1 shows an image of a document that does not have HTML tags, viewed through a browser, as an example of the difference these tags make.

With some HTML tags added to it, the same document looks like Figure 1.2.

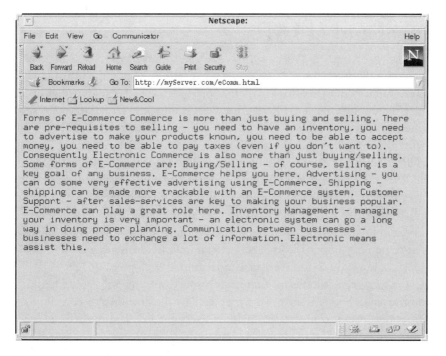

Figure 1.1

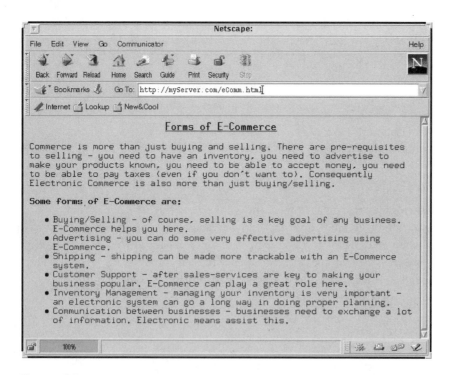

Figure 1.2

Web Servers and HTTP

But then how does a Web page become "available" to a browser? To make your Web site and its pages available to other people on the Internet, you first need to get your site on the Internet. You can get a location on the Internet by either signing up with an Internet Service Provider (ISP) or hooking up your machine directly to the Net. Look at the last section of this chapter for more details.

ISPs run software called a Web server on their machines If you have your own machine, you will have to install and start a Web server on your machine.

This software listens for "requests" coming from clients (like browsers). The "requests" can be of the form "I want to see a Web page on this machine whose name is products.html." The Web server interprets this request and takes appropriate action. In the case a Web page has been requested, it reads the corresponding HTML file and sends the contents back to the client who originated the request.

Web servers listen for requests coming from clients on a particular port of a machine. Most Web servers are capable of handling several simultaneous requests, thus allowing more than one user to connect to one Web site simultaneously.

Web servers and clients need a protocol in order to talk to each other. The protocol in use is commonly known as HTTP (*Hyper-Text Transfer Protocol*). This protocol determines the "handshake" between the client and the server. So when a client requests a Web page, it sends the request in an HTTP-compliant format. The Web server, also HTTP-compliant, understands this and sends the data back, transmitting an HTTP-compliant signal to the browser at the same time so that the browser knows what kind of data is coming back, its length, and possibly other information.

URLs

URL (*Uniform Resource Locator*) is the address of a file on the Internet. This file can be of any type supported by HTTP—a Web page, an image file, a sound file, and so on. Here's an example of a URL:

http://www.javasoft.com

This is what you would type in your browser in order to access the main page of Javasoft's Web site. A URL has a specific format. It identifies the machine from which you're requesting something, the port on which the Web server on that machine is listening, and the file that you are interested in. There are defaults for some of these. Here's the format of an HTTP-compliant URL:

http://<machine>:<port>/<file>

The default port, 80, is the port at which most people run their Web servers. So if you don't specify a port, the browser will try to make a connection to port 80 on the machine you specified. The <file> also has a default; this is index.html. If the Web server finds that a <file> is missing in the URL request, it returns a file called index.html, which lies in the document root directory.

FORMs and CGI

A Web site would be very dull if it contained just static text and images. HTML allows you to give the look and feel of an application to your Web page. Using certain tags in HTML you can create the appearance of a paper form containing text fields, buttons, checkboxes, and more.

The <FORM> tag of HTML allows you to do this. But, you may ask, what's the use of having a Web page that *looks* like an application if it can't behave like one? The answer is that development of a Web site doesn't stop at HTML. Whereas HTML is good for display purposes, it does not provide application logic. This gap can be filled by an application written in a language like C or the Unix-Shell or a DOS batch script. The <FORM> tag of HTML allows you to specify an application that a user can execute. A <FORM> can contain a special button called the Submit button; if a user viewing the FORM presses this button, the application associated with it is executed.

This execution is achieved by the Common Gateway Interface (CGI), which is the standard way for the Web server to pass a request from a browser to an application and send the resulting data from the application back to the client. CGI is part of the HTTP protocol.

Thus, if your Web page contains a form and the user presses the Submit button, the application specified in the FORM is executed. All the data in the FORM is sent to the application, which can then process it. The application can then send data back to your browser. This data may be in the form of an HTML page displayed by the browser.

Here's an example of an HTML page containing a FORM:

```
<HTML>
  <HEAD></HEAD>
  <BODY>
     Please enter your information and press the Go button.
     This will execute the application myApplication.exe.
      <FORM ACTION='/cgi-bin/myApplication.exe'>
             First Name: <INPUT TYPE='text' NAME='first' VALUE=' '>
             Last Name: <INPUT TYPE='text' NAME='last' VALUE=' '>
             Address: <INPUT TYPE='text' NAME='address' VALUE=' '>
             Phone: <INPUT TYPE='text' NAME='phone' VALUE=' '>
             Fax: <INPUT TYPE='text' NAME='fax' VALUE=' '>
             <INPUT TYPE='submit' NAME='submit' VALUE='Go'>
      </FORM>
  </BODY>
</HTML>
```

Figure 1.3 shows how this page looks in a browser.

The HTML page contains a FORM, whose "ACTION" is "/cgi-bin/myApplication.exe."

ACTION is an attribute of the <FORM> tags specifying the backend application that should be invoked. The FORM also contains a submit button (<INPUT TYPE='submit'), whose name is "Go." When the Go button is pressed, a request will be sent from the browser to the server on which the application "myApplication.exe" resides. This request causes the application to be executed and the results to be sent back to the browser.

We've added text fields to the form in which a user can type something. Each text field is added as a result of a tag that looks like <INPUT TYPE='text' . . . Further, each text field has been given a name. For instance, the text field in which you're supposed to enter "First Name" has been named as "first" and its value has been initialized to a blank.

When the Go button is pressed, the values of these variables are sent to the application so that it can find out what information the user entered and process it accordingly. The application may do anything that a regular executable does. At the end it is expected to send a result back to the browser. This result could be another HTML page.

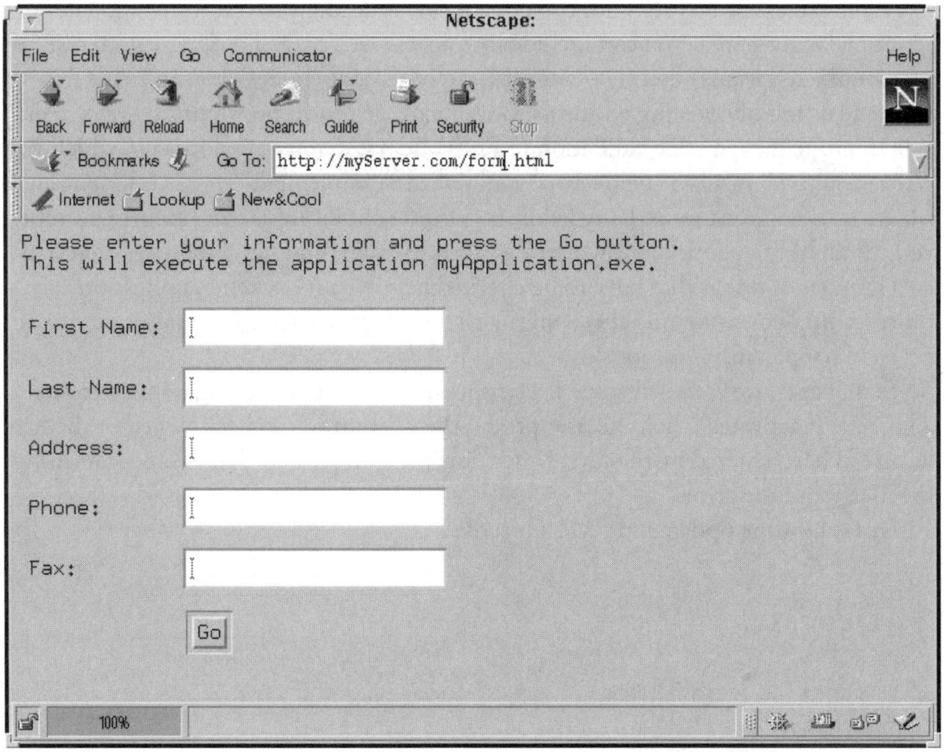

Figure 1.3

In the ACTION attribute earlier, instead of just writing the name of the backend application, we pre-pended "/cgi-bin/." The reason for this is that when a request is sent, the Web server has to be able to distinguish whether the request is for an HTML page or for an application, as they are treated differently. In the Web server configuration you can specify that if the request contains a specific keyword (like "/cgi-bin/"), it means that the request is for a CGI. Appendix A provides more details on Web server configurations.

Javascript

In the early days of the Web, having a static HTML page containing formatted text and images was considered the coolest thing in the world. However, by nature humans are insatiable. Dynamism in Web pages started becoming a necessity. You can achieve some amount of dynamism with a CGI backend; if the user presses a button, you can generate a new page through your CGI program. However, this step involves a time lag, as a request needs to be sent to the server, an application needs to be executed, and the results need to be interpreted by the browser before they are displayed.

This problem gave birth to client-side languages, that is, scripts or executables that could be part of the HTML page and could modify the page based on certain events like mouse clicks or text selections. Netscape introduced Javascript—a client-side scripting language that you can include in your HTML page. The language allows you to manipulate various objects in your HTML page. It also allows you to create new windows or modify existing windows. But one of the most important uses of a client-side language is client-side validation of FORM data. If you have a form in which you want users to fill in all the fields, you would need to implement error checking to make sure that they haven't missed any fields. In a form containing a social security number, you would like to check that the user has filled in only numerics. Likewise, there can be a number of things that have to be checked before your backend application can proceed. Implementing this check on the client side helps detection and reporting of errors to happen instantaneously.

To illustrate, we've added some Javascript code to the HTML page shown earlier. This code is activated when the user presses the Go button. It checks whether the first name has been entered by the user. If not, it throws up an alert dialog box, informing the user about the error.

This is how the updated HTML file looks:

```
<HTML>
    <HEAD></HEAD>
    <SCRIPT>
        function verify(frm)
        {
            if(frm.first.value.length == 0)
            {
```

```
                alert('First name not specified');
                return false;
            }
            return true;
        }
    </SCRIPT>
    <BODY>
        Please enter your information and press the Go button.
        This will execute the
        application myApplication.exe.
         <FORM ACTION='/cgi-bin/myApplication.exe'
                             onSubmit='return verify()'>
                First Name: <INPUT TYPE='text' NAME='first' VALUE=' '>
                Last Name: <INPUT TYPE='text' NAME='last' VALUE=' '>
                Address: <INPUT TYPE='text' NAME='address' VALUE=' '>
                Phone: <INPUT TYPE='text' NAME='phone' VALUE=' '>
                Fax: <INPUT TYPE='text' NAME='fax' VALUE=' '>
                <INPUT TYPE='submit' NAME='submit' VALUE='Go'>
        </FORM>
    </BODY>
</HTML>
```

In this form, if the user presses the Go button without entering something in the First Name field, an error box is thrown up. This looks like Figure 1.4.

So how does this all work? If you look at the FORM tag, we've added:

onSubmit='return verify(this).'

Here, "onSubmit" is a Javascript keyword and **verify()** is a Javascript function that we have written. Most Javascript operations are carried out as a result of some event that occurs in the Web page. There can be several different kinds of events, for example, a mouse click, a keyboard stroke, or the loading of an HTML page in the browser. Although there is a default behavior associated with each event, you can override these defaults with your own functions. To do so, you must use Javascript reserved words that denote these events to specify what function should be invoked when the event occurs. Thus, "onSubmit" is the keyword for the submit event (that is, when the Submit button is pressed). "onSubmit = 'return verify()'" means that when the Submit button is pressed, the function **verify()** should be invoked. We're passing a "this" as an argument to this function. "this" is a reserved word and in the context of "onSubmit" it refers to the current FORM.

Actual Javascript functions are defined within a <SCRIPT> and </SCRIPT> tag in an HTML file. We have defined the function **verify()**. In this function we're checking the value of the FORM element "first." If its length is 0, the user has not entered anything in this field. Hence, we're using a Javascript global function called **alert()**, which throws an alert dialog box. By returning a false "here," we're saying that normal

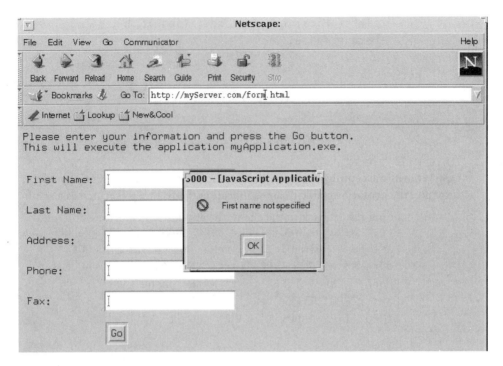

Figure 1.4

processing of the Submit button should not be carried out—in other words, if this error occurs, don't invoke the backend application.

Cookies

In an application running on your system, if you move from one screen to another, state is automatically maintained as all the screens belong to that application. So if the application asked for your name in the first screen, it need not ask for the same information in a subsequent screen. However, when you connect to the different pages of a Web site, each request is treated as separate. Any information gathered in one page is not available by default in subsequent requests. This is a very serious drawback.

Fortunately, there is a way out: cookies. Cookies are pieces of data that are stored on the client side and can be sent to servers along with page requests. Cookies are created by server-side or client-side code. Normally, personalization data or any other data that the site refers to frequently is stored in a cookie. Once a cookie has been created, it resides on the client machine.

Cookies are associated with the servers from which they originated. Besides storing the cookie data, they also store information about the server from which the particular cookie came. When the client connects to the same server again, all cookies that originated from that server are sent back along with the new request.

This is how a cookie exchange typically takes place:

The client (browser), while making a request to a Web site, checks whether it has a cookie that is applicable to the server to which the request is being sent. If so, the cookie is sent along with the request. If not, only the request for the page is sent.

While receiving results from the server, the client checks whether a cookie has been sent as part of the result. If so, the cookie is stored for future use.

The server, while accepting a request, checks whether the client has sent a cookie. If so, it makes the cookie available to any application that is being executed as a result.

Also, while sending results back to the client, the application can create and send a new cookie (or modify an existing one) along with other results, which will then be stored on the client.

Client-side code can also set and read cookies. Actual code for setting and getting cookies is discussed in detail in Chapters 4 and 5.

Let us look at an example where cookies can be very useful. If you create your Web site in such a way that there is a section in which users can type in personal information in a FORM (name, city, etc.), when a user has entered this information, you can use Javascript to set a cookie that contains these values. The next time the user tries to access your site, you can read the name and city from the cookie. Then you can write a message like "Welcome back John Doe." You can apply more complex logic if you want; for example, you can have logic that says

if(city == 'San Francisco')

write ('There is a conference coming up in San Francisco that you may want to attend');

In this way you can, with very little effort, achieve personalization for all users of your Web site.

Java and Servlets

Java is a language developed by Sun Microsystems to make it easier to write applications for the Internet. It is platform independent and quite straightforward and easy to learn, but it allows you to write very complex applications. All the backend code in this book is written in Java.

In the discussion of CGI earlier, we mentioned that CGI is a way of executing backend applications. Even though you can execute Java applications using CGI, there are performance downsides. One specific disadvantage is that because Java is an interpreted language, every time a Java application is to be executed, a Java interpreter needs to be spawned. If a large number of users are trying to execute this CGI at the same time, this will have a big impact on performance.

A solution to this problem comes in the form of Servlets. These are Java applications that are written in accordance with the Servlet API from Javasoft. The applications run in the context of a Servlet engine that provides optimizations. The Servlet engine can be integrated with your Web server. The backend applications in this book are mostly written as servlets.

Databases

Almost every application needs to manipulate data. Though data can be stored in flat files, this method is not recommended especially if you have a lot of data. It is preferable to use a Database Management System (DBMS) specifically geared toward managing complex data.

Databases facilitate addition, modification, and retrieval of data. A database is essentially a collection of spreadsheets, in which data is stored in rows and columns. Each row represents information for one entity. The row itself is divided into columns. Each column of a row contains some specific data about that entity. Thus, in an employee database, there would be a row for each employee. The row for each employee would contain name, date of hire, social security number, salary, and so on in individual columns. The advantage of the database becomes evident when the volume of data becomes great. Database systems are optimized for storing and retrieving data so that the operations do not take too much time.

A language called Structured Query Language (better known by its abbreviation, SQL) is used for issuing commands to the database system. There is an INSERT command for inserting new information into the database. An UPDATE command is used for modifying existing information, whereas a DELETE command can be used for deleting some data. For retrieving data there is a SELECT command. You can put WHERE clauses with some of these commands to help search specific sets of data.

JDBC

Since our applications are going to be in Java, we need a way for them to communicate with databases. Java contains some prebuilt facilitator code that allows you to connect to a database and execute SQL commands against it; this is JDBC. Javasoft has defined some APIs for connecting to databases that are independent of the database vendors. Each vendor then supplies an implementation of these APIs. You can get this implementation from the vendor from whom you got your database. The APIs contain methods for executing all types of standard SQL commands, such as INSERT, SELECT, DELETE, and UPDATE.

XML

We saw earlier how HTML tags can be used for making plain text look appealing by displaying certain items in bold, italics, etc. This result was achieved by putting specific tags around the data elements. Whereas HTML tags tell us how the element should be displayed, they don't tell us what the element is. "<B>Leptukinavia</B>," for example, means that "Leptukinavia" should be displayed in bold text, but it doesn't tell us whether this is the name of a city, a country, or the forty-eighth bone of a human being. On the other hand, if we write this as "<City>Leptukinavia </City>," the piece of data suddenly acquires a meaning. XML, e*X*tensible *M*arkup *L*anguage, is all about giving meaning to data. Individual elements of any piece of data can be described by putting suitable tags around them.

XML is a set of specifications that can be used for creating new tags to give meaning to data. You have the flexibility of defining your own XML-based languages. We will look at a number of examples in the XML chapter to show how it can be used effectively for business-to-business communication.

e-Commerce Systems

Commerce is more than just buying and selling. There are prerequisites to selling—you need to have an inventory, you need to advertise to make your products known, you need to be able to accept money, you need to be able to pay taxes (even if you don't want to). Consequently, electronic commerce is also more than just buying and selling, because so many other components form part of a complete system. Here is a brief introduction to some systems that have been developed in the complete example of Part IV.

Inventory Management Systems

An inventory management system is one that stores information about the products and services you are selling. In this system you can use a backend database for storing all pertinent information. This information can include, but is not limited to, the following:

Names of your products

Description of your products

Price

Quantity in stock

Quantity sold till date

If you have all this information in a database, you can present your customers with a catalog that is drawn from this database. This catalog can be built dynamically by a backend Servlet that pulls data and builds a Web page based on the products that are available. Also, if there is any price change, it is reflected immediately, as your Servlet is pulling the latest data every time a user wants to look at the catalog.

An inventory management system allows you to add new products to your database, as well as to modify existing products (for instance, if the price or name of a product has changed).

A well-designed system also allows you to bundle several products together and present them as one item. In general, it helps you to organize your data very effectively.

Another advantage you can derive from an inventory management system is the ability to maintain your inventory above danger levels. Thus, if a user purchases five products of the same kind, your ordering system can update the inventory to reflect this. If it notices that this order has reduced the inventory to a very low level, it can send mail to the production department. This capability saves you from the possibility of losing customers for lack of product availability. The best thing about this is that it is all automated.

Still another advantage is that you can monitor how many units of a particular product have been sold over a period of time. This ability is clearly enormously helpful for forecasting, and also suggests your customers' shopping trends. For example, if the sale of a product has been close to 0 in the last n months, you may want to reevaluate your strategy and determine the root cause.

Profile Management Systems

Maintaining a profile of your customers can be a very rewarding experience for both the buyer and the seller. A Profile Management System allows your customers to become registered users. The system consists of two major parts: a Registration System and an Update Profile System. Users can register using the Registration System. This system asks for things like name, address, credit card number (which could be optional), and other data. This data is then stored in a database so that next time the customer orders something, you don't have to ask for the same information again. However, addresses and other information about customers are subject to change. You can allow customers to update this information themselves by providing an Update Profile system where users can log in and change the information as required. This ability avoids the necessity of having a customer support person to update customer data. There are some hidden benefits as well; for example, when a person enters his or her address, there is less likelihood of errors than when these details are dictated over the phone.

A profile management system can maintain the following data (more or less, depending on your business needs):

Name

Contact info

    Address

        Billing address

        Shipping address

    Phone

    Fax

    E-mail

Payment info

    Credit card information

Orders list

"Orders list" is a pointer to another data set that contains information about the orders this customer has placed so far. You can use this information both to do targeted advertising and to serve your customer better. You may also use this information to give discounts to customers who have been loyal.

You can also add utilities to a Profile Management System that would be not only beneficial to the customer but would also save your company some customer support time by providing a self-service interface.

One such utility is a password-finding system. It often happens that users register at a particular site and use it for some time. At some point, though, they may no longer have a reason to visit that site. In that case they forget about it till some event makes them come back. Chances are that by then they will have forgotten their previous password, forcing them either to register again or call up your customer support. In the first case your database will then contain duplicate information and the customer will also have a negative user experience as a result of having to go through the registration process again. And if the user calls up customer support, some of your employees will spend a lot of valuable time trying to locate passwords, a step that can easily be automated.

A properly designed feedback system is also of importance in any Web site. At the very least you can use a "mailto" HTML tag to provide a link that pops up a mail window in which customers can type their questions. However, a more efficient way of doing this is to present a FORM in which users select the category in which their feedback fits, so that an email is sent to the correct customer support representative.

Ordering Management Systems

The Ordering Management System, which encompasses the front end that customers use to place orders or buy products and the backend that fulfills these orders, is crucial. An Ordering Management System is tightly coupled with the Inventory Management

System. It pulls data from the Inventory Management System to provide a list of products that you are selling and present them to the customer, who can then select one or more of these products.

One common way of implementing an Ordering Management System is to follow the shopping cart model with which we are all familiar from visiting a grocery store. When we visit a supermarket, we normally pick up a cart and walk through the aisles that contain the products we are interested in. We then pick items and put them in the cart. Once we're done, we go to the checkout counter, where we pay and take the items home.

The Ordering Management System is just a transformation of the same model in terms of Web technology. Being a computer-driven system, it can be enhanced by some intelligence to provide a richer user experience. For instance, if we can identify a customer, we don't need to ask for the credit card information again, because we stored it when the person shopped at the site for the first time. Also, we can allow a user to define a regular cart, that is, a list of items that are purchased on a regular basis. This is an option we don't have in grocery stores today. You may buy two pounds of onions, one dozen eggs, and one bottle of milk every week, but every time you go to the grocery store you have to explicitly pick up these items; you cannot merely go to the checkout stand and tell them you need the items on this list. However, in the Web-based system you can establish a history and provide each user with a one-to-one experience.

Another advantage is that while presenting the products you can provide links to files and images that contain more information about those products, which is a great benefit for customers who have questions on their minds.

Maintaining order history can provide other benefits to customers. Customers can, for example, easily check what items they have bought and how much they have spent purchasing products from your site. If your products involve lengthy shipping times, customers can check the status of their order—whether it is being processed or has been shipped and, if so, on what date and by what means.

One advantage of the Inventory Management System is that when a purchase is made, you can update the inventory levels online. This capability helps you detect falling quantities early in the game.

The orders list that we saw in the Profile Management System can point to a list maintained by the Ordering Management System. This list contains information such as the following:

Products ordered by a customer

Price at which the product was purchased

Quantity that was purchased

Total amount that was billed to the customer

Date order was placed

Date order was shipped (if it has been shipped)

Status of the order

Interfaces to the Profile Management System need to be provided in the Ordering Management System so that users can enter or update their credit card information. The system also needs to be able to contact a credit card verification agency to claim payment for goods sold.

Shipping Management Systems

Unlike a regular store where customers buy goods and most often take the goods home with them, an Internet store needs to send the goods to the customers. For this reason a shipping system needs to be in place that allows the shipping department to look at pending orders. Information required by the department includes the products to be sent and the shipping address. A shipping system can use the orders list updated by the Ordering System to find out where pending orders are and can then update the order depending on the action taken. The customer can then view the status of his or her order.

Reporting Systems

One big advantage of doing business using databases is that you have a lot of data. One big disadvantage of doing business using databases is that you have a LOT of data. Data is more or less useless unless it can be translated into meaningful information. For this you need a proper reporting system that analyzes and presents data in a way that you can use to generate more business. A reporting system can do some of the following:

Provide information about total sales in a given period.

Split up sales information on a monthly or weekly basis.

Provide a comparison of revenues generated from different products.

This information can be used to find out where your business is doing well and where it could use some improvement. Consequently, you can do better forecasting and inventory management. Another area in which reporting can be useful is in studying customer patterns. For example, identifying areas in which most of your customers are concentrated can help you make decisions like setting up a warehouse in that region so as to reduce shipping costs and improve delivery time.

Getting on the Internet

In order to deploy an e-commerce system you will need a computer running a Web server that is connected to the Internet. You will also need a permanent Web address for this computer. This section discusses some of the things you need from a technical point of view.

You have essentially two options—you may either buy your own computer and connect it to the Net, or you may sign up with an Internet Service Provider (ISP) that allows application hosting. Each approach has its own advantages and disadvantages. If you use an ISP, your investment is minimal. ISPs typically charge a low monthly fee proportional to the amount of disk space you are using. The biggest gain here is that the responsibility of maintaining the machine is theirs. The downside is that you have less control over the machine. So, for example, if you want to use a particular backend tool or technology, you will be limited to those supported by the ISP. Besides, ISPs typically don't encourage heavy-duty applications that will slow down their other operations.

If you have your own machine, you can either maintain it yourself or you can have it hosted by companies that specialize in doing this. The former approach gives you maximum flexibility but is not recommended unless you're thoroughly familiar with system administration. The latter is a safer approach. Even though the machine is being hosted by somebody else, it is yours. You have the flexibility of installing any software and applications on the system. However, there is a flip side. Since computer hosting companies typically provide good physical security for the machines, this approach rules out direct physical access to the machine, which you would probably have to access through a remote login. Depending on the speed of your connection with the hosting company, this process can prove frustrating at times. Note that not all hosting companies provide the service of system administrators, and you may want to get this information before deciding on this option.

Here are some tips on how to approach the three options:

Using an ISP

You can find a list of ISPs that host Java servlets at the following site: *http://www. adrenalinegroup.com/jwsisp.html*. When you sign up with an ISP, you will be asked what name you want to give to your site. You can choose something like *www.myCompany. com*. The ISP will then contact an organization called interNIC that maintains a central database where names are registered. Once the name has been established, you can start using this address as a normal Internet URL. The ISP will also give you a way of transferring data to the ISP machine so you can maintain your Web site.

Using a Hosting Service

One of the hosting companies we found by doing a search on the Internet is *www.abovenet.com*. You can find more companies by searching on the Internet. Once you've finalized an agreement, your computer will be moved to their facility. They will provide you with a username and password that you can use for accessing the computer remotely, and they will also help you get a Web address through interNIC.

Keeping the Computer with You

If you want to keep the computer yourself, the best place to start is your phone company. Companies such as Pacific Bell and Bell Atlantic are now providing DSL services. DSL is a technology that offers high-speed Internet connection. The phone company should be able to help you set up your computer.

A Note about Speed

The speed of your connection is very crucial, because customers invariably hate waiting for responses from Web sites. The higher your connection speed, therefore, the better chance you have of retaining customers.

A T1 speed is considered reasonably good for most businesses. ISPs and big businesses with a lot of traffic may want to go for a fractal T3, full T3, or an OC-3 line, all of which are much faster.

However, speed comes at a price. A fractal T3 may cost as much as $4,000 a month. Determining the speed required for a business is a complex business decision based on a number of factors such as the amount of traffic that is expected, the kind of customers, the cost, and more.

One important fact about speed is that companies providing Internet connectivity offer different options. Each option has two kinds of speed listed in it: an upload speed and a download speed. If your primary concern is to make your system available to customers (as opposed to accessing the Internet yourself from this computer), then you should be concerned about the upload speed. Download speed is the speed at which you can access other sites. Upload is the maximum speed at which others can access your site. In most options the upload speed is significantly lower than the download speed, so you need to choose carefully.

Disclaimer

The code is provided as reference material, with no express or implied warranties. Extreme care has been taken to make the code free of bugs, but as with any software system, it may contain some problems.

Part II

Chapter 2

HTML

I'm quite hyperactive—even the language I speak is Hyper-Text Markup Language!

Introduction

This chapter introduces you to HTML and covers most of the elements of HTML that will be used in the following chapters. It assumes no prior knowledge of HTML.

Any person who has written a Graphical User Interface (GUI) in a traditional language like C will tell you that it is by no means the easiest task in the world. However, in the age of the Internet, the task of building a GUI has been greatly simplified by a language that makes the work of building interfaces look like child's play. Hyper-Text Markup Language, more commonly known as HTML, is by far the most popular Internet language.

HTML is used for creating Web pages. Browsers, as popular client-side software is known, understand HTML and display these pages. Documents are the most common type of Web pages. If you are using Windows and want to read a Microsoft Word document, you can do so by starting up Word. But this document cannot be viewed by somebody on Unix. Browsers and HTML solve this and other problems on the Internet.

HTML documents are stored in the ASCII format. But an ASCII document doesn't contain formatting by default, so you can't have one line in bold and another in italics. HTML allows you to add formatting to the document. HTML is based on a set of pre-defined tags that can be used for controlling the appearance of a document. For instance, there are tags that can make some words underlined, others blinking, and so on. This chapter examines a number of these tags.

First HTML File

We begin with a simple HTML document. This is a file called **firstPage.html**. You can view it using a browser like Netscape or Internet Explorer. In Netscape go to the "File" menu and select the "Open page" option. Then select the file. Its contents will be displayed in the browser's window. The page looks as shown in Figure 2.1.

Let's examine this HTML page. The code is shown below:

```
<HTML>
<HEAD><TITLE>First Page</TITLE></HEAD>
<BODY BGCOLOR='#0000FF'>
    <FONT FACE="Arial, Helvetica" COLOR='#FFFFFF'>
        <CENTER>
            I'm quite hyper - even the language I speak is Hyper-
Text-Markup-Language <B>- Vivek</B>
        </CENTER>
    </FONT>
</BODY>
</HTML>
```

It begins with the tag <HTML>, which indicates that this is an HTML file. HTML tags have corresponding ending tags. In some cases these may be optional, but in most cases the ending tag must be explicitly specified. As you can see, the last line closes the <HTML> tag with the corresponding </HTML> tag. A closing tag is the same as the starting tag except that it has a "/" after the first bracket. Next comes the <HEAD> tag,

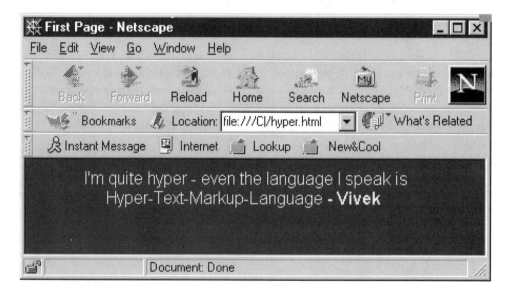

Figure   2.1

which can be used to specify a heading for the document. A <TITLE> can be specified—any text specified between the <TITLE> and </TITLE> tags appears in the top bar of the browser.

Then comes the <BODY> tag. The body of the document is present between the <BODY> and </BODY> tags. A <BODY> tag can take parameters—we're specifying the background color of the document by using the BGCOLOR parameter. The value of this parameter is the usual RedGreenBlue color combination. In this case, we want the document to have a blue background so we specify the color as the Hex value **#0000FF** (red would be **#FF0000**, green would be **#00FF00**).

In the body of the document we want to display a few words. But before we do so, we want to do some formatting, so that the document doesn't look like a boring ASCII file. We're first specifying a font that should be used for displaying the document. For this we use the "Arial, Helvetica" font by using the <FONT> tag. This tag also takes arguments. FACE specifies the typeface to be used. We can also specify the color in which the foreground text is to be displayed by using the COLOR tag; we're setting this to **#FFFFFF** so that the text is displayed in white.

Next we've put the <CENTER> tag. This ensures that the text is displayed in the center of the browser window. If you resize the window, the text will shift so that it is always centered. Lastly, we want the name of the author to appear in bold letters. This is done by using the <B> tag. Note how we're closing the bold, center, and font tags. Then we close the <BODY> and <HTML> tags and we're done. This is a complete HTML document that can be displayed by a browser.

Some Formatting Tags

I discovered a great weight watchers' program for my PC—
it's called Format!

See how simple it was to make a plain ASCII file look pretty? You can play around with these tags and add more text to see the effect on the output page. Colors and font faces can be changed very easily.

Here are some of the common formatting tags:

<I>—Italics

<U>—Underlined

<blink>—Blinking text

There are six standard size tags that control sizes of the characters that are displayed: <H1>, <H2>, <H3>, <H4>, <H5>, and <H6>. Figure 2.2 shows the HTML file that uses these tags and its output.

```
<HTML>
<HEAD><TITLE>Size Tags</TITLE></HEAD>
```

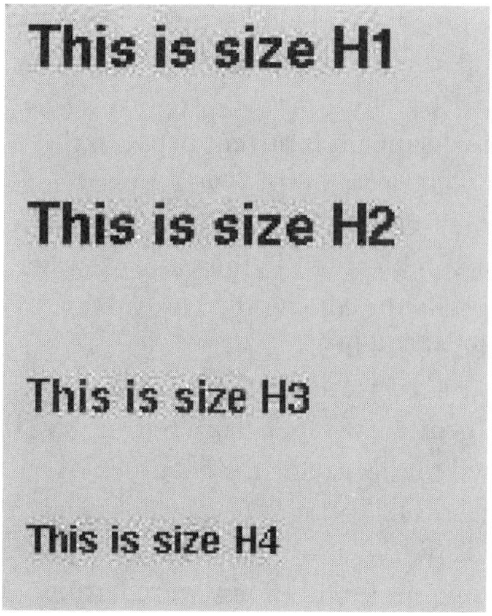

This is size H1

This is size H2

This is size H3

This is size H4

Figure   2.2

```
<BODY>
   <FONT FACE="Arial, Helvetica">
   <H1>This is size H1 </H1><BR>
   <H2>This is size H2 </H2><BR>
   <H3>This is size H3 </H3><BR>
   <H4>This is size H4 </H4><BR>
   </FONT>
</BODY>
</HTML>
```

In this case we're printing the four sizes using the <Hn> tags where n is 1 through 4. (HTML allows H1–H6). We've also introduced another element, <BR>. In HTML, extra spaces are ignored. So whether you write "Spaced text" or "Spaced   text," they will both appear in the Web page with a single space between "Spaced" and "text." Similarly, even if you hit a new line, it will be ignored. To introduce a new line you need to specify the break tag, <BR>. It has an optional </BR> closing tag. Since it is optional, we can ignore it, as we're doing in the HTML file above. Note that if we didn't specify the <BR> tags above, all the lines of text would appear on a single line.

There's another tag, called <P>, which can be used for creating a new paragraph. Anything included between a <P> and a </P> appears as a paragraph. You can use the <PRE> tag if you want the text to appear as it is, spaces and all; anything between a <PRE> and a </PRE> tag appears as you've written it in the HTML page; if there are spaces they will be displayed; if there are new lines, these too will be displayed; Try putting the following lines in the body of an HTML document:

```
<PRE>
    With the Pre tag you can have all the          space in the world.
</PRE>
```

You will see a number of spaces between *the* and *space*.

Try the same without the <PRE> tag. Now you will see just one space. Another interesting tag worth mentioning here is the <HR> tag, which creates a horizontal line on the page. Try putting this tag in your HTML page and look at the results in the browser.

Links

I have links in high places—the president is my third nephew's second wife's fourth cousin's maternal aunt's sixth husband's fourth cousin's foster son!

Navigation in a traditional document can sometimes become difficult. Take the case of a book. If there is something in Chapter 1 that refers to something in Chapter 20, a line in the book will tell you to go to Chapter 20. If there are too many references like this, however, you will soon get tired of flipping chapters. One of the most useful things that HTML brought to documents was links. A link is a "pointer" to another document (it could be an HTML file or image or something else). When you click this link, the document that it points to is displayed. You don't have to type in the location of that document to see it. Usually a link appears as an underlined text (or image) and if you move your mouse over it, the shape of the cursor changes to that of a hand. On clicking, you're transported to the document this link points to.

We now create a link in an HTML file **Link.html**:

```
<HTML><HEAD></HEAD>
<BODY>
<A HREF='First.html'>Link to First.html</A>
</BODY>
</HTML>
```

A link starts with the anchor tag <A HREF='.....'>. Within the quotes you specify the document to which users should be transported if they click on this link. The tag is closed by a </A>. Between the starting and ending tag you can specify text or an image. The text will appear underlined.

But you may not always want the "link" document to appear in the same browser window, as this will make your original content disappear. This point is particularly important if the link points to a document that you want the reader to view alongside the text in the current document, such as help on a particular feature of your product. You can use the "target" attribute with the <A> tag.

Try the following: in **Link.html**, change

```
<A HREF='First.html'>Link to First.html</A>
```

to read:

```
<A HREF='First.html' target='anotherFrame'>Link to First.html</A>
```

Now if you click the link, the document **First.html** will be displayed in another window.

Now you may ask, how do I include images? An image can be included in an HTML file by using the <IMG SRC> tag. In this you specify the location of an image (a GIF/JPEG file) that you want to display. The example **LinkImage.html** shows how an image can be specified with a link:

```
<HTML><HEAD></HEAD>
<BODY>
<A HREF='First.html'><IMG SRC='help.jpg' BORDER='0'></A>
</BODY>
</HTML>
```

Here **help.jpg** is the name of a JPEG file that we want to display as a link. By default, if you specify an image as a link, browsers tend to put an outline around the image. You can prevent this by specifying BORDER='0'—this means "don't create a border around the image."

You can also use the <A> tag to create a link that, if clicked, brings up a mail window and allows users to send email. If you want to create a link that will allow a user to send email to "abc@def.com," you can write the following in your HTML file:

```
<A HREF='mailto:abc@def.com'>Send mail to abc</A>
```

In **First.html,** we saw how to set the background color of your HTML page. You can also set an image as the background of your page. As you can see in **BackgroundImage.html**, this is pretty straightforward to do.

```
<HTML><HEAD></HEAD>
<BODY BACKGROUND='help.jpg'>
</BODY>
</HTML>
```

We're specifying that the JPEG file **help.jpg** should be the background of this page. If the JPEG file is smaller than the size of window, the browser will automatically create multiple copies of the image and display them next to each other so that the complete window has this image as the background.

Lists

I finally made it to the underworld's most prestigious list—
I'm fifth on America's Most Wanted!

Sometimes you want to display data in the form of points. This concept is referred to as a bullet in Word. You can create an equivalent in HTML using ordered and unordered lists. In the next example we're creating an unordered list (see Figure 2.3).

```
<HTML><HEAD></HEAD>
<BODY>
   Apples
    <UL>
        <LI>Red
        <LI>Green
    </UL>
   Mangoes
    <UL type=square>
        <LI>Green
        <LI>Yellow
    </UL>
</BODY>
</HTML>
```

An unordered list starts with the <UL> tag and ends with the </UL> tag. Each bulleted item in a list starts with an <LI> tag. The browser creates bullets for every <LI> item. All the <LI> bullet items between the <UL> and </UL> tag are grouped together. By default the bullet is a disc, but you can specify it to be either a circle or a square. In the example above we're specifying the bullets of the Mangoes list to be square.

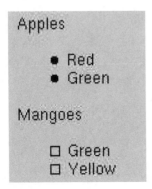

Figure   2.3

Tables

A table is another way of organizing related data. One common example of a document that requires a table is a spreadsheet. Tables help you put data in cells that are organized in the form of rows and columns. A table starts with a <TABLE> tag and ends with the </TABLE> tag. You can have multiple rows and columns in a table. A row starts with the <TR> tag and ends with the </TR> tag. Between the <TR> and </TR> tags you can specify the columns using the <TD> and </TD> tags. Data present between the <TD> and </TD> tags in a given row (<TR> </TR>) constitutes one cell of the table.

A table can also have a heading for each of the columns. This is specified by using the <TH> and </TH> tags.

Figure 2.4 illustrates the example **Table.html.**

```
<HTML>
<HEAD></HEAD>
<BODY>
        <TABLE BORDER='2'>
            <TH>Column 1</TH><TH>Column 2</TH>
            <TR>
                <TD>Cell 1</TD><TD>Cell 2</TD>
            </TR>
            <TR>
                <TD>Cell 3</TD><TD>Cell 4</TD>
            </TR>
        </TABLE>
</BODY>
</HTML>
```

In this example we are creating a table with two rows and two columns. The first cell has "Cell 1" written in it, the second has "Cell 2," and so on. Also, we've used an attribute of <TABLE> called BORDER that specifies the width of the border around the table.

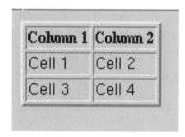

Figure   2.4

A table can contain one or more tables in it to create complex interfaces. You can also use the "WIDTH" attribute with the <TD> tag to specify the width of a column. The "BGCOLOR" attribute can be used to control the background color of a row with the <TR> tag.

Frames

In the Links section we saw how the <A> tag can be used with the TARGET attribute to display an HTML file in a popped-up window. But pop-ups are not always the best design; they may end up confusing users. A better approach is to divide your browser window into parts, each one displaying its own page. This can be achieved using Frames, a very powerful feature of HTML that can be used to split the display into a number of windows, each of which can display an HTML page of its own. This feature is very helpful for providing easy navigation. For instance, if you wanted to display this book in HTML, you could create two frames, with the left frame containing the names of the chapters as links. On clicking the link, a user would see the chapter in the right frame. However, the left frame would still contain the list of chapters, so that another chapter could easily be accessed by clicking on its link.

You construct Frames using two tags: <FRAMESET> and <FRAME>. The first tag, <FRAMESET>, defines how the screen needs to be split, while <FRAME> determines what should be displayed in each of these portions. A <FRAMESET> can have other <FRAMESET> tags in it, thus enabling you to create a complex layout. You can use a COLS or ROWS attribute with this tag to specify how many rows or columns the Frameset needs to be split in and what should be the size of each. For example, a <FRAMESET ROWS='50,80,*'> would split the screen horizontally into three parts. The first part would be 50 units high, the second would be 80 units high, and the * indicates that the rest would be taken up by the third part. You can also specify percentages. A <FRAMESET COLS='10%, *'> would split the screen vertically into two parts; the first would take up 10 percent of the screen, and the rest would belong to the second part.

Now we see what goes into each of these parts, as specified by the <FRAME> tag. You can provide an SRC attribute in this to determine the HTML file that should be displayed there. There should be one <FRAME> for each of the parts into which the screen has been split.

A small example—if you view the following HTML file, the browser will display a screen that is split into two parts. The first 20 percent will display **left.html** and the remainder will display **right.html**.

```
<FRAMESET COLS='20%, *'>
   <FRAME SRC='left.html'>
   <FRAME SRC='right.html'>
</FRAMESET>
```

A <FRAMESET> may contain other <FRAMESET> tags. The following example would split the screen into three parts. The top 20 percent will display **topPart.html.** The lower portion will be split vertically into two parts, with the first 10 percent displaying **lowerLeft.html** and the remainder containing **lowerRight.html**.

```
<FRAMESET ROWS='20%, *'>
        <FRAME SRC='topPart.html'>
        <FRAMESET COLS='10%,*'>
            <FRAME SRC='lowerLeft.html'>
            <FRAME SRC='lowerRight.html'>
        </FRAMESET>
</FRAMESET>
```

<FRAME> can have a name, defined by the NAME attribute. By giving a name to a Frame you can use it in other ways. For example, you may use the TARGET attribute of the <A> tag so that any click on a link causes the page to be displayed in another Frame.

Here's a more complex example. **shady.html** contains a frame at the top that displays a logo (**shadyLogo.html**). Below this the screen is split into two parts—the left part shows a menu (**shadyMenu.html**) and the right part displays the link in the menu that is clicked. If you click on any of the links in **shady.html,** the corresponding HTML file will be displayed in the Frame named "display," because we've used the TARGET attribute of the <A> tag.

The logo and the menu always remain there—it's only the "display" area that changes when you click links.

Figure 2.5 shows how the front page looks.

Figure 2.6 shows what you will see if you click the "Robbery Assistance" link.

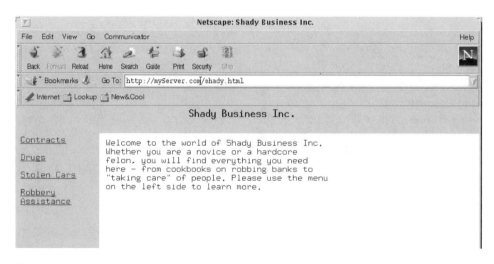

Figure   2.5

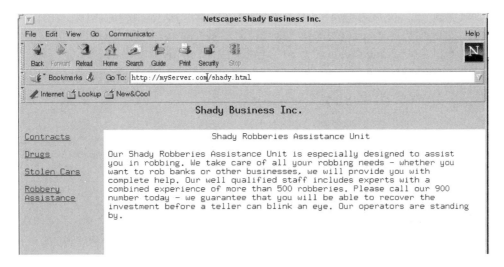

Figure   2.6

shady.html

```
<HTML><HEAD><TITLE>Shady Business Inc.</TITLE></HEAD>
<FRAMESET ROWS='50,*' BORDER='0'>
    <FRAME NAME='logo' SRC='shadyLogo.html'>
    <FRAMESET COLS='150,*' BORDER='0'>
        <FRAME NAME='menu' SRC='shadyMenu.html' TARGET='display'>
        <FRAME NAME='display' SRC='shadyDisplay.html'>
    </FRAMESET>
</FRAMESET>
<BODY>
</BODY>
</HTML>
```

shadyLogo.html

```
<HTML><HEAD></HEAD>
<BODY>
    <CENTER><H1>Shady Business Inc.</H1></CENTER>
</BODY>
</HTML>
```

shadyMenu.html

```
<HTML><HEAD></HEAD>
<BODY>
    <A HREF='shadyContracts.html' TARGET='display'>Contracts<P>
```

```
        <A HREF='shadyDrugs.html' TARGET='display'>Drugs<P>
        <A HREF='shadyCars.html' TARGET='display'>Stolen Cars<P>
        <A HREF='shadyRobbery.html' TARGET='display'>Robbery
             Assistance<P>
</BODY>
</HTML>
```

shadyDisplay.html

```
<HTML><HEAD></HEAD>
<BODY BGCOLOR='#FFFFFF'>
        <TABLE>
          <TR><TD WIDTH='400'>
        Welcome to the world of Shady Business Inc. Whether you are a novice
        or a hardcore felon, you will find everything you need here—from
        cookbooks on robbing banks to "taking care" of people. Please use
        the menu on the left side to learn more.
             </TD></TR>
        </TABLE>
</BODY>
</HTML>
```

shadyRobbery.html

```
<HTML><HEAD></HEAD>
<BODY BGCOLOR='#FFFFFF'>
        <CENTER>Shady Robberies Assistance Unit</CENTER><P>
        <TABLE>
          <TR TD WIDTH='400'>
        Our Shady Robberies Assistance Unit is especially designed to assist
        you in robbing. We take care of all your robbing needs. Whether you
        want to rob banks or other businesses, we will provide you with
        complete help. Our well-qualified staff includes experts with a
        combined experience of more than 500 robberies. Please call our
        900 number today. We guarantee that you will be able to recover
        the investment before a teller can blink an eye. Our operators
        are standing by.
             </TD></TR>
        </TABLE>
</BODY>
</HTML>
```

Forms

They say it takes just twenty minutes for an average person to fill in my state's tax form.
Gee, I must be at the very bottom of the gene pool!

All that we've looked at earlier is good for formatting text and making documents look pretty. However, the Web has moved from the age of static pages to acting as a front end for complex applications. This makes it necessary for HTML to support elements that are found in stand-alone desktop applications and link the frontend HTML page with a backend application that can be invoked by clicking a button on the page.

This is supported by the <FORM> element of HTML. Forms are used for creating front ends that can contain elements like buttons, text fields in which you can type, radio buttons, checkboxes, and select lists.

A form can have a name as one of its attributes. It can—and usually does—have an ACTION attribute. In this you specify the application that should be invoked when you click the Submit button. All the elements to be included in a form are specified between the <FORM> and </FORM> tags. When the Submit button is clicked, data in these elements that has been selected or typed in by the user is passed to the application specified in the ACTION attribute of the form. This application can then process the data and send results back to the browser.

We begin by creating a very simple form, **FirstForm.html** (see Figure 2.7).

```
<HTML>
<HEAD></HEAD>
<BODY>
    <FORM ACTION='/ProcessApplication.exe'>
     Please type your email address below:<P>
```

Figure   2.7

```
      <INPUT TYPE='text' NAME='email' VALUE=' ' SIZE='20'
                                      MAXLENGTH='25'><P>
      <INPUT TYPE='submit' NAME='submit' VALUE='Send'>
   </FORM>
</BODY>
</HTML>
```

In the ACTION attribute of this form we've specified that when this form is submitted, the application "ProcessApplication.exe" should be invoked.

Next we have a line of text followed by a paragraph separator (<P>). Then we create a text field in which users can type in text. Look at the line of code that we've used for creating this text field:

```
      <INPUT TYPE='text' NAME='email' VALUE=' ' SIZE='20'
                                      MAXLENGTH='25'><P>
```

It begins with the <INPUT> tag. We're using it to create a text field. This has been specified in the "TYPE" attribute of the tag.

This tag, as we will see later, can be used for creating not just text fields but also several other elements.

All elements of a form have a name associated with them. As we mentioned earlier, when the form is submitted, the current state of all elements in the form is passed to the application that is invoked. The application needs to parse this data to see which element has what value(s). This is why the elements need to have names. Although you can create nameless elements without having a visual impact, the form becomes useless if the backend application cannot process it properly.

In this case we've given this element the name "email." We've initialized its value to an empty string. Any string you typed in would appear as the default value of the text field.

A text field element's size can be controlled using the SIZE tag. We've specified this value to be 20. This means that the length of the field when it is displayed should be such that twenty characters are displayed. Even if you enter more than twenty characters, only twenty will be displayed. You can, of course, scroll in the text field to see the remaining characters.

Another attribute, MAXLENGTH, allows us to limit the maximum number of characters a user is allowed to type in this field. In this example MAXLENGTH is set to 25. The browser won't allow you to type more than 25 characters in this text field.

In the next line we've specified a Submit button. This special type of button, unlike a normal button, acts as the Next button that we see in most stand-alone applications. The Submit button is also specified using the <INPUT> tag. In this case, however, the TYPE is Submit. It has a NAME and can have a VALUE. This value is displayed as the name of the Submit button.

As we saw above, the <INPUT> tag can be used to specify a text field or a Submit button by specifying the correct type in the TYPE attribute. Other elements can be specified in the TYPE attribute to create different GUI elements, including the following:

password—used for creating a Password text field in which the value that is being typed is not displayed.

```
<INPUT TYPE='password' NAME='myPassword' VALUE=' ' SIZE='10'>
```

button—a normal button that doesn't result in a call to the backend application

```
<INPUT TYPE='button' NAME='myButton' VALUE='Click this button'>
```

reset—a button that can be used to clear the contents of the form and set them to their default values.

```
<INPUT TYPE='reset' NAME='resetButton' VALUE='RESET'>
```

image—this can be used to create a Submit button in which there is an image instead of a button. The effect of clicking this image is the same as that of clicking the Submit button, i.e., the backend application is invoked.

```
<INPUT TYPE='image' SRC='/submitImage.jpg'>
```
Here, the SRC attribute specifies the location of the image that is to be used.

radio—used for creating a set of radio buttons. A radio button is a set of buttons, only one of which can be checked at a time. You can specify the one that is checked by default by using the CHECKED attribute:

```
<INPUT TYPE='radio' NAME='radioButtons' VALUE='value1' CHECKED>
<INPUT TYPE='radio' NAME='radioButtons' VALUE='value2'>
```
All radio buttons that have the same NAME belong to the same set of buttons. In this example, we've created a set called "radioButtons"; the first one is checked by default. If you check the second one, the first is "unchecked." When this form is submitted, the value of the button that is checked is sent to the backend application. So if you checked the second button and pressed Submit, the value "Value 2" would be sent.

checkbox—used for creating a set of checkboxes. Checkboxes are like radio buttons except that you can check zero, one, or more of these. Values of all checkboxes that are "checked" are sent to the backend application.

```
<INPUT TYPE='checkbox' NAME='radioButtons' VALUE='value1' CHECKED>
<INPUT TYPE='checkbox' NAME='radioButtons' VALUE='value2' CHECKED>
```

hidden—used for creating a hidden element, an element that is not displayed but can contain a value that is passed to the backend application. Whereas use of this element may not be so intuitive for a person new to forms, you will gradually learn the importance of this element in the following chapters, where we use it extensively.

```
<INPUT TYPE='hidden' NAME='aHiddenField' VALUE='value1'>
```

Try putting these elements in an HTML file and see the output.

A text field can be used for supplying an element in which a user can type in a line of text. But what if you want somebody to be able to type in multiple lines of text? For this you can use the <TEXTAREA> tag. This allows you to create an area with a specified number of rows and columns in which a user can type text.

Look at **TextArea.html** for an example:

```
<HTML><HEAD></HEAD>
<BODY BGCOLOR='#FFFFFF'>
   <FORM>
      <TEXTAREA ROWS='5' COLS='30'>
          Default text
      </TEXTAREA>
    </FORM>
</BODY>
</HTML>
```

The ROWS attribute of the text area specifies how many rows should be displayed, while the COLS parameter specifies how many characters per line are to be displayed. You can use the horizontal and vertical scrollbars to view text that may have overflowed. If there is any text between the <TEXTAREA> and </TEXTAREA> tags, it is displayed as the default text of this text area.

Another commonly used form element is the Select list. A Select list is similar in nature to radio buttons or checkboxes, but the appearance is different, and of course the syntax is different too. The tag for this is <SELECT>. In this you can specify the NAME attribute to give a name to the list. You can also specify whether users are allowed to pick just one item (as with a radio button) or multiple items. By default, users are allowed to pick only one item. However, if you want to allow multiple items, you can specify the MULTIPLE attribute.

Well, you may ask, why Select lists? But if you think carefully about radio buttons or checkboxes, if there are a lot of them that need to be specified in a page, they would easily clutter up the page. It is far better to display just a few of the options and view the rest by using scroll bars. This is what Select lists offer. The SIZE tag can be used to specify the maximum number of options that are displayed. If there are more, scroll bars are created, and the user can see other options by using these.

The options of a Select list are specified with the <OPTION> tag, and the value is the text written after the <OPTION> tag. If you want to send a value to the backend application that is different from the displayed value, you can do so by using the VALUE attribute of option. For example:

SelectList.html

```
<HTML><HEAD></HEAD>
<BODY>
     <FORM>
```

```
            <SELECT NAME='mySelectList' MULTIPLE SIZE='2'>
                <OPTION VALUE='1'>USA
                <OPTION VALUE='2'>Canada
                <OPTION VALUE='3'>Mexico
            </SELECT>
        </FORM>
</BODY>
</HTML>
```

In our Select list named "mySelectList," we have three options: USA, Canada, and Mexico. The MULTIPLE attribute makes it possible for a user to select one or more of these options. However, the display only shows two of the three options at a time, because we've specified the SIZE of the Select list to be two.

If an option is selected, the value that is passed is not the displayed value but the one that is specified using the VALUE attribute. Thus, if USA and Mexico are selected, the backend application will receive the values 1 and 3.

Putting Comments in HTML

Comments in HTML start with a <!-- and end with a -->. Here's an example of commented HTML:

```
<!-- This is Comments.html -->
<HTML>
<HEAD></HEAD>
    <BODY>
<!-- This is where we have
    the body of the html file -->
    </BODY>
</HTML>
```

Conclusion

Although this brings to an end our discussion of HTML, the scope of the language is much richer than could be covered in this chapter. Several elements and attributes could not be discussed in the limited space. However, this chapter contains most of the elements that we will be using in subsequent chapters. You should by now be well equipped to take the plunge into creating your own Web pages.

If you need more information on HTML, there is more than enough available on the Web itself.

You can also pick up several books that deal with the subject extensively. A number of tools, such as HotMetal PRO, can be used for creating HTML pages. These are pretty helpful if you're creating complex pages with lots of nested tables and links.

Chapter 3

Java

Introduction

This chapter is meant for you if you belong to one of the following three categories:

1. You know Java and just want a quick refresher course

2. You know C and would like an introduction to Object Oriented Programming and Java

3. You know C++ and want to see how programming in Java is different

If you don't yet know any of these three languages, you would be better off learning at least one of them before reading this book.

A few years ago a new computer language was born that took the world by storm. Java, as we know it today, is one of the fastest-growing languages. Ease of programming makes it a natural choice, but it is platform independence that is Java's biggest selling point. Code written in pure Java is cross-platform and can be used on any platform complying with Sun's Java Development Kit (JDK) implementation. Java is also a very rich language, allowing you to do a myriad things with ease.

But to coin a phrase, every silver lining has a cloud! Java is a semi-interpreted language. This means that compiled Java code is not "as" compiled as an executable produced by compiling a C program. And this translates to slower execution. In fact speed is the biggest point that critics raise whenever Java is being scrutinized. Some work has been done to alleviate this problem. For instance, just-in-time compilers can be installed to do a compilation of the program just before execution. The resulting compiled program typically executes faster.

You may now ask why the program is not compiled and stored in the first place. The answer is that a fully compiled program conforms to the instruction set of the computer on which it is to run. It may not work on another machine with a different operating system. A C executable that has been compiled on Solaris will not execute on

Windows 95. The platform dependence of languages like C forces software companies to devote considerable resources to porting their products. One of the fundamental goals of Java was to solve this problem. And that problem does not go away if you compile the program fully.

Instead, the Java "compiler" converts the source code to byte code. This is an instruction set developed by Sun. On each platform there is a "java" interpreter that understands this byte code. When you execute your Java program using this interpreter, it reads the byte code and issues the corresponding machine-specific instructions. The interpreter behaves like a virtual machine, as it has its own instruction set. It is referred to as the Java Virtual Machine (JVM).

In this chapter we're going to take a whirlwind tour of Java. The language is so extensive that covering it in one chapter is like fitting the universe in a matchbox. We will give a brief overview of its most commonly used features and concentrate on aspects that will be used in the remaining chapters. We will also illustrate the use of the language with some practical examples.

So pick up a mug of *real* Java and get ready for the tour of your, well, book!

The JDK, can be downloaded from *www.javasoft.com.* Installation is quite straightforward and is explained on the Web site for each of the platforms for which the kit is available. These include Unix, Mac, and Windows. You will need to download and install the JDK in order to compile your own Java programs.

Java programs end with the extension **java**. The "compiler" executable is called **javac**. To compile a file called "Test.java" you need to execute **javac Test.java**. This action will produce a "class" file called "Test.class," which contains the compiled code that can be executed by a Java interpreter. The JDK comes with a default interpreter called "java." In order to execute "Test.class," you need to issue a command like **java Test**. Note that you don't specify the extension (**.class**).

The JDK "java" interpreter uses an environment variable called CLASSPATH to locate class files. This can be considered equivalent to the PATH environment variable used by most operating systems to locate executables. In most cases, if you want to execute a class using "java," you need to set CLASSPATH to include the directory containing "Test.class." (Normally, if you are in the directory in which the **.class** is present and execute "java," the interpreter will be able to find and execute the class even if your CLASSPATH is not set).

But what exactly is a class? Here is a small primer on Object Oriented Programming.

Object Oriented Programming

I'm very object oriented—
my living room is full of Oriental objects.

Traditional languages laid a lot of stress on structure but were still far from representing objects as they exist in the real world. Object Oriented Programming languages, however, try to model the world more closely. A **struct** in C can contain variables.

However, this is not sufficient to represent an object like a dog, which has not only state but also behavior. The variables can hold the state the dog is in (sleeping/awake) and parameters like the color of its eyes.

But there is no convenient way of making this dog move or bark. If we add functions (methods) to this struct that are capable of making the dog move or bark, then we will have a better representation. These functions may be very simple—for instance, all that a **bark()** function needs to do is set the state of a variable to "barking." Of course we could do this without putting the **bark()** function inside the struct. However, putting functions applicable to an object along with its variables together in one representation makes a lot of sense, as it adds to the completeness of the object. This changes the represented thing from being a state holder to something that can have both state and behavior; in Object Oriented Programming, this is referred to as an object.

When houses are built, usually a blueprint is prepared that lays down the floor plan. Then a number of houses are built based on this plan. The actual houses can be looked upon as objects. A "Class" in Object Oriented Programming is the equivalent of the blueprint. An object is an instantiation of a class.

Besides making code more modular, as it consists of self-contained entities, the concept of objects gives us another advantage—encapsulation. There are some things about an object that need not be exposed to the external world, things that only the object itself needs to know. This can be easily done in objects by making some variables and methods private (as opposed to public ones that are exposed to the world). Take the example of a calculator. While you may want to use a calculator to figure out how much you made in the stock market, you would not necessarily be interested in learning the circuitry that's doing the calculations. Since this circuitry, however, is what the machine uses to do the calculation, it is important to the calculator itself. So the circuitry can be represented in private variables and methods. Methods for addition and subtraction, etc.—such as **add(), subtract()**—could be public methods.

Now we move on to see how these concepts are represented in Java. Let us begin with a test program.

First Java Program

Create a file called "Test.java" in an ASCII text editor (like "vi" on Unix, "Notepad" on Windows) and save the following lines of code in it:

```
public class Test
{
    public static void main(String[] args)
    {
        System.out.println("The CEO of Beverages Cheaper!
                testified before a grand jury that Java is
                    not addictive");
    }
}
```

Put your **javac** executable in your path. This executable will be present in the "bin" directory under the directory where you installed the JDK. For instance, assuming you installed the JDK in /JDK1.1.4, you can do this on Solaris (c-shell) as follows:

set path=(/JDK1.1.4/bin:$path).

On Windows you can say:

PATH=C:\JDK1.1.4\bin;<rest Of your path>

Now compile **Test.java** as follows:

javac Test.java

A class file called "Test.class" will be produced in the same directory. Now set your CLASSPATH environment variable to include the current directory. Assuming the directory is /home/me/test, you would do this as follows on Solaris:

setenv CLASSPATH /home/me/test

To execute the class file simply issue the following command:

java Test

This will print out the following line:

The CEO of Beverages Cheaper! testified before a grand jury that Java is not addictive.

So let's see how this all happened. Look at the code above. It begins with this line:

public class Test

This means that we're creating a new class whose name is "Test." This is a public class, which roughly means that any other class can create an instance of this class and invoke methods of it that have been declared "public." (A method is the equivalent of a function in a programming language like C.) Note that if you declare your class to be public, the name of the class should be the same as that of the Java file in which it is being saved. So if you open a file "NotTest.java" and save the class Test in it, **javac** will exit with an error.

Then there is the main method. Stand-alone applications need to have a **main()** method in them, as this is where execution begins when the "java" interpreter starts executing the class. The main method takes a String array as an argument. Any command line arguments supplied when the class is executed can be accessed through this array. If you say **java Test arg1**, you can access **arg1** in your main method; this will be the first element in the String array called **args (args[0])**.

The next line is **System.out.println()**. This is the way you print something to the standard output. It takes a String as an argument.

A String is close to a character array in C. The main difference between Java and C is that Java is an Object Oriented language. Most of the basic datatypes have classes wrapped around them. Instead of dealing with a character array, therefore, in most cases you will be using a String. This is a class that comes as part of the JDK. It contains methods that allow you to perform some of the common char array manipulation operations, such as string comparisons and concatenations.

At this point, we would suggest you take a brief look at the JDK documentation. There are a number of useful classes that come along with the JDK and make your life much easier. The String class already mentioned is one such example. Similarly, there are classes that help you do varied things like date comparisons, connecting to databases, generating random numbers, creating complex GUIs, do file I/O, and much more. Classes are organized in "packages." A package is a collection of classes. You can create your own packages and also use packages that come as part of the JDK. In fact, you've already used a package called **java.lang** that comes with the JDK and contains **String.class**. (As we shall see later, you need to explicitly "import" packages in your Java file to inform the compiler of the packages your class needs. You don't have to "import" **java.lang** as that is implicitly included). Some of the packages that are present in the JDK are **java.lang, java.sql, java.util**, and so on. The JDK documentation discusses all these packages and the classes that they contain. A detailed description of all these classes tells you the methods in these classes that you can use. A quick perusal of these packages will give you a feel for the kind of power already at your disposal.

Applets and Applications

There are essentially two types of Java programs. We've already looked at the first type, which is called an application. An application is a Java program that is explicitly executed on your system by an interpreter such as "java." Typically, these types of programs are executed on a server. However, another area in which Java has played a prominent role is client side execution. Client-side executable code is written in the form of applets. An applet is a Java program that is typically executed on the client side in a Web browser. Web browsers such as Netscape and Internet Explorer have mini Java interpreters built inside them. When a browser accesses an HTML page that contains a reference to an applet, it loads the class file containing the applet and executes code in it. This execution occurs on the client side (on the machine on which the browser is running) as opposed to the server (on which the applet class file is present). This is a way of reducing load on your server. However, since applets come with some security restrictions, they may not be the ideal choice. Also, applets execute on the client side, which means that you have no control over the execution environment. And that can sometimes become pretty frustrating, as some browsers may implement Java slightly differently. This book concentrates mainly on server-side applications. Applets cannot just be wished away, however. Client-side functionality has its own advantages, the most prominent being that it reduces the load on your server. We will therefore look at applets later in this chapter.

Let us first delve a bit deeper into Java applications by creating a few more classes. The aim here is to introduce you to some of Java's concepts and JDK packages that we will eventually be using.

Instances

The following example, a class called TwoInstances, introduces you to the concept of instances, As described, this class needs to be saved in a file called **TwoInstances.java**.

```java
public class TwoInstances
{
    int i = 0;
    static int j = 0;
    public static void main(String[] args)
    {
        TwoInstances a1 = new TwoInstances();
        a1.incrementValues();
        TwoInstances a2 = new TwoInstances();
        a2.incrementValues();

        a1.printIt("From a1:");
        a2.printIt("From a2:");
    }
    public void printIt(String header)
    {
        System.out.println(header);
        System.out.println("i is : " + i);
        System.out.println("j is : " + j);
    }
    public void incrementValues()
    {
        i++;
        j++;
    }
}
```

In the main method (where execution begins), we're creating two "instances" of this class.

In Object Oriented Programming, there is a distinction between a class and an object. Typically, an object is instantiation of a class. Methods and variables defined in the class can belong either to the class or to an instance of the class. The methods and variables that belong to a class have only one instantiation. All instances of this class running in the same environment share only one copy of these methods and variables. However, this is not desirable in most cases. Ideally, each instance of a class should have its own set of variables and methods. That is exactly what we're doing in the above example.

We're using "new" to create two instances of the class "TwoInstances." These instances are **a1** and **a2**:

```
AnInstance a1 = new AnInstance();
AnInstance a2 = new AnInstance();
```

There are two methods and two variables defined in this class. The variables **i** and **j** are both of the type **int** and have been initialized to 0. The method **incrementValues()** increments the value of both these variables by 1. **printIt()** is a method that prints the values of both these variables. It first prints a "header," which is a String that we're passing to distinguish between the two instances.

To access the methods and variables, we're using the "." operator. This operation would be familiar to someone who knows C—it is used in the same way you use "." to access variables in a structure. Thus, **a.printIt()** means invoke the method **printIt()** in instance **a**, and **a.i** means the variable **i** in instance **a**.

Both the methods defined in this class are instance methods in this class. This means that the methods in the instance **a1** are isolated from the same methods in instance **a2**. So how did we define these to be instance methods as opposed to class methods? If you notice, the method "main" is defined as a "static" method. The "static" qualifier declares a method (or variable) to be a class method. If we declare a method in this class with the static keyword, it will be a class method. The variable **j** is defined like this. This implies that there is only one copy of **j**, which is shared by both **a1** and **a2**.

Now let's see what happens during execution. After creating the instances **a1** and **a2**, we're invoking the method **incrementValues()** in both instances. When the method is invoked in the instance **a1**, the value of the variable **i** is changed from 0 to 1. Similarly, the value of **j** is changed from 0 to 1. Then the method in **a2** is executed. Since **i** is an instance variable, **a2** has its own copy of this variable, which is not accessible to **a1**. This means that the value of **i** is still 0 in this instance, so when the method **incrementValues()** is executed in **a2**, the value of **i** is changed from 0 to 1. However, because **j** is a static variable (class variable), only one copy of this variable is shared by both **a1** and **a2**. Therefore, when **incrementValues()** is executed in the instance **a2**, the value of **j** is already set to 1 (as it was incremented by the instance **a1**). **a2** now increments it to 2.

This can be verified by invoking the **printIt()** method from both the instances. If you execute this program, you get the following output:

From **a1**:

i is : 1

j is : 2

From **a2**:

i is : 1

j is : 2

One more thing needs clarification. Look at the following line:

```
System.out.println("i is : " + i);
```

As we learned earlier, **System.out.println()** takes in a String argument. But what is a **+** operator doing there? In Java, the definition of the **+** operator has been extended beyond its use in arithmetic operations, and it can also imply String concatenation. In the previous code, first the words "i is:" are printed and then the value of the variable **i** is appended to them because of the **+** operator.

Method Overloading

I'm always overloaded with work—
a twenty-hour workday sounds like a vacation to me!

Another useful feature of object oriented languages is method overloading, whereby a class can have two or more methods of the same name provided their input and output arguments are not of the same type. The following example shows a Java class containing two methods with the same name. The interpreter calls the appropriate method based on the arguments used when the methods are invoked. Let's look at the Java file "Overloading.java":

```java
public class Overloading
{
    public static void main(String[] args)
    {
        Overloading a1 = new Overloading();
        a1.printArgs(args);
        a1.printArgs(args[0]);
    }
    public void printArgs(String[] theArgs)
    {
        int length = theArgs.length;
        System.out.println("From printArgs(String[]):");
        for(int i=0; i<length; i++)
            System.out.println(theArgs[i]);
    }
    public void printArgs(String arg)
    {
        System.out.println("From printArgs(String): " + arg);
    }
}
```

This class contains two methods, each called **printArgs**. The first one takes a String array as its input argument, while the second takes a single String object. We're creating an instance of this class and then invoking the two methods. First we pass the entire command-line arguments to this method. Since this is a String array, the Java interpreter knows that the first implementation of **printArgs()** (the one that takes a String array as input) should be invoked. As a result, all the command-line arguments are printed on the standard output.

Then we call **printArgs()** by passing just the first command-line argument (the first element in the array **args[]**, which is **args[0]**). Now the second **printArgs()** is invoked, and this first element is printed.

Let us look at the implementation of the first **printArgs()** in some more detail. First, it calculates the length of the array that has been passed to it as an argument. An array has a "length" variable associated with it that contains the length of the array, that is, the number of elements in it.

```
int length = theArgs.length;
```

In order to print these elements, we're looping through all the elements using a "for" loop. Just like C, Java supports several control structures, like "for" and "while" loops.

```
for(int i=0; i<length; i++)
```

If you execute the class as "java Overloading argument1 argument2," you get the following output:

From printArgs(String[]):

argument1

argument2

From printArgs(String): argument1

Inheritance

Grandpa left me all he had—
a list of loan sharks he owed money to!

Another feature of object oriented languages is inheritance, which allows us to create new classes that inherit features of some other classes. Inheritance can be used effectively to create reusable code. To understand this, look at a theoretical example. Let's say you want to create representations of mammals. All mammals share some features in common. They are warm-blooded, they have a four-chambered heart, and females give birth to live young. However, other characteristics are not shared. Whereas humans live and breathe on land, whales live in water. If we want to represent all mammals, one way of doing this is to create a class for each type of mammal containing all characteristics of that mammal. But that would be really crude, because we're simply repeating all the common information in all the classes. A better way is to create a class called "Mammal," which contains all the common characteristics. Then we can create separate classes containing unique characteristics for each of the individual types of mammals. And we can have these classes inherit characteristics of the parent mammal class. This way, if you need to change common information, you can change it in just one place and see its effect everywhere.

The example below illustrates this concept's application in Java. We're creating representations of two countries, the United States and Great Britain. Since they're both countries, they both have names and capital cities. So we have created a class called "Country.java," which has variables for both of these common characteristics. It also has methods for returning these two variables.

```java
public class Country
{
    private String name;
    private String capital;

    Country(String nm, String cp)
    {
        name = nm;
        capital = cp;
    }
    public String getName()
    {
        return name;
    }
    public String getCapital()
    {
        return capital;
    }
}
```

However, there is at least one striking difference between the United States and Great Britain. The latter has a queen, whereas the former doesn't. So we've created two separate classes, for each of these countries. The "GreatBritain" class contains a variable called "queen" and a method that returns this variable.

```java
public class GreatBritain extends Country
{
    private String queen = "Queen Elizabeth";
    GreatBritain()
    {
        super("Great Britain", "London");
    }
    public String getQueen()
    {
        return queen;
    }
}


public class USA extends Country
{
```

```
USA()
{
        super("USA", "Washington DC");
}
}
```

As you can see, both of these classes have an "extends Country" in their declaration, which simply means that these classes inherit the class "Country." Public methods and variables of "Country" are available to these classes. Any class can create an instance of these classes and invoke the public methods of that class as well as the public methods of "Country."

Both the classes have "constructors." A constructor is a method with the same name as the class. When you create an instance of a class, the constructor is invoked by default. So if some class creates an instance of the class "USA" (it can do so by saying **new USA()**), the method **USA()** is invoked. Constructors can also be overloaded. The different implementations, however, should have different input and output arguments.

The constructors of both "USA" and "GreatBritain" use the keyword **super()** to invoke the constructor of the parent, "Country." They pass two arguments—the name of the country and the capital city. The constructor of "Country" stores these in its private variables. Since these variables are private, no other class can access these variables, including classes that are inheriting from "Country." So we've created public methods in "Country" that return the required values.

Now let's look at a class that creates an instance of these two countries:

```
public class Inheritance
{
    public static void main(String[] args)
      {
            GreatBritain gb = new GreatBritain();
            USA us = new USA();
            System.out.println("Name: " + gb.getName());
            System.out.println("Queen: " + gb.getQueen());
            System.out.println("Name: " + us.getName());
      }
}
```

When this class is compiled and executed, first an instance of "GreatBritain" is created. This means that the method **GreatBritain()** (the constructor) is invoked. This action calls the constructor of "Country" and sets the name of this country as Great Britain with London as its capital.

Then an instance of "USA" is created. Now, there are two instances, **gb** and **us**, which represent the two countries. If you now invoke **gb.getName()**, "Great Britain" is printed, but if you invoke **us.getName()**, "USA" is printed. **gb.getQueen()** prints "Queen Elizabeth." This method is not applicable to the instance **us**, however, because there is no such method in either "Country" or "USA."

The output of this program is

Name: Great Britain
Queen: Queen Elizabeth
Name: USA

Interfaces

Whereas some object oriented languages like C++ allow multiple inheritance (one class can inherit from multiple classes), Java allows inheritance from just one class. Though multiple inheritance is a useful feature, it is often confusing, and Java has only made life simpler by avoiding it. However, Java has another concept called interfaces that "simulates" multiple inheritance, though not fully. Interfaces are very useful for designing your entire system. An interface is a collection of variables and method declarations. Interfaces contain only declarations of methods—they can't and don't contain definitions. Other classes need to implement these interfaces and provide definitions for these methods. A class that implements an interface needs to define all the methods declared in the interface. It can also implement its own methods and have its own variables in addition.

The following example uses an interface called Fruit. Since all fruits have a name and a color, we've created an interface containing declarations of methods that are supposed to return the name and color of the fruit.

```
public interface Fruit
{
        public String getName();
        public String getColor();
}
```

Note that the interface contains only declarations. Definitions are provided by classes that implement these interfaces. We have two such fruits that implement this interface, Apple and Orange.

```
public class Apple implements Fruit
{
    public String getName()
    {
        return "Apple";
    }
    public String getColor()
    {
        return "Red";
    }
}
```

```java
public class Orange implements Fruit
{
    public String getName()
    {
        return "Orange";
    }
    public String getColor()
    {
        return "Orange";
    }
}
```

Since they both implement the Fruit interface, they need to define the two methods, **getName()** and **getColor()**, declared in that interface. Now we create a class that instantiates Orange and Apple:

```java
public class Interfaces
{
    public static void main(String[] args)
    {
        Apple a = new Apple();
        Orange o = new Orange();
        printNameColor(a);
        printNameColor(o);
    }
    public static void printNameColor(Fruit f)
    {
        System.out.println("Name:" + f.getName() +
                            " Color: " + f.getColor());
    }
}
```

This class contains a method called **printNameColor()** that invokes the methods **getName()** and **getColor()** on the object passed to it as an input parameter. As you can see, we're first passing the apple object (**a**) to this method and then we're passing the orange object (**o**). So how come apples and oranges are being treated alike by the method **printNameColor()**? Because the input argument is of the type "Fruit." This method can thus take as input any object that implements the Fruit interface, be it an Orange or an Apple. However, you can only invoke those methods in the object that belong to the interface. (As an exercise, add a method **public void getValue()**{} to **Apple.java**. In **Interface.java**, call this method inside **printNameColor()** as **f.getValue()**. You will see that the **javac** compiler quits with an error.)

On compiling and executing you get the following output:

Name:Apple Color: Red

Name:Orange Color: Orange

Packages

Good things come in small packages—
except pet elephants!

Imagine going to the supermarket to buy fruits and discovering that apples are in aisle 1, oranges in aisle 12, and bananas in aisle 26. Obviously, putting similar things together has its own advantages. Packages in Java are a collection of similar classes. A package is a way of organizing your classes. Along the way you end up with more benefits. For instance if you have put classes of your product in a package, you are in your own namespace and don't have to worry about other products that may have classes with the same name. This approach can also be related to something we see on a day-to-day basis—real estate! There could be a 4800 Hastings Drive in both San Francisco and Boston, but we know exactly which one we're talking about if we specify 4800 Hastings Drive, San Francisco, CA, USA. In other words, you can think of USA as a package that contains cities. These cities in turn have streets and drives that have houses in them. If all parameters are specified, you know exactly which house somebody is talking about.

Let us create a package to see how one is introduced and used. We go back to the supermarket example to establish the model of supermarket. There are several sections in this supermarket. We are representing the vegetable and fruit sections. Our vegetable section will contain a Potato, while the fruit section will contain a Pineapple and a Banana.

This is how **Potato.java** looks:

```
package supermarket.vegetables;
public class Potato
{
    public Potato()
    {
        System.out.println("Potato");
    }
}
```

We begin by declaring that this class belongs to a package, **supermarket.vegetables**. In other words, there is a directory called Supermarket that contains a directory called Vegetables. The class Potato resides in that directory.

The two fruits reside in the package **supermarket.fruits**, that is, they exist in the directory Fruits under Supermarket. These two classes look like this:

```
package supermarket.fruits;
public class Pineapple
{
    public Pineapple()
```

```
    {
        System.out.println("Pineapple");
    }
}

package supermarket.fruits;
public class Banana
{
    public Banana()
    {
        System.out.println("Banana");
    }
}
```

Now that we have seen how packages can be created, let's look at how they can be used. For this we create a class that calls the constructors of these packages.

```
import supermarket.vegetables.Potato;
import supermarket.fruits.*;
public class Packages
{
    public static void main(String[] args)
    {
        Banana b = new Banana();
        supermarket.fruits.Pineapple  a =
                    new supermarket.fruits.Pineapple();
        Potato p = new Potato();
    }
}
```

In this class we're using the "import" keyword, which indicates that this class needs to use some classes defined in a package. The first line in our class is

```
import supermarket.vegetables.Potato;
```

This means that we want to use the class Potato, which belongs to the package **supermarket.vegetables**. But what if there were more classes in that package? Would we have to import each class separately? The answer, fortunately, is no. We can use the wildcard character, "*," to import multiple classes. We're doing this in the second line to import all classes in the **supermarket.fruits** package.

After that you can use the classes as if they were regular classes residing in your CLASSPATH. However, sometimes there may be conflicts; you might have two packages containing classes with the same name. Here you need to provide resolution. You can see this in JDK packages also: one Date class is defined in the **java.util** package, and another Date class is defined in the **java.sql** package. To resolve the conflict, you need to provide a package name along with the class name. We've illustrated this in the previous example by referring to Pineapple with its fully qualified name (even though it was not necessary in this case):

```
supermarket.fruits.Pineapple a = new supermarket.fruits.
    Pineapple();
```

To use this package, create a directory called Supermarket. In this create two subdirectories called Fruits and Vegetables. Copy **Pineapple.java** and **Banana.java** to the Fruits directory and **Potato.java** to the Vegetables directory. Put **Packages.java** in another directory. Add the directory that contains "supermarket" to your CLASSPATH. If Supermarket exists in the directory : /home/me/packageExample, then add this directory to your CLASSPATH. Also, you may want to include the directory in which the class Packages resides (as this could be different from /home/me/packageExample).

Compile all the Java files and start execution by invoking **java Packages**. This is what you will see in the output:

Banana

Pineapple

Potato

Note that if you want to invoke a class inside a package directly, you can do so by providing the qualified name of the class as

java supermarket.fruits.Banana

This would execute the class Banana, which resides in the package **supermarket.fruits** (i.e., the class has been implemented with a **package supermarket.fruits** line and resides in a directory Supermarket/Fruits under a directory that is in your CLASSPATH.

Exceptions

*Every rule has an exception—
except for Murphy's law.*

One problematic aspect of programming in C is that you need to check for errors almost everywhere, especially if you want to recover from them. This requirement tends to make the code very messy. Java provides a solution to this problem in the form of Exceptions. An exception is typically an error condition, though in the true sense it is anything interrupting the normal flow of execution. Java allows you to catch exceptions and do some processing afterwards. You can enclose a block of code by one or more exception catchers. An error occurring in any line in this block is caught by one of the exception catchers, which saves you the trouble of checking for errors after every line. The following simple example illustrates this point:

```
public class AnException
{
    public static void main(String[] args)
    {
        try
        {
            int i=5, j=20;
            for(int k=i; k>-5; k-)
            {
                int m = j/k;
            }
        }catch(Exception e)
            {
                System.out.println("Exception");
                e.printStackTrace();
            }
        System.out.println("After the for loop");
    }
}
```

In this class we're deliberately creating an error condition. There is an **int** variable, **m**, in which we try to store the result of a division. During the course of this division, we set the denominator to 0. This happens when the counter **k** reaches 0 as it is decremented. In this example, we know beforehand that this division by 0 will happen, so we can avoid it.

However, if we were using a random number as the denominator, this result might or might not occur. The code above has been written to handle a division by 0 (or any other error). We've done this by putting a "try{", "}catch()" block around the code. In the catch we need to specify what kind of Exception we're catching. There are predefined exceptions in Java that can be used to handle some common error conditions (like **FileNotFound** while trying to read a file). You may also define your own exceptions. One try can have multiple **catch()** blocks associated with it to handle different types of exceptions that may be thrown by the same or different lines of code.

However, if you want to catch any and every sort of exception, you should catch the exception named "Exception" (as we've done above). After the **catch()** there is a block in which you can write some error recovery/handling routines. In our example we're first printing the word "Exception" to the standard output. Next we're using a method of Exception, **printStackTrace()**, which gives details of the kind of exception that occurred (including the line of code where this exception occurred). Whenever an exception occurs in a line, the rest of the code till the appropriate catch block is skipped. Then code that is outside this try-catch block (after the outermost catch) is executed. In our example, after the exception's stack trace has been printed, the line "After the for loop" is printed.

Here is the result of executing **java AnException**:

Exception
java.lang.ArithmeticException: / by zero
    at AnException.main(Compiled Code)
After the for loop

File I/O

In the next example we look at more exceptions in the context of File I/O. The class "Copy" reads from one text file and writes to another.

It takes two input arguments: the name of an existing text file and the name of the file to which you want to copy its data.

```
import java.io.*;
public class Copy
{
      public static void main(String[] args)
      {
            String inFile = args[0];
            String outFile = args[1];
            try
            {
                BufferedReader br =
                    new BufferedReader(new FileReader(inFile));
                PrintWriter pw =
                    new PrintWriter(new FileWriter(outFile));
                String s;
                while((s = br.readLine()) != null)
                    pw.println(s);
                br.close();
                pw.close();
            }catch(FileNotFoundException fn)
                {System.out.println("Unable to find file: " +
                    inFile);}
            catch(IOException ioex)
                {System.out.println("I/O Error");}
      }
}
```

Here we begin by importing an I/O package that comes with the JDK: **java.io**. If you look at the documentation for this package, you will see that it contains a large number of classes. There are different classes optimized for doing different types of I/O operations. You can use specialized classes for doing byte reading and writing, doing random access, and so on. In our example we're using classes for reading and writing text files line by line. **BufferedReader** is being used for reading. The constructor of this class takes a Reader object as its input. For this we're creating a **FileReader** object and passing this in the constructor of **BufferedReader()**. **FileReader** itself takes the name of a file as input. Similarly we're creating a **PrintWriter()** object for writing to the output file.

BufferedReader contains a method called **readLine()** which reads a line in the file and returns it as a String. It also advances the pointer so that a new call to **readLine()** returns the next line in the file. If there are no more lines available (**End Of File** has been reached), it returns a null.

PrintWriter contains a method for writing a line to a file (the **println()** method). It writes the given line to the output file and outputs a new line character.

We're using these two methods to read the input file line by line and for writing these lines to the output file. Then we use **close()** methods of both these objects so that these objects are released.

In this example there are two types of exceptions that can occur. If we supply a nonexistent input file, there would be an obvious error. To catch this, we've put a try-catch block in which we're catching an exception defined in the JDK—**FileNotFoundException**.

There could also be a generic I/O error; as an example, when we're copying the file, the disk could become full. To catch this type of an exception we have added another **catch()**, which takes care of IOException. As you can see in this example, you can have more than one "catch" with a "try." If an exception occurs, control goes to the most specific block that handles this exception.

Threads

A stitch in time saves nine!

Most real-world Web applications need to be able to handle concurrent users and share data resources. Threads help you do jobs concurrently instead of sequentially. Generally, operating systems themselves use the concept of threads, enabling you to open multiple windows that may simultaneously be executing different applications. This operation is managed by timesharing. The operating system gives each process or application a slice of time to execute. When a process's slice is over, OS allows another process to execute and then comes back to the first one. These slices are so small that to a user it appears as if all the processes were executing simultaneously. Another common application that uses threads is the Web browser. While you're viewing a page's written content, one of the threads of the browser might be fetching an image.

One way of creating threads in Java is by inheriting from the Thread class. However, if you have multiple threads that need to share a common resource, you need to take extreme care to prevent these threads from stepping on each other. Look at a case where you have two threads, one of which is reading data from a source (like a file) and the other, writing data to it. What if the reader is reading at the same time the other thread is writing? There is a good chance the reader will get incoherent data. Or worse, if there are two writer threads, they would end up corrupting the file. To avoid this, you can use the "synchronized" keyword, which can be used to prevent two threads from accessing the same resource at the same time.

We explain all this with the help of an example. In the following example, we look at a class called MultiThread, which creates two threads. It creates an instance of a class AResource, which contains a String variable. This instance is passed to both the threads. The first thread will read the String variable in the AResource object while the second will modify it. Obviously we don't want these two threads to step on each other. To avoid this, we're making the read and write methods "synchronized." When a thread enters a method that is "synchronized," it locks the object that contains this method. This prevents any other thread from executing this or other synchronized methods in this object. The lock is released when the method has been fully executed by the thread that locked the object. Another way of releasing the lock is by calling **wait()** inside the method. Threads that are waiting for the lock to be released on an object can be informed by calling **notifyAll()**. The Java VM then wakes up one of the threads so it can lock the object. To make things more clear, we step through the code.

```java
public class MultiThread
{
    public static void main(String[] args)
    {
        AResource ar = new AResource();
        AThread at1 = new AThread(ar, "Thread 1");
        AThread at2 = new AThread(ar, "Thread 2");
        at1.start();
        at2.start();
    }
}


class AThread extends Thread
{
    AResource theResource;
    String name;
    AThread(AResource a, String n)
    {
        theResource = a;
        name = n;
    }
    public void run()
    {
```

```
        int i=0;
        while(true)
        {
            if(name.equals("Thread 1"))
            {
                theResource.addElement("Element " + i);
                i++;
                if(i == 100)
                    break;
            }
            else
                System.out.println("Got element: " +
                            theResource.getElement());
            try{
                    sleep(200);
            }catch(InterruptedException ie){}
        }
    }
}
```

This file contains a public class, MultiThread, and another, nonpublic class called AThread.

MultiThread contains the main routine and creates an instance of the class AResource. It also creates two instances of AThread and passes the instance of AResource to both of them.

The class AThread actually represents a thread. this is because it "extends" the Thread class. Execution of a thread object starts when the **start()** method is invoked. Threads contain a **run()** method in them. When a thread is "started," the **run()** method is executed. The thread dies when the **run()** method's execution has finished. In our example, after creating the two threads, MultiThread starts their execution by invoking **start()**.

As you can see, the first thread's name is "Thread 1" and the second one is "Thread 2." Inside the run method we call the **addElement()** method of AResource if it is the first thread that is being executed and the **getElement()** if it is the second. After doing this, each thread sleeps for 200 milliseconds, so it is quite likely that while the first thread is executing **addElement()**, the second is calling **getElement()**. We now look at **AResource.java** to see how this problem is solved.

```
import java.util.*;
public class AResource
{
    String theElement = "";
    boolean somebodyReadingElement = false;
    public synchronized void addElement(String s)
    {
        while(somebodyReadingElement)
```

```
        {
            try{
                    wait();
            }catch(InterruptedException ie){}
        }
        System.out.println("Adding element " + s);
        theElement = s;
        somebodyReadingElement = true;
        notifyAll();
    }
    public synchronized String getElement()
    {
        while(somebodyReadingElement == false)
        {
            try{
                    wait();
            }catch(InterruptedException ie){}
        }
        somebodyReadingElement = false;
        notifyAll();
        return theElement;

    }
}
```

In this class, besides the String "theElement," in which data is stored, we're maintaining a variable to determine whether a thread is reading the String or writing to it. Both **addElement()** and **getElement()** have been declared "synchronized" methods. Let's say first the **read** thread gets control and tries to invoke **getElement()**. As soon as it enters the method, the thread has "locked" this object. In this method we're first checking if the Boolean **somebodyReadingElement** is false. Since this is the case initially, the **wait()** method is invoked. This means that the lock is released. Now, if the **write** thread wants to write, it can invoke **addElement()** as the object is no longer locked. As soon as the method is invoked, the "lock" is obtained by the **write** thread. While it is writing the data, no other thread (including the **read** thread) can invoke **getElement()**, as it is a synchronized method.

Once writing has been done, we set **somebodyReadingElement** to true so that when the **read** thread gets control, it can go past the **while()** loop in which it was forced to wait. But before the **write** thread returns, it must notify the **read** thread (and possible other threads) that it is releasing the lock. This is done by invoking the **notifyAll()** method. Now the **read** thread can safely go and read the data.

Output of this program:

Adding element Element 0

Got element: Element 0

Adding element Element 1

Got element: Element 1

Adding element Element 2

Got element: Element 2

....

Some Useful Classes and Methods

Before we take a look at some other features of Java, here's a quick overview of two utility classes that you could find pretty useful.

Vectors

When faced with a situation where you have to store objects for future use, you may often encounter a situation where you wouldn't know beforehand how many objects you want to store. Vectors provide a convenient storage mechanism. A vector can contain any type of object, and you don't need to specify the maximum number of objects to be stored in it. The size of a vector automatically expands or contracts as you add or remove objects. This provides some of the benefits of a linked list and at the same time hides most of the complexity behind the scenes. Here is an example illustrating the use of a vector.

This class takes a number as input. It creates as many objects as are specified in the command line and stores them in a vector. It then prints the size of the vector. Then it retrieves the objects and prints them.

```java
import java.util.*;
public class AVector
{
    public static void main(String[] args)
    {
        Integer in = new Integer(args[0]);
        int total = in.intValue();

        Vector v = new Vector();
        System.out.println("Before adding elements,
                            size of vector is " + v.size());
        for(int i=0; i<total; i++)
            v.addElement("Element " + i);

        int size = v.size();
        System.out.println("After adding elements,
```

```
                                          size of vector is " + size);
        for(int i=0; i<size; i++)
        {
                String s = (String)v.elementAt(i);
                System.out.println(s);
        }
    }
}
```

The class "Vector" is in the **java.util** package, so we're importing it. In the main method we need to know how many objects are to be created, as this is being specified as a command-line argument. However, the argument comes to the program as a String object, and we need to convert it to an **int**. For this, we first create an **Integer()** object, which is the closest object to an **int**. This object contains a method that returns the **int** value. This method is appropriately named **intValue()**.

Then we create a new vector object. To see the initial size of the vector, we're printing it out. Vector has a **method size()** in it that returns the number of elements present in the vector. As expected, this number is 0.

Then we loop through an array and add a String object to the vector. Elements are added to a vector using the **addElement()** method.

After that we again calculate the size of the vector and print it out. We then retrieve the elements that we have stored in this vector and print them out. One common method of retrieving elements from a vector is **elementAt()**. This method takes a number as input and returns the object present at that location. Objects are present at the same location where they were stored (assuming some elements weren't removed). As a result, the first element that we added can be accessed using **v.elementAt(0)**, and so on.

Since we can store any type of object in a vector, we need to explicitly cast the value returned by **elementAt()** before we can assign it to a variable. This is why we're casting our elements to the String datatype (as we had stored String objects earlier using **addElement**).

If you invoke this class as

java AVector 2

you get the following output:

Before adding elements, size of vector is 0

After adding elements, size of vector is 2

Element 0

Element 1

You can experiment by invoking it with a number other than 2.

Hashtables

If you want to store an indefinite number of objects and are looking at fast retrieval, Hashtable is the way to go. This class allows you to store objects, associating them with a unique key. When an object is to be retrieved, you need to specify that key.

Here's an example:

```java
import java.util.*;
public class AHashtable
{
    public static void main(String[] args)
    {
        Hashtable h = new Hashtable();
        h.put("Key1", "value1");
        h.put("Key2", "value2");

        String s = (String)h.get("Key1");
        System.out.println("Key1's value is " + s);

        System.out.println("Here are all the keys and values");
        Enumeration e = h.keys();
        while(e.hasMoreElements())
        {
            String key = (String)e.nextElement();
            String val = (String)h.get(key);
            System.out.println("Key: " + key + " Value: " + val);
        }
    }
}
```

We're importing **java.util**, as that package contains Hashtable. We're putting two String objects, **value1** and **value2**, in this Hashtable. We're associating the key **Key1** with the first and **Key2** with the second. These keys can be anything so long as they are unique. Hashtable has a **put()** method for storing objects. The first argument of this is the key; the second is the object that is to be stored.

Retrieval can be done by using the **get()** method, which takes the name of a key as input and returns the associated stored object as output. However, in some cases you may not be sure of the names of the keys but would like to retrieve all the objects stored in a Hashtable. To do this, we use the **keys()** method of Hashtable, which returns an **Enumeration** object.

This **Enumeration** object contains a list of all the keys.

Enumeration has two important methods: **hasMoreElements()**, which returns a Boolean that tells if there are any more elements left in the **Enumeration** object that haven't been retrieved, and **nextElement()**, which returns the next element. We're using these two methods to retrieve the keys one by one. Then we use the **get()** method of Hashtable and pass the retrieved key to get the associated value. This way we're retrieving all the keys and values stored in the Hashtable.

Object Serialization

One peculiarity of this serial killer
is that he begins his day with a killer cereal!

At times you may find the need to store your objects for reuse. Or you may want to pass them around in a network. One way of doing this is to retrieve values of individual elements of the object and send them one by one. The receiving end could then reconstruct the object using these values. However, this is a rather cumbersome and crude way of dealing with objects.

Object serialization allows you to serialize your objects, and an object that has been serialized can be stored in a file and retrieved later in a straightforward way. Similarly, it can be passed around in a network; you can write the object to a stream and read it from the stream transparently.

In Java an object can become serializable by implementing the **java.io.Serializable** interface. It must contain only serializable objects in it. Most Java objects (String, Integer, etc.) are serializable and thus can be included in your serializable objects.

An instance of a class that implements the **java.io.Serializable** interface can be stored in a stream and later retrieved from it. The retrieved instance will be exactly like the stored instance, and values of the variables that were set before the class was stored will be available.

Let's look at it with an example. We begin by creating a serializable object called **SerialObject**. This object contains two variables, a String and an Integer. It contains methods for setting and retrieving values of these variables.

SerialObject.java

```java
public class SerialObject implements java.io.Serializable
{
    String s;
    Integer i;
    public void setValues(String st, Integer it)
    {
        s = st;
        i = it;
    }
    public String getS()
    {
        return s;
```

```
    }
    public Integer getI()
    {
        return i;
    }
}
```

Now we create an instance of this class and store it in a file named **SerialFile**.

As we will see later, another class can then retrieve the object from the file. The values of the String and the Integer in the object would be the same as they were when the object was written using **WriteObject**.

WriteObject.java

```
import java.io.*;
public class WriteObject
{
    public static void main(String[] args)
    {
        SerialObject  s = new SerialObject();
        s.setValues("String Object", new Integer(5));
        try
        {
            FileOutputStream f = new FileOutputStream
                ("SerialFile");
            ObjectOutputStream os  =  new  ObjectOutputStream(f);
            os.writeObject(s);
            os.flush();
            os.close();
        }catch(IOException e){}

    }
}
```

This class creates an instance of **SerialObject** and sets the values of the String and Integer variables to "String Object" and 5, respectively.

```
        SerialObject  s = new SerialObject();
        s.setValues("String Object", new Integer(5));
```

It then uses the **ObjectOutputStream** (which is another I/O stream in the **java.io** package for writing objects) to write the object created above into a file named **SerialFile**.

```
        FileOutputStream f = new FileOutputStream
            ("SerialFile");
        ObjectOutputStream os  =  new  ObjectOutputStream(f);
        os.writeObject(s);
```

Next we see how this object can be retrieved and used.

ReadObject.java

```java
import java.io.*;
class ReadObject
{
    public static void main(String[] args)
    {
        SerialObject so;
        try
        {
            FileInputStream f = new FileInputStream("SerialFile");
            ObjectInputStream is = new ObjectInputStream(f);
            try
            {
                so = (SerialObject)is.readObject();
                String s = so.getS();
                Integer i = so.getI();
                System.out.println("Value of s: " + s);
                System.out.println("Value of i: " + i.toString());
            }catch(ClassNotFoundException c){c.printStackTrace();}
            is.close();
        }catch(IOException e){}
    }
}
```

This class uses the ObjectInputStream's **readObject()** method to read the object from **SerialFile**. After this we can invoke the methods of SerialObject as if it was an instance created by us. The values of the two variables would still be "String Object" and 5, values that were set in the "WriteObject" class.

If you run the following commands:

java WriteObject

java ReadObject

the output would be

Value of s: String Object

Value of i: 5

A couple of things to note: The value of any static variables is not stored when you write the object. So if you want to store the object and be able to retrieve values for all variables, none of them should be static. Another type that is not stored is variables that are declared as "private transient."

Remote Method Invocation (RMI)

Times have changed—
now man's best friend is the remote!

As enterprise systems grow bigger, the need for applications to interact with each other arises. Applications residing on different systems often need to exchange data. Also, a system may comprise several applications, each performing a specialized task. However, these applications may need to communicate among themselves to keep the whole system going. This brings us to the topic of Remote Method Invocation (RMI), a Java API that allows applications to invoke methods of one or more applications residing on the same or different machines.

You can write RMI programs quite easily using Java. First you create a server containing methods that can be invoked remotely by other applications. The server makes itself available by registering itself on the network using a name. Other applications can then look up this server using the name and invoke methods implemented by it.

For this to work, an executable called **rmiregistry** (which comes with the JDK) is started on the server. This starts up a registry that maintains information about remote objects available on this machine. Once a server binds itself to this, it becomes available for clients, which can obtain a reference to it using the name with which it registered.

The JDK comes with a utility called **rmic**. Once a server class has been compiled, you can run **rmic** on it. This creates a surrogate object (known as a stub). The stub needs to be transferred to the client side. Any client can then invoke methods in the server through this stub object. The communication is transparent as far as the client is concerned; it can invoke the methods as if they belonged to a class residing on the client machine.

The following steps are required for creating an RMI implementation:

1. An interface is written containing declarations of methods that can be remotely invoked.

2. A server class that implements this interface and extends the UnicastRemoteObject class is created.

3. rmic is executed on this server class and stubs are generated.

4. rmiregistry is started.

5. The server is started using javac. The server binds itself to the registry using a unique name.

6. Stubs and the interface are moved to all client machines that need to invoke methods of this server.

7. The client Java classes can now invoke methods on the server as if they belonged to a local object.

RMI classes and interfaces are defined in the **java.rmi** and **java.rmi.server** packages.

We look at this with the help of the following example. Here we are creating a message server containing methods that can be invoked remotely by clients and allowing clients to write messages that can be read by the same or other clients.

There are two methods on the server that can be invoked by clients: **writeMessage()** accepts a username and a message String. The message String is stored in a Hashtable with the username as its key so a client can write a message that will be stored by the server. Another client can then retrieve this message by calling the method **readMessage()** and passing in the same username.

A typical invocation would be like this:

Client 1: calls writeMessage("client1Username," "message from client 1");

Client 2: calls readMessage("client1Username") to read message written by client 1; calls writeMessage("client2Username," "response to message from client 1");

Client 1: calls readMessage("client2Username") to read message written by client 2.

Here's a look at the server-side code:

MessageServer.java

```
public interface MessageServer extends java.rmi.Remote
{
    String readMessage(String user) throws java.rmi.RemoteException;
    void   writeMessage(String user, String message)
                                    throws java.rmi.RemoteException;
}
```

This is the interface that our server will implement. It extends java.rmi.Remote, as our server is going to be a remotely callable object. The interface tells us that the server object will have two methods, **readMessage()** and **writeMessage()**, that can be remotely called by a client. Each remote method has to be defined in such a way that it can throw the **java.rmi.RemoteException**.

MessageServerImpl.java

```
import java.util.*;
import java.rmi.*;
import java.rmi.server.UnicastRemoteObject;

public class MessageServerImpl
        extends UnicastRemoteObject
        implements MessageServer
{
    Hashtable messages = new Hashtable();

    public MessageServerImpl() throws java.rmi.RemoteException
```

```
    {
        super();
    }

    public static void main(String args[])
    {
        // Create and install the security manager
        System.setSecurityManager(new RMISecurityManager());

        try
        {
            MessageServerImpl ms = new MessageServerImpl();
            Naming.rebind("MessageServer", ms);
            System.out.println("Name MessageServer bound to
                registry");

        } catch (Exception e)
          {
            System.out.println("Exception occurred in
                                        MessageServerImpl: ");
            e.printStackTrace();
          }
    }


    public String readMessage(String user)
                        throws java.rmi.RemoteException
    {
        String message = (String)messages.get(user);
        return message;
    }
    public void writeMessage(String user, String message)
                                throws java.rmi.RemoteException
    {
        messages.put(user, message);
    }
}
```

This is the actual implementation. It implements the interface defined earlier and thus contains implementations for the two methods defined in the interface. It contains a Hashtable called "messages," which is used for storing messages received from a client.

The main method binds the server object to the registry so that it becomes available to clients.

First we need to define the security manager that controls security on the server.

```
System.setSecurityManager(new RMISecurityManager());
```

An instance of the server object is then created and bound with the name MessageServer. You can use any name so long as there is no other object in this registry with this name.

```
MessageServerImpl ms = new MessageServerImpl();
Naming.rebind("MessageServer", ms);
```

Now our object is available for use by clients.

When a client calls the **writeMessage()** method with a username and the message content, the message content is stored in the message's Hashtable.

```
messages.put(user, message);
```

If a client calls **readMessage()**, the message content is retrieved from the Hashtable and returned to the client.

```
String message = (String)messages.get(user);
return message;
```

This completes discussion of the server-side code. Now we take a look at the client-side code.

We have implemented two client classes, "WriteMessage" and "ReadMessage." The first can be used for writing messages to our server, while the second can be used for retrieving messages from it that have been written by a client class on the same machine or somewhere else.

```
import java.rmi.*;

public class WriteMessage
{
    public static void main(String args[])
    {
        if(args.length != 2)
        {
            System.out.println(
                "Usage: java WriteMessage <username>
                        <message>");
            System.exit(0);
        }
        try
        {
            String n = "//myServer.com/MessageServer";
            MessageServer obj = (MessageServer) Naming.lookup(n);
            obj.writeMessage(args[0], args[1]);
```

```
        } catch (Exception e)
            {
                e.printStackTrace();
            }
    }
}
```

The client-side code first obtains a reference to the server object by using the
lookup() method in the Naming class (which is part of the JDK).

```
            String n = "//myServer.com/MessageServer";
            MessageServer obj = (MessageServer) Naming.lookup(n);
```

Here "myServer.com" is the name of the machine on which the server is running.
"MessageServer" is the name with which our server has bound itself to the registry.
Naming.lookup() thus looks for a server object bound to the name "MessageServer"
on the machine "myServer.com."

```
            obj.writeMessage(args[0], args[1]);
```

Once a reference to the remote server object has been obtained, remote methods
defined in it can be invoked as if they were methods of any other local object.

```
import java.rmi.*;

public class ReadMessage
{
    public static void main(String args[])
    {
        if(args.length != 1)
        {
            System.out.println("Usage: java ReadMessage
                <username>");
            System.exit(0);
        }
        try
        {
            String n = "//myServer.com/MessageServer";
            MessageServer obj = (MessageServer) Naming.lookup(n);
            String message = obj.readMessage(args[0]);
            System.out.println(message);
        } catch (Exception e)
            {
                e.printStackTrace();
            }
    }
}
```

ReadMessage class obtains a server object reference like WriteMessage. It then invokes the **readMessage()** method and prints the returned result on the standard output.

Setting this all up to work happens as follows:

On the Server Side

1. javac MessageServer.java MessageServerImpl.java

2. rmic MessageServerImpl

3. Create a directory in which you want to store the server objects—let's call it /home/vsharma/RMI_DIR:

   mkdir /home/vsharma/RMI_DIR

4. Copy classes to /home/vsharma/RMI_DIR:

   cp *.class /home/vsharma/RMI_DIR

5. Start up the rmiregistry:

   rmiregistry&

6. cd /home/vsharma/RMI_DIR

7. Start up the server so that it binds itself to the registry and becomes available:

   java -Djava.rmi.server.codebase=http://myServer.com/home/vsharma/RMI_DIR/ MessageServerImpl&

On the Client Side

On each of the client machines

1. copy MessageServer.class and MessageServerImpl_Stub.class from /home/vsharma/ RMI_DIR on server

2. javac ReadMessage.java WriteMessage.java

Usage

   java WriteMessage <username> <message>
   java ReadMessage <username>

So, if a client on machine A invokes:

   java WriteMessage johndoe "This is a message from John Doe. How are you?"

a client on machine B can retrieve this message as follows:

   java ReadMessage johndoe

This would print out the following on machine B:

   This is a message from John Doe. How are you?

Reading a URL

While on a topic related to networking, we look at a JDK class that allows you to connect to a URL (such as a Web page or a CGI program) and retrieve results from it. The following example connects to a URL specified in the command line. It opens an input stream so that it can read data from the URL. The contents are read line by line and displayed on standard output.

```java
import java.net.*;
import java.io.*;
class ReadURL
{
    public static void main(String[] args)
    {
        try
        {
            URL myURL = new URL(args[0]);
            InputStreamReader inpStream =
                    new InputStreamReader(myURL.openStream());
            BufferedReader br = new BufferedReader(inpStream);
            String inpLine;

            while ((inpLine = br.readLine()) != null)
            {
                System.out.println(inpLine);
            }
            br.close();
        } catch (Exception ex)
          { ex.printStackTrace(); }
    }
}
```

We make use of the URL class; a URL object is created.

```java
URL myURL = new URL(args[0]);
```

The argument in this is the complete URL to which we want to connect. Then we obtain an input stream to this URL so that we can read its contents.

```java
InputStreamReader inpStream = new
InputStreamReader(myURL.openStream());
```

Now we can simply read the contents using normal I/O routines. An example invocation of this would be

java ReadURL *www.somewebsite.com*

This would return the *index.html* of *somewebsite.com*.

Working with Proxies

In typical companies the internal machines need to be isolated from the rest of the world to prevent people in other companies from connecting to these machines and stealing secrets. However, the company's employees would still want somehow to connect to the Internet. One solution to this paradoxical problem is to install a gateway machine, that is, a machine that sits between internal machines and the rest of the world. It allows people from inside to connect to the outside world but does not allow anybody from outside to connect to internal machines. This is a proxy server, or firewall. If the ReadURL class described earlier is not working when you try to access an external URL, chances are you are behind a firewall. There is a simple solution to this problem.

First find out the name of your proxy machine and the port on which it is accepting connections. A system administrator should be able to supply this information to you. You will need to modify the ReadURL class a little bit. The JVM needs to know your proxy machine and port so that the URL class can route the request appropriately through the proxy machine. For this add the following lines of code before creating the URL object:

```
Properties p = System.getProperties();
p.put(""ttp.proxyHost", "YOUR_PROXY_MACHINE");
p.put("http.proxyPort", "YOUR_PROXY_PORT");
System.setProperties(p);
```

Also, you will need to import the package java.util.*, which contains the Properties class used here.

Now things should be fine and you should be able to connect to the outside world.

Internationalization

I'm a very learned person. I know many languages—
English, French—and then there's Pascal, Fortran, C++ . . .

Once your business is on the Net, like it or not, it becomes available worldwide. But to truly increase your reach to far-flung corners of the world, you have to provide information in languages other than English. While this is not a strict requirement, it can help increase the outreach of your business to a wider audience. Fortunately, Java provides a simple way to present language- or country-specific text based on a user's preference. The important thing to note, however, is that you would have to provide translations for all languages you want to support. Java merely helps pick the right translation based on a user's choice. So you don't have to write a different executable for displaying text in different languages; the same executable picks up the relevant text.

How does this all work? In a noninternationalized executable you would probably put hard-coded text like this:

```
System.out.println("System Error! Please reboot your computer");
```

However, with internationalization you would use a key to retrieve the message in the appropriate language and then put that retrieved message in **System.out.println()**. Translations for each of the languages you support would be present in a set of "properties" files. There would be one properties file for each language, containing key value pairs. The key is the one you would use in your program, and the value would be the translated text.

Here's an example. Let's say we want to display two lines of text to a customer. The customer may want to view these in English or French, depending upon his or her preference.

We begin by creating two properties files, one for U.S. English and another for French. The first one is named "myText_en_US.properties." Here "en" represents the language, and "US" represents the country. The second one is named "myText_fr_FR.properties." We will put two key value pairs in both of them, one for each of the text lines we want to display. The name of the keys needs to be the same in both the files. Let's say the keys are named **text1** and **text2**. For the sake of simplicity, even the French version contains English text; however, you are free to put French words here.

myText_en_ US.properties

text1 = How does the guy who drives a snowplow get to work in the morning?

text2 = If a cow laughed, would milk come out of its nose?

myText_fr_FR.properties

text1 = Comment le type qui conduit un chasse-neige obtient-il de travailler le matin?

text2 = Si une vache riait, le lait sortirait-il de son nez?

Next we look at our Java program. As you can see, there is only one **International. java**, which will display either the French text or the English text based on the preference specified by the user on the command line. The program takes two command-line arguments: the country or language in which the user wants to see the messages.

The Java class "ResourceBundle" is the one that helps in picking the text from the appropriate properties file based on a **Locale** object created using the country or language specified by the user. The static method **getBundle()** returns an instance of "ResourceBundle," which can be queried to retrieve the appropriate text using the keys specified in your properties files.

```
import java.util.*;
public class International
{
```

```
public static void main(String[] args)
{

    String country="", language="";

    if(args.length == 2)
    {
        country = new String(args[0]);
        language = new String(args[1]);
    }

    Locale currentLocale;
    ResourceBundle messages;

    currentLocale = new Locale(language, country);

    messages = ResourceBundle.getBundle("myText",
                                        currentLocale);
    System.out.println(messages.getString("text1"));
    System.out.println(messages.getString("text2"));
}
}
```

The program begins with storing the country or language specified by the user on the command line in the variables country and language. Then a **Locale** object is created.

```
    currentLocale = new Locale(language, country);
```

Next we obtain an instance of the "ResourceBundle" for this country or language. The method **getBundle()** takes two arguments. The first is the base name of our properties files. In this case that would be "myText" (as our properties files are named "myText_<something>.properties"). The second argument is the **Locale** object, which contains information about the country/language selected by the user.

```
    messages =
        ResourceBundle.getBundle("myText", currentLocale);
```

Now that we know the correct resource bundle, we can retrieve the text for both keys, text1 and text2, which are present in our properties files, and display the retrieved Strings.

```
    System.out.println(messages.getString("text1"));
    System.out.println(messages.getString("text2"));
```

Here are results of invoking this application:

java International US en

How does the guy who drives a snowplow get to work in the morning?

If a cow laughed, would milk come out of its nose?

java International FR fr

Comment le type qui conduit un chasse-neige obtient-il de travailler le matin?

Si une vache riait, le lait sortirait-il de son nez?

Similarly, you can create properties files for other languages you want to support on your site. For each language you would create a file named

myText_<language>_<country>

Of course you can use a name other than "myText"!

But what happens if a user types in, say "java International hu HU" and you don't have a properties file for that country or language. For this **getBundle()** looks for the default file, in this case "myText.properties."

So, you can create "myText.properties" as follows:

text1 = Text 1 in default language

text2 = Text 2 in default language

Now, here's the result of invoking it:

java International hu HU

Text 1 in default language

Text 2 in default language

Note that the properties files need to be in your CLASSPATH. **ResourceBundle. getBundle()** looks for the properties files in all directories in your CLASSPATH.

If you want to learn more about internationalization, you can look at a couple of other classes provided by Java for internationalization: "ListResourceBundle" and "PropertyResourceBundle."

Applets

We've looked at a lot of Java applications. Now it's time to move to Java applets. These are Java programs that execute on the client's machine and can be used for relieving some of the stress on your server. An applet is quite different from a typical Java application. There is no **main()** method in an applet. The entry point is different. Also, applets are generally used for displaying pretty pictures and text, so they are graphics-intensive.

In order to make use of applets on your site, you would create an applet class and put it on your Web server along with your HTML files. The HTML files can then "include" this applet with an <APPLET> tag. When a client reads the HTML file and encounters the <APPLET> tag, it loads the applet class(es) for execution. The client sets aside an area in its window where the applet can display text and graphics that coexist with the rest of the HTML page.

If a customer is viewing the following HTML file through, say, Netscape:

```
<HTML><HEAD></HEAD>
<BODY>
   <H1>My Applet</H1><BR>
       <APPLET CODE=MyApplet.class WIDTH=350 HEIGHT=30>
       </APPLET>
</BODY>
</HTML>
```

The browser would display the line "My Applet" and would then allocate a rectangle of height 30 and width 350 for the applet. It would load the class **MyApplet.class**, which is assumed to exist in the same directory as your HTML file, unless you specify otherwise (for more information on this see the CODEBASE attribute of the APPLET tag). The Applet class is then executed by the browser. Whatever the applet writes is displayed in the rectangular area set aside by the browser.

In the Java file we begin by importing two packages that are required by applets: **java.awt** and **java.applet**.

Each applet extends the Applet class that comes with the JDK. It may implement several methods—**init(), start(), stop(), paint()**, and **update()**. You may override the default implementations by providing implementations for these methods in your applet.

The first time an applet is loaded, the **init()** method is invoked. You can override the default **init()** by writing your own. This method can be used to set some initializing parameters. The **init()** method is called only once in the life of an applet.

Every time an applet becomes visible, the **start()** method is called. Every time it goes out of visibility, the **stop()** method is called. So if you minimize a Netscape window displaying an applet, the **stop()** method will be called. When you reopen it, **start()** will be called (but **init()** won't be). Similar behavior will be initiated if you press the Forward and Back buttons of your browser.

The **paint()** method is the one in which the text and graphics to be displayed are specified. You would almost always want to override this method so that you can display something on the Web page.

Now we look at an actual applet. FirstApplet is an applet that displays a String in the display area. The String is displayed in white with a red background. To view this, move firstApplet.html and FirstApplet.class to your webserver. Now if you try to access firstApplet.html through your browser, the applet will be loaded and executed, as illustrated in Figure 3.1.

Figure 3.1

FirstApplet.java

```java
import java.awt.*;
import java.applet.*;

public class FirstApplet extends Applet
{
    String message = "";
    public void init()
    {
        message = getParameter("message");
    }

    public void paint(Graphics g)
    {
        g.setColor(new Color(255, 0, 0));
        g.fillRect(0,0,200,30);
        g.setColor(new Color(255, 255, 255));
        g.drawString(message, 10, 15);
    }
}
```

firstApplet.html

```html
<HTML><HEAD></HEAD>
<BODY>
    <APPLET CODE=FirstApplet.class WIDTH=350 HEIGHT=30>
        <PARAM NAME="message" VALUE="Message from HTML File">
    </APPLET>
</BODY>
</HTML>
```

The <APPLET> tag not only allows you to specify the width and height of the display area and the applet class file's name, it also allows you to pass parameters to the applet. In this example we're passing a parameter named "message":

```
<PARAM NAME="message" VALUE="Applets are not mini apples">
```

In our applet class we begin by reading this value in the **init()** method.

```
message = getParameter("message");
```

Here **getParameter()** is an Applet method that retrieves the value of a named parameter from the HTML file.

We've also overridden the **paint()** method. Anything we display here will be written in the rectangular window allocated for this applet by the browser.

```
public void paint(Graphics g)
```

The method gets a handle to a Graphics object. This object contains methods like **drawString()** and **drawImage()** that can be used for writing text or displaying images. It also has methods for setting the color in which text is going to be written.

The Graphics object can also be used for drawing shapes like lines and rectangles. We're drawing a filled rectangle of red color by first setting the color to red and then invoking **fillRect()**.

```
g.setColor(new Color(255, 0, 0));
g.fillRect(0,0,200,30);
```

Here colors are RGB values ranging from 0–255. The **fillRect()** takes four arguments. The first two are the x and y position of the left top corner of the rectangle, relative to the position of the applet. The next two parameters are the width and height of the applet.

Next we set the color to white and draw the message string at an x offset of 10 and a y offset of 15 from the top left corner of the applet.

```
g.setColor(new Color(255, 255, 255));
g.drawString(message, 10, 15);
```

Threads in Applets

The applet in Figure 3.1 is pretty static. What if you want some animation in it? For instance, you may want the text message to scroll across the applet window instead of just staying where it was (after all, you could achieve the static effect using plain old HTML itself). We illustrate one way of doing this with an example using an applet that creates a thread. The thread can be started when the applet becomes visible and stopped when it becomes invisible. This thread can then scroll the message infinitely by repeatedly invoking the **paint()** method of the applet, making it write the message at a different x position every time.

In this example we also illustrate another concept, events and event handling in Java. This applet recognizes mouse clicks. If a user clicks the mouse in the applet area and the message is scrolling, it will stop scrolling. If the user wants to restart the scrolling, (s)he can click the mouse in the applet area again.

In order to create a thread, an applet can implement the Runnable interface. As a result of implementing this interface, the applet would have to implement the **run()** method. This method will be automatically invoked when the thread is started.

To capture events like mouse clicks, the applet can implement methods like **mouseDown()**, **mouseUp()**, **mouseEnter()**, and **mouseExit()**.

```java
import java.awt.*;
import java.applet.*;

public class AnimationApplet extends Applet implements Runnable
{
    int xPos = 0;
    int delay = 500;
    boolean stopped = false;
    String message = "";

    Thread ap = null;

    public void init()
    {
        message = getParameter("message");
    }

    public void start()
    {
        ap = new Thread(this);
        ap.start();
    }
    public void stop()
    {
        ap = null;
    }
    public void run()
    {
        Thread.currentThread().setPriority(Thread.MIN_PRIORITY);
        while(ap != null)
        {
            repaint();
            try{
                Thread.sleep(delay);
```

```
                }catch(Exception ex){}
                if(stopped == false)
                {
                        xPos += 10;
                        if(xPos > 200)
                                xPos = 0;
                }
            }
    }
    public void paint(Graphics g)
    {
            g.setColor(new Color(255, 255, 255));
            g.drawString(message, xPos, 10);
    }

    public boolean mouseDown(Event e, int x, int y)
    {
        if(stopped == false)
                stopped = true;
        else
                stopped = false;
        return false;
    }
}
```

As you can see, this applet implements the Runnable interface. In the **start()** method we create a Thread and start it:

```
        ap = new Thread(this);
        ap.start();
```

As a result of this, the **run()** method is invoked. Inside the **run()** method we're repeatedly calling the **repaint()** method. Calling the **repaint()** method has the effect of invoking the **paint()** method.

```
        while(ap != null)
        {
                repaint();
```

We then make the thread sleep for some time.

```
        try{
                Thread.sleep(delay);
        }catch(Exception ex){}
```

Then we advance the **xPos** so that next time **g.drawString()** in the **paint()** method draws the string at a different location.

```
if(stopped == false)
{
    xPos += 10;
    if(xPos > 200)
        xPos = 0;
}
```

Here the variable "stopped" determines whether **xPos** value should be changed. We want to make sure that if the user has clicked the mouse and wants to stop the scrolling, the message should not be written at a different x position.

And the value of "stopped" is controlled in the method **mouseDown()**. This method is called automatically when the user presses the mouse inside the applet area. We're simply reversing the value of the variable "stopped" so that the scrolling can stop or start depending on how many times the user has clicked the mouse.

```
public boolean mouseDown(Event e, int x, int y)
{
    if(stopped == false)
        stopped = true;
    else
        stopped = false;
```

Here are two snapshots of this applet; as you can see in Figures 3.2 and 3.3, the text has scrolled across the page in the second case.

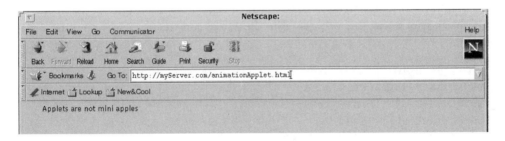

Figure   3.2

Figure   3.3

This completes our discussion of applets. You can use the techniques we described to create different types of animation. If you want to use images in your applet, you can do so by looking up the JDK documentation for the **drawImage()** method.

Java Mail API

You've Got Mail!

Another topic of interest to people developing e-commerce systems would be the Java Mail API, an API that allows you send emails. We will look at some practical examples that use this API in the following chapters. In the meantime, here is a quick overview of how you can start using the API.

You can download the API, which is an extension of the standard JDK, from the Java Web site. You will also need to download the Java Activation Framework (JAF), as the Mail API uses some classes from the JAF API. To compile and use classes that use the Java Mail API, you will need to have the following two files in your CLASSPATH:

activation.jar

mail.jar

These jar files come with the JAF and the JavaMail API, respectively.

To be able to send emails, your system must have access to an SMTP host. Check with your system administrator to find out which SMTP host you can use.

Here's a program that uses the JavaMail API to send mail. It accepts four command-line arguments: the "From" address, the "To" email address, the subject of the mail, and the body of the mail. It uses classes in the API to construct a message and to send it.

```java
import java.io.*;
import java.net.InetAddress;
import java.util.Properties;
import java.util.Date;

import javax.mail.*;
import javax.mail.internet.*;
import javax.activation.*;

public class SendEmails
{
    String smtphost = "YOUR_SMTP_HOST";
    public static void main(String[] args)
            throws Exception
    {
        if(args.length != 4)
```

```
            {
                System.out.println(
                    "Usage: java SendEmails <from> <to>
                        <subject> <body>");
                System.exit(0);
            }
            SendEmails se = new SendEmails();
            se.start(args[0], args[1], args[2], args[3]);
        }
        public void start(String from, String to,
                            String subject, String body)
            throws Exception
        {
            Properties props = new Properties();
            props.put("mail.smtp.host", smtphost);
            Session session = Session.getDefaultInstance(props, null);
            Message msg = new MimeMessage(session);
            msg.setFrom(new InternetAddress(from));
            InternetAddress[] address = {new InternetAddress(to)};
            msg.setRecipients(Message.RecipientType.TO, address);
            msg.setSubject(subject);
            msg.setSentDate(new Date());
            msg.setText(body);
            Transport.send(msg);
        }
    }
```

First the SMTP host is specified as a property named "mail.smtp.host."

```
    props.put("mail.smtp.host", smtphost);
```

A Message object is created, and different methods, like **setSubject()**, **setRecipients()**, **setText()**, and **setFrom()**, are called to set the components of the mail such as the "To" list, the "From" address, subject, and body. Finally, the **send()** method in the Transport class is used to send the email.

Here's a look at the **setRecipients()** method where we specified the To address.

```
    msg.setRecipients(Message.RecipientType.TO, address);
```

The first argument is the recipient type. If you want to CC (carbon copy) email or send a blind copy (BCC), you can set the appropriate recipient type, for example:

```
    Message.RecipientType.CC
```

If you download the API, you will notice that it contains a number of usage examples. The examples demonstrating how you can send HTML mail are definitely worth reading.

Commenting Code in Java

Java supports two types of comments (the standard C style of comments): Anything between "/*" and "*/" is considered commented. Also, there is a convenient way of creating small comments; anything followed by a "//" up to the end of a line is considered commented.

Here's a small example:

```
public class Comments
{
    /* This is the class Comments in which we've commented code  -
        this is the 'C' style of comments*/
    public static void main(String[] args)
    {
        int i = 0; // and this is the other style supported by Java
    }
}
```

Some Useful Tools

There are a number of useful tools that come with the JDK. You've already used two of them—**javac**, which is the Java compiler, and "java," which is the interpreter. Here is an introduction to two more useful tools:

jar

The **jar** tool is a Java application that combines multiple files into a single JAR archive file. It is a general-purpose archiving and compression tool. If you've seen the "tar" command on Unix, **jar** will appear very familiar.

Usage examples

Putting all the class files in the current directory into a **jar** file called "myClasses.jar":

jar cf myClasses.jar *.class

Extracting all the files in a **jar** file:

jar xf myClasses.jar

javadoc

This tool is very useful for creating documents describing your Java packages, classes, and their methods and variables. By putting special tags in your Java file and running **javadoc** on it, you can create useful documents.

javadoc generates one **.html** file for each **.java** file and each packages it encounters. It also produces a class hierarchy (**tree.html**) and an index of those members (**AllNames.html**). Anybody can easily navigate these HTML files to know more about your classes.

You can learn more about Java tools from the Java tools documentation:

http://java.sun.com/products/jdk/1.1/docs/tooldocs/solaris/javadoc.html

Some Practical Examples

Before we end this chapter, let us look at a couple of practical examples developed using some of the concepts we have learned. We are intentionally providing very little explanation for these examples, as most of the code is based on theory discussed here and in the first two chapters.

The first example shows how you can create an applet to display advertisements on your Web site. The second example uses RMI to keep track of how many times somebody has clicked on the advertisement. We use a Frames environment.

Example 1: Displaying Multiple Advertisements on Your Site

The user connects to frontPage.html. This creates two frames. The applet, AdTicker. class, comes in the upper frame and displays messages read from the HTML file in which it resides, **adTicker.html**. If you click on one of the messages, the corresponding URL is displayed in the lower frame (**displayArea.html**).

These are the messages displayed:

Advertisement page 1

Advertisement page 2

These messages will be alternately displayed with a delay of two seconds.

If you click on the first one, *myServer.com/ad1.html* will be displayed in the lower frame. *MyServer.com/ad2.html* will be displayed if you click on the second message.

When you initially view this, it will look something like Figure 3.4.

The message in the ticker bar will keep on changing. If you click on the message, the corresponding page will be displayed below. This may look like Figure 3.5.

frontPage.html

```
<HTML><HEAD></HEAD>
<FRAMESET ROWS='40,*'>
    <FRAME NAME='adTicker' SRC='adTicker.html'>
    <FRAME NAME='displayArea' SRC='displayArea.html'>
</FRAMESET>
```

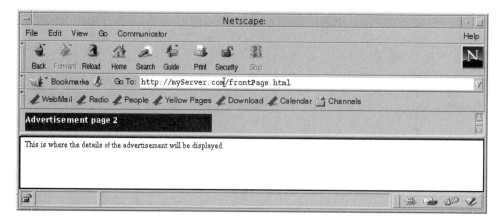

Figure 3.4

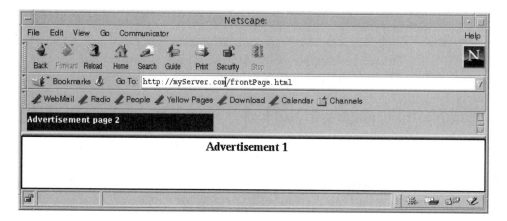

Figure 3.5

adTicker.html

```
<HTML><HEAD></HEAD>
<BODY>
    <APPLET CODE=AdTicker.class WIDTH=350 HEIGHT=30>
        <PARAM NAME="message0" VALUE="Advertisement page 1">
        <PARAM NAME="url0" VALUE="http://myServer.com/ad1.html">
        <PARAM NAME="message1" VALUE="Advertisement page 2">
        <PARAM NAME="url1" VALUE="http://myServer.com/ad2.html">
    </APPLET>
</BODY>
</HTML>
```

displayArea.html

```
<HTML><HEAD></HEAD>
<BODY BGCOLOR='#FFFFFF'>
This is where the details of the advertisement will be displayed.
</BODY>
</HTML>
```

AdTicker.java

```java
import java.awt.*;
import java.awt.image.*;
import java.net.*;
import java.applet.*;
import java.util.*;
import java.io.*;

public class AdTicker extends Applet implements Runnable
{
    Vector tickerMessages = new Vector();
    Vector tickerUrls = new Vector();

    Thread tickerThread;

    int curAdTickerPos = 0;
    int totalAdTickers = 0;
    int delay = 2000;
    boolean mouseInside = false;
    int MAX_ADS = 10;

    public void init()
    {
        for(int i=0; i<MAX_ADS; i++)
        {
            String paramName = "message" + i;
            String nm = getParameter(paramName);
            if(nm == null)
                    continue;
            tickerMessages.addElement(nm);
            paramName = "url" + i;
            nm = getParameter(paramName);
            tickerUrls.addElement(nm);
        }
```

```java
        totalAdTickers = tickerMessages.size();
    }

    public void start()
    {
        tickerThread = new Thread(this);
        tickerThread.start();
    }
    public void run()
    {
        Thread.currentThread().setPriority(Thread.MIN_PRIORITY);
        int k = 0;
        while(k == 0)
        {
            if(tickerThread == null)
                break;
            if(curAdTickerPos == totalAdTickers)
                curAdTickerPos = 0;
            repaint();
            try{
                Thread.sleep(delay);
            }catch(Exception ex){}
            curAdTickerPos++;
        }
    }
    public void paint(Graphics g)
    {

        if(mouseInside == false)
            g.setColor(new Color(0, 0, 255));
        else
            g.setColor(new Color(255, 0, 0));

        g.fillRect(0, 0, 300, 30);

        Font f = getFont();
        g.setFont(new Font(f.getName(), Font.BOLD, f.getSize()));

        g.setColor(new Color(255, 255, 255));
        g.drawString(
            (String)tickerMessages.elementAt(curAdTickerPos), 0,
                15);
    }
```

```
    public boolean mouseEnter(Event e, int x, int y)
    {
        mouseInside = true;
        repaint();
        return true;
    }
    public boolean mouseExit(Event e, int x, int y)
    {
        mouseInside = false;
        repaint();
        return true;
    }
    public boolean mouseDown(Event e, int x, int y)
    {
        try{
            URL u = new URL((String)tickerUrls.elementAt
                (curAdTickerPos));
            AppletContext ac = getAppletContext();
            ac.showDocument(u, "displayArea");
            try{
                    Thread.sleep(2000);
            }catch(Exception ex){}
        }catch(Exception exy){}
        return false;
    }
}
```

In this applet we've implemented the methods **mouseEnter**() and **mouseExit**(). This is because we want the color of the displayed message to change when the mouse enters or exits the applet area.

Another new thing in this applet is the code in the **mouseDown**() method; this code displays a URL in the lower frame.

```
        URL u = new URL((String)tickerUrls.elementAt
            (curAdTickerPos));
        AppletContext ac = getAppletContext();
        ac.showDocument(u, "displayArea");
```

The first line retrieves the name of the URL that is to be displayed from the tickerUrls vector and creates a URL object.

The second line gets a hold of the AppletContext, which contains a method **showDocument**() that causes a URL to be loaded and displayed. This method takes two arguments. The first is the URL object that is to be displayed, and the second is the name of the frame in which it is to be displayed. Since our lower frame is named "displayArea," the URL will be displayed in it.

While we've shown how you can use this technology to place advertisements on your site, it has other uses as well. For instance, you could use an applet like this to flash new product information to your customers, or to display news items and press articles about your company.

Example 2: Keeping Track of Clicks on Advertisements

Now that you have a way of displaying advertisements on your page, you will want to keep track of how many times they were clicked so that you can charge the advertisers accordingly. For this your applet somehow needs to connect to the server and inform it when somebody has clicked a URL. This example shows how you can do this using RMI.

Since we still have to look at databases and how they can be used, we will simulate a database. This is in the class CounterDatabase. It contains a Hashtable. The Hashtable will contain the number of times a URL has been clicked; the URL would be the key, and the value would be the count of clicks on this URL from the applet. It contains a method called **setClickCount**(), which can be used for setting the click count for a URL; a method **getClickCount**(), which can be used for seeing how many times a URL has been clicked; and a method called **getCounter**(), which can be used for retrieving the entire Hashtable. The CounterDatabase class is a serializable class, which we will store in a file "/home/vsharma/counter.db." Every time the count needs to be updated, the serial file will be read, the value will be modified, and the CounterDatabase object will be written back in the file.

The RMI server is implemented in the class TickerDatabaseImpl, and the applet would invoke the **incrementClickCount**() method there remotely whenever a user clicks one of the messages. This method gets the instance of the CounterDatabase using the method **getCounterDatabase**(), which reads the serial file. It then updates the click count and uses **setCounterDatabase**() to write the updated CounterDatabase into the file.

The server also contains a method **getCounter**(), which reads the **Counter Database** object using **getCounterDatabase**() and returns the Hashtable using the **getCounter**() method of CounterDatabase. This method is invoked by a utility **SeeClickCount**, which can be used to see how many times a URL has been clicked.

A very important point to note here is that this code is not multi-user safe. We are not doing any explicit locking to ensure data integrity if two clients simultaneously call **incrementClickCount**(). But then, this implementation uses only a pseudo-database and should be replaced by one that connects to a real database, say, using JDBC. In that case the database should be able to handle the concurrency issues.

The applet itself has changed, as it now needs to make an RMI connection. This is in the class "AdTickerRmi." To use this example, you will have to follow the steps described in the previous RMI section (including running rmic and generating stubs). You will need to place the following classes along with **AdTickerRmi.class** on your Web server:

TickerDatabaseImpl_Stub.class

TickerDatabase.class

Now if a user loads the HTML page and clicks on a message, **increment ClickCount()** will be called, and the CounterDatabase object will be updated. To see how many times each URL has been clicked, you can execute the SeeClickCount class. Typical results are like this:

Click count for *http://myServer.com/ad1.html* is 5

Click count for *http://myServer.com/ad2.html* is 15

And here's the complete code:

CounterDatabase.java

```
import java.util.*;
public class CounterDatabase implements java.io.Serializable
{
        Hashtable counter = new Hashtable();
        public Integer getClickCount(String url)
        {
            Integer i = (Integer)counter.get(url);
            if(i == null)
                i = new Integer(0);
            return i;
        }
        public void setClickCount(String url, Integer i)
        {
            counter.put(url, i);
        }
        public Hashtable getCounter()
        {
            return counter;
        }
}
```

TickerDatabase.java

```
import java.util.*;
public interface TickerDatabase extends java.rmi.Remote
{
    public void incrementClickCount(String url)
                                    throws java.rmi.RemoteException;
    public Hashtable getCounter() throws java.rmi.RemoteException;
}
```

TickerDatabaseImpl.java

```java
import java.rmi.*;
import java.rmi.server.UnicastRemoteObject;
import java.io.*;
import java.util.*;

public class TickerDatabaseImpl
        extends UnicastRemoteObject
        implements TickerDatabase
{
    static String counterDbFile;
    public TickerDatabaseImpl()  throws java.rmi.RemoteException
    {
        super();
    }

    public static void main(String args[])
    {
        // Initialize database connection pool

        System.setSecurityManager(new RMISecurityManager());

        try{
            counterDbFile = "/home/vsharma/counter.db";
            TickerDatabaseImpl obj = new TickerDatabaseImpl();
            Naming.rebind("TickerDatabase", obj);
        } catch (Exception e)
          {
            e.printStackTrace();
          }
    }
    private CounterDatabase getCounterDatabase()
    {
        CounterDatabase cdb = null;
        try{

            if( (new File(counterDbFile)).exists() == false)
            {
                    cdb = new CounterDatabase();
            }
            else
            {
                FileInputStream f =
                            new FileInputStream(counterDbFile);
```

```java
                ObjectInputStream is = new ObjectInputStream(f);
                cdb = (CounterDatabase)is.readObject();
                is.close();
            }
        }catch(Exception ex){}
        return cdb;
    }
    private void setCounterDatabase(CounterDatabase cdb)
    {
        try{
            FileOutputStream fo = new FileOutputStream(counter
                DbFile);
            ObjectOutputStream os  =  new ObjectOutputStream(fo);
            os.writeObject(cdb);
            os.flush();
            os.close();
        }catch(Exception ex){}
    }
    public void incrementClickCount(String url)
        throws java.rmi.RemoteException
    {
        try{

            CounterDatabase cdb = getCounterDatabase();
            Integer countTillNow = (Integer)cdb.getClickCount(url);
            int c = countTillNow.intValue() + 1;
            countTillNow = new Integer(c);

            cdb.setClickCount(url, countTillNow);
            setCounterDatabase(cdb);

        }catch(Exception ex){ex.printStackTrace();}
    }
    public Hashtable getCounter()
        throws java.rmi.RemoteException
    {
        CounterDatabase cdb = getCounterDatabase();
        return cdb.getCounter();
    }
}
```

AdTickerRmi.java

```java
import java.awt.*;
import java.awt.image.*;
```

```
import java.net.*;
import java.applet.*;
import java.util.*;
import java.io.*;
import java.rmi.*;

public class AdTickerRmi extends Applet implements Runnable
{

    Vector tickerMessages = new Vector();
    Vector tickerUrls = new Vector();

    Thread tickerThread;

    int curAdTickerPos = 0;
    int totalAdTickers = 0;
    int delay = 2000;
    boolean mouseInside = false;
    int MAX_ADS = 10;
    String dbLocation = "//myServer.com/TickerDatabase";

    TickerDatabase db;

    public void init()
    {
        for(int i=0; i<MAX_ADS; i++)
        {
            String paramName = "message" + i;
            String nm = getParameter(paramName);
            if(nm == null)
                continue;
            tickerMessages.addElement(nm);
            paramName = "url" + i;
            nm = getParameter(paramName);
            tickerUrls.addElement(nm);
        }
        totalAdTickers = tickerMessages.size();
          try
          {
                db = (TickerDatabase) Naming.lookup(dbLocation);
          } catch (Exception e)
            {
            }
    }
```

```java
public void start()
{
    tickerThread = new Thread(this);
    tickerThread.start();
}
public void run()
{
        Thread.currentThread().setPriority(Thread.MIN_PRIORITY);
        int k = 0;
        while(k == 0)
        {
            if(tickerThread == null)
                break;
            if(curAdTickerPos == totalAdTickers)
                curAdTickerPos = 0;
            repaint();
            try{
                Thread.sleep(delay);
            }catch(Exception ex){}
            curAdTickerPos++;
        }
}
public void paint(Graphics g)
{

    if(mouseInside == false)
        g.setColor(new Color(0, 0, 255));
    else
        g.setColor(new Color(255, 0, 0));

    g.fillRect(0, 0, 300, 30);

    Font f = getFont();
    g.setFont(new Font(f.getName(), Font.BOLD, f.getSize()));

    g.setColor(new Color(255, 255, 255));
    g.drawString(
        (String)tickerMessages.elementAt(curAdTickerPos), 0,
            15);
}

public boolean mouseEnter(Event e, int x, int y)
{
    mouseInside = true;
```

```
        repaint();
        return true;
    }
    public boolean mouseExit(Event e, int x, int y)
    {
        mouseInside = false;
        repaint();
        return true;
    }
    public boolean mouseDown(Event e, int x, int y)
    {
        try{
            String urlClicked =
                        (String)tickerUrls.elementAt(curAdTickerPos);
            URL u = new URL(urlClicked);
            AppletContext ac = getAppletContext();
            ac.showDocument(u, "displayArea");

            db.incrementClickCount(urlClicked);

                try{
                    Thread.sleep(2000);
                }catch(Exception ex){}
        }catch(Exception exy){}
        return false;
    }
}
```

SeeClickCount.java

```
import java.util.*;
import java.io.*;
import java.rmi.*;

public class SeeClickCount
{
    static String dbLocation = "//myServer.com/TickerDatabase";
    static TickerDatabase db;

    public static void main(String[] args)
    {
        try
        {
            db = (TickerDatabase) Naming.lookup(dbLocation);
```

```
            Hashtable counter = db.getCounter();
            Enumeration allUrls = counter.keys();
            while(allUrls.hasMoreElements())
            {
                String url = (String)allUrls.nextElement();
                Integer i = (Integer)counter.get(url);
                System.out.println("Click count for " + url +
                                        " is " + i.toString());
            }
        } catch (Exception e)
          {
                e.printStackTrace();
          }
    }
}
```

Conclusion

As we mentioned earlier, Java is by no means a limited language. Several tomes can be written describing different features and internals of the Java Virtual Machine. However, we've tried to cover most of the commonly used features, especially the ones that will be used throughout this book. You can get more information from the primary Web site, *www.javasoft.com*. This site contains a Java tutorial that you can refer to, with several useful examples that can help you learn details of the language. Also, there are a large number of books you can consult.

Some Handy Classes and Methods in Some Useful Packages

Package **java.io**:

BufferedReader—for reading text from a character-input stream. Useful for reading of characters and lines.

— Methods: **readLine()**—for reading a line of text.
read()—for reading a single character.
read(char[], **int**, **int)**—for reading specified numbers of chars.

BufferedWriter—the counterpart of BufferedReader for writing characters/arrays. Contains a **newLine()** method useful for writing a new line character.

DataInputStream—for reading primitive Java data types, e.g., for reading **int**, **float**, String, etc.; stored using **DataOutputStream**.

—Methods: **read(byte[])**—for reading a specific number of bytes.
          readChar()—for reading a Unicode character.
          readDouble()—for reading a double.
          readInt()—for reading a signed 32-bit integer.

DataOutputStream—the counterpart of **DataInputStream**, for writing primitive data types. Contains methods for writing ints, chars, doubles, etc.

File—represents a file with the specified name.

—Methods: **exists()**—checks if the file exists.
          length()—length of the file.
          canRead()—checks if you can read from this file.
          canWrite()—checks if you can write to this file.
          mkdir()—creates a directory whose pathname is specified by this.

ObjectOutputStream—allows writing of primitive data types to an **OutputStream** and is used for achieving serialization. Using this, you can save an entire object with the current state of its variables. The object can then be reconstructed by reading it using the **ObjectInputStream**. Useful for storing state and for passing objects over the network.

—Methods: **writeObject(Object)**—for writing a specified object.

ObjectInputStream: the counterpart of **ObjectOutputStream**—used for reading objects stored using **ObjectOutputStream**.

PrintWriter: Useful for writing formatted representation objects to a text stream.

—Methods: **write(String)**—for writing out a string.
          println(String)—for writing the string followed by a new line.
          close()—for closing the stream.

RandomAccessFile—useful for reading/writing a random access file.

—Methods: **seek(long)**—sets the file-pointer offset at which the next read/write begins.
          skipBytes(int)—skips specified numbers of bytes.

Package **java.lang**:

Classes: Boolean, Float, Double, Integer, Long—useful for creating object wrappers around primitive types like Boolean, float, etc.

Math—useful for mathematical computations.

—Methods: **sqrt(double)**—square root.
          sin(double)—trignometric sine of an angle.
          random()—returns random numbers between 0.0 and 1.0.

Runtime—useful for doing some runtime operations like executing a command from a Java program.

—Methods: **exec(String[])**—executes the specified command in a separate process.

String—a representation of character strings. Contains methods for manipulating strings, like comparing, searching for a substring, creating substrings, changing case, etc.

—Methods: **charAt(int)**—gets the character at the given index.
equals(Object)—compares String to a given object.
indexOf(String)—returns index in string of first occurrence of specified substring.
length()—length of the string.
replace(char, char)—replace occurrences of first char with second.
substring(int, int)—returns a substring of this String.
toUpperCase()—converts string to uppercase.

System—contains utilities for using the standard input/output and error streams, getting the current time, etc.

—Methods: **currentTimeMillis()**—returns the current time in milliseconds.
exit(int)—for terminating the current application.

Thread—represents a thread of execution. Contains methods for changing the priority of threads, for starting execution, suspending a thread, making it sleep, and so on.

—Methods: **start()**—causes a thread to begin execution.
sleep(long)—causes a thread to sleep for specified milliseconds.
stop()—causes a thread to stop executing.
setPriority(int)—changes priority of the thread.

Package **java.net**:

URL—represents a Uniform Resource Locator. Used for connecting to Web site or other resource.

—Methods: **openConnection()**—returns a URLConnection object representing connection to the remote object referred to by this URL.

URLConnection—used for reading or writing to a resource referenced by a URL.

—Methods: **connect()**—used to open a connection to a URL.
getContent()—gets contents of this URL.
getInputStream()—gets an input stream that reads from this connection.
getOutputStream()—gets an output stream that writes to this connection.
setDoOutput(boolean)—specifies whether any output will be written to this connection.

URLEncoder—used for converting a String into a MIME format. This format is used for transmitting data over the Net. You will see this being used in CGI programs where FORM data are transmitted.

—Methods: **encode(String)**—translates the String into the MIME format.

Package **java.util**:

Hashtable—for efficient storage and retrieval of objects.
—Methods: **get(Object)**—get an object from the Hashtable.
put(Object, Object)—store an object in the Hashtable.
elements()—an enumeration of all the values of the Hashtable.
keys()—an enumeration of all the keys in the Hashtable.
remove(Object)—remove an object from the Hashtable.
size()—number of keys in the Hashtable.

StringTokenizer—used for splitting a string into parts by specifying separator chars. These parts are referred to as tokens.
—Methods: **hasMoreTokens()**—tests if more tokens are available.
nextToken()—returns the next token.

Vector—works like an array except that its size can grow and shrink as needed. Contains methods for adding or removing elements, etc.
—Methods: **addElement(Object)**—adds an element to end of vector.
elements()—an enumeration of all elements of the vector.
elementAt(int)—returns object in vector at the specified index.
insertElementAt(Object, int)—inserts the specified object at the specified index.
removeElementAt(int)—removes the object at the specified index.

Chapter 4

Servlets

HTML FORMs

I marked the wrong column in the DMV form—
they told me the easiest way out was a gender change surgery!

In the chapter on HTML we briefly looked at the FORM element of HTML. This element is the basis of most Web applications. A quick recap—a typical FORM looks like this:

```
<FORM ACTION='someApplication'>
    ... elements like buttons, text fields etc
    <INPUT TYPE='submit' NAME='submit' VALUE='Go'>
</FORM>
```

The FORM tag has an ACTION attribute—this contains reference to an application that typically resides on the server on which this Web page resides (the machine running the Web server). The FORM normally has a Submit button in it—when you press this Submit button, the application mentioned in the ACTION attribute is invoked on the server where it resides. This application receives all data present in the form such as the current value of the text fields, which radio buttons have been checked, and so on. The application can then process this information and return results back to the client. The client (typically a browser) can then display these results in a new Web page.

POST and GET METHODs

Another attribute of the FORM tag worth mentioning here is the METHOD attribute. The value of this attribute determines "how" FORM data is sent from the browser to the server. Two commonly used methods are GET and POST. The default method is GET.

In the case of GET, the user agent appends a "?" to the application link, appends FORM data to it, and then traverses that link. A user can thus see the values of all the variables that were passed to the application. An example:

```
<FORM ACTION='http://myServer/cgi-bin/processIt'>
    <INPUT TYPE='text' NAME='txt' VALUE='This'>
    <INPUT TYPE='submit' NAME='submit' VALUE='Go'>
</FORM>
```

If you press the Submit button, you will see that your browser is trying to access something like this:

http://myServer/cgi-bin/processIt?txt=This&submit=Go

So everything after the "?" is the set of FORM variables and their values. In this case "txt" is the name we gave to the text field and "This" was its default value. If you changed the value of the text field, the URL that the browser accesses would be changed to reflect the new value of the text field.

At the server end, the Web server reads these variables and makes them available in the form of an environment variable, QUERY_STRING. Your application then needs to read and parse these to get the value of the FORM elements.

In the case of POST, however, the user agent creates a message that contains the values of the FORM elements. This message is posted on the data stream that is established between the client and the server. The Web server makes this data available to the application in the form of an input stream. The application can read the message from this input stream and parse it to get the values of the FORM elements. In the case of the above example you would specify the FORM like this:

```
<FORM ACTION='http://myServer/cgi-bin/processIt' METHOD='POST'>
```

The rest is the same as above.

All you would see in the browser is that it has tried to access the URL *http://myServer/cgi-bin/processIt*.

It is advisable to use POST as opposed to GET—one major reason is that GET imposes some limitations. You cannot transmit more than 1024 characters using GET on most systems. This is because the GET method relies on environment variables that have limitations on most systems.

We will be using POST in all our operations.

Anatomy of a Request and a Response

In this section we take a closer look at the HTTP protocol to see how a handshake occurs between the client (browser) and the server. The process begins with a request initiated from the client side. Thus, if you try to request a Web page from your browser, the browser will send an HTTP request to the server on which the page resides. Now the ball is in the Web server's court. It has received a request and has to process it. At this stage it determines the type of request.

While sending the request, the client can specify the type of request. The type indicates whether the request is for an HTML page, a FORM application, and so on. If it's a request for a Web page, the server reads the page and returns its contents to the client. If it is a FORM request, then the server determines the METHOD by which data has been sent by the client. The requested application is invoked, and the data is made available to it. It is up to the application to generate the response data. The data (whether a Web page or application is generated) is sent to the client, which then displays it or takes some other action.

As part of the handshake process, the client and the server exchange some more information as well. Information about the client is made available by the Web server to applications on the Web server. This information is available in the form of CGI variables that can be queried. The variables that are available for applications to use include the following:

REMOTE_ADDR—the IP address of the client machine

REMOTE_HOST—the fully qualified name of the client machine

CONTENT_LENGTH—the length of data sent by the client (this would be the FORM data)

When the application returns a response, it must include some basic information so that the client can interpret it properly. One of the things that needs to be set is the type of content that is being sent back. An application can send back an HTML page as response, but that is not a requirement. It may send an Acrobat file or data in some other media format. The only way a client can efficiently determine the proper display format is if the server tells it beforehand what kind of data it is sending in the response to a request. For this a response header called "Content-type" is used. If the application is returning an HTML page as the response, it should set this type to "text/html"; if it's sending plain text, the type would be "text/plain." Similarly, the application can set this value to a number of other MIME types. The client would read the value of "Content-type" and display results based on this.

CGI Scripts

What kind of applications can be specified in the ACTION attribute? Any application that can be executed directly on the server is fine. You could have a C executable or a Perl script or a Shell script specified in this attribute. When you press the Submit button, the Web server will recognize this to be an application request (typically called a CGI request). It will then spawn off a new process in which the application will be executed. The application may then return results back to the browser in the form of an HTML page or some other form. Now the question is, how does the Web server recognize that the request is for an application and not for a static HTML page? In the configuration of your Web server you can specify that one or more directories are CGI directories. You can set an alias for them. Whenever a request to a URL is received that contains a reference to this alias, the Web server knows that this is a CGI request and that it needs to spawn an application as opposed to reading an HTML file and returning it back. The directive for CGI in an Apache configuration file is shown below:

ScriptAlias /cgi-bin/ /home/vsharma/cgi-bin/

This means that if somebody tries to access "http://myServer/cgi-bin/Something," the Web server should execute "Something," which resides in the directory "/home/vsharma/cgi-bin/."

Drawbacks of CGI

I paid a lot of money to get my new green millennium car—
the only drawback is it's a Y2K Bug!

If your application is a Java executable, it has to be invoked indirectly. This is because it needs the **java** interpreter in order to run (unlike a C executable). One way of achieving this is on Solaris is by creating a shell script that invokes the **java** interpreter. Let's say our backend application is a class called "MyClass.class." We can create a script—let's name it "MyShell.sh":

```
#!/bin/sh
java MyClass
```

In your FORM you would have something like:

```
<FORM ACTION='/cgi-bin/MyShell.sh'>
```

When the user presses the Submit button, "MyShell.sh" is executed, spawning off a JVM that executes "MyClass.class."

However, there is an obvious drawback here, namely, that every time a user submits the FORM, a new JVM is started. Each JVM takes up a considerable amount of memory and resources, so if you had a large number of users pressing the Submit button simultaneously, your system would soon come to its knees.

Efficiency with Servlets

If Efficiency=(Work done)/(Time spent at work),
can I become infinitely efficient by spending 0 time at work?

This is where Servlets come in. Servlets help in improving application efficiency by conserving resources. Java Servlets are Java programs that run on the backend like CGI programs—the difference is that they execute in the environment of a Servlet engine, which helps in increasing efficiency of the system. A request to a Servlet looks exactly like a CGI request. The difference is that instead of spawning off an application, the Web server directs the request to the Servlet engine. This engine then directs the request to a Servlet, which is executed.

Several Servlet engines are available as add-ons to popular Web servers like Apache. Some examples are **JServ** and **JRun**. Once the Servlet engine environment has been set up and integrated with the Web server, you can start using Servlets as your backend applications.

The Servlet engine loads a class in the Java Virtual Machine (JVM) process and creates one instance of the Servlet class. This instance may be created when the engine is started or when the first request to the Servlet arrives. Every time a request comes in, a new thread is created using the same Servlet instance. The same Servlet instance is thus used to handle multiple requests; new instances are not created for subsequent requests. Since there is only one instance of the Servlet that is serving different Web requests, it is important to understand that any instance (global) data is shared by all the requests. If you need to store data that can be changed, you will have to provide synchronization. The data that is local (variables defined inside methods) is, however, not shared by the threads, so you can maintain any local data here. Let's look at an example:

```
public class MyServlet extends HttpServlet
{
    int globalVar;
    public void myMethod()
    {
        int localVar;
    }
}
```

Since **globalVar** will be shared by all threads that are serving the instance of MyServlet, if you change the value of this without synchronizing, the data might get corrupted. On the other hand, since **localVar** is declared within a method, it is a local variable not shared by the different threads. Any changes to this in one thread will not affect the other threads using the same Servlet instance.

Anatomy of a Servlet

Servlets implement and use interfaces and classes defined in the javax.servlet package. All Servlets must "extend" the Servlet class or one of its children. For our purposes, because we will be using Servlets for HTTP requests, we can use the specialized "HttpServlet" class.

Servlets can define an **init()** method. This method is executed only once in the lifecycle of a Servlet. This may happen when the Servlet engine is started or when the first request to the Servlet is made. You can do some initializations here. It is not necessary to implement this method. Similarly, when the Servlet engine is shut down, a **destroy()** method is called. You can put code here that will free up any resources you may have initialized. This method is also called only once in the lifecycle of a Servlet.

The most important method as far as we are concerned is the **doPost()** method, which is called when a POST request comes in (i.e., if a user has submitted a FORM in which METHOD='POST'). You can put all your processing code here or in methods that are called from this method. The Servlet engine passes two objects to this method by default:

1. HttpServletRequest, which can be used to get information about the request such as the IP address it came from and the names and values of the FORM from which this request was initiated.

2. HttpServletResponse, which can be used to generate a response back to the client.

Normally the response is another HTML page (which may contain a FORM). However, you can send other types in the response. One popular type is Acrobat files, which spawn off the Acrobat Reader on the client machine. You need to specify the output content type before you send the actual response. This is specified using one of the methods of HttpServletResponse.

Note that if the FORM uses the GET method instead of POST, your backend application will need to implement the **doGet()** method instead of the **doPost()** method; fortunately the two methods are exactly alike except for the name.

JServ—Servlet Engine

Before we look at a real Servlet, let's digress a little bit to understand the JServ environment we will be using for our Servlets. This is a Servlet engine available for download at *http://java.apache.org/*. Installation instructions are available at the site. In addition to downloading and installing this, you will need to download and install the Java Servlet Development Kit (JSDK), available at *http://java.sun.com*. Appendix A contains detailed instructions on installing and configuring **JServ**.

Once installation has been done and the Servlet engine has been started, it is ready to accept Servlet requests. As mentioned earlier, a request to a Servlet looks like a CGI request. Just as we need to declare the CGI directory and the corresponding alias in a configuration file of the Web server, Servlet directories and the corresponding aliases (refered to as "zones") are defined in the configuration files of **JServ**. There is a **jserv.conf** file in which all zones are declared. Each zone has a properties file in which the corresponding physical directory (in which the Servlets reside) is declared. As an example, if you have a zone called "testZone" with an alias "testZone," **jserv.conf** would look like this:

ApJServMount /testZone /testZone

You would need to create a file called "testZone.properties." One of the elements in this would look like this:

repositories=/home/vsharma/SERVLETS/JSERV/Apache-JServ-1.0b1/testZone

Your Servlets would reside in this directory:

/home/vsharma/SERVLETS/JSERV/Apache-JServ-1.0b1/testZone

You can have multiple zones. This is a way of having different types of applications in their own "areas." All the zones are specified in the **jserv.properties** file.

For example, the following line in this file shows that this installation has two zones:

zones=example,testZone

testZone.properties=/local/vsharma/SERVLETS/JSERV/Apache-JServ-1.0b1/ testZone/testZone.properties

It also shows where **testZone.properties** exists.

Another important element in **jserv.properties** is the list of directories and **jar** files that need to be included in the CLASSPATH. (After all, **JServ** runs a JVM that looks for classes in directories specified in the CLASSPATH.) This parameter is the wrapper.classpath parameter. There can be one line for each directory or file you want to include in the CLASSPATH. Here's an example:

wrapper.classpath=/local/vsharma/SERVLETS/JSERV/Apache-JServ-1.0b1/src/java/Apache-JServ.jar

wrapper.classpath=/local/vsharma/SERVLETS/JSDK/JSDK2.0/lib/jsdk.jar

wrapper.classpath=/local/vsharma

wrapper.classpath=/local/vsharma/JAF/jaf/activation.jar

wrapper.classpath=/local/vsharma/JAVAMAIL/javamail-1.1/mail.jar

Every time you add a new classpath entry or make other changes to this file, you will need to restart JServ, which can be done by restarting Apache if you install it as instructed in Appendix A, in order for the changes to take effect.

In this configuration, if you try to access http://myServer/testZone/MyServlet, this will be recognized as a request to a Servlet that belongs to the zone "testZone." The Servlet engine will see if an instance of **MyServlet.class** exists. If yes, it will create a thread in which this instance is executed (its **doPost()** method will be called if the request originated from a POST FORM). If the instance does not exist, a new instance will be created, and the **init()** method of the class will be called. Then the **doPost()** method will be called.

MyServlet.class is expected to be in the physical path specified in **testZone. properties**:

/home/vsharma/SERVLETS/JSERV/Apache-JServ-1.0b1/testZone

A Basic Servlet

Here's an example of a Servlet, assuming it has been put in the "testZone." First the HTML:

firstServlet.html

```
<HTML><HEAD></HEAD>
  <BODY>
    <FORM ACTION='http://myServer/testZone/FirstServlet'
        METHOD='POST'>
        <INPUT TYPE='submit' NAME='Submit' VALUE='Execute'>
    </FORM>
  </BODY>
<HTML>
```

When the Submit button is pressed, the following class (Servlet) is executed:

```
import java.io.*;
import javax.servlet.*;
import javax.servlet.http.*;
public class FirstServlet extends HttpServlet
{
    public void doPost (HttpServletRequest req,
                    HttpServletResponse res)
        throws ServletException, IOException
    {
            PrintWriter out;

            res.setContentType("text/html");
            out = res.getWriter();
```

```
        out.println("<HTML><HEAD></HEAD>");
        out.println("<BODY bgcolor=\"#FFFFFF\">");
        out.println("<B>First Servlet </B>");

        out.println("</BODY></HTML>");
        out.close();
    }
}
```

To use this, move **firstServlet.html** to your Document Root. Compile **Testing.java** (note that you will need to have the **jsdk.jar** in your CLASSPATH in order to compile) and move **Testing.class** to a zone called "testZone." Then you can visit **firstServlet.html** through a browser and click on the Execute button.

Figure 4.1 shows how it looks.

When you press the Execute button, the Servlet is invoked. Figure 4.2 illustrates what we see as a result.

We begin by importing a few packages. The "io" package is required, as we are writing out an HTML page to the output. The javax.servlet and javax.servlet.http packages contain the Servlet classes that we are using. We've implemented the **doPost()** method, which takes two input parameters: an HttpServletRequest object and an HttpServletResponse object. The class testing itself extends HttpServlet. Note that all Servlets need to implement the Servlet interface. HttpServlet extends GenericServlet, which implements the Servlet interface.

In the **doPost()** method we're getting a handle to the outptut stream by using the **getWriter()** method of HttpServletResponse, which returns a PrintWriter object.

```
        out = res.getWriter();
```

Whatever we write to this object will be sent back to the browser (client) from which the request was initiated. As mentioned above, we need to set the output content type of this response. In this example we're sending back an HTML page as a response. So the content type is "text/html."

```
        res.setContentType("text/html");
```

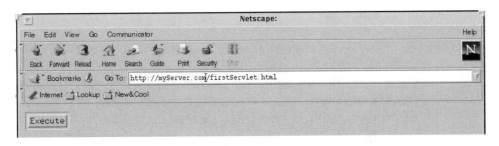

Figure   4.1

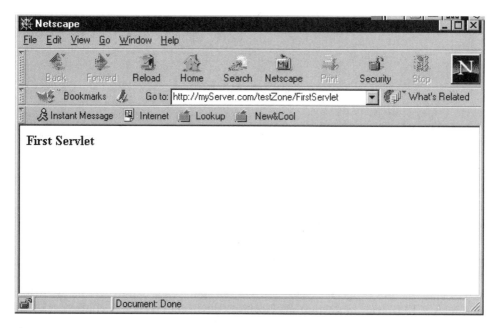

Figure 4.2

For a more detailed discussion of response types, see the discussion about MIME types in Appendix A.

All the **out.println()** statements are simply writing HTML, which will be displayed by the browser just like a regular Web page.

FORM Variables

Next we see how you can extract values of the FORM variables using methods defined in HttpServletRequest. In this example we have an HTML FORM in which there is a text field and a set of radio buttons. The Servlet will read the values of all the FORM variables and display them.

```
<HTML><HEAD></HEAD>
  <BODY>
    <FORM ACTION='http://myServer/testZone/ShowFormVariables'
        METHOD='POST'>
      <INPUT TYPE='text' NAME='firstName' VALUE=' '><BR>
      <INPUT TYPE='radio' NAME='rd' VALUE='val1'><BR>
      <INPUT TYPE='radio' NAME='rd' VALUE='val2'><BR>
      <INPUT TYPE='submit' NAME='Submit' VALUE='Execute'>
    </FORM>
```

```
    </BODY>
<HTML>

import java.io.*;
import java.util.*;
import javax.servlet.*;
import javax.servlet.http.*;
public class ShowFormVariables extends HttpServlet
{
    public void doPost (HttpServletRequest req,
                        HttpServletResponse res)
        throws ServletException, IOException
    {
            PrintWriter out;
            res.setContentType("text/html");
            out = res.getWriter();

            out.println("<HTML><HEAD></HEAD>");
            out.println("<BODY bgcolor=\"#FFFFFF\">");

            String txt = req.getParameterValues("firstName")[0];
            out.println("Value of text field, firstNames, is: " + txt);

            out.println("<BR>Here are all variables and their
                        values<BR>");
            Enumeration names = req.getParameterNames();
            while(names.hasMoreElements())
            {
                String name = (String)names.nextElement();
                String value = req.getParameterValues(name)[0];
                out.println("NAME: " + name + " VALUE: " + value
                            + "<BR>");
            }
            out.println("</BODY></HTML>");
            out.close();
        }
}
```

HttpServletRequest contains a method called **getParameterValues()**, which can return the value of any FORM variable by name. This method returns a String array (because a FORM variable can have multiple values; for instance, you could have a set of four checkboxes with the same name, and if the user selects three of them, three values would be returned for this name). If there is only one value associated with the variable, you can retrieve it as the first element of the array returned by the method.

We're doing this to retrieve the value of firstName in this example:

```
        String txt = req.getParameterValues("firstName")[0];
```

The class also provides another way of accessing the names and values without knowing the names beforehand. Using the **getParameterNames()** method returns an Enumeration of all the FORM variables (including the Submit button).

```
Enumeration names = req.getParameterNames();
```

You can then traverse this Enumeration and retrieve elements from it. The elements will be String objects containing names of the FORM variables. You can then use this name with the **getParameterValues()** method to get the value of the variable.

The output of this looks like this:

Value of text field, firstNames, is: This is the text field

Here are all variables and their values

NAME: rd VALUE: val2

NAME: Submit VALUE: Execute

NAME: firstName VALUE: This is the text field

Cookies

I used to hate cookies—
till Netscape started baking them!

By default, each request to a Web page or Servlet is independent of previous requests from the same client. This puts some severe limitations on the kind of user experience that can be provided. For instance, if you've asked a user's name in one of your Servlets, you wouldn't know it if the user invokes another Servlet. This means that you can't provide a personalized greeting to the user in the second Servlet. The concept of cookies was developed to overcome this type of limitation. We will look at another approach (Sessions) in the next section. A cookie is a piece of data created by the applications on your site. It resides on the client's machine and is sent along with every request the client makes to your site. You can store information like first name, last name, etc., in the first Servlet. In subsequent requests, your Servlets will have access to this cookie, can derive the first name and last name from it, and can provide personalized messages.

However, before we explain how to use cookies, you must be aware that cookies have their own limitations. Most client browsers put limitations on the size of a cookie and how many cookies can be accepted from a particular server. Therefore, you can't store arbitrarily large amounts of data in cookies. If you need to be able to access huge amounts of information, you can use Sessions, described in the next section.

In this example we see how a cookie can be set and retrieved. To see this work you need to move **cookieExample.html** to your Document Root. The classes SetCookie and GetCookie need to be compiled and moved to the example zone.

When you access **cookieExample.html**, you're presented with a FORM asking for your first name and last name. The Submit invokes the SetCookie Servlet. This Servlet reads the first and last names and constructs a cookie called MYSITE. A cookie has a name and a value. Since one cookie has only one value and we want to store the first as well as the last name in it, we're creating a String containing both, separated by a delimiter. This delimiter can be used later to separate the first name from the last in the cookie value String.

The SetCookie Servlet then redirects the user to the GetCookie Servlet. This Servlet reads the value of the cookie named MYSITE and extracts the first and last name from it. The first and last names are then displayed to the user in an HTML page (along with names of any other cookies received by GetCookie from the client).

cookieExample.html

```
<HTML><HEAD></HEAD>
<BODY>
```
This example demonstrates how a cookie can be set and retrieved using servlets.
The first name and last name you provide will be stored in a cookie and later
retrieved from the cookie by another servlet.

```
    <FORM ACTION='/example/SetCookie' METHOD='POST'>
        <TABLE>
            <TR><TD>First Name</TD>
                <TD><INPUT TYPE='text' NAME='firstName'
                                    SIZE='10'></TD></TR>
            <TR><TD>Last Name</TD>
                <TD><INPUT TYPE='text' NAME='lastName'
                                    SIZE='10'></TD></TR>
            <TR><TD></TD>
                <TD><INPUT TYPE='submit' NAME='submit'
                                    VALUE='Ok'></TD></TR>
        </TABLE>
    </FORM>
</BODY>
</HTML>
```

SetCookie.java

```java
import java.util.*;
import java.io.*;
import javax.servlet.*;
import javax.servlet.http.*;
public class SetCookie extends HttpServlet
{
    String cookieName = "MYSITE";
    String cookieDomain = "YOUR_DOMAIN";
    String delim = "DLM:";
```

```
    int maxAge = 3600; // 3600 seconds = 1 hour
    String redirectUrl = "/example/GetCookie";
    public void doGet (HttpServletRequest req, HttpServletResponse
        res)
    {
        doPost(req, res);
    }
    public void doPost (HttpServletRequest req,
                        HttpServletResponse res)
    {
        try{
            String firstName = "", lastName = "";
            Enumeration values = req.getParameterNames();
            while(values.hasMoreElements())
            {
              String name = (String)values.nextElement();
              String value = req.getParameterValues(name)[0];
              if(name.equalsIgnoreCase("firstName"))
                    firstName = value;
              if(name.equalsIgnoreCase("lastName"))
                    lastName = value;
            }
            String cookieVal = firstName + delim + lastName;
            Cookie ck = new Cookie(cookieName, cookieVal);
            ck.setDomain(cookieDomain);
            ck.setMaxAge(maxAge);
            ck.setPath("/");
            res.addCookie(ck);
            res.sendRedirect(redirectUrl);
        }catch(Exception ex){}
    }
}
```

The JSDK comes with a Cookie class, which represents a cookie. You can construct a new cookie using this class and add it to the response. At the very least the cookie will have a name and a value. You can also specify when this cookie expires using the **setMaxAge()** method. This method expects the number of seconds from NOW when you want the cookie to expire.

You can also specify the domain and path for the cookie. The domain determines the set of servers to which this cookie should be returned. By default, if you set a cookie, it would be returned only to you. However, if you're running a bunch of servers in the same domain, you can specify that the cookie be returned to all of them. As an example, if your domain is ".xyz.com," your machines would be something like "abc.xyz.com," "def.xyz.com," and so on. If the machine def.xyz.com has created a cookie and wants that the browser to send that cookie whenever it tries to acess abc.xys.com, def.xyz.com, or any other machine in this domain, it could use the **setDomain()** method as shown:

```
cookie.setDomain(".xyz.com");
```

Similarly, you can specify that the cookie be sent only if the user tries to access a URL in a certain section of your site. By default a cookie is sent only to applications or pages in the directory where the application or page that set it resides. However, if you want the cookie to be available to all applications on your site (or a specific directory only) you can use the **setPath()** method. In the line of code shown below, the cookie will be available to all applications or pages on your server:

```
cookie.setPath("/");
```

Here's the code for creating and setting the cookie from SetCookie.java:

```
// Create the cookie with a name and value
Cookie ck = new Cookie(cookieName, cookieVal);

// Set domain, age and path
ck.setDomain(cookieDomain);
ck.setMaxAge(maxAge);
ck.setPath("/");

// Add the cookie to the response
res.addCookie(ck);
```

We're using the method **sendRedirect()** of ServletResponse instead of sending an HTML page or other response to the client you want to tell it to access another URL. In this case we're telling the client that it should access the /example/GetCookie Servlet.

```
res.sendRedirect(redirectUrl);
```

GetCookie.java

```
import javax.servlet.*;
import javax.servlet.http.*;
import java.io.*;
public class GetCookie extends HttpServlet
{
    String cookieName = "MYSITE";
    String delim = "DLM:";
    public void doGet (HttpServletRequest req, HttpServletResponse
        res)
    {
        doPost(req, res);
    }
```

```
public void doPost (HttpServletRequest req,
                    HttpServletResponse res)
{
    try{
        PrintWriter out = null;
        res.setContentType("text/html");
        out = res.getWriter();
        Cookie[] cookieList = req.getCookies();
        int size = cookieList.length;
        for(int i=0; i<size; i++)
        {
            Cookie c = cookieList[i];
            String name = c.getName();
            String value = c.getValue();
            out.println("Cookie Name " + name + "<BR>");
            if(name.equals(cookieName))
            {
                int ind = value.indexOf(delim);
                String firstName = value.substring(0, ind);
                String lastName = value.substring(ind +
                        delim.length());
                out.println("Values retrieved from the
                    cookie:
                        <BR>");
                out.println("First Name: " + firstName +
                        " Last Name: " + lastName);
            }
        }
        out.close();
    }catch(Exception ex){}
}
}
```

The request to a Servlet can be queried for a list of cookies sent to the server by the client. If you use the **getCookies()** method for this, it returns an array of cookies. You can then loop through this array and use methods of Cookie like **getName()** and **getValue()**, which will tell you the name and value of the cookie. In the GetCookie Servlet we print the names of all the cookies. When we find the MYSITE cookie we parse its value (using the delimiter we used in SetCookie) to separate the first name from the last and display these.

Sessions

All the sessions with my shrink were well worth it—
for him. He's richer by a fortune!

This leaves us with one final topic of discussion on Servlets: sessions. The Web is a stateless system. By default, the Web server does not allow maintenance of session information, which is a big drawback for applications that can span multiple screens. If you have an application consisting of three screens, all of which need to be filled out, and the data is written into the database when the last screen has been submitted by the user, you have to pass all the data gathered in the first and second screens, in the form of hidden variables, to the third screen. This process can get very cumbersome and unnecessarily burdensome, as all of the data needs to be gratuitously transmitted over and over again. A better solution would be one in which the data is maintained on the server for a configurable period of time. The JSDK comes with an HttpSession interface that allows you to do exactly this.

A session is essentially a connection between the client and the server that persists over multiple requests—something Web servers do not offer by default. Sessions can be used to maintain persistent data over multiple page requests or FORM submissions. The most common method used for maintaining sessions is through the use of cookies. Any application can join this session and get or set data belonging to the session.

A new session can be established by using the **getSession()** method of the Servlet request. This takes a Boolean as input; if "true," the engine checks whether there is already a session established with this client. If so, a handle to that session is returned by the method. Otherwise a new session is created. The call looks like this:

```
HttpSession session = request.getSession(true);
```

Now you can use methods defined in HttpSession to store or retrieve values that belong to this session, which can be done either by this Servlet or any other Servlet running in the context of this Servlet engine.

You can store variables in the session using the **putValue()** method of HttpSession and retrieve them using **getValue()**. If you want to store an integer in the session context so that it can be retrieved and modified later, you can do this:

```
Integer i = new Integer(22);
session.putValue("myinteger", i);
```

We've given a name, "myinteger," to this session variable and stored it using the **putValue()** method. Now any other Servlet that has bound itself to this session can retrieve the value as follows:

```
Integer theVal = (Integer)session.getValue("myinteger");
```

If there is no session variable of this name (myinteger), then **getValue()** returns a null.

You can remove variables from the session by using **removeValue(name)**. A list of names of all variables stored in this session can be obtained using

```
String [] getValueNames ()
```

If you want to end the session, you can use the **invalidate()** method to terminate the session. As a result, a call to **getSession(true)** will return a new session, and the servlets will not have access to data stored in the previous session.

Now it's time to look at a small session example. The Servlet is invoked for the first time when you click the submit button in the HTML file below.

```
<HTML><HEAD></HEAD>
  <BODY>
    <FORM ACTION='http://myServer/testZone/SessionServlet'
        METHOD='POST'>
      <INPUT TYPE='submit' NAME='Submit' VALUE='Execute'>
    </FORM>
  </BODY>
<HTML>
```

In this Servlet we create a session (HttpSession) with the client. We're using the **getSession(true)** method of HttpServletRequest. The "true" parameter means first check if a session is already there, and if so return a handle to that session; otherwise, create a new session.

We're storing and retrieving an integer object from this session. The value of this Integer is incremented each time the Servlet is invoked.

The Servlet then prints an HTML page and displays the current value of this integer, showing the number of times the same client has accessed this servlet in the current session. The HTML page also contains a FORM whose ACTION is this Servlet itself, so that when the user presses the Submit button, the same Servlet is executed again.

One last thing about sessions before we see the actual code. A session is established between a client and the Web server. There is a separate session for each client. So, if you access this Servlet from machine A and execute it four times, the values of the integer displayed as a result will be 1, 2, 3, and 4. And if you access it again from the same machine, the integer's value will be incremented to 5. However, if you access it from machine B, a new session will be established, and you will see the value 1 (not 6, which you will see from machine A).

Try the following:

Create an HTML FORM for the SessionServlet whose code appears below.

Access this form from one machine and press the Submit button.

Do this a number of times.

Now go to another machine and submit the FORM from there. You will notice that the displayed value on the second machine will start from 1, not from the last value displayed on the previous machine.

However, if you go back to the first machine and resubmit the form, values will start from where you left them on that machine.

This is just a demonstration of the fact that a different session is established with each client.

```java
import java.io.*;
import javax.servlet.*;
import javax.servlet.http.*;
public class SessionServlet extends HttpServlet
{
    public void doPost (HttpServletRequest req,
                        HttpServletResponse res)
        throws ServletException, IOException
    {
            PrintWriter out;

            // Get a handle to the session or create a new one
            HttpSession session = req.getSession(true);

            res.setContentType("text/html");
            out = res.getWriter();
```

/* Get the value of the variable "totalAccesses". If this is the first time the Servlet is being accessed in this session, **getValue()** will return null */

```java
            Integer accesses =
                    (Integer)session.getValue("totalAccesses");
```

/* If this is the first time (a newly established session), create an integer with the value 1. Otherwise retrieve the value of the integer and increment it by 1 */

```java
            if(accesses == null)
                    accesses = new Integer(1);
            else
            {
                    int total = accesses.intValue();
                    total++;
                    accesses = new Integer(total);
            }
```

/* Put the integer object back in the list of variables belonging to the session */

```java
            session.putValue("totalAccesses", accesses);
```

/* Print an HTML page—show the value of the integer */

```
out.println("<HTML><HEAD></HEAD>");
out.println("<BODY bgcolor=\"#FFFFFF\">");
out.println("<H3>Total accesses in this session so far: "
            + accesses.toString() + "</H3>");
```

/* Add a FORM to this HTML page—when Submit is pressed in the FORM, this Servlet is executed */

```
out.println("<FORM
ACTION='http://myServer/testZone/SessionServlet'
METHOD='POST'>");
out.println("<INPUT TYPE='submit'
            NAME='Submit' VALUE='Execute'>");
out.println("</FORM>");

out.println("</BODY></HTML>");
out.close();
    }
}
```

Some Practical Examples

We conclude this chapter with a few practical examples that you can leverage for your site. The examples are based on concepts we've learnt in this chapter, as well as those in Chapters 2 and 3. Very little explanation has been provided, as very few new concepts are introduced in the examples. We have provided detailed explanation in such cases.

Example 1: Bulk Email Sender

This Servlet allows you to send mass emails to customers. Email addresses are read from a file. The name of the addresses file, return address, and subject and body of the mail are specified in an HTML page containing a FORM. When the Submit button is pressed, the Servlet SendMailsServlet is invoked. It reads mail addresses from the file and uses the class EmailSender to send individual mails to each of the addresses in the file. EmailSender uses the JavaMail API for sending emails.

The mail addresses file is expected to contain one email address per line. A typical file would look like this:

vivek_sharma_99@yahoo.com

vivek_sharma_99@hotmail.com

You can put as many email addresses in this as you want. The Servlet will read each line and send an email to that address.

The front end for this tool is the HTML file **sendBulkMails.html**. Figure 4.3 shows how it looks as viewed from a browser.

In order to use this you would move the HTML file **sendBulkMails.html** to your DocumentRoot directory. The Servlet classes should be moved to the physical path corresponding to the "example" zone. Also, you would need to include **activation.jar** and **mail.jar** in the CLASSPATH of your JServ (the **wrapper.classpath** parameter in the "jserv.properties" file). Note that you will need these two **jar** files in order to compile the Servlets also.

The code is as follows:

sendBulkMails.html

```html
<HTML><HEAD></HEAD>
<CENTER><H1>Bulk Mail Sender</H1></CENTER>
<BODY>
<FORM ACTION='/example/SendMailsServlet' METHOD='POST'>
<TABLE>
    <TR><TD>"To" addresses file</TD>
        <TD><INPUT TYPE='text' NAME='toFile' SIZE='20'>
        </TD></TR>
    <TR><TD>Subject</TD>
        <TD><INPUT TYPE='text' NAME='subject' SIZE='50'>
        </TD></TR>
    <TR><TD>Body</TD>
        <TD><TEXTAREA NAME='body' ROWS='8' COLS='50'></TEXTAREA>
        </TD></TR>
    <TR><TD>Return Address</TD>
        <TD><INPUT TYPE='text' NAME='returnAddress' SIZE='20'>
        </TD></TR>
    <TR><TD></TD>
        <TD><INPUT TYPE='submit' NAME='send' VALUE='Send Mails'>
        </TD></TR>
</TABLE>
</FORM>
</BODY>
</HTML>
```

SendMailsServlet.java

```java
import java.io.*;
import javax.servlet.*;
import javax.servlet.http.*;
import java.util.*;
public class SendMailsServlet extends HttpServlet
{
```

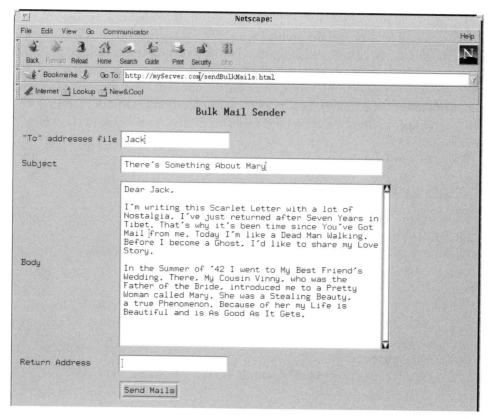

Figure   4.3

```java
public void doGet (HttpServletRequest req, HttpServletResponse
    res)
{
    doPost(req, res);
}
public void doPost (HttpServletRequest req,
                    HttpServletResponse res)
{
    try{
        PrintWriter out = null;
        res.setContentType("text/html");
        out = res.getWriter();

        Enumeration values = req.getParameterNames();

        String returnAddress = "", body="",
            subject="", toFile="";
        while(values.hasMoreElements())
```

```
            {
                String name = (String)values.nextElement();
                String value = req.getParameterValues(name)[0];
                if(name.equalsIgnoreCase("returnAddress"))
                    returnAddress = value;
                if(name.equalsIgnoreCase("body"))
                    body = value;
                if(name.equalsIgnoreCase("subject"))
                    subject = value;
                if(name.equalsIgnoreCase("toFile"))
                    toFile = value;
            }

            int count = 0;
            try{
                File f = new File(toFile);
                FileReader fr = new FileReader(f);
                BufferedReader bis = new BufferedReader(fr);
                String to;
                while((to = bis.readLine()) != null)
                {
                    EmailSender es =
                        new EmailSender(returnAddress, to,
                                        subject, body);
                    es.send();
                    count++;
                }
                bis.close();
            }catch(Exception ex){}
            out.println("<HTML><HEAD></HEAD><BODY>");
            out.println("Sent " + count + " mails");
            out.println("</BODY></HTML>");
            out.close();
        }catch(Exception ex){}
    }
}
```

EmailSender.java

```
import java.io.*;
import java.net.InetAddress;
import java.util.Properties;
import java.util.Date;

import javax.mail.*;
```

```
import javax.mail.internet.*;
import javax.activation.*;

public class EmailSender
{
    static String smtphost = "SMTP_HOST";
    String from, to, mailHeader, mailBody;
    EmailSender(String f, String t, String mh, String mb)
    {
        from = f;
        to = t;
        mailHeader = mh;
        mailBody = mb;
    }
    public void send()
        throws Exception
    {
        Properties props = new Properties();
        props.put("mail.smtp.host", smtphost);
        Session session = Session.getDefaultInstance(props, null);
        Message msg = new MimeMessage(session);
        msg.setFrom(new InternetAddress(from));
        InternetAddress[] address = {new InternetAddress(to)};
        msg.setRecipients(Message.RecipientType.TO, address);
        msg.setSubject(mailHeader);
        msg.setSentDate(new Date());
        msg.setText(mailBody);
        Transport.send(msg);
    }
}
```

Example 2: Internationalized Help Screens for Your Worldwide Customers

In this example we see how you can implement an internationalized help system. Using this kind of technology, your customers can view information in the language of their choice, provided you support that language.

Customer experience begins with selectLanguage.html, where (s)he selects the country and language. This contains select boxes from which customers can select. The Submit button in this FORM invokes SelectLanguageServlet, which creates a session and stores the customer's preferred language and country. It also presents links to different help topics that the customer can view. Each of these links refers to the DisplayHelpServlet Servlet and passes a unique id as a parameter to the Servlet so that the Servlet knows which help page is to be displayed.

The base name of the resource bundles is "help." The properties files contain values for each of the id values of the links displayed by SelectLanguageServlet. We have played a small trick here. Instead of containing text that is to be displayed, the value of these keys in the properties files is the name of an HTML file that should be displayed.

The French file looks like this:

01 = /home/vsharma/HTML/HELP/FR/help01.html

02 = /home/vsharma/HTML/HELP/FR/help02.html

Therefore, if a customer who has selected French clicks on the link with id=01, DisplayHelpServlet will read the value of 01 from the properties file. This value is as follows:

/home/vsharma/HTML/HELP/FR/help01.html

Now, instead of sending this value to the browser, the Servlet reads the file "/home/vsharma/HTML/HELP/FR/help01.html" and sends the contents of the file. Similarly, if the customer clicked on the link with id=02, help02.html from the FR directory would be displayed. This procedure allows your translation department to create HTML files in different languages so that the entire content may be internationalized, not just individual Strings.

As shown in Figure 4.4, the user starts by selecting preferred country and language.

As shown in Figure 4.5, the SelectLanguageServlet, which is invoked if the OK button is pressed, displays links to two help topics.

Figure 4.6 shows what the user sees if US/English is chosen.

And Figure 4.7 shows what a French user would see.

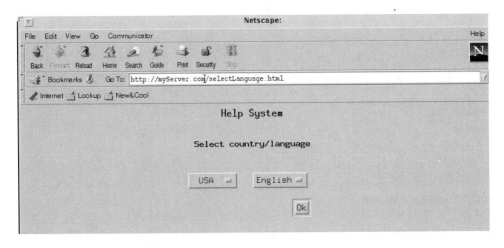

Figure   4.4

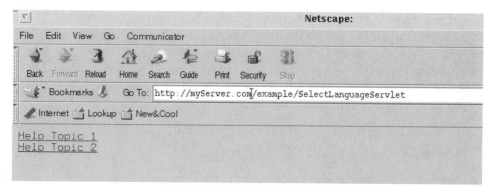

Figure 4.5

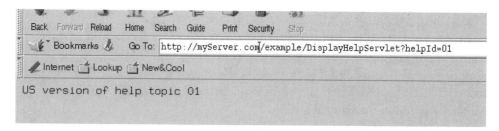

Figure 4.6

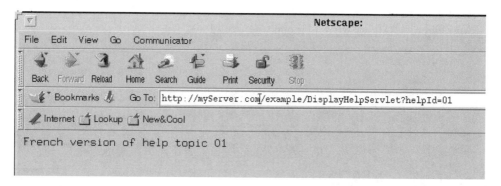

Figure 4.7

Here's the source code:

selectLanguage.html

```
<HTML><HEAD></HEAD>
<BODY>
    <H1><CENTER>Help System</H1></CENTER><BR>
    <H3><CENTER>Select country/language</H3></CENTER><BR>
```

```
                  <FORM ACTION = '/example/SelectLanguageServlet'
                           METHOD='POST'>
<CENTER>
    <TABLE>
        <TR><TD>
            <SELECT NAME='country'>
                    <OPTION VALUE='US'>USA
                    <OPTION VALUE='FR'>France
            </SELECT>
        </TD><TD>
            <SELECT NAME='language'>
                    <OPTION VALUE='us'>English
                    <OPTION VALUE='fr'>French
            </SELECT>
        </TD></TR>
        <TR><TD></TD><TD ALIGN='right'>
                <INPUT TYPE='submit' NAME='submit' VALUE='Ok'>
        </TD></TR>
    </TABLE>
</CENTER>
</FORM>
</BODY>
</HTML>
```

SelectLanguageServlet.java

```java
import java.io.*;
import javax.servlet.*;
import javax.servlet.http.*;
import java.util.*;
public class SelectLanguageServlet extends HttpServlet
{
    public void doGet (HttpServletRequest req, HttpServletResponse
        res)
    {
        doPost(req, res);
    }
    public void doPost (HttpServletRequest req,
                        HttpServletResponse res)
    {
        try{
            PrintWriter out = null;
            res.setContentType("text/html");
            out = res.getWriter();
```

```java
            HttpSession session = req.getSession(true);
            Enumeration values = req.getParameterNames();

            String language = "";
            String country = "";
            while(values.hasMoreElements())
            {
                    String name = (String)values.nextElement();
                    String value = req.getParameterValues(name)[0];
                    if(name.equalsIgnoreCase("country"))
                        country = value;
                    if(name.equalsIgnoreCase("language"))
                        language = value;
            }
            session.putValue("language", language);
            session.putValue("country", country);

            out.println("<HTML><HEAD></HEAD><BODY>");
            out.println("<A HREF=
                    '/example/DisplayHelpServlet?helpId=01'>
                        Help Topic 1</A><BR>");
            out.println("<A HREF=
                    '/example/DisplayHelpServlet?helpId=02'>
                        Help Topic 2</A><BR>");
            out.println("</BODY></HTML>");
            out.close();
        }catch(Exception ex){}
    }
}
```

DisplayHelpServlet.java

```java
import java.io.*;
import javax.servlet.*;
import javax.servlet.http.*;
import java.util.*;
public class DisplayHelpServlet extends HttpServlet
{
    public void doGet (HttpServletRequest req, HttpServletResponse
        res)
    {
        doPost(req, res);
    }
    public void doPost (HttpServletRequest req,
                    HttpServletResponse res)
```

```
{
    try{
        PrintWriter out = null;
        res.setContentType("text/html");
        out = res.getWriter();

        HttpSession session = req.getSession(false);
        Enumeration values = req.getParameterNames();

        String helpId = "";
        while(values.hasMoreElements())
        {
                String name = (String)values.nextElement();
                String value = req.getParameterValues(name)[0];
                if(name.equalsIgnoreCase("helpId"))
                    helpId = value;
        }
        String country = (String)session.getValue("country");
        String language = (String)session.getValue("language");

        if(country == null)
            country = new String("US");
        if(language == null)
            language = new String("us");

        Locale currentLocale;
        ResourceBundle messages;

        currentLocale = new Locale(country, language);
        messages =
            ResourceBundle.getBundle("help", currentLocale);
        String htmlFile = messages.getString(helpId);

        displayHtmlFile(htmlFile, out);
        out.close();
    }catch(Exception ex){}
}
public void displayHtmlFile(String fileName, PrintWriter out)
{
    try
    {
        File f = new File(fileName);
        FileReader fr = new FileReader(f);
        BufferedReader bis = new BufferedReader(fr);
        String inpu;
        while((inpu = bis.readLine()) != null)
        {
```

```
            out.println(inpu);
        }
        bis.close();
    }catch(Exception e){
        out.println("<HTML><HEAD></HEAD><BODY>");
        e.printStackTrace();
        out.println("</BODY></HTML>");
    }
  }
}
```

Example 3: Stocks Reader

This is a Java class that posts a request to a Servlet and receives results from it. We've simulated a stocks Servlet that returns the value of a stock based on its symbol (similar to the way *quote.yahoo.com* works). Our stocks Servlet can return stock values for the symbols MSFT and ORCL, both of which are hard-coded. The Java class, StocksReader, accepts a symbol as an argument and posts a request on StocksServlet. Since StocksServlet is typically expected to be called through a browser, it returns an HTML page that the browser can display, containing the value of the stock. But our Java class is being invoked on the command line. If it displayed contents of the HTML file, it would be difficult to find the value of the stock we're interested in. So it parses the HTML file, looks for the value of the stock, and displays it.

You can use this type of a utility in conjunction with a site like *quote.yahoo.com* to provide your own stock reader. Or you may even build a tool that monitors stocks automatically by querying *quote.yahoo.com* (or some other stock site) and picking the stocks that have performed best in the last year, two months, and so on. This type of utility may also be used to create a service like helping customers find the cheapest insurance or the best car value by querying sites of different insurance companies and car dealers.

First we present the StocksServlet, which simulates a stock quote site. Next we take a look at StocksReader, which connects to this site. Before that, however, we see the kind of HTML page that StocksServlet returns when you query it through a browser, illustrated in Figure 4.8.

StocksServlet.java

```
import java.io.*;
import javax.servlet.*;
import javax.servlet.http.*;
import java.util.*;
public class StocksServlet extends HttpServlet
{
    public void doGet (HttpServletRequest req, HttpServletResponse
        res)
```

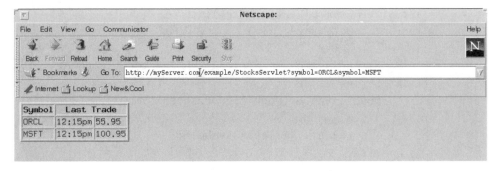

Figure 4.8

```
{
     doPost(req, res);
}
public void doPost (HttpServletRequest req,
                    HttpServletResponse res)
{
     PrintWriter out = null;
     res.setContentType("text/html");
     try{
        out = res.getWriter();
     }catch(Exception ex){}

     Hashtable quotes = new Hashtable();
     quotes.put("MSFT", new Double(100.95));
     quotes.put("ORCL", new Double(55.95));

     Enumeration values = req.getParameterNames();
     Vector symbolVector = new Vector();
     while(values.hasMoreElements())
     {
          String name = (String)values.nextElement();
          String[] value = req.getParameterValues(name);
          if(name.equalsIgnoreCase("symbol"))
          {
               int len = value.length;
               for(int i=0; i<len; i++)
                   symbolVector.addElement(value[i]);
          }
     }

     out.println("<HTML><HEAD></HEAD><BODY>");
     out.println("<TABLE BORDER='2'><TH>Symbol</TH>
                    <TH COLSPAN='2'>Last Trade</TH>");
```

```java
        int size = symbolVector.size();
        for(int i=0; i<size; i++)
        {
                String symbol = (String)symbolVector.elementAt(i);
                String value = "";
                Double val = (Double)quotes.get(symbol);
                if(val == null)
                    value = "Illegal symbol";
                else
                    value = val.toString();
                out.println("<TR><TD>" + symbol +
                    "</TD><TD>12:15pm</TD><TD>" + value +
                    "</TD></TR>");
        }
        out.println("</TABLE>");
        out.println("</BODY></HTML>");
        out.close();
    }
}
```

StocksReader.java

```java
import java.net.*;
import java.io.*;

public class StocksReader
{
    String theURL = "http://myServer.com/testZone/StocksServlet";
    public static void main(String[] args)
    {
        String symbol = args[0];
        StocksReader sr = new StocksReader();
        sr.start(symbol);
    }
    public void start(String symbol)
    {
        try
        {
            URL myURL = new URL(theURL);
            URLConnection conn = myURL.openConnection();
            conn.setDefaultUseCaches(false);
            conn.setDoOutput(true);
            conn.setRequestProperty("Content-type",
                        "application/octet-stream");
```

```java
            String message="symbol=" + symbol;
            conn.setRequestProperty("Content-length", "" +
                        message.length());
            OutputStreamWriter outStream =
                new OutputStreamWriter(conn.getOutputStream());
            PrintWriter pout = new PrintWriter(outStream);
            pout.write(message);
            outStream.flush();
            outStream.close();
            InputStreamReader inpStream =
                    new InputStreamReader(conn.getInputStream());
            BufferedReader br = new BufferedReader(inpStream);

            String oneLine;

            while ((oneLine = br.readLine()) != null)
            {
                parseIt(oneLine, symbol);
            }
            br.close();
        } catch (MalformedURLException mex)
        {
                mex.printStackTrace();
        } catch (IOException ioex)
        {
                ioex.printStackTrace();
        }
    }
    public void parseIt(String line, String symbol)
    {
        int index = line.indexOf(symbol);
        if(index != -1)
        {
            String delim = "<TD>";
            int ind2 = line.indexOf(delim, index);
            ind2 = line.indexOf(delim, ind2+1);
            int ind3 = line.indexOf("</TD>", ind2);
            String value = line.substring(ind2 +
                delim.length(), ind3);
            System.out.println("Value of " + symbol  + " is " +
                                value);
        }
    }
}
```

In this we're using the URL class to connect to StocksServlet. However, instead of just reading an HTML file as we did in the Java chapter, this URL is a Servlet to which we want to post a request. Hence the code is slightly different. We first open a connection to the URL. Then we specify that we want to use the output stream to supply some data (CGI variables) to the URL.

```
URLConnection conn = myURL.openConnection();
conn.setDefaultUseCaches(false);
conn.setDoOutput(true);
```

We set the request property for this connection to application/octet-stream, as we're connecting to a Servlet (which is an application). Next we construct the CGI variables that we need to post and set the Content-length header to inform the Servlet of the length of our CGI input so that it can handle the request properly.

```
conn.setRequestProperty("Content-type",
                "application/octet-stream");
String message="symbol=" + symbol;
conn.setRequestProperty("Content-length", "" +
                            message.length());
```

The CGI variables are then written to the output stream obtained from this connection, making the CGI variables available to the Servlet.

```
OutputStreamWriter outStream =
    new OutputStreamWriter(conn.getOutputStream());
PrintWriter pout = new PrintWriter(outStream);
pout.write(message);
```

Next we obtain an input stream from this connection so that we can read results sent by the Servlet.

```
InputStreamReader inpStream =
        new InputStreamReader(conn.getInputStream());
```

Subsequently, the results are parsed and the value of the stock is derived from that. One thing to note is that this implementation assumes that StocksServlet is always going to return data in the same format. While this may be a valid assumption if you also control StocksServlet, it may not work in the real world. For instance, if you are using *quote.yahoo.com* and they change the output HTML page to add another column to the table, your program will stop working correctly. In Chapter 7 we will see a more sophisticated solution that can work with sites supporting XML.

Example: Session-Based Shopping Cart

In this example we create a simple shopping-cart Servlet. The Servlet displays a list of products that you can add to your shopping cart. It also shows a button that can be clicked to view current contents of the cart, including the total price of items you've added to the cart.

Each product in the store is represented by the Product object (in Product.java). We've simulated a ProductDatabase containing a list of all products that this virtual store sells. Every item that a customer purchases is represented by the Item object (Item.java).

Product.java defines the Product class. Each product can have a name, price, and a unique id, with methods to get and set the values.

ProductDatabase.java contains a vector called Products, which contains Product objects for each of the products the store sells. In a real world these would be retrieved from a database. However, since we still have to look at databases, we've simulated this stage by creating some dummy products like "Product 1" with price 29.95 (look at the method **retrieveAllProducts()**).

ProductDatabase contains a method to get a Product by its id and a method to get the products vector (the list of all products in the database).

Item.java contains the Item class that represents an item added to the cart. An item consists of a product and the quantity of this product that has been added to the cart. Each item is assigned a unique id. The class contains methods for getting and setting these values.

For each customer who connects to the ShoppingServlet, a ShoppingCart object is created and maintained. All items selected by the customer are added to the ShoppingCart object.

The **init()** method of ShoppingServlet retrieves a list of products from the ProductDatabase. When a customer first connects to the ShoppingServlet, a session is established. A ShoppingCart object is created and stored as a session variable. Names of all products are displayed. Next to each of these is a text field in which the customer can type the quantity (s)he wants to purchase. Each line contains one product's name, a text field, and a Submit button. On pressing the Submit button, ShoppingServlet is invoked again. This time a different portion of the ShoppingServlet code is executed (the method **addToCart()**), which creates a new Item object containing the product and quantity specified by the customer. The Item object is then added to the customer's cart.

If the customer presses the Show Cart link, ShoppingServlet is invoked. This time it calls the method **showCart()**, which retrieves the Item objects in this customer's shopping cart. Product information and price for each of these Item objects is retrieved and calculated, and then displayed.

All code is assumed to exist in a package book.cart, inside the Servlet zone "example." You can deploy it in a Servlet zone called "example." Note that you will have to create the directories book and book/cart in your "example" zone. The classes will need to be moved to the book/cart directory as the package is named **book.cart**.

Here's a visual look at the shopping cart behavior. User experience begins by invoking the URL: *http://myServer.com/example/book.cart.ShoppingServlet* (see Figure 4.9).

If the customer presses the Add to Cart button, the item is added to the shopping cart, and the same page is displayed again.

Figure 4.10 shows what is displayed if the customer presses the Show Cart link.

Here is the complete code.

Product.java

```
package book.cart;

public class Product
{
    String name = "";
    Integer id;
    Double price;

    Product(Integer i, String n, Double p)
    {
        id = i;
        name = n;
        price = p;
    }
    public Integer getId()
    {
```

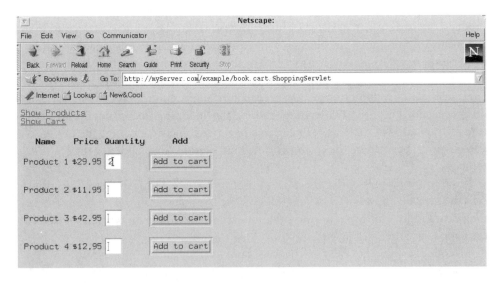

Figure 4.9

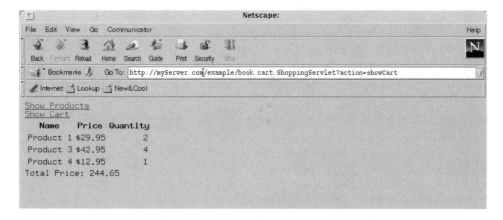

Figure 4.10

```
            return id;
      }
      public String getName()
      {
            return name;
      }
      public Double getPrice()
      {
            return price;
      }
}
```

ProductDatabase.java

```
package book.cart;
import java.util.*;
public class ProductDatabase
{
      Vector products = new Vector();
      ProductDatabase()
      {
            retrieveAllProducts();
      }
      public Product getById(int id)
      {
            Product theProduct = null;
            int size = products.size();
            for(int i=0; i<size; i++)
            {
```

```java
                Product p = (Product)products.elementAt(i);
                int pid = (p.getId()).intValue();
                if(pid == id)
                {
                        theProduct = p;
                        break;
                }
            }
            return theProduct;
        }
        public Vector getAllProducts()
        {
            return products;
        }
        public void retrieveAllProducts()
        {
            // This should retrieve from database. For the sake of
              an example
            // we supply dummy values here.
            Product p = new Product(new Integer(1),
                        "Product 1", new Double(29.95));
            products.addElement(p);
            p = new Product(new Integer(2), "Product 2",
                        new Double(11.95));
            products.addElement(p);
            p = new Product(new Integer(3), "Product 3",
                        new Double(42.95));
            products.addElement(p);
            p = new Product(new Integer(4), "Product 4",
                        new Double(12.95));
            products.addElement(p);
        }
}
```

Item.java

```java
package book.cart;

public class Item
{
        Product prod;
        Integer qtty;
        Integer id;
```

```
        Item(Integer i, Product p, Integer q)
        {
                id   = i;
                prod = p;
                qtty = q;
        }
        public Integer getId()
        {
                return id;
        }
        public Product getProduct()
        {
         v      return prod;
        }
        public Integer getQuantity()
        {
                return qtty;
        }
}
```

ShoppingCart.java

```
package book.cart;

import java.util.*;
public class ShoppingCart
{
        int lastItemId = 0;
        Vector items = new Vector();
        public void addItem(Item i)
        {
                items.addElement(i);
        }
        public int getNewItemId()
        {
            lastItemId++;
            return lastItemId;
        }
        public Vector getAllItems()
        {
                return items;
        }
}
```

ShoppingServlet.java

```java
package book.cart;
import java.io.*;
import java.util.Enumeration;

import javax.servlet.*;
import javax.servlet.http.*;
import java.util.*;
public class ShoppingServlet extends HttpServlet
{
   ProductDatabase pd;
   PrintStream ps = null;

     public void init(ServletConfig s)
             throws ServletException
     {

         pd = new ProductDatabase();
     }
     public void doGet (HttpServletRequest req, HttpServletResponse
         res)
     {
         doPost(req, res);
     }
     public void doPost (HttpServletRequest req,
                         HttpServletResponse res)
     {
         PrintWriter out = null;
         String action = "showProducts";
         String prodId = "", prodQtty = "";
         HttpSession session = req.getSession(true);
         Enumeration values = req.getParameterNames();

         while(values.hasMoreElements())
         {
             String name = (String)values.nextElement();
             String value = req.getParameterValues(name)[0];
             if(name.equalsIgnoreCase("action"))
                 action = value;
             if(name.indexOf("qtty") != -1)
             {
                 int ind = name.indexOf("_");
                 prodId = name.substring(0, ind);
                 prodQtty = value;
```

```java
            }
        }

        res.setContentType("text/html");
        try{
            out = res.getWriter();
        }catch(Exception ex){}

        ShoppingCart cart =
            (ShoppingCart)session.getValue("book.cart.shopping
                Cart");
        if(cart == null)
            cart = new ShoppingCart();

        showCommonPart(out);
        if(action.equalsIgnoreCase("addToCart"))
        {
            cart = addToCart(prodId, prodQtty, cart);
            action = "showProducts";
        }
        if(action.equalsIgnoreCase("showCart"))
            showCart(out, cart);
        if(action.equalsIgnoreCase("showProducts"))
            showProducts(out);
        session.putValue("book.cart.shoppingCart", cart);

        out.println("</BODY></HTML>");
        out.close();
    }
    public ShoppingCart addToCart(String prodId, String prodQtty,
                                  ShoppingCart cart)
    {
        int itemId = cart.getNewItemId();
        int pid = (new Integer(prodId)).intValue();
        Product prod = pd.getById(pid);
        Item i = new Item((new Integer(itemId)), prod,
                          new Integer(prodQtty));
        cart.addItem(i);
        return cart;
    }
    public void showCommonPart(PrintWriter out)
    {
        out.println("<HTML><HEAD></HEAD><BODY>");
        out.println("<A HREF=
'/example/book.cart.ShoppingServlet?action=showProducts'>
                Show Products</A><BR>");
```

```java
            out.println("<A HREF=
'/example/book.cart.ShoppingServlet?action=showCart'>
                    Show Cart</A><BR>");
    }
    public void showProducts(PrintWriter out)
    {

            Vector prods = pd.getAllProducts();

            int size = prods.size();
            out.println("<TABLE><TH>Name<TH>Price</TH>
                    <TH>Quantity</TH><TH>Add</TH>");
            for(int i=0; i<size; i++)
            {
                Product p = (Product)prods.elementAt(i);
                String name = p.getName();
                String id = (p.getId()).toString();
                String price = (p.getPrice()).toString();
                out.println("<TR><FORM ACTION=
              '/example/book.cart.ShoppingServlet' METHOD='POST'>");
                out.println("<INPUT TYPE='hidden' NAME='action'
                        VALUE='addToCart'>");
                out.println("<TD>" + name + "</TD><TD>$" +
                        price + "</TD>");
                out.println("<TD><INPUT TYPE='text' NAME='" + id +
                        "_qtty" + "' SIZE='2'></TD>");
                out.println("<TD><INPUT TYPE='submit' NAME='
                        submit' VALUE='Add to cart'></TD>");
                out.println("</FORM/TR>");
            }
            out.println("</TABLE>");
    }
    public void showCart(PrintWriter out, ShoppingCart cart)
    {
            out.println("<TABLE><TH>Name</TH><TH>Price</TH>
                    <TH>Quantity</TH>");
            double totalPrice = 0.0;
            Vector items = cart.getAllItems();
            int size = items.size();
            for(int i=0; i<size; i++)
            {
                Item it = (Item)items.elementAt(i);
                Product p = it.getProduct();
                Integer qtty = it.getQuantity();
```

```
            int quantity = qtty.intValue();

            String name = p.getName();
            Double price = p.getPrice();

            totalPrice += price.doubleValue()*quantity;

            out.println("<TR><TD>" + name + "</TD><TD>$" +
                    price.toString() + "</TD><TD>" +
                    qtty.toString() + "</TD></TR>");
        }
        out.println("</TABLE>");
        out.println("Total Price: " + totalPrice);
    }
}
```

Conclusion

This completes our discussion of Servlets. In the previous chapters we have covered HTML and Java. A combination of these technologies, along with some other technologies like JDBC and Javascript that will be discussed later, can be used to create very useful and powerful Web applications. If you are new to any of the technologies, you may initially need to come back and refer to these chapters. However, as you play around with the code, it should not take too long for you to integrate the information in your system. It would also be useful to consult the sites and books mentioned for additional information that would be helpful in making useful additions to the applications.

Some Useful Interfaces/Classes and Some of Their Methods

package javax.servlet

Servlet.java—interface

Every Servlet implements this interface.

> —Methods: **init()**—method for initializing the Servlet. Executed once automatically when the Servlet is loaded.
> **getServletConfig()**—returns a Servlet config object that contains initialization parameters for the Servlet.
> **service()**—method for serving a request from the client. In specialized Servlets for serving HTTP requests, you would implement a doPost() or doGet() method.

destroy()—method for cleaning up resources when Servlet is unloaded. Executed only once, automatically.

ServletRequest.java

Represents the request from the client. Can be used for getting more information about the request.

—Methods: **getRemoteAddr()**—IP Address of the client from which request came
getRemoteHost()—name of host from which request came
getParameterValues()—get value of a CGI parameter
getParameterNames()—names of all the CGI parameters

ServletResponse.java

Represents the response from the Servlet to the client.

—Methods: **setContentType()**—set the content type of the response.
getWriter()—get a handle on the output stream so that you can send data back to the client

package javax.servlet.http

Cookie.java

Class representing a Cookie—can be used for setting and getting cookies.

—Methods: **Cookie**(String name, String value)—constructor for creating a Cookie.
setDomain()—method for setting the domain for which this Cookie is applicable.
setMaxAge()—sets the age of the cookie. If a negative value is specified, cookie is not treated as persistent.
setPath()—sets the path for which Cookie is applicable.
setName()—sets the name of the Cookie.
setValue()—sets the value of the Cookie.
The set methods have corresponding get()s.

HttpServlet.java

Abstract class that is "extended" by Http Servlets

—Methods: **doGet()**—method that is called if a GET request is posted. You can read data, process it, and send a response back using two objects passed in as input parameters.
doPost()—method for POST operations.

HttpServletRequest.java—interface that extends ServletRequest.

Represents the request from the client—can be used for getting more information about the request.

—Methods: **getCookies()**—returns a list of all cookies in this request.
getMethod()—returns the HTTP method (e.g., GET, POST).
getRequestURI()—name of the requested URI, without the query String.
getRemoteUser()—name of the user making request (if known). Useful if the user has authenticated.
getSession()—gets a handle on an existing session or creates a new session.

HttpServletResponse.java

Represents the response from the Servlet to the client.

Extends ServletResponse

—Methods: **addCookie()**—for sending cookies to the client.
sendRedirect()—send a redirect response to client so the client tries to open that URL instead.

HttpSession.java

Represents a session between the client and the server.

—Methods: **getId()**—get identifier assigned to this session.
getCreationTime()—time at which this session was created.
getLastAccessedTime()—last time this session was accessed.
invalidate()—invalidate the session.
putValue()—store an object in the session.
getValue()—retrieve an object previously stored in the session.
removeValue()—remove an object from the session.
getValueNames()—get names of objects stored in the session.

HttpServletRequest is actually an extension of ServletRequest, which resides in the **javax.Servlet** package. Similarly, HttpServletResponse is an extension of ServletResponse. These base interfaces provide some methods that can be of great use. Here are some methods from ServletRequest:

Interface ServletRequest

getContentLength()—CGI variable CONTENT_LENGTH (size of data being transmitted to the Servlet).

getContentType()—CGI variable CONTENT_TYPE (media type of requested entity).

getServerName()—CGI variable SERVER_NAME (host name of server that received the request).

getRemoteAddr()—CGI variable REMOTE_ADDR (IP address of client machine).

Chapter 5

Javascript

Introduction

Javascript is a cross-platform scripting language developed by Netscape.It can be used for creating both server-side and client-side applications. In this chapter, however, we will focus only on the client-side aspects of the language. Client-side Javascript is typically executed in a browser that supports the language. It is an interpreted object-oriented language that can be included in HTML pages. You can access a number of elements in your HTML page and manipulate them using Javascript. This helps in the creation of dynamic HTML pages capable of responding to user events like mouse clicks, key presses, selection of elements in a form, and so on.

Different components of an HTML page (including elements belonging to a FORM) are represented as objects that can be accessed by Javascript. These objects are organized in a hierarchy that begins at the top with the window object. A window represents a browser window or frame. Objects have properties and methods associated with them, and the properties may actually be references to other objects contained in an object. A window thus has several properties such as frames (representing frames present in this window) and a history property (containing information about the URLs that the client has visited within this window). Other properties contain information about the window itself, for example, its height and width.

Objects may also have methods associated with them. For instance, a window object has an **alert** method that can be used for throwing an Alert dialog box, a **moveTo** method that allows you to move the window, a **resizeTo()** method that allows you to change the size of the window, and so on.

Objects can also have events with associated event handlers. In the case of a window, therefore, when the window is loaded, a load event occurs, which can be handled by a user-defined function. The "onLoad" event handler is used to specify the function that will handle this. Similarly you can provide your own functions to handle events like unload, window move, window resize, etc.

Documents

My life is well documented—
in the annals of internal medicine!

One of the properties of a window is the document, which represents the current document and provides methods for displaying HTML output to the user. The Javascript runtime engine creates a document object for each HTML page. A document in turn contains links, images, and—most important, from our point of view—"a forms" property that represents all the FORMs in it. Other properties can be used to control the appearance of the document—the bgColor (background color), fgColor, etc. A document also has a cookie property used for specifying/retrieving cookies.

A cookie is a piece of data that can be sent from the client to the server whenever a page request is made. Cookies are used primarily for maintaining state and personalizing site experience. We will learn more about them later.

document.forms

As mentioned above, the "forms" property of a document gives you access to all the Form objects in the document. You can then access elements of this form, which are included in the properties of the Form object. You can access these elements by name. A Form also has an "elements" array as one of its properties. This array contains all the elements in the form, which you can access by referring to an element in this array by position.

Event handlers of a form are "onReset" and "onSubmit." Using these, you can specify functions that will be invoked when the user presses the Submit button or the Reset button.

Statements

All statements and opinions expressed here are my boss's,
not my own—please sue my boss!

Javascript supports a number of constructs found in languages like C. Here are some commonly used Javascript statements:

break, continue, do...while, for, function, if...else, return, var

Examples

Following are a number of examples through which we will show how to use different features of Javascript.

```
<HTML><HEAD></HEAD>
<BODY>
This is static text<P>
   <SCRIPT LANGUAGE="Javascript">
       document.write('Random number:' + Math.random());
   </SCRIPT>
</BODY>
</HTML>
```

This is a very simple example containing some Javascript code inside the BODY tag of the HTML file. Javascript code is enclosed by <SCRIPT LANGUAGE=" "Javascript"> and </SCRIPT> tags.

When this page is displayed, there are two lines in it. The first is "This is static text"; the second displays a random number. The difference is that while the first line is a regular static HTML element, the second line is generated as a result of execution of the Javascript code. When the browser encounters the <SCRIPT> tag, it interprets and executes the code. In this case, we're using the "write" method of document. If you recall from our discussion earlier, "document" represents the current document (HTML page). The **write()** function can be used to write data to this document. We're also using the **random()** function in math for generating a random number.

This small script has in essence made the HTML page dynamic. If you reload it, you will see a different random number. The reason for this is that the code has executed again, resulting in the display of a new random number.

Functions

As a manager, my main function is to keep the staff happy—
they hired me because I'm so smooth at making false promises!

Next we look at how functions (methods) are defined and used in Javascript.

```
<HTML><HEAD></HEAD>
<SCRIPT LANGUAGE="Javascript">
   function printIt(txt)
   {
       document.write(txt + Math.random());
   }
```

```
    </SCRIPT>
<BODY>
This is static text<P>
    <SCRIPT LANGUAGE="Javascript">
        printIt("Random number:");
    </SCRIPT>
</BODY>
</HTML>
```

In this example we've split our Javascript code into two distinct parts. The second part is specified in BODY section as in our previous example, but the first part is before it. Code that is present in the body is executed as it is encountered. However, the code before the body needs to be specifically invoked either by an event or by an explicit call from the body. This example behaves exactly like the first example. In the prebody part we've specified a function called **printIt()**, which takes a variable named "txt" as argument. Note that Javascript is not a strongly typed language, so you don't have to specify whether "txt" is an integer, a Boolean, or a String. In this function we're printing this input argument followed by the random number.

The script in the body has changed. Instead of using **document.write()**, it calls the function **printIt()** and passes "Random number:" to it for display. Simple, isn't it?

Objects in Javascript

The next example creates an object. Note that in Javascript, an object is also declared as a function. The function then uses "this" keyword for storing instance variables. All methods that belong to the object are declared using "this."

```
<HTML>
<HEAD>
<SCRIPT LANGUAGE="JavaScript">
    function writeIt(b)
    {
        document.write("Value of variable myVar:
            <B>"+this.myVar+"</B><BR>");
        document.write("Value passed to function Printer:<B>"+ b +
            "</B><BR>");
    }
    function Printer(a)
    {
        this.myVar = a;
        this.writeIt = writeIt;
        document.write("Value passed to object:<B>"+a+"</B><BR>");
    }
```

```
</SCRIPT>
</HEAD>
<BODY>
<SCRIPT LANGUAGE="JavaScript">
    mm = new Printer(20);
    mm.writeIt(55);
</SCRIPT>
</BODY>
</HTML>
```

In this script we're creating an object of the type Printer and invoking a method called **writeIt()** that belongs to this object. We're using the familiar dot notation "." to invoke methods of the object.

The "new" keyword is used for creating objects.

The object and its method are defined in the first script. As you can see, Printer is declared as a normal function and accepts an input argument. We're also declaring a variable in this of the name "myVar" and assigning to this the value that is passed to **Printer()** as input.

Next we're declaring that the function **writeIt()** belongs to Printer.

```
    this.writeIt = writeIt;
```

This means that the function **writeIt()** can be invoked as an instance method of a Printer object. **writeIt()** itself is declared as a normal function. Since it belongs to the **Printer()** object, it has access to variables of **Printer()**. As a result, it can access "myVar," which we declared in Printer. In fact, we're displaying the value of this variable in the first line of the **writeIt()** function.

When this page is loaded, the following lines appear in the output:

Value passed to object:20

Value of variable myVar:20

Value passed to function Printer:55

The first two are values passed to **Printer()** at creation time that we stored in the variable "myVar." The third is the value passed as an input argument to **writeIt()**.

In this example, we're invoking **writeIt()** by first declaring an object "mm" of the type **Printer()** and then calling **mm.writeIt()**. However, just because **writeIt()** belongs to **Printer()** doesn't mean it is not accessible outside the context of **Printer()**. At the same time, though, if this method accesses any variables that belong to Printer, they will be undefined unless it is invoked as an instance method of Printer. In this case, therefore, you can call **writeIt()** directly, but the first line that tries to print "this.myVar" will print "undefined" instead of the number 20.

Events and Event Handling

I lead a very eventful life—
my friends call me Bond, James Bond!

In the next example we look at events and how they can be handled. Most objects can respond to events using Javascript. You can write your own event-handling functions. You could write code that pops up a window when a button is clicked. For most events that occur in HTML elements—buttons, checkboxes, text fields, etc.—you can specify the name of the event-handling function inside the HTML tag for that element (just as you write attributes). There are reserved words in Javascript that you can use for specifying the kind of event you are interested in. So, "onClick" refers to a click event occurring on a button (or a link). If you have written a function **A()** to handle this, your button declaration would look like this:

```
<INPUT TYPE='button' NAME='bt' VALUE='v1' onClick='A()'>
```

In this example we're looking at a link and how we can control what happens on a mouse click.

```
<HTML>
<HEAD>
<SCRIPT LANGUAGE="JavaScript">
function openHelp()
{
    window.open("file://myDir/helpmain.html", "helpWindow",
        "toolbar=no,directories=no,menubar=no,location=no,
        scrollbars=yes,width=50,height=50");
    return false;
}

</SCRIPT>
</HEAD>
<BODY>
  <A HREF=" onClick='return openHelp();'>Help</A>
</BODY>
</HTML>
```

In the body of this example, we've created a link using the <A> tag. Unlike the links we've seen earlier, this one doesn't contain anything in the HREF attribute. At the same time, we've written an "onClick" statement, that is, a directive to the Javascript interpreter that when the link is clicked, the function **openHelp()** should be invoked and the value returned by **openHelp()** returned to the event handler. If this user-defined function returns a false value, the event handler doesn't do any more processing. If it returns true, however, that is an indication to the event handler that it needs to process the link as it would process a normal link.

Now look at the function **openHelp()**. In this we're using the **open()** method of window to create a new window in which some other document can be displayed. **open()** takes three arguments: (1) the location of the document you want to display in the new window, (2) the name of the window, and (3) a list of parameters that determine the shape and size of the window. In this case we've specified the window to be 50 pixels by 50 pixels with no menubar. When the user clicks the Help link, **openHelp()** is invoked to open this window and display "helpmain.html" in it. It then returns a false so that the default event handler does nothing more.

You can write handling code besides onClick for other events. Some common ones are onMouseOver, onMouseOut, onKeyDown, and onKeyUp.

You can use another event, associated with the document, to display help automatically. In the BODY tag you can include an "onLoad" statement. The "onLoad" event occurs when the document is loaded.

In this example you can do so by changing the <BODY> statement to read as follows:

```
<BODY onLoad='return openHelp();'>
```

Try it and see the effect. The help window will automatically show up every time you open this HTML file.

Arrays

Arrays offer a powerful way of storing objects and variables in Javascript, as illustrated in the following example. Here we're creating an array in which we're storing three String objects. Then we're using the built-in functions of "Array" for sorting and reversing elements of the array.

```
<HTML><HEAD></HEAD>
<BODY>
<SCRIPT LANGUAGE="JavaScript">
    gr = new Array();
    gr[0] = "First Item";
    gr[1] = "Second Item";
    gr[2] = "Third Item";
    document.write(gr[1] + "<BR>");
    document.write(gr + "<BR>");
    document.write(gr.sort() + "<BR>");
    document.write(gr.reverse() + "<BR>");
</SCRIPT>
</BODY>
</HTML>
```

A new array is created using **new Array()**. As we mentioned earlier, object instances are created using the "new" keyword. That is exactly what we're doing here—creating an instance of the Array object. You don't need to specify an initial size for the array (but you can if you want by passing a number).

In this example we're creating an array named "gr" and then adding elements to it. Elements of an array can be accessed using the [number] notation. Here "number" starts from 0, which represents the first element of the array. If an assignment is being done, the element at that location is replaced or created (if one didn't exist before). In this example, therefore, **gr[0]** = "First Item" means that a String whose value is "First Item" is added as the first element of the array "gr." Similarly, we're adding two more Strings to the array.

Next we're printing the second element, **(gr[1])**, and then we're printing the contents of the entire array. (Note that if you print "gr" instead of referring to individual elements, all the elements of "gr" are printed.)

After this we're using the **sort()** function of Array to sort the elements before printing them. Finally, we're sorting them in the reverse order.

Following is the output of loading this page in the browser:

Second Item

First Item,Second Item,Third Item

First Item,Second Item,Third Item

Third Item,Second Item,First Item

Arrays have a property called "length," which can be used to determine the number of elements in the array.

FORMs

Now we move on to FORMs. You can very effectively use Javascript here to create elements not directly supported by HTML. As we will see, Javascript can be used to manipulate FORM elements. As a first example, we will create a FORM containing a Select list. Every time an element is selected, we will display a list of all elements in the Select list and also show the element that has been selected. The display is being done in a separate "confirm" window. The global function **confirm()** creates a dialog box with an OK button and a Cancel button. As it is a modal dialog box, users cannot proceed unless they click either OK or Cancel. **confirm()** takes a String as an argument—this is the text that is displayed in the dialog box.

Select Lists

You've been exclusively selected to receive our $5 million prize!!!!
(Fine print: You must be nuts! We say that to every potential customer.)

```
<HTML><HEAD>
<SCRIPT>
function handleClick(frm)
{
    var optionsLen = frm.mySelect1.options.length;
    for(i=0; i<optionsLen; i++)
    {
        confirm('Element at ' + i + ' is ' +
                    frm.mySelect1.options[i].text);
    }
    var selIndex = frm.mySelect1.selectedIndex;
    confirm('Selected ' + frm.mySelect1.options[selIndex].text);
    return false;
}
</SCRIPT>
</HEAD>
<BODY>
<FORM NAME="myForm1">
<SELECT NAME="mySelect1" SIZE=4 onChange="handleClick(this.form)">
<OPTION NAME="op1">First Option
<OPTION NAME="op2">Second Option
<OPTION NAME="op3">Third Option
<OPTION NAME="op4">Fourth Option
</SELECT>
</FORM> </BODY> </HTML>
```

We have created the Select list named "mySelect1" using the normal syntax (the <SELECT> tag). In this we've put a Javascript directive: onChange= "handleClick(this.form)." This means that whenever there is a user-initiated change (if an element in the Select list is selected or deselected), the function **handleClick()** should be invoked.

Here "this.form" is a reference to the form in which this select list is present. This handle is being passed to the function **handleClick()** so that it can access the values of all elements (including the Select list) in this form.

Now look at **handleClick()**. A reference to the form is coming in as an input argument named "frm."

```
function handleClick(frm)
```

A form's elements can be accessed by name. In this case we're trying to access the Select list named "mySelect1."

We determine the total number of options in the Select list. Options in a Select list can be accessed using the options property, which is an array. To determine the length of this options array, we're using "length," which is equal to the number of options in the Select list.

```
var optionsLen = frm.mySelect1.options.length;
```

Then we loop through all the options of the list and display the name of the option in a "confirm" dialog box. Each option has a "text" property containing the value that is displayed.

After looping, we display the option that has been selected. Select lists have a property called "selectedIndex" showing the element that has been selected. (Note that this works only if one element in the list can be selected; if it is a multiple Select list, you will have to loop through all the options and use the "selected" property—this property is true for elements that have been selected and false for others.) The index of the element that has been selected is being stored in a variable called "selIndex." We then find the "text" of the option in the "options" array at the location "selIndex." It is displayed in the "confirm" dialog box.

Buttons

Buttons have a click event associated with them. You can capture this and invoke a function or do something else. To see how this works, modify the previous example. Create two buttons in your form, one named "Show all" and the other named "Show selected." If the first one is clicked, all options of the forms should be displayed. If the second one is clicked, only the selected option should be displayed.

Here's a hint on how to do this: Add the following to the FORM:

```
<INPUT TYPE='button' VALUE='Show all'
                      onClick='handleAll(this.form)'><BR>
<INPUT TYPE='button' VALUE='Show selected'
                    onClick='handleSelected(this.form)'><BR>
```

In the <SELECT> tag remove the directive "onChange=...". Split the **handleClick()** function into two: (1) **handleAll()**, which uses the logic that displays all the options, and (2) **handleSelected()**, which displays only the selected option.

Submit and Radio Buttons

In this example we see the basis for an important area in which Javascript is used: form validation. When you want users to submit a form, it is important to make sure that they fill out all the required fields. One way to do this is to have your backend code do the checking, but this causes a delay because the backend code resides on a server that is different from the user's machine. This problem leads to a bad user experience. A better design is one in which the checking is done on the client machine itself so that the user gets to know the errors immediately. Javascript is an ideal means of accomplishing this goal.

Submit buttons are treated differently from normal buttons. Instead of using a click event associated with the button itself, it is more useful to capture the "submit" event. This event occurs when a user tries to submit the form by clicking the Submit button. To capture this event, you need to have the following in the <FORM> tag—"onSubmit='...'". You could execute a function here. Another difference with the Submit button is that when it is clicked, the browser sends a request to execute the backend code. However, with Javascript you can prevent this from happening. This capability is very important in cases like form validation, where you don't want the backend code to be executed if the user has missed something out or has entered invalid data in the form. With onSubmit, you can return either a true or a false value. True indicates that everything is fine and the backend code should be executed; false indicates that the backend code should not be executed.

Now look at the following example. Here we create two radio buttons and a Submit button. There is a variable called **oneSelected** which is initially set to false. Radio buttons have a click event that can be captured using **onClick**. We will make the variable **oneSelected** true if the user selects one of the radio buttons. This is done in the function **setSelected()**.

In the <FORM> tag we've added "onSubmit='return validate(this).'" This means that when the form is submitted, the function **validate()** is called. If this function returns a true, the backend code will be invoked; otherwise it will not. The "this" here is a reference to the current form.

Take a look at the function **validate()**. In this we're examining the variable "oneSelected." If it is false, this means that the user didn't select any radio button. In this case we're alerting the user about this and returning a false. On the other hand, if this is true, it means that the user has selected one of the buttons. We retrieve the display value of this button and show it in an "alert" dialog box. See how we're doing this:

```
frm.rd[0].value
```

rd is the name of the radio button. This is actually an array with each element corresponding to one of the buttons whose name is **rd**, **rd[0]** being the first button. The radio buttons have a "checked" property, which is true if the button has been selected. There is also a "value" property, which is the display value associated with the button.

```
<HTML><HEAD>
<SCRIPT>
var oneSelected = false;
function setSelected()
{
```

```
        oneSelected = true;
    }
    function validate(frm)
    {
        if(oneSelected)
        {
            if(frm.rd[0].checked)
                alert('You selected ' + frm.rd[0].value);
            if(frm.rd[1].checked)
                alert('You selected ' + frm.rd[1].value);
            return true;
        }
        else
        {
            alert('Error: You need to select one radio button');
            return false;
        }
    }
    </SCRIPT>
    </HEAD>
    <BODY>
    Please select one:<P>
    <FORM NAME="myForm1" onSubmit='return validate(this)'>
    <INPUT TYPE='radio' NAME='rd' VALUE='rd1' onClick='setSelected()'>
                                                    Radio 1<BR>
    <INPUT TYPE='radio' NAME='rd' VALUE='rd2' onClick='setSelected()'>
                                                    Radio 2<BR>
    <INPUT TYPE='submit' VALUE='Submit'><BR>
    </FORM> </BODY> </HTML>
```

Checkboxes

Check this box if you're a software developer—
check that box if you're a normal person!

Checkboxes are treated like radio buttons in Javascript. You can use the "onClick" event handler and the "selected" and "value" properties as we used them in the previous example.

Text Fields and Text Areas

Like other Form elements, text fields and text areas can be manipulated as well. In this example we have a text field, a text area, and a button. When the user enters some text in the text field and presses the Add button, the text is appended to the text area and the text field is cleared. To achieve this goal, we've put an "onClick" directive in the Add button to invoke the function **addToTextArea()**. Inside this function we're using the "value" property of the text field. This contains the current value of the text field, that is, whatever the user has entered in the text field.

We retrieve this in a variable called **val**. The value of the text field is then set to blank:

```
frm.txt.value = ' ';
```

The value "val" is then appended to the text area. In the case of text area there is also a property called "value," which refers to its current value. We're also appending a new-line character so that the new text appears on a separate line.

```
<HTML><HEAD>
<SCRIPT>
function addToTextArea(frm)
{
    var val = frm.txt.value;
    frm.txt.value = ' ';
    frm.area.value += val + '\n';
}
</SCRIPT>
</HEAD>
<BODY>
<FORM NAME="myForm1">
<INPUT TYPE='text' NAME='txt'>
<INPUT TYPE='button' VALUE='Add'
onClick='addToTextArea(this.form)'><BR>

<TEXTAREA NAME='area' ROWS='5' COLS='65'>
</TEXTAREA><BR>
</FORM> </BODY> </HTML>
```

Frames

I know who framed Roger Rabbit—
the art shop across the corner!

Javascript can be used with Frames to store and retrieve information applicable to multiple sections of a Web site. As we saw in Chapter 2, a Frames-based site has a main entry point in which framesets and frames are declared. This entry page can be used for storing Javascript variables that can be accessed by the different frames. That is exactly what we're doing in this example. The entry point page is **Frames.html**. In this we have two frames, one called left and the other called right. We've also declared a Javascript variable called **totalAccessed**, whose value is initialized to 0. Whenever a page link is clicked in the link frame, this variable will be incremented.

left.html contains a link called "Show Accesses." When you click on this, the value of the variable **totalAccessed** is displayed, showing how many pages on this site have been accessed by the user.

Figure 5.1 shows a snapshot of the browser taken after loading **Frames.html** and clicking "Show Accesses."

Frames.html:

```
<HTML><HEAD></HEAD>
<SCRIPT>
var totalAccessed=0;
</SCRIPT>
<FRAMESET COLS='200,*' BORDER='0'>
    <FRAME NAME='left' SRC='left.html' TARGET='right' BORDER='0'>
    <FRAME NAME='right' SRC='right.html' BORDER='0'>
</FRAMESET>
<BODY> </BODY> </HTML>
```

Here's how **left.html** looks. It contains links to three HTML files. The first two links have an **onClick()** directive that invokes the function **increment()**. This is a function we have defined that increments the value of **totalAccessed** by 1. Since the variable resides in the parent frame, we're accessing it using the "parent" property of the current document (document has a property called "parent" that refers to the frame that contains it).

```
parent.totalAccessed++;
```

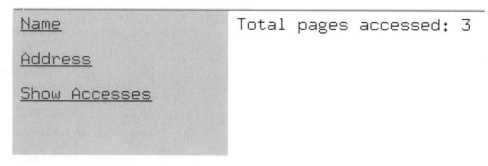

Figure 5.1

The third link is to **show.html**, an HTML file that will display the current value of the variable.

```
<HTML><HEAD></HEAD>
<SCRIPT>
function increment()
{
    parent.totalAccessed++;
}
</SCRIPT>
<BODY>
<A HREF='name.html' TARGET='right'
                        onClick='increment()'>Name</A><BR><BR>
<A HREF='address.html' TARGET='right'
                        onClick='increment()'>Address</A><BR><BR>
<A HREF='show.html' TARGET='right'>Show Accesses</A><BR>
</BODY> </HTML>
```

Here's **show.html**. This contains a script that accesses the value of **totalAccessed** and displays it. Note that **show.html** also belongs to the right frame and can thus use the "parent" property to access the parent frame and all variables declared in it.

```
<HTML><HEAD></HEAD>
<BODY>
    <SCRIPT>
        document.write('Total pages accessed: ' + parent.
            totalAccessed);
    </SCRIPT>
</BODY> </HTML>
```

Cookies

My fortune cookie advised me to never eat at a Chinese restaurant!

This example demonstrates the use of cookies. It shows both how to set cookies and how to retrieve data stored in cookies. When you run it the first time, it asks you for your name. When you press OK, it sets a cookie in which this name is stored. On subsequent calls, it doesn't bring up the form asking for your name—instead it says "Welcome: < your_name >." You can delete the cookies by clicking on the Delete Cookies button.

We have defined a function called **getCookie()** to be used to retrieve a cookie if it is available.

In this example, we're setting (and checking for) a cookie named "firstName." Cookies can be accessed in a document using the "cookie" property of the document.

This is a String that contains data on all the cookies that have been passed to the server from the browser. The function **getCookie** parses all available cookies to find the one whose name is passed in as an argument. When it finds that cookie, it calls the function **GetCookieValue()**, which returns the value of this cookie. This value is then passed to the calling function. If no such cookie is found, it returns null.

Also, we have defined a function called **setCookie()**, which sets a cookie with the given name and an expiration date 24 hours hence. The actual setting of the cookie is done in the **SetCookie()** function.

When you load the page initially, the Javascript code in the body is executed. This looks for a cookie named "firstName." However, as there is no such cookie initially, **getCookie()** returns null. As a result, a form is written in which there is a text field and a Submit button. When you type your name and press Submit, the function **setCookie()** is executed. This sets a cookie called "firstName" on the client (browser). Now if you reload the page, the cookie is sent by the browser, so when the page is loaded and the Javascript is executed, **getCookie()** returns the value that you typed in the text field.

Also, it executes the first part of the "if" condition; it shows a form with the message "Welcome <your_name>," followed by a Delete Cookie button. If you press this, the cookie is deleted by the **deleteCookie()** function. The way to delete a cookie is to give it an expiration date earlier than the current date.

```
<HTML>
<HEAD>
<SCRIPT LANGUAGE="JavaScript">
function SetCookie(name, value, expdate)
{
        document.cookie = name + "=" + value + "; expires=" +
                        expdate.toGMTString();
}
function getCookie(name)
{
  var i = 0;
  var arg = name + "=";
  var cookieLen = document.cookie.length;
  var nameLen = arg.length;
  while (i < cookieLen)
  {
    var j = i + nameLen;
    if (document.cookie.substring(i, j) == arg)
       return GetCookieValue(j);
    i = document.cookie.indexOf(" ", i) + 1;
    if (i == 0) break;
  }
```

```
    return null;
}
function GetCookieValue(start)
{
  var end = document.cookie.indexOf (";", start);
  if (end == -1)
    end = document.cookie.length;
  var val = unescape(document.cookie.substring(start, end));
  return val;
}
function getFirstName()
{
    var currentDate = new Date();
    var expires = new Date()
    expires.setTime(currentDate.getTime() + 60*60*24);
    SetCookie("firstName", document.firstNameForm.firstName.value,
              expires);
    return false;
}

function deleteCookie(name)
{
    document.cookie = name + "=" + "; expires=Thu,
                                   01-Jan-70 00:00:01 GMT";
    return false;
}
</SCRIPT>
</HEAD>
<BODY>
<SCRIPT>
var firstName = getCookie("firstName");
if(firstName == null)
{
    document.write("<FORM NAME='firstNameForm'
                         onSubmit='return getFirstName();'>");
    document.write("Type in your first name please:");
    document.write("<INPUT TYPE='text' NAME='firstName'
        VALUE=' '>");
    document.write("<INPUT TYPE='submit'  VALUE='OK'>");
    document.write("</FORM>");
}
else
{
```

```
        document.write("Welcome back, " + firstName);
        document.write("<FORM NAME='deleteForm'
                        onSubmit='deleteCookie (\"firstName\");'>");
        document.write("Press button to delete cookie");
        document.write("<INPUT TYPE='submit' VALUE='DELETE_COOKIE'>");
}
</SCRIPT>
</BODY> </HTML>
```

A Practical Example

One thing that a Web-based system can do is to provide personalized service to customers. If we have enough information, we can write Servlets that can provide one-to-one service. Such service could range from greeting customers by their name when they log on to the site to presenting Web pages based on their personal likes, purchase history, and so on. In fact we've already seen two examples of personalization. In Chapter 4 we saw how Java's internationalization feature can be used for presenting Help pages to a customer in that customer's preferred language. And we saw how we can greet somebody by name using cookies in the section above. In this example we go one step further. We show a system that provides true personalization by making use of Servlets, Java internationalization, HTML Frames, and of course Javascript. Nothing new is being introduced here. This is just a practical demonstration of how several technologies can be combined to build a really useful application.

Example: Personalized One-to-One
Service to Customers

In this example we will demonstrate a site built using Frames. The customer visits the **mySite.html** URL, which contains a frameset. This frameset splits the screen into two parts: a left frame, **leftFrame.html**, and a right frame, **rightFrame.html**. **mySite.html** contains some "global" Javascript variables such as firstName, lastName, city, state, country, and language. The HTML files that are displayed in the frames use these variables.

One of the variables is "loggedIn," which is initially false. **leftFrame.html** uses this to determine whether the customer has logged in with his or her username (assuming each customer who visits the site has an assigned, unique username). If the value of "loggedIn" is false, **leftFrame.html** uses Javascript to display a FORM containing a text field in which the customer can type his or her username. On pressing the OK button, the Servlet MySiteLogin is invoked. This servlet retrieves the firstName, lastName, city, and other information about the customer based on the username entered. It stores the values in the parent frame **mySite.html**, so that they can be accessed by any other HTML page that belongs to this parent. It also sets the value of "loggedIn" to true and causes **leftFrame.html** to reload.

This time **leftFrame.html** does not display the login text field, as the value of "loggedIn" is true. Instead it contains two links: (1) Events and (2) Promotions. If the customer clicks on these links, (s)he gets a personalized page. In the case of Events, the customer receives a listing of events related to your company that are occurring in the state to which the user belongs. Each customer is also assumed to have a preassigned rating. (S)he could have a rating from 0 (lowest category) to 5 (highest category). The MySiteLogin also retrieves this information and stores it in the rating variable of **mySite.html**. This variable is used by our promotions link. It presents different promotions to different customers based on their rating, thus offering a discount of 20 percent to a five-star customer but only a 10 percent discount to others.

To top it all, both promotions and events are presented in the preferred language of the customer. For this we use a technique similar to the one we used in the internationalization example in Chapter 4; there are properties files for each language. The base name of the properties files is "htmlIndex." They include keys containing names of HTML files that should be displayed, depending on the link clicked by the customer. The events and promotions links point to the Servlet DisplayFile. They both pass in id variable to the Servlet; events has an id = events, and promotions has an id = promotions. The properties files contain values for both the keys.

This is how the properties files look:

French version

promotions = /home/vsharma/HTML/promotions/FR/promotions.html

events = /home/vsharma/HTML/events/FR/events.html

U.S. version

promotions = /home/vsharma/HTML/promotions/US/promotions.html

events = /home/vsharma/HTML/events/US/events.html

If a customer from France clicks on the promotions links, the DisplayFile Servlet will present /home/vsharma/HTML/promotions/FR/promotions.html. A customer in the United States would be presented with /home/vsharma/HTML/promotions/US/promotions.html. Both versions make use of variables in the parent frame to display a personalized message to the customer.

Two more Java classes belong to this system: the Customer and the CustomerDatabase system. They are based on principles similar to the ProductDatabase we used in the shopping cart example in Chapter 4. The Customer class represents a Customer who has a name, city, rating, etc. The CustomerDatabase maintains a list of Customer objects. The constructor of this class creates a few dummy Customer objects.

All Java code is assumed to reside in the book.personalization package. You can deploy it in a Servlet zone called "example." Note that you will have to create the directories book and book/personalization in your "example" zone. The classes will need to be moved to the Book/Personalization directory, as the package is named book.personalization.

Before compiling the Java classes, you will need to replace **myServer.com** with the machine/port on which your Servlets-enabled Web server is running.

The HTML files need to go in your document root.

Figure 5.2 shows what is displayed when a user first visits the site.

Figure 5.3 shows how it looks after the customer has logged in.

Figure 5.4 illustrates the Promotions page displayed to a five-star customer. It is different from the one viewed by customers with a lower rating.

Figure 5.5 shows how the Events page looks as seen by a French customer.

A U.S. California-based customer sees the page illustrated in Figure 5.6 on clicking the Events link.

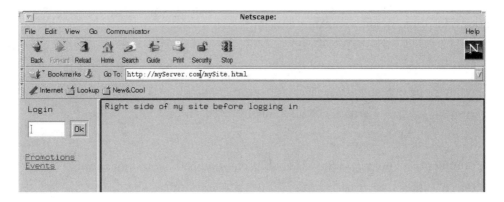

Figure   5.2

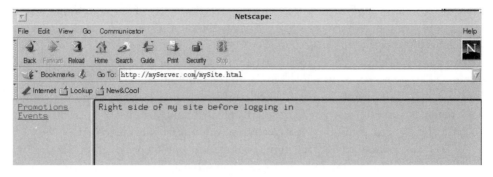

Figure   5.3

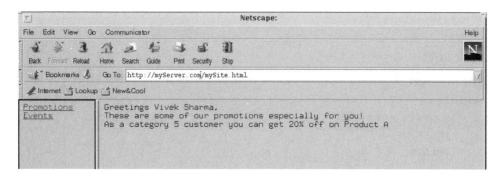

Figure 5.4

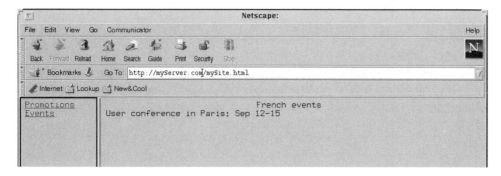

Figure   5.5

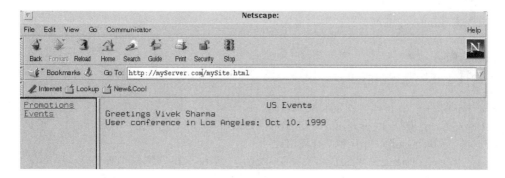

Figure   5.6

Here's the complete code:

mySite.html

```
<HTML><HEAD>
<SCRIPT>
    loggedIn = false;
    firstName = "";
    lastName = "";
    city = "";
    state = "";
    country = "";
    rating = 0;
</SCRIPT>
</HEAD>
<FRAMESET COLS='150,*'>
    <FRAME NAME='left' SRC='http://myServer.com/leftFrame.html'>
    <FRAME NAME='right' SRC='http://myServer.com/rightFrame.html'>
</FRAMESET>
<BODY>
</BODY>
</HTML>
```

leftFrame.html

```
<HTML><HEAD></HEAD>
<BODY>
<SCRIPT>
   if(parent.loggedIn == false)
   {
   document.write("<FORM ACTION=
   '/example/book.personalization.MySiteLogin' METHOD='POST'>");
        document.write("<TABLE>");
        document.write("<TR><TD>Login</TD><TD></TD></TR>");
        document.write("<TR><TD><INPUT TYPE='text' NAME='username'
        SIZE='6'></TD><TD><INPUT TYPE='submit' VALUE='Ok'></TD>
            </TR>");
        document.write("</TABLE>");
        document.write("</FORM>");
   }
</SCRIPT>
   <A HREF='/example/book.personalization.DisplayFile?id=
        promotions'
```

```
    TARGET='right'>Promotions</A><BR>
    <A HREF='/example/book.personalization.DisplayFile?id=events'
    TARGET='right'>Events</A><BR>
</BODY>
</HTML>
```

rightFrame.html

```
<HTML><HEAD></HEAD>
<BODY>
    Right side of my site before logging in
</BODY>
</HTML>
```

promotions.html

```
<HTML><HEAD></HEAD>
<BODY>
<SCRIPT>
    document.write("Greetings " + parent.firstName + " " +
                                  parent.lastName + ",<BR>");
    document.write("These are some of our promotions especially for
                   you!<BR>");
    if(parent.rating == 5)
        document.write("As a category 5 customer you can get 20%
            off on Product A");
    else
        document.write("As a category 5 customer you can get 10%
            off on Product A");
    document.close();
</SCRIPT>
</BODY>
</HTML>
```

events.html

```
<HTML><HEAD></HEAD>
<BODY>
   <CENTER>US Events</CENTER>

   <SCRIPT>
    document.write("Greetings " + parent.firstName + " " +
```

```
                              parent.lastName + "<BR>");
    if(parent.state == 'CA' || parent.state == 'NV')
        document.write('User conference in Los Angeles:
                          Oct 10, 1999');
    else
    if(parent.state == 'MA')
        document.write('User conference in Boston: Sep 30,
                          1999');
    else
        document.write('No events in your neighborhood in
                          the near future');
  document.close();
 </SCRIPT>
</BODY>
</HTML>
```

MySiteLogin.java

```java
package book.personalization;
import java.io.*;
import java.util.Enumeration;

import javax.servlet.*;
import javax.servlet.http.*;
import java.util.*;
public class MySiteLogin extends HttpServlet
{
    CustomerDatabase cd;
    public void init(ServletConfig s)
            throws ServletException
    {
        cd = new CustomerDatabase();
    }
    public void doGet (HttpServletRequest req, HttpServletResponse
        res)
    {
        doPost(req, res);
    }
    public void doPost (HttpServletRequest req,
                        HttpServletResponse res)
    {
        PrintWriter out = null;
        String username = "";
        HttpSession session = req.getSession(true);
```

```
Enumeration values = req.getParameterNames();
while(values.hasMoreElements())
{
      String name = (String)values.nextElement();
      String value = req.getParameterValues(name)[0];
      if(name.equalsIgnoreCase("username"))
            username = value;
}
res.setContentType("text/html");
try{
   out = res.getWriter();
}catch(Exception ex){}

Customer c = cd.getByUsername(username);
String firstName = c.getFirstName();
String lastName = c.getLastName();
String city = c.getCity();
String state = c.getState();
String country = c.getCountry();
String language = c.getLanguage();

Integer rating = c.getRating();

session.putValue("book.personalization.username",
    username);
session.putValue("book.personalization.language",
    language);
session.putValue("book.personalization.country",

    country);
out.println("<HTML><HEAD></HEAD><BODY>");
out.println("<SCRIPT>");
   out.println("parent.firstName='" + firstName + "';");
   out.println("parent.lastName='" + lastName + "';");
   out.println("parent.city='" + city + "';");
   out.println("parent.state='" + state + "';");
   out.println("parent.country='" + country + "';");
   out.println("parent.language='" + language + "';");
   out.println("parent.rating=" + rating.toString()
       + ";");
   out.println("parent.loggedIn=true;");
   out.println("parent.left.location.replace(
               'http://myServer.com/leftFrame. html');");
out.println("</SCRIPT>");
out.println("</BODY></HTML>");
```

```
            out.close();
      }
}


```

CustomerDatabase.java

```java
package book.personalization;
import java.util.*;
public class CustomerDatabase
{
      Vector customers = new Vector();
      CustomerDatabase()
      {
            retrieveAllCustomers();
      }
      public Customer getByUsername(String username)
      {
            Customer theCustomer = null;
            int size = customers.size();
            for(int i=0; i<size; i++)
            {
                  Customer c = (Customer)customers.elementAt(i);
                  String u = c.getUsername();
                  if(u.equalsIgnoreCase(username))
                  {
                        theCustomer = c;
                        break;
                  }
            }
            return theCustomer;
      }

      public Vector getAllCustomers()
      {
            return customers;
      }
      public void retrieveAllCustomers()
      {
          /* This should retrieve from database.
             For the sake of an example
             we supply dummy values here. */

            Integer rating = new Integer(5); // Most prized customer
            Customer c = new Customer("Vivek", "Sharma",
                        "Los Angeles", "CA",
```

```
                              "US", "us", "vivek", "vivek", rating);
            customers.addElement(c);

            rating = new Integer(3);
            c = new Customer("Bill", "Peterson", "New York", "NY",
                        "US", "us", "bill", "bill", rating);
            customers.addElement(c);

            rating = new Integer(1);
            c = new Customer("John", "Doe", "Paris", "",
                        "FR", "fr", "john", "john", rating);
            customers.addElement(c);
        }
}
```

Customer.java

```java
package book.personalization;

public class Customer
{
    String firstName = "", lastName = "", city = "", state = "",
            country = "";
    String language = "", username = "", password = "";
    Integer rating;

    Customer(String f, String l, String c, String s, String ct,
            String ln, String u, String p, Integer r)
    {
        firstName = f;
        lastName  = l;
        city = c;
        state = s;
        country = ct;
        language = ln;
        username = u;
        password = p;
        rating = r;
    }
    public Integer getRating()
    {
        return rating;
    }
    public String getFirstName()
    {
```

```
                return firstName;
        }
        public String getLastName()
        {
                return lastName;
        }
        public String getCity()
        {
                return city;
        }
        public String getState()
        {
                return state;
        }
        public String getCountry()
        {
                return country;
        }
        public String getLanguage()
        {
                return language;
        }
        public String getUsername()
        {
                return username;
        }
        public String getPassword()
        {
                return password;
        }
}
```

DisplayFile.java

```
package book.personalization;
import java.io.*;
import javax.servlet.*;
import javax.servlet.http.*;
import java.util.*;
public class DisplayFile extends HttpServlet
{
        public void doGet (HttpServletRequest req, HttpServletResponse
            res)
```

```java
{
     doPost(req, res);
}
public void doPost (HttpServletRequest req,
                    HttpServletResponse res)
{
     try{
          PrintWriter out = null;
          res.setContentType("text/html");
          out = res.getWriter();

          HttpSession session = req.getSession(false);
          Enumeration values = req.getParameterNames();

          String id = "";
          while(values.hasMoreElements())
          {
               String name = (String)values.nextElement();
               String value = req.getParameterValues(name)
                   [0];
               if(name.equalsIgnoreCase("id"))
                    id = value;
          }
          String country =
(String)session.getValue("book. personalization.country");
          String language =
(String)session.getValue("book.personalization.language");

          if(country == null)
              country = new String("US");
          if(language == null)
              language = new String("us");

        Locale currentLocale;
        ResourceBundle messages;

         currentLocale = new Locale(country, language);
         messages = ResourceBundle.getBundle("htmlIndex",
                     currentLocale);
         String htmlFile = messages.getString(id);

         displayHtmlFile(htmlFile, out);
         out.close();
      }catch(Exception ex){}
 }
 public void displayHtmlFile(String fileName, PrintWriter out)
```

```
{
    try
    {
        File f = new File(fileName);
        FileReader fr = new FileReader(f);
        BufferedReader bis = new BufferedReader(fr);
        String inpu;
        while((inpu = bis.readLine()) != null)
        {
            out.println(inpu);
        }
        bis.close();
    }catch(Exception e){
        out.println("<HTML><HEAD></HEAD><BODY>");
        e.printStackTrace();
        out.println("</BODY></HTML>");
    }
}
}
}
```

Some Useful Methods, Properties, and Event Handlers of Some Useful Objects

Array—used for creating arrays in Javascript. "length" indicates length of the array. Contains methods for joining, sorting, reverse sorting.

Methods: **concat**, **join**, **sort**, **reverse.**

Properties: length.

Button—the Button element of an HTML Form. Name and value available through similarly named properties. Reference to the form it belongs to can be obtained by the "form" property. When the mouse comes over the button (it comes into focus), leaves the button (blur), or is clicked, events are raised that can be captured.

Properties: form, name, value.

Event Handlers: onFocus, onBlur, onClick.

Checkbox—the checkbox element of an HTML form. "checked" property indicates whether this checkbox has been selected by the user or not.

Properties: form, name, value, checked.

Event Handlers: onFocus, onBlur, onClick.

Date—a global object that can be used for obtaining/setting the current date. Methods available for getting and setting date and creating a String representation of the same.

Methods: **getDate**, **getDay**, **getHours**, **getMonth**, **getSeconds**, **getYear** (and corresponding set functions), toGMTString.

document—the current HTML page. Contains methods for writing to the page, opening a new one, or closing it. Contains properties that can be used to obtain and set foreground and background colors and cookies. Also contains properties that can be used to access forms, images, or links in the document.

Methods: **write**, **writeln**, **open**, **close**.

Properties: bgColor, cookie, fgColor, forms, images, links.

Form—represents the <FORM> element of HTML. Contains methods for resetting values of the form and for submitting it.

Contains an "elements" property that can be used to access all elements in the form. Action can be taken by capturing the reset and submit events.

Methods: **reset**, **submit**.

Properties: elements, name.

Event Handlers: onReset, onSubmit.

Location—contains information about the current URL. Contains methods for reloading the page and for replacing it with a different URL.

Methods: **replace**, **reload**.

Link—represents a link (<A> tag) in the document. Events associated with this are those occurring when the mouse comes over the link or leaves or clicks the link. Events can be captured and appropriate action taken.

Event Handlers: onMouseOver, onMouseOut, onClick.

Math—global object with methods for doing math operations like calculating tan, sin, cos and for generating random numbers.

Methods: **asin**, **acos**, **atan**, **random**.

Option—represents an <OPTION> in a <SELECT> list. "selected" is a property that tells whether this option has been selected by the user. "text" is the value that is displayed, and "value" is the actual value of the option that is passed to the back end when the form is submitted.

Properties: selected, text, value.

Password—represents the Password element of HTML.

Properties: form, name, value.

Radio—represents a Radio button element of HTML. "checked" is true or false, depending on whether the button has been selected or not.

Properties: form, name, value, checked.

Event Handlers: onFocus, onBlur, onClick.

Select—represents the <SELECT> element of HTML. "options" contains a reference to all the <OPTION> elements that belong to the list. "selectedIndex" is the index of the option that has been selected. The change event, which can be captured using "onChange," occurs when a change like an option has been selected or deselected.

Properties: form, name, length, options, selectedIndex.

Event Handlers: onFocus, onBlur, onChange.

String—an object representing a series of characters. The "length" property shows the number of characters in the String. "charAt" method can be used to find the character at a given position. "indexOf" can be used to locate the position at which a given substring is present in the String. Methods also available to convert the String to upper/lower case. "substr" can be used to obtain a substring from the given String.

Methods: charAt, indexOf, lastIndexOf, toLowerCase, toUpperCase, substr.

Properties: length.

Text—represents the text field of HTML. The "change" event occurs when the text field loses focus and its value has been modified. The "select" event occurs when a portion of the text in the field has been selected.

Properties: form, name, value.

Event Handlers: onFocus, onBlur, onChange, onSelect.

Text area—represents the <TEXTAREA> element of HTML. The onKeyUp event occurs when the user releases a key in the text area.

Properties: form, name, value.

Event Handlers: onFocus, onBlur, onChange, onSelect, onKeyDown, onKeyUp.

Window—represents a browser window or frame. It is the top-level object for a document. The "parent" property is the window or frame whose frameset contains the current frame.

Methods: alert, close, open, confirm.

Properties: frames, history, location, outerHeight, outerWidth, parent.

Event Handlers: onLoad, onUnload, onResize.

Reference

http://developer.netscape.com/docs/manuals/javascript.html

Chapter 6

SQL and JDBC

In Chapter 3 we saw how the language can be easily used for writing complex applications. However, a good percentage of real-life applications depends on a backend data storage mechanism—a database—with which they need to interact. Information needs to be stored, queried, and retrieved. The **java.sql** package was designed to allow this Java-database interaction.

Structured Query Language (SQL) is the most popular (and standard) language for interacting with databases.

There are several major players in the database market, among them Oracle, IBM, Informix, Sybase, and Microsoft.

They have their own ways of connecting to the database and front ends for issuing SQL statements. Java provides a standard way of doing this through the JDBC API. This API consists of a set of interfaces. Each database vendor supplies an implementation of these interfaces that provides corresponding functionality for connecting to and manipulating its database. Vendors provide drivers that help in achieving this.

To use JDBC, you need to do the following: download the JDK (as it contains the JDBC interfaces), install a database, and install the JDBC driver of that database. Drivers are normally available free of charge on the Web sites of the vendors. For instance, if you have installed Oracle, you can go to the company's main Web site, *www.oracle.com,* and download the appropriate driver.

Two of the major types of drivers are the thin-client and the thick drivers. Thin-client drivers are written in pure Java, whereas thick drivers have native code in them. Though thick drivers are relatively faster, they are platform-dependent. In regard to programming in JDBC, there are very minor differences between them. We will focus our discussion on thin drivers, as they are platform-independent.

Databases and SQL

Finally, the details of my shady accounts are organized in a database—
that makes an IRS conviction only a few SQL statements away!

Before we delve into JDBC, we will cover some basic database concepts and SQL statements. In relational databases data is organized in the form of tables, which consist of rows and columns. You can visualize this concept in terms of a spreadsheet. A Database Management System (DBMS) can be looked at as a system for creating and maintaining a collection of spreadsheets. You can specify the tables that need to be created, information that needs to be stored or manipulated, and data that needs to be retrieved using SQL commands.

Here is an example. Let's say you want to store information about customers of your store. Each customer has a name, city of residence, and state. This is how it would look in a spreadsheet:

Name	City	State
John	Los Angeles	CA
Jill	Boston	MA
Peter	San Francisco	CA

. . . .

While spreadsheets are good if you have small amounts of data, once your data size grows, you will feel the need for a DBMS to provide efficiency in data insertion, lookup, and modification. Also, it is relatively straightforward to execute complex searches.

Let's say you want to use a database for storing this type of data. You would first create a table in which this data would be stored and give it a name. The table is the equivalent of the spreadsheet above. Let's name the table "Customers." Next you would specify that this table has three columns; "Name," "City," and "State." Now your empty table (spreadsheet) is ready. You can now use SQL to insert records into this and to retrieve information. For example, if you want to find out the names of all customers in California, you can execute a simple SQL command like this:

```
SELECT Name FROM Customers WHERE State = 'CA'
```

Schemas

One term you're likely to hear often in the context of databases is "Schemas." A database schema is a username that can be used for logging into a database and performing operations on it. All multi-user systems like Unix workstations maintain a list of authorized users. To work on the machine, you need to log in with a valid username and password. Similarly, databases can be used by multiple users. The different users are distinguished from each other by unique usernames. Each such unique space is called a schema. A database can support multiple schemas. Different schemas can have different privileges. An administrator can restrict the activity of a particular schema user by means of some simple SQL commands.

Next we take a look at datatypes supported by SQL; then we look at actual SQL statements that can be used for inserting, retrieving, modifying, and deleting data.

Datatypes

The first step after installing the database is to decide how your data is going to be organized. You can create arbitrarily complex tables and establish relationships among them. When you create a table, you need to specify a name for it and the data types of its columns. Some of the common types supported by most databases are CHAR (for character data like Strings), NUMBER (for numeric data), and DATE (for storing date/time). Some support a variation of CHAR, known as VARCHAR, which is a space saver. If you declare the data type to be CHAR(100), the database will allocate enough space to save 100 characters of information. If you end up putting in less information, the rest of the space will be wasted. On the other hand, if the datatype is VARCHAR, the extra space is made available for storing other data. Not all databases support this option, however.

In most databases the maximum size of a character column is 2000. So how do you store large amounts of information? Well, most databases support the LONG datatype, which has a huge capacity for information (typically in the order of gigabytes). However, this capacity does not come without a drawback. You cannot do searches for Strings in LONG columns as you can do in CHAR or VARCHAR columns. Some companies have developed tools that allow you to do searches in LONG columns, but they are beyond the purview of this book.

Some databases support subtypes; for example, in Oracle, NUMBER represents any type of number, and you can make it more specific by using subtypes such as INTEGER, DECIMAL, REAL, etc. You may also specify precision by declaring a column like NUMBER(10, 2). Such a column can contain a ten-digit number followed by two digits after the decimal.

You will need to refer the manuals of the database you're using to see the exact names of the supported datatypes.

Table Creation

Changing professions from a carpenter to a database administrator didn't help much—
I'm still creating tables!

Here's a simple SQL statement that creates a table named "Employee." As you will see later, you can use JDBC to issue this statement. Otherwise you can connect to the database using its client utility and execute the SQL (Oracle provides SQL*PLUS and MSQL provides the mSQL monitor for connecting to the database).

```
CREATE TABLE product   (id            NUMBER,
                        name          CHAR(50),
                        creation_date DATE);
```

With this statement we have created a table in the database whose name is "Product." It consists of three columns. The first is named "id" and can store numeric values in it. The second is "name" and can store character data up to a maximum of 50 characters. The third is "creation_date" and store a date.

In this example, it would be better to use VARCHAR instead of CHAR if the database supports it. Likewise, you could create other tables and put different columns in them.

Column Constraints

You can also put constraints on table columns to ensure that only the right kind of data is stored in them. If you've specified a constraint on a column, every time you insert, delete, or update information in that column, the DBMS checks whether the data violates any constraints. If so, it throws an error and does not allow the operation to succeed.

One common constraint is the "NOT NULL" constraint, which ensures that null data is not entered. Different database systems may have different ways of specifying these constraints. For instance, in Oracle, a "not null" constraint is specified in the column declaration. To make the id field not null you would declare it as follows:

```
id NUMBER NOT NULL
```

Now if you try to insert a null value in this column, the DBMS will not accept that record and throw an error.

The "UNIQUE" constraint ensures that a column doesn't get the same value multiple times. To make the field unique you would declare it as

```
id NUMBER CONSTRAINT uq_nm UNIQUE
```

In mSQL, you would declare the unique constraint in a separate statement:

```
create unique index uq_nm on product(id)
```

This ensures that you cannot have two rows in the table with the same id. If you try to insert two rows with the same id, the database system will throw an error.

Keys

*I know who holds the key to my happiness—
the person who stole my Ferrari!*

Uniqueness can also be guaranteed by making one column the primary key of the table. A primary key is a column of the table that is unique, is used for referencing the table, and uniquely identifies each record in the table. For instance, if you're creating a database for storing employee names, you need to be able to distinguish between two John Does working in the company. To do this, you assign them employee ids and then create your table to include the first name, last name, and this employee id as its primary key.

Another type of key is the foreign key, normally used for creating a relationship among multiple tables. If you're creating an employee database, you may want to split information in different tables. The name and other personal info can be in a table called "Employee," but the salary could be in a table called "Salary." You need a way to link the information in the two tables so that John Doe doesn't run away with the salary of his boss. This goal can be achieved by using primary and foreign keys. The employee table would have the employee id as a primary key. The salary table would have a column (let's call it "empid") that references this id, and this column would be the foreign key. The value of "empid" for John's record in the salary table would be the same as the value of "id" for his record in the employee table.

Now, if John's employee id is 22, when you search for John's salary your query would be for the record where "Employee.id = 22 and Employee.id = Salary.empid."

Here is an example of creating a foreign key:

```
CREATE TABLE employee (id   NUMBER PRIMARY KEY,
                       name VARCHAR2(80));
CREATE TABLE salary (empid CONSTRAINT emp_fkey REFERENCES employee,
                     amount  NUMBER);
```

We've declared the "id" field to be a primary key in the employee table. In the salary table we've used the CONSTRAINT keyword to declare the column "empid" to be a foreign key (the name of the constraint being **emp_fkey**). The REFERENCES keyword indicates that this field is a foreign key to the primary key in the employee table. This means that the salary table cannot contain a record that has an empid that doesn't correspond to an id in the employee table. Therefore, if you try to delete John Doe's record from the employee table before deleting his record from the salary table, the database will complain. In this way foreign keys help you to ensure data integrity. After all you don't want John to keep on receiving his salary even after he has left the company just because somebody forgot to remove him from the salary table!

Indexes

It was a really big book—
volume I contained the material, and volume II contained the index!

Thick books normally have an index at the end to help you quickly locate what you're looking for. Similarly, databases use indexes for faster retrieval of data. You can declare that a certain column (or columns) should act like an index. If the employee table is set up and most of your queries are by last name, you can declare the last name field to be an index. Now searches based on last name will work much faster than otherwise. However, you have to be cautious with indexes, because they consume a lot of space. Also, there is a performance degradation if you insert rows in a table with indexes, as the indexes then need to be updated independent of the table itself.

Normally an index is created like this:

```
CREATE INDEX abcd ON product(id)
```

Here "abcd" is the name of the index, "Product" is the name of the table, and "id" is the name of the column on which the index has been created. Indexes are created on primary keys and unique columns by default. It is often a good idea to create indexes on foreign keys, as these are almost invariably used in queries.

Dropping Tables

If you're not satisfied with a table, you can drop it and recreate it. The syntax for dropping a table is

```
DROP TABLE <tableName>
```

You can also use ALTER TABLE to modify a table, but discussion of this is beyond the scope of the book.

Most commercial databases come with tools that allow you to design your database. Oracle comes with Designer. If you have a sufficiently complex database, it is worth using such tools.

Data Insertion and Modification

If you modify datinformation it may become disinformation!

Now that we've looked at how you can create your tables, let's move on to see how data is actually stored and retrieved from the tables. Data insertion is done with the "INSERT" SQL statement.

Here's the syntax for this:

```
INSERT INTO <table_name> (<colName>, <colName>....)
        VALUES (<value>, <value>....)
```

Thus, if you want to insert a product named "Product 1" in the product table we created above and assign it an id 1, you would issue the following SQL statement:

```
INSERT INTO product(id, name) VALUES (1, 'Product 1')
```

Note that we didn't insert a creation date, even though the table contains a field for this; in such cases the database automatically puts a null value on the fields not specified. This worked because the field does not have a NOT NULL constraint on it. Similarly, you could insert multiple records into this table. But because of the UNIQUE constraint on the "id" field you cannot issue the same SQL statement again, as the "id" has to be unique.

Dates work differently in different databases. In Oracle, you could convert a String to DATE format for inserting into the DATE column. In the above example you could say something like this:

```
INSERT INTO product(id, name, creation_date) VALUES
    (1, 'Product 1', TO_DATE('31-MAR-1999', 'DD-MON-YYYY'))
```

Oracle provides a convenient mechanism for calculating the current date; you can use the keyword SYSDATE.

So the above statement could be as follows:

```
INSERT INTO product(id, name, creation_date) VALUES
    (1, 'Product 1', SYSDATE)
```

In mSQL you can get the current date by issuing this statement:

```
SELECT _sysdate FROM <someTable>
```

This will return the current date, which you can use in the INSERT statement.

If you want to update data in one or more records (as opposed to creating new records using INSERT), you need to use the UPDATE statement. The syntax is like this:

```
UPDATE <table> SET <colName> = <value>, <colName> = <value> .....
    [WHERE <condition>]
```

As an example, if you want to set the creation_date of all the products in the product table to be 31-MAR-1999, you can issue the following update statement:

```
UPDATE product SET creation_date = TO_DATE('31-MAR-1999',
    'DD-MON-YYYY')
```

But what if you wanted this to happen for products whose id is less than 20? You can use the WHERE clause of the UPDATE statement to restrict updates to affect selective records. In this case you would say this:

```
UPDATE product SET creation_date = TO_DATE('31-MAR-1999',
                                            'DD-MON-YYYY')
       WHERE id < 20
```

Here "id < 20" is a condition that says only records in the product table that have an id of less than 20 should be affected. The conditions can be complex with AND/OR operators. If you wanted to affect products that have an id of less than 20 and those with an id of greater than 30, you could say this:

```
WHERE id < 20 OR id > 30
```

Transactions

In typical database applications you may want to follow a transaction model where a group of SQL statements should act as a logical unit—either they should all be applied, or none should be applied. As an example, consider the case where money is being transferred from your money market account to your checking account. There would be an SQL statement that debits from the money market account and a statement that increments the checking account. What if the first statement works but then there is a power failure, as a result of which you end up losing money? You would certainly want either both statements to take effect or none, as this is one complete transaction. Databases allow you to group statements together with a COMMIT statement. By default, a statement that is issued does not make changes in the underlying tables until you explicitly issue a COMMIT statement. Thus, you could issue the statement that debits the money market account, prepare the statement that credits the checking account, and then type in COMMIT. These steps would make both the debiting and crediting happen.

Data Retrieval

Data retrieval is done using the SELECT statement with the following syntax:

```
SELECT <colName>, colName,.... FROM <tableName> [WHERE
    <condition>]
```

You could also say SELECT * FROM <tableName> [WHERE <condition>]. This will return date in all the columns of the table.

To retrieve the id and name of all the products in the product table, you would issue the following command:

```
SELECT id, name FROM product
```

You can put conditions in the WHERE clause (as we saw in the UPDATE) to restrict results. The WHERE clause is very powerful. We now discuss some of the operators that can be used in this clause. Note that this discussion is applicable to the Oracle database—other databases may have the same or similar syntax. At a minimum, you need to refer to the documentation for those databases.

Operators

Please call 1-800-SURGEONS—
operators are standing by!

We've already seen how to use the > and < comparisons and the **AND/OR** operators. You can similarly use the =, >=, and <= operators on numeric columns. You can also use the = comparison for String comparisons. So, SELECT id FROM product WHERE name = 'Product 1' will return the id of the product whose name is "Product 1." Note that this comparison is case-sensitive, so if there is a product with the name "PRODUCT 1," its id will not be returned. To overcome this you can use the NLS_UPPER() function to first convert the field value to uppercase before the comparison is applied. Now your statement would be as follows:

```
SELECT id FROM product WHERE NLS_UPPER(name) = 'PRODUCT 1'
```

But what if you want the id of all products whose name begins with 'Product.' You can use the LIKE operator for this. Your statement would be: SELECT id FROM product WHERE name LIKE 'Product%.' Here "%" is a special character, and "Product%" denotes any string that begins with "Product." So, if you want to search for products that end with this word, you would say this:

```
SELECT id FROM product WHERE name LIKE '%Product'
```

You can also use the **NOT** operator. Thus, if you don't want products that contain the word "Product" in their name, you would say this:

```
SELECT id FROM product WHERE name NOT LIKE '%Product%'
```

You can also do powerful date comparisons; the >, =, and < operators can be used there as well. To search for all products whose creation date is before 31-March-1999, you would say this:

```
SELECT id FROM product WHERE creation_date <
                TO_DATE('31-MAR-1999', 'DD-MON-YYYY')
```

Functions

Oracle also provides a convenient way of just counting the number of records in one or more tables. So, if you just want to see how many products there are that start with the name "Product," you would say this:

```
SELECT COUNT(*) FROM product WHERE name LIKE 'Product%'
```

Here **COUNT()** is a function available in the database. Other common functions supported by many databases include **AVG()**, **MIN()**, **MAX()**, **SIN()**, **COS()**, **TAN()**, and **SQRT()**. If you want to calculate the average salary of all employees in the database you would say this:

```
SELECT AVG(amount) FROM Salary
```

Retrieving Records from Multiple Tables

You can also select records from multiple tables and present them as one record. This step would be required in the employee and salary tables we created earlier if we want to display both the name and the salary of one or more employees. To get the correct results, we need to specify the relationship between the two tables. The statement would be as follows:

```
SELECT employee.name, salary.amount FROM employee, salary
                WHERE employee.id = salary.empid
```

Note that in the FROM section we specify both the tables that we're using in the query. The SELECT section specifies the columns that we need to retrieve—we want "name" to come from the employee table and "amount" to come from the salary table. In the WHERE clause we've specified the linkage between the two tables, as established using the primary key id and the foreign key empid.

Let's say the two tables contain the following records:

Employee		Salary	
id	name	empid	amount
1	John	1	20000
2	Peter	2	25000
3	Tom	3	40000

The select statement above would print the following:

John	20000
Peter	25000
Tom	40000

If you want to print salaries where the amount is less than 25000, you can say this:

```
SELECT employee.name, salary.amount FROM employee, salary
       WHERE employee.id = salary.empid
       AND salary.amount < 25000
```

In this case it will just print the following: John   20000.

Deleting Records

You can also delete records in a table. Here's the syntax for this:

```
DELETE FROM <tableName> WHERE <condition>
```

Thus, to delete rows containing information about all products that have an id of less than 10, you would say this:

```
DELETE FROM product WHERE id < 10
```

Sequences

In the discussion of primary keys, we mentioned that this key is a column in a table that has unique values. In a large number of cases it makes sense to have this unique field contain a numeric value. For instance, people can be identified by a unique Social Security number, orders in a store can be identified by a unique Order Id, and so on. But if large numbers of people are trying to write the database simultaneously, there needs to be a foolproof way of generating these numbers so that they are unique. Most databases come with a sequence number generator that helps you generate unique sequential numbers using SQL. For this you need to create a sequence and give it a name. Then you can "get" values from this sequence.

This is how it's done in Oracle:

```
CREATE SEQUENCE id_seq START WITH 1 CACHE 20
```

This creates a sequence named **id_seq** that starts with the value 1. When you get the next value, it will return 2, the next will be 3, and so on. CACHE keyword is optional—it tells the sequence generator to pregenerate chunks of sequence numbers to improve performance. In this case we're asking it to generate chunks of 20. There is also a STEP option you can use to specify how much the next number should be incremented. So if you add "STEP 2" in the above statement, the numbers generated will be 1, 3, 5, 7, and so on.

To retrieve values you use the following:

```
SELECT <sequenceName>.NEXTVAL FROM dual
```

"dual" is a reserved table used for sequences and some other things. Every time you execute this statement, the next number in the sequence will be returned.

In this case you would say this:

```
SELECT id_seq.NEXTVAL FROM dual
```

And this is how you do it in mSQL (note that in mSQL a sequence is tied to a table):

```
CREATE SEQUENCE ON product
SELECT _seq FROM product
```

Stored Procedures

Our strict procedures are meant to help our customers
(and our customer support department, which is woefully understaffed!).

When an SQL statement is issued, the database system compiles it and then executes it. However, most database systems also allow you to precompile statements so that they execute faster at runtime. This can be done by creating stored procedures. Stored procedures in SQL are like methods in Java; they can contain a number of SQL statements. They can receive both input parameters and return values. And the best thing is that at the time of creation they are compiled into the database. When a procedure is invoked, the SQL statements it contains are invoked.

A procedure can have three types of parameters: IN parameters are those that supply a value to the procedure/function. OUT parameters can be used for returning information to the caller. And there can be INOUT parameters also, which work as a combination of IN and OUT parameters. When the procedure is invoked, the parameter can be used for sending a value to the procedure. The procedure can then set its value so that the calling program can read results returned by the procedure.

A procedure can be created by using the CREATE PROCEDURE command. The syntax is like this:

```
CREATE PROCEDURE <name> AS
BEGIN
   [SQL statements]
END <name>;
```

The SQL statements section can have any valid SQL statements in it. You can issue these commands in the command-line monitor of your database system. The DBMS will compile the statements. Now you can invoke this procedure from the command-line monitor, resulting in the execution of all SQL statements contained in this procedure.

Here's a simple procedure:

```
CREATE PROCEDURE reg(
            username_in    IN  VARCHAR2,
            result_out     OUT NUMBER) AS
BEGIN
      INSERT INTO customer(id, username)
            VALUES (1, username_in);
      result_out := 1;
END reg;
```

It takes an IN parameter and has an OUT parameter. Once this procedure has been created and compiled, the insert SQL statement will not need to be recompiled. If you want to perform complex database operations that need a bunch of SQL statements to be executed, putting them in procedure can help in improving performance.

As you can see, you can do assignments also. In this example we're assigning a value to the **result_out** parameter.

Procedures can make use of variables. We now look at a slightly more complex procedure. This procedure creates records in two tables—"customer" and "telecom_address." It makes use of a sequence called **customer_seq**. The tables and sequences are defined as follows:

```
CREATE TABLE customer(
            id          NUMBER,
            username    VARCHAR2(30));
CREATE TABLE telecom_address(
            phone       VARCHAR2(20));
CREATE SEQUENCE customer_seq START WITH 1;
```

The procedure, named **register()**, takes a username and phone number as input. It inserts the username into a table called "Customer" and the number into another table, called "telecom_address." It also retrieves the next value of the **customer_seq** **SEQUENCE** and inserts it into the customer table. It finally returns a result, which is a count of the number of customers with this username.

```
CREATE OR REPLACE
PROCEDURE register(
          username_in            IN        VARCHAR2,
          phone_in               IN        VARCHAR2,
          result_out             OUT       NUMBER) IS

          v_customer_id          NUMBER;
BEGIN
          result_out := 0;
          SELECT customer_seq.NEXTVAL INTO v_customer_id FROM dual;
          INSERT INTO customer(id, username)
```

```
            VALUES (v_customer_id, username_in);
    INSERT INTO telecom_address(phone)
            VALUES (phone_in);
    SELECT count(*) INTO result_out FROM customer
            WHERE username=username_in;
END register;
```

Some of the interesting lines in this code are described in brief here. In the definition of the procedure we've declared a variable that this procedure will use:

```
v_customer_id          NUMBER;
```

The procedure begins by setting the value of the out variable to 0. It then employs a variation of the SELECT statement, making use of the INTO clause that can be used for storing the result to be stored in a variable. The next value of **customer_seq** is retrieved and stored in the variable **v_customer_id**.

```
SELECT customer_seq.NEXTVAL INTO v_customer_id FROM dual;
```

Next a record is created in the customer table. The "id" field of this record will contain the value just retrieved from **customer_seq** (and stored in **v_customer_id**):

```
INSERT INTO customer(id, username)
        VALUES (v_customer_id, username_in);
```

Then there are two more SQL statements. The second one stores the result in the **result_out OUT** variable. The calling program can read this value to determine how many people with this username (username_in) exist in the customer table.

Procedures are beneficial in such cases, where a large number of statements need to be executed as a batch. Being precompiled into a procedure, the statements will execute much faster than if invoked one by one.

JDBC

Now that we've looked at databases, it is time to see how they can be manipulated from your Java applications. We're going to see how you connect to the database and how you can insert, update, and retrieve data. We will discuss some of the JDBC interfaces that help you achieve this. These interfaces and classes are present in the java.sql package that comes with the JDK.

Connecting to the Database

Before any data manipulation is done, you need to connect to the database. As mentioned earlier, each database vendor provides a driver that Java uses to connect to the database and to perform actions on it. So the first step is to inform your Java application which driver is going to be used. The next step is to use this driver to obtain a connection to the database. After that, you create a statement object that is used for issuing the actual SQL statements.

Drivers

Our fleet has 10 drivers. The city's population being 10 million makes each of them 1 in a million!

A database driver is an object specific to a database that defines how connections to the database are made and how SQL statements can be executed against it. There are two methods for registering a driver. For Oracle drivers you can use the **registerDriver()** method of the DriverManager class.

```
DriverManager.registerDriver(new oracle.jdbc.driver.
    OracleDriver());
```

The other method involves loading the driver using the **forName()** method of Class. The mSQL driver from Imaginary can be registered as follows:

```
Class.forName("com.imaginary.sql.msql.MsqlDriver");
```

The driver vendor would have supplied this information to you in the documentation. Drivers normally come as a "zip" file that needs to be included in your CLASSPATH. This zip file contains vendor-specific implementation of the JDBC classes and interfaces. For instance, Oracle's JDBC driver for use with JDK1.1 is called "classes111.zip" and is present in a directory "jdbc/lib." If you've installed it in your root directory (Solaris), you would include it in your CLASSPATH as follows:

```
setenv CLASSPATH /jdbc/lib/classes111.zip:$CLASSPATH
```

Connection Object

Next we obtain a connection to the database. For this you can use the **getConnection()** method of DriverManager. This returns a Connection object that represents one connection to the database. You need to tell the **getConnection()** method about the physical database that you want to connect to and the username/password that you wish to use to log in. In the case of Oracle, assume you are connecting to a database whose name (ORACLE_SID) is PRODUCTION, with the database listener running on port 1521 of the machine "www.myserver.com." Let's say you're logging in as the user "me" with the password "mypassword." Also, assuming you're using the "thin" driver of Oracle. Your getConnection would be like this:

```
Connection conn = DriverManager.getConnection(
                "jdbc:oracle:thin:@www.myserver.com:1521:
                    PRODUCTION",
                "me", "mypassword");
```

Here "jdbc:oracle:thin" indicates that the thin driver of Oracle that has been registered above (using **DriverManager.registerDriver()**) is to be used for obtaining a connection.

For mSQL also you would have a similar, though not identical, statement.

```
Connection conn = DriverManager.getConnection(
                "jdbc:msql://www.myserver.com:1521/
                    PRODUCTION",
                "me", "mypassword");
```

Once you have used the Connection object and don't require it any longer, you can close it using the **close()** method.

Statement Object

A Connection represents a session with the database. SQL statements are executed within this context. You need to create a Statement object in order to issue SQL commands. This can be easily obtained from the Connection object using its **createStatement()** method.

```
Statement stmt = conn.createStatement();
```

The Statement interface contains two important methods in it: **executeQuery()** and **executeUpdate()**. The former is used for issuing queries that return results like SELECT statements. The latter is used for updating and modifying the database (e.g., INSERT, UPDATE, DELETE).

Retrieving Data

We can help you retrieve any data about any person—
the only data we don't have is your credit card number!

executeQuery() returns a ResultSet object that contains the results returned by the query. You can explore this object to find out results of your query.

Let's say you execute the following query:

```
ResultSet rset =
            stmt.executeQuery("SELECT empid, amount FROM Salary");
```

This query is expected to return the employee id and salary of all employees.

Results are available through the **rset** object, which is of the type ResultSet. This object actually points to a row in the table(s) you queried. Initially it is positioned one location before the first row in the result. The pointer is advanced using the **next()** method of the ResultSet. Thus **rset.next()** would make the result set object point to the next row in the result. This method returns a Boolean value, which is false if there are no more rows available in the query. As a result, you can essentially loop through all the rows in the result by doing a **: while(rset.next())**—this while loop will end when **rset.next()** returns a false, and that will happen when all the rows that resulted from the query have been traversed.

ResultSet also contains methods for extracting data in individual columns. There are several methods you can use for extracting the data in a format you want, including **getInt()**, **getLong()**, **getFloat()**, **getDate()**, **getByte()** and **getTime()**. We will limit discussion to the **getString()** method, which behaves similarly to other methods and returns a String representation of the column data. The most efficient way of retrieving column data is to reference it by position. Positions start with 1. So in the previous query, the employee id would be at position 1 and amount would be at position 2.

To retrieve and print all the employee ids and amounts, we would have the following code:

```
while(rset.next())
{
        String empId = rset.getString(1);
        String amount = rset.getString(2);
        System.out.println("EMPLOYEE ID: " + empId +
                        " AMOUNT: " + amount);

}
```

When **rset.next()** is called the first time, it positions the pointer to the first row in the result. Now when you say **rset.getString(1)**, the data in the first column of the first row is returned. **rset.getString(2)** returns the data in the second column of this row. The next time **rset.next()** is called, the pointer has advanced to the second row. Now **rset.getString(1)** returns the first column of the second row. When all rows have been examined, **rset.next()** returns a Boolean false, because of which the **while()** loop ends.

Here's how the complete program would look:

```
import java.sql.*;
public class RetrieveEmployee
{
        public static void main(String[] args)
        {
            try{
                        Connection conn = DriverManager.getConnection(
                        "jdbc:oracle:thin:1521:PRODUCTION",
                                "me", "mypassword");
                    Statement stmt = conn.createStatement();

                    ResultSet rset =
                            stmt.executeQuery(
```

```
                              "SELECT empid, amount FROM
                                   Salary");
               while(rset.next())
               {
                     String empId = rset.getString(1);
                     String amount = rset.getString(2);
                     System.out.println("EMPLOYEE ID: " +
                               empId + " AMOUNT: " +
                                    amount);
               }
               conn.close();
          }catch(Exception ex){}
     }
}
```

The output of this program would look like this:

EMPLOYEE ID: 1 AMOUNT: 20000

EMPLOYEE ID: 2 AMOUNT: 25000

EMPLOYEE ID: 3 AMOUNT: 40000

Note that to compile and use this class, you will need to include the JDBC driver (zip or jar file) in your CLASSPATH.

JDBC allows you to write any valid SQL statement. This means you can do table joins. So, if you want the name of the employee in addition to the employee id, you can modify the code as follows:

```
          ResultSet rset =
               stmt.executeQuery("SELECT Employee.id,
                              Salary.amount, Employee.name
                              FROM Salary, Employee
                              WHERE Employee.id =
                              Salary.empid");
          while(rset.next())
          {
               String empId = rset.getString(1);
               String amount = rset.getString(2);
               String name = rset.getString(3);
               System.out.println("EMPLOYEE ID: " +
                         empId + " AMOUNT: " + amount
                         + " NAME: " + name);
          }
```

Now your output would look as shown:

    EMPLOYEE ID: 1 AMOUNT: 20000 NAME: John
    EMPLOYEE ID: 2 AMOUNT: 25000 NAME: Peter
    EMPLOYEE ID: 3 AMOUNT: 40000 NAME: Tom

Inserting/Modifying Data

Next we see how you can insert rows into the database or update existing rows. Once again the Statement object is used. This time, however, we use the **executeUpdate()** method of this object. This method takes a String as an argument (the SQL statement you want to execute) and returns an **int**. This **int** value shows the number of rows in the database that were affected as a result of this execution. Note that if you're issuing a CREATE TABLE kind of statement, this number will be 0.

As we saw earlier, you need to register the JDBC driver and establish a connection before you can issue any SQL statement. Once we've done this, execution of an insert/update statement is pretty straightforward.

```
Statement stmt = conn.createStatement();
int totalInserted =
                stmt.executeUpdate("INSERT INTO product(id,
                        name, creation_date)
                        VALUES(5, 'Product 5',
                        TO_DATE('31-MAR-1999', 'DD-MON-
                            YYYY'))");
int totalUpdated =
        stmt.executeUpdate("UPDATE product SET name=
            'Product'");
```

The first executeUpdate will return 1, as we're inserting one statement into the product table. The second will return the total number of rows that were affected by this update.

PreparedStatement

Don't worry, it's not just you. This statement was prepared by my lawyer, and even he doesn't understand it!

There are two more types of statement objects—PreparedStatement and CallableStatement. The former is useful if you want to execute the same SQL statement multiple times, as the statement is precompiled and stored in the Prepared-Statement object, which improves efficiency. A CallableStatement is used to execute stored procedures.

We illustrate the use of PreparedStatement with a couple of examples:

For the first example we create a table called email_address, which contains two NUMBER fields and 5 VARCHAR fields. The reason we've created such a big table in this example is because we're going to reuse this table in the practical examples toward the end of the chapter.

```
CREATE TABLE email_addresses(
        id              NUMBER,
        first_name      VARCHAR2(50),
        last_name       VARCHAR2(50),
        email           VARCHAR2(50),
        state           VARCHAR2(50),
        ok_to_send_email NUMBER);
```

Now we see how a PreparedStatement can be used for inserting information into this table. In using a statement to execute insert operations we first create an instance of the Statement object using **createStatement()** of Connection and then invoke **executeUpdate()**, passing the SQL code to this method. In the case of a PreparedStatement, however, we first give an instruction for compiling the statement. This is done by calling Connection's **prepareStatement()** method. This method takes a semi-SQL statement as input and returns a PreparedStatement object that can be used for executing queries or updates.

So what is this semi-SQL statement? It is your regular SQL statement, except that no values have been specified in it. It contains placeholders (denoted by question marks); the actual values are supplied using **setXXX** methods of PreparedStatement just before the statement is executed. If you want to create a PreparedStatement to be used for querying the id of people in different states from the above table, you would proceed as follows:

1. Create the semi-SQL statement:

```
String semiSQL =
        "SELECT id FROM email_addresses WHERE state=?";
```

2. Create a PreparedStatement object:

```
PreparedStatement psmt = conn.prepareStatement(semiSQL);
```

3. Supply the value for the placeholder. Since state is a VARCHAR type field, we will use the **setString()** method. If it were NUMBER, we would use **setInt()**. Similarly, depending on the datatype, you can use different set methods like **setDate()**, etc.

```
psmt.setString(1, "CA");
```

Here the first parameter is the position of the question mark, for which the value "CA" should be substituted. If there were more question marks in this, we would have to provide a **setXXX** method for specifying values for each of them.

4. Execute the query.

```
psmt.executeQuery();
```

Now if you want to execute for "MA," you can say

```
psmt.setString(1, "MA");
psmt.executeQuery();
```

As the statement is precompiled, it should execute faster than a regular **Statement. executeQuery()**.

Based on this background the following example should be self-explanatory. It inserts two records in the email_addresses table. The PreparedStatement is prepared in the **start()** method. The **insertRecord()** method supplies values for the six question marks using the appropriate **setXXX** methods and then calls **executeUpdate()**.

```
import java.sql.*;
public class PreparedStatementExample
{
    String host="HOST", port="PORT", sid="SID";
    String login="LOGIN", password="PASSWORD";

    PreparedStatement psmt;
    public static void main(String[] args)
    {
        PreparedStatementExample ps = new PreparedStatement
            Example();
        ps.start();
    }
    public void start()
    {
        try{
            Connection conn = getConnection();
            String insertSQL = "INSERT INTO email_addresses
                (id, first_name, last_name, email, state,
                 ok_to_send_email) VALUES(?,?,?,?,?,?)";
            psmt = conn.prepareStatement(insertSQL);
            insertRecord(1, "John", "Doe", "john@doe.doe", "CA",
                1);
            insertRecord(2, "Jill", "Doe", "jill@doe.doe", "CA",
                1);
            psmt.close();
```

```
            conn.close();
        }catch(Exception ex){}
    }
    public void insertRecord(int id, String fName, String lName,
                String email, String state, int okToSendEmail)
    {
        try{
            psmt.setInt(1, id);
            psmt.setString(2, fName);
            psmt.setString(3, lName);
            psmt.setString(4, email);
            psmt.setString(5, state);
            psmt.setInt(6, okToSendEmail);
            psmt.executeUpdate();
        }catch(Exception ex){}
    }
    public Connection getConnection()
    {
        Connection conn = null;
        try{
                String connection = "jdbc:oracle:thin:@" + host +
                            ":" + port + ":" + sid;
                DriverManager.registerDriver(
                    new oracle.jdbc.driver.OracleDriver());
                conn =
                    DriverManager.getConnection (
                            connection,
                            login, password);
        }catch(Exception ex){}
        return conn;
    }
}
```

Insert into a LONG Column

He lived a pretty long life—
in moth years he lived to be 300,000!

Inserting data in a LONG column is done in a significantly different way than inserting data in a VARCHAR column. This is because data that goes in a VARCHAR column cannot be too big, whereas a LONG column can accept a very large amount of data. We use the **setAsciiStream()** or **setBinaryStream()** methods of PreparedStatement, and the data that goes into the column is fed from a stream. For example, if you want to store a file on the machine in a LONG column in the database, you can open an input stream to the file and then use the **setAsciiStream()** method or the **setBinaryStream()** method. When you do an **executeUpdate()**, data will be read from the stream and stored in the database.

To illustrate this, here's a simple example. We create a table "long_example," containing two columns: "id," which is a NUMBER, and "val," which is LONG. We then show the class InsertLong, which generates a huge amount of data, converts it into a stream, and uses the **setAsciiStream()** method of PreparedStatement before calling execute**Update()**.

```
CREATE TABLE long_example(
    id          NUMBER,
    val         LONG);
```

```java
import java.io.*;
import java.sql.*;
public class InsertLong
{
    String host="HOST", port="PORT", sid="SID";
    String login="LOGIN", password="PASSWORD";

    PreparedStatement psmt;
    public static void main(String[] args)
    {
        InsertLong ps = new InsertLong();
        ps.start();
    }
    public void start()
    {
        try{
            Connection conn = getConnection();
            String insertSQL =
                    "INSERT INTO long_example(id, val) VALUES(?,?)";
            psmt = conn.prepareStatement(insertSQL);

            int id = 30;
            // Simulating big chunk of data—consisting of 10000
                characters
            String theValue = "";
            for(int i=0; i<10000; i++)
                theValue +="A";
            psmt.setInt(1, id);

            /* Convert the data in the String theValue to a byte array so we
               can create a ByteArrayInputStream from it. This will be
```

used as the second argument to setAsciiStream() which
expects an InputStream as the second argument. The third
argument is the length of this stream */

```
        byte[] data = theValue.getBytes();
        psmt.setAsciiStream(2,
                new ByteArrayInputStream(data), data.length);

        psmt.executeUpdate();

        psmt.close();
        conn.close();
    }catch(Exception ex){}
}
public Connection getConnection()
{
    Connection conn = null;
    try{
        String connection = "jdbc:oracle:thin:@" + host +
                    ":" + port + ":" + sid;
        DriverManager.registerDriver(
                new oracle.jdbc.driver.OracleDriver());
        conn =
            DriverManager.getConnection (
                    connection,
                    login, password);
    }catch(Exception ex){}
    return conn;
}
}
```

CallableStatement

We saw how stored procedures can be created. Now let's see how they can be invoked from your Java applications. A CallableStatement can be used for calling stored procedures. This object is similar to a PreparedStatement. The parameters are defined using the **setXXX** methods. A stored procedure can also have out parameters, but these have to be explicitly indicated if you're using a CallableStatement. The **registerOutParameter()** method is used for this purpose. The first argument of this is the position of the parameter. The second argument is its type. The SQL for calling the procedure looks like this:

```
    {call <procedure>(<paramters>)}
```

You begin by defining this SQL statement and using the **prepareCall()** method of CallableStatement. Next you define values for all the IN parameters and datatypes of all the OUT parameters. Then the procedure is executed using the **execute()** method. Results of OUT parameters can be retrieved using the **getXXX** methods.

This is illustrated by an example that invokes the **register()** procedure we created in the Stored Procedures section of this chapter. The following program can be invoked on the command line to invoke **register()** and insert records into the "customer" and "telecom_address" tables. It takes two arguments: a username and a phone number. The program prints a count of total number of records in the customer table with this username.

```java
import java.sql.*;
public class Register
{
    static String host="HOST", port = "PORT", sid="SID";
    static String login="LOGIN", password="PASSWORD";
    public static void main(String[] args)
    {
        if(args.length < 2)
        {
            System.out.println("Usage: java Register <username>
<phone>");
            System.exit(0);
        }
        Connection conn = getConnection();
        try{
            String sql = "{call register(?,?,?)}";
            CallableStatement cs = conn.prepareCall(sql);
            cs.setString(1, args[0]);
            cs.setString(2, args[1]);
            cs.registerOutParameter(3, Types.INTEGER);
            cs.execute();
            String retVal = cs.getString(3);
            System.out.println("Return value is " + retVal);
        }catch(SQLException sqlE){sqlE.printStackTrace();}
    }
    public static Connection getConnection()
    {
        Connection conn = null;
        try{
            DriverManager.registerDriver(
                new oracle.jdbc.driver.
                    OracleDriver());
```

```
                    String connectString = "jdbc:oracle:thin:@" +
host
                                        + ":" + port + ":" +
sid;
                    conn =  DriverManager.getConnection (
                                        connectString,
                                        login, password);
          }catch(SQLException sqlE){sqlE.printStackTrace();}
          return conn;
    }
}
```

First, an instance of CallableStatement is prepared. Here we're saying that we want to invoke a stored procedure called register, which takes three parameters (these could be IN, OUT, INOUT or any combination).

```
        String sql = "{call register(?,?,?)}";
        CallableStatement cs = conn.prepareCall(sql);
```

Next we specify values for the first two parameters. These are the username and phone number that are passed as command-line arguments to this program and will be stored as VARCHARs in the database.

```
        cs.setString(1, args[0]);
        cs.setString(2, args[1]);
```

The third parameter is an OUT parameter of the type INTEGER.

```
        cs.registerOutParameter(3, Types.INTEGER);
```

Now that all parameters have been specified, the stored procedure is executed.

```
        cs.execute();
```

The return value is retrieved from the procedure. This is the third parameter in the procedure.

```
        String retVal = cs.getString(3);
```

Transactions in JDBC

Our transactions are like an open book—
everything happens beneath the covers!

In most applications database updates are done in the form of logical units. An update consists of several SQL statements, which may affect multiple tables. It is a requirement that either all or none of these SQL statements should affect the database. This concept of transactions has already been explained.

We've seen that databases allow you to COMMIT transactions so that all the SQL statements take effect together. In a JDBC statement, however, the default action is to issue a COMMIT after every **executeUpdate()**.

If you want to group your statements together and then issue a COMMIT, you need to do some more work.

The Connection interface has a method called **setAutoCommit(boolean)**. If you invoke this method by passing a "false" argument to it, the connection enters a non-auto-commit mode. This means that any statement you execute will not be COMMITted unless you explicitly do it. You can commit the statements by using the **commit()** method of Connection. There is another method called **rollback()**, which can be used to ROLLBACK your changes. This means that any changes made by statements since the last **commit()** or **rollback()** will be discarded by the database.

We can see this with the help of an example. We'll again use the product table as our base. In this example we will see how **rollback()** works (**commit()** works on the same principles). We will set the autoCommit to false so that no updates actually take effect in the database. Then we will insert five rows into the product table. We will get a count of rows in the database to confirm that five rows were inserted in this connection. After that we will roll back the changes. Because of this the five rows will be removed from the database, and we will confirm this by getting a new count of rows.

```java
import java.sql.*;
public class JdbcTest
{
    public static void main(String[] args)
    {
        try{
            // Register the driver and establish connection

            DriverManager.registerDriver(
                new oracle.jdbc.driver.OracleDriver());
            String connString =
             "jdbc:oracle:thin:@www.myserver.com:1521:
                PRODUCTION";
            Connection conn =
                    DriverManager.getConnection(connString,
                    "me", "mypassword");
            // Turn off autoCommit so inserts are not
                automatically COMMITed
            conn.setAutoCommit(false);

            // Count number of rows in database
            Statement stmt = conn.createStatement();
            String query = "SELECT COUNT(*) FROM product";
            ResultSet rset = stmt.executeQuery(query);
```

```
                        rset.next();
                        System.out.println("Initially, total rows in
    product:
                                          " + rset.getString(1));
                        rset.close();

                        // Insert 5 rows
                        for(int i=20; i<25; i++)
                        {
                            String upd = "INSERT INTO product (id, name)
                                        VALUES(" + i + ", 'Product')";
                            int tot = stmt.executeUpdate(upd);
                            System.out.println("Total inserted: " +
    tot);
                        }
```

/* Count number of rows—this will return initial number of rows + 5
   Important thing to note here is that even though this count seems to indicate
   that the 5 rows have been COMMITted, that is not really the case. This query
   returns "initial + 5" because we're in the same connection in which the inserts
   were done—if you view the database using another connection you will still
   see that there are "initial" number of rows in the product table.
*/

```
                        rset = stmt.executeQuery(query);
                        rset.next();
                        System.out.println("Before rollback, total rows
                            in product: " + rset.getString(1));
                        rset.close();
```

/* Now we roll back our changes—this ensures that the 5 rows are not
   added to the product table */

```
                        conn.rollback();
```

/* We again count the number of rows in the
      database—
   this time the result will
   be "initial" number of rows. */

```
                        rset = stmt.executeQuery(query);
                        rset.next();
                        System.out.println("After rollback, total rows in
                                        product: " + rset.
                                            getString(1));
                        rset.close();
                        stmt.close();
```

```
            conn.close();
        }catch(SQLException ex){ex.printStackTrace();}
    }
}
```

In this example we inserted five rows in the database but rolled them back. Similarly, you could **commit()** those rows so they would all be added to the database as a logical unit.

Some Practical Examples

Here are some practical examples that make use of Servlets and JDBC. In all the examples we use the "email_addresses" table created above. In addition to that we will make use of a sequence for generating unique values for the id field in the table. This sequence can be created as shown:

```
CREATE SEQUENCE email_addresses_seq START WITH 1
```

Example 1: A Customer Registration System

The first example is a small customer registration system, which allows your customers to register themselves with your site. The data is captured by a Servlet and stored in the database using JDBC. This type of system can be used for several other things as well; for instance, you can create an inventory of your products using the same technology.

Figure 6.1 shows how the registration screen looks.

Once a customer has registered successfully, the screen shown in Figure 6.2 is displayed.

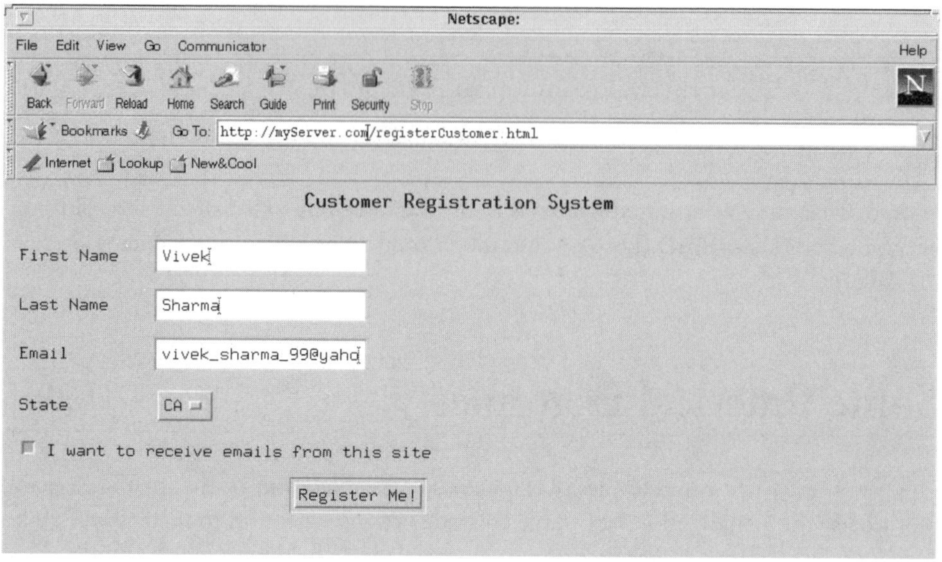

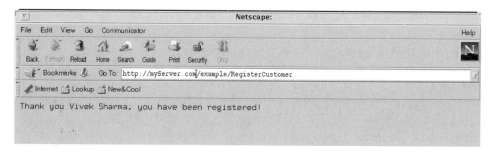

Figure 6.1

Figure 6.2

The customer registers by visiting the following Web page:

registerCustomer.html

```
<HTML><HEAD></HEAD>
<BODY>
    <CENTER><H1>Customer Registration System</H1></CENTER>
    <FORM ACTION='/example/RegisterCustomer' METHOD='POST'>
        <TABLE>
            <TR><TD>First Name</TD>
                <TD><INPUT TYPE='text' NAME='firstName'
                                        SIZE='20'></TD></TR>
            <TR><TD>Last Name</TD>
                <TD><INPUT TYPE='text' NAME='lastName'
                                        SIZE='20'></TD></TR>
```

```
<TR><TD>Email</TD>
    <TD><INPUT TYPE='text' NAME='email'
                            SIZE='20'></TD></TR>
<TR><TD>State</TD>
    <TD><SELECT NAME='state'>
            <OPTION>CA <OPTION>MA <OPTION>NY <OPTION>TX
        </SELECT></TD></TR>
<TR><TD COLSPAN='2'><INPUT TYPE='checkbox'
            NAME='okToSendEmail' VALUE='1' CHECKED>
        I want to receive emails from this
            site</TD></TR>
<TR><TD></TD><TD ALIGN='right'><INPUT TYPE='submit'
            NAME='submit' VALUE='Register Me!'></TD>
            </TR>
    </TABLE>
  </FORM>
</BODY>
</HTML>
```

In this FORM the customer can fill out first name, last name, and email address. The customer can also specify whether (s)he wants to receive emails from your site by clicking on a checkbox. We are going to use this value in the next example.

When the customer presses the Submit button, the Servlet RegisterCustomer (which, according to our FORM, should be in the "/example" zone) is invoked. We now present the code for this Servlet. It reads the values supplied by the customer, creates a database connection, and sets up a record in the "email_addresses" table:

```
import java.sql.*;
import java.io.*;
import javax.servlet.*;
import javax.servlet.http.*;
import java.util.*;

public class RegisterCustomer extends HttpServlet
{
    String host="HOST", port="PORT", sid="SID";
    String login="LOGIN", password="PASSWORD";
    public void doGet (HttpServletRequest req, HttpServletResponse
        res)
    {
        doPost(req, res);
    }
    public void doPost (HttpServletRequest req, HttpServletResponse
        res)
    {
```

```
try{
        String firstName="", lastName="", email="", state="";
        String okToSendEmail="0";

        PrintWriter out = null;
        res.setContentType("text/html");
        out = res.getWriter();
        Enumeration values = req.getParameterNames();
        while(values.hasMoreElements())
        {
                String name = (String)values.nextElement();
                String value = req.getParameterValues(name)
                    [0];
                if(name.equalsIgnoreCase("firstName"))
                    firstName = value;
                if(name.equalsIgnoreCase("lastName"))
                    lastName = value;
                if(name.equalsIgnoreCase("email"))
                    email = value;
                if(name.equalsIgnoreCase("state"))
                    state = value;
                if(name.equalsIgnoreCase("okToSendEmail"))
                    okToSendEmail = "1";
        }
        Connection conn = getConnection();
        String querySQL =
                "SELECT email_addresses_seq.NEXTVAL FROM
                    dual";
        Statement stmt = conn.createStatement();
        ResultSet  rset = stmt.executeQuery(querySQL);
        rset.next();
        String id = rset.getString(1);

        String insertSQL = "INSERT INTO email_addresses(id,
            first_name, last_name, email, state,
            ok_to_send_email) VALUES(" + id +  ", '" +
            firstName + "', '" + lastName + "','" + email +
            "','" + state + "'," + okToSendEmail + ")";
        stmt.executeUpdate(insertSQL);
        stmt.close();
        conn.close();
        out.println("<HTML><HEAD></HEAD><BODY>");
        out.println("Thank you " + firstName + " " + lastName
```

```
                        + ", you have been registered!");
                out.println("</BODY></HTML>");
                out.close();
            }catch(Exception ex){}
    }
    public Connection getConnection()
    {
            Connection conn = null;
            try{
                    String connection = "jdbc:oracle:thin:@" + host +
                                    ":" + port + ":" + sid;
                    DriverManager.registerDriver(
                                    new oracle.jdbc.driver.
                                        OracleDriver());
                    conn =
                        DriverManager.getConnection (
                                    connection,
                                    login, password);
            }catch(Exception ex){}
            return conn;
    }
}
```

Example 2: Bulk Email Sender—JDBC Version

In Chapter 4 we saw how we can use the JavaMail API to send bulk mails. The email addresses were read from a file. However, if you have a registration system as shown earlier, you can directly query the database and send emails to all customers in the database. And it does not end there. By having information in the database, you gain considerable flexibility. You can then execute a query that returns the email addresses of only those customers who are in a particular state or region and send a targeted email to them.

Another thing we illustrate in this example is a way for people to specify that they don't want to receive emails from you. Spam mailings have unfortunately become very frequent, and as a result legislation is being passed to prevent them. Some places already have a law requiring that if you send bulk mailings, you have to provide a way for the receiver to block emails from you in the future. We are going to achieve that by modifying our original email sender.

In this new version we extract email addresses from the email_addresses table and send messages to those people. But we extract only those records for which the value of "ok_to_send_emails" is 1. We have created another Servlet, UpdateOkToSendMails, which sets the value to 0 or 1.

To achieve this, we're extracting the id and email address of each person in the email_addresses table whose "ok_to_send_emails" value is 1. Then we append the following link to the mail body:

http://myServer.com/example/UpdateOkToSendMails?id=<ID>&ok=0

Here <ID> is the id of the customer. If the user clicks this link, UpdateOkToSend Mails is invoked. This servlet reads the "id" and the value of "ok." It then updates the "ok_to_send_emails" field and sets its value for this person's record. Since we're specifying ok = 0 in the link above, the value of "ok_to_send_emails" will be set to 0 for each person who clicks that link. Thus, next time we send out a mailing using our mail utility, that person's record will not be picked up. Of course we need to tell the customer that if ever (s)he wants to start receiving mailings from our site, (s)he can invoke the following URL:

http://myServer.com/example/UpdateOkToSendMails?id=<ID>&ok=1

Note that now the value of "ok" is set to 1.

Here's the complete code:

SendMailsJdbcServlet.java

```java
import java.io.*;
import javax.servlet.*;
import javax.servlet.http.*;
import java.util.*;
import java.sql.*;
public class SendMailsJdbcServlet extends HttpServlet
{
    String host="HOST", port="PORT", sid="SID";
    String login="LOGIN", password="PASSWORD";

    public void doGet (HttpServletRequest req, HttpServletResponse
        res)
    {
        doPost(req, res);
}
    public void doPost (HttpServletRequest req,
                        HttpServletResponse res)
    {
        try{
            PrintWriter out = null;
            res.setContentType("text/html");
            out = res.getWriter();

            Enumeration values = req.getParameterNames();
```

```java
        String returnAddress = "", baseBody="", subject="";
        while(values.hasMoreElements())
        {
                String name = (String)values.nextElement();
                String value = req.getParameterValues(name)[0];
                if(name.equalsIgnoreCase("returnAddress"))
                        returnAddress = value;
                if(name.equalsIgnoreCase("body"))
                        baseBody = value;
                if(name.equalsIgnoreCase("subject"))
                        subject = value;
        }

        int count = 0;
        Connection conn = getConnection();
        Statement stmt = conn.createStatement();
        String query =
                "SELECT id, email FROM email_addresses
                WHERE ok_to_send_email = 1";
        ResultSet rset = stmt.executeQuery(query);
        while(rset.next())
        {
                String id = rset.getString(1);
                String to = rset.getString(2);
                String footNote = getFootNote(id);
                String body = baseBody + footNote;
                EmailSender es =
                        new EmailSender(returnAddress, to,
                                                subject, body);
                es.send();
                count++;
        }
        out.println("<HTML><HEAD></HEAD><BODY>");
        out.println("Sent " + count + " mails");
        out.println("</BODY></HTML>");
        out.close();
    }catch(Exception ex){}
}
public String getFootNote(String id)
{
    String footNote = "\n\nIf you don't want to receive
        emails from us you can click the following link:\n";
    footNote +=
```

```
                "http://myServer.com/example/
                    UpdateOkToSendMails? id=" + id + "&ok=0";
            return footNote;
    }
    public Connection getConnection()
    {
        Connection conn = null;
        try{
                DriverManager.registerDriver(
                    new oracle.jdbc.driver.OracleDriver());
                String connectString = "jdbc:oracle:thin:@" +
                                    host + ":" + port + ":" +
                                        sid;
                conn =  DriverManager.getConnection (
                                    connectString,
                                    login, password);
        }catch(SQLException sqlE){}
        return conn;
    }
}
```

UpdateOkToSendMails.java

```
import java.io.*;
import javax.servlet.*;
import javax.servlet.http.*;
import java.util.*;
import java.sql.*;
public class UpdateOkToSendMails extends HttpServlet
{
    String host="HOST", port="PORT", sid="SID";
    String login="LOGIN", password="PASSWORD";

    public void doGet (HttpServletRequest req, HttpServletResponse
        res)
    {
        doPost(req, res);
    }
    public void doPost (HttpServletRequest req,
        HttpServletResponse res)
    {
        try{
            PrintWriter out = null;
```

```java
            res.setContentType("text/html");
            out = res.getWriter();

            Enumeration values = req.getParameterNames();

            String id = "", ok = "";
            while(values.hasMoreElements())
            {
                    String name = (String)values.nextElement();
                    String value = req.getParameterValues(name)
                        [0];

                    if(name.equalsIgnoreCase("id"))
                            id = value;
                    if(name.equalsIgnoreCase("ok"))
                            ok = value;
            }

            Connection conn = getConnection();
            Statement stmt = conn.createStatement();
            String update = "UPDATE email_addresses SET
                ok_to_send_email = " + ok + " WHERE id = " +
                    id;
            stmt.executeUpdate(update);
            out.println("<HTML><HEAD></HEAD><BODY>");
            if(ok.equals("0"))
            {
                out.println("Your record has been udpated. You
                        should not receive any more mails from
                        us<BR>If you want to start receiving mails
                        again, click the following link:<BR>");
                out.println("<A HREF='http://myServer.com/
                        example/UpdateOkToSendMails?id=" + id +
"&ok=1'>http://myServer.com/example/UpdateOkToSendMails?id=" + id +
    "&ok=1</A>");

            }
            else
                out.println("Your record has been udpated. Now
                        you will be receiving mails from us");
            out.println("</BODY></HTML>");
            out.close();
        }catch(Exception ex){}
    }
    public Connection getConnection()
```

```
        {
                Connection conn = null;
                try{
                        DriverManager.registerDriver(
                                new oracle.jdbc.driver.OracleDriver());
                        String connectString = "jdbc:oracle:thin:@" +
                        host + ":" + port + ":" + sid;
                        conn =  DriverManager.getConnection (
                                                connectString,
                                                login, password);
                }catch(SQLException sqlE){}
                return conn;
        }
}
```

Some Useful Classes and Interfaces in the Java.sql Package

Driver.java

Interface that represents the driver of the database to which connection is being established.

—Methods: **connect()**—gets a Connection to the database.
acceptsURL()—a method for testing if driver thinks it can open a connection to the database.
getMajorVersion()—gets major version number of the driver.

DriverManager.java

Provides service for managing a set of database drivers.

—Methods: **getConnection()**—gets a connection to the database.
registerDriver()—makes a driver known to the manager.
getDrivers()—gets a list of all the drivers.

Connection.java

Represents a specific connection to the database. SQL statements can be executed within the context of a Connection.

—Methods: **createStatement()**—creates a Statement object that can be used for issuing SQL.
prepareStatement()—creates a PreparedStatement object.

prepareCall()—creates a CallableStatement object.
setAutoCommit()—turns autoCommit mode on or off.
getAutoCommit()—gets the current state of autoCommit.
commit()—commits all changes made since last commit/rollback.
rollback()—rolls back all changes made since last commit/rollback.
close()—closes the connection to the database and releases resources.
isClosed()—checks whether connection is closed or open.
getMetaData()—gets DatabaseMetaData objects, which contains more information about the database.

DatabaseMetaData.java

Provides information about the database.

—Methods: **getDatabaseProductVersion()**—version of the database.
getNumericFunctions()—gets list of math functions supported.
getStringFunctions()—gets list of supported String functions.
getMaxColumnNameLength()—limits column name length.

Date.java

Represents dates. Extends java.util.Date.

—Methods: **setTime()**—sets time of the Date object.
valueOf()—converts String in "yyyy-mm-dd" format to Date object.
toString()—converts Date to String in format "yyyy-mm-dd."

CallableStatement.java

Used to execute SQL-stored procedures.

—Methods: **registerOutParameter()**—declares a parameter to be of the type OUT.
getString()—gets the value of a parameter as a String.

PreparedStatement.java

Used for SQL statements that are precompiled. Useful if the same SQL statement needs to be executed a number of times. It is an interface that extends Statement.

—Methods: **executeQuery()**—executes an SQL query.
executeUpdate()—executes an SQL update/insert/delete.

setBoolean()—sets a parameter to be of the type Boolean.
setNull()—sets a parameter to be of the type NULL.

ResultSet.java

This represents the data returned from an SQL query.

—Methods: **next()**—moves the pointer to point to the next row in the result.
close()—closes the result set.
getString()—gets value of a column in the result as a String.
getBoolean()—gets value of a column in the result as a Boolean.
getByte()—gets value of a column in the result as a byte.
getInt()—gets value of a column in the result as an int.
getMetaData()—gets a ResultSetMetaData object that contains more information about the result.

ResultSetMetaData.java

Contains more information about the result obtained in a ResultSet.

—Methods: **getColumnCount()**—number of columns in the ResultSet.
isSearchable()—can the column be used in a where clause?
getColumnDisplaySize()—max width of column in chars.
getColumnName()—name of column at a given index.
getTableName()—name of table that has this column.
getColumnType()—SQL datatype of the column.

Statement.java

Interface that can be used to execute SQL statements.

—Methods: **executeQuery()**—executes an SQL query.
executeUpdate()—executes an SQL update/insert/delete.
close()—closes the Statement and releases resources.
getMaxFieldSize()—current max column size limit.
getMaxRows()—gets max rows the result set can contain.
setMaxRows()—sets max rows the result set can contain.
setQueryTimeout()—time the driver will wait for Statement to execute. If time exceeds, an SQLException is thrown.

Chapter 7

XML

Introduction

This chapter introduces you to XML, the latest buzz word in the software industry. The chapter does not assume prior knowledge of XML but does assume that you have some understanding of a language like HTML and have a basic idea about databases.

We have looked at a lot of HTML in previous chapters and have seen how it can magically transform a plain-looking document into a well-organized, good-looking one. The key to all these transformations is a set of tags that are inserted between the text items, giving meaning to the way these text items appear. These tags are interpreted by the browser, and the document is displayed as dictated by them. Obviously, this system has a lot of advantage, but it is not without its drawbacks.

If you are using a text editor, a plain document is much easier to read than an HTML document, because of the formatting tags that your brain must skip in order to weed out the real information.

Look at the following line in plain text.

Patrick Joe

4444, NoStreet

MyCity, 44444

415-555-1212

The equivalent information could be written in an HTML file like this:

<H1><U><B>Patrick Joe</B></H1></U>
<I>4444,
NoStreet</I>
<H5>MyCity, 44444</H5>
<B><U>415-555-
1212</B></U><P>

Viewed through a browser, this would look great. But look what it has done to the information itself. The data has been obscured by these formatting tags. So if you just want to process the information, the plain version of the document looks more attractive. But is that enough? Looking at it, can you tell whether Patrick is the first name or the last? Also, can you tell whether the number at the end is a regular phone number, a cell phone number, a fax number, or something else?

This brings us to the concept of information about information—data that describes a piece of information and gives meaning to it. And if this meta-information can be given in such a way that it can be processed by a computer, all the better. This is the basic underlying concept behind eXtensible Markup Language, commonly known as XML.

You have the concept of meta-information in databases. If you were to create a database table to store this information, you would probably create the following fields:

firstName, lastName, StreetAddress, City, Zip, and Phone.

Alternatively, you could store them in one single line, but splitting the data into multiple fields has given it an organization. The same thing can be achieved through XML. Data can be organized in a hierarchical fashion.

XML is not a language in itself. You can look at it as a set of specifications based on which other languages can be defined—in fact, you have the liberty of defining your own language based on XML rules. You can create your own set of tags that may give information about information.

To illustrate the concept, let us see how we would represent the information we saw above using an XML syntax.

```
<?xml
version="1.0"
?>
<People>
  <Person>
    <Name>
        <First>Patrick</First>
        <Last>Joe</Last>
    </Name>
    <Address>
        <Street>4444, NoStreet</Street>
        <City>MyCity</City>
        <Zip>44444</Zip>
    </Address>
    <Phone>415-555-1212</Phone>
  </Person>
</People>
```

We have created our own tags, similar to names of database fields. These tags have been embedded around the data, just as tags were embedded when we created the

HTML document. The presence of these new tags has certainly not made the document any easier to read, but by inserting appropriately named tags we have given it more meaning. Now you can easily look for the last name, and you can easily tell that the 415 number is a phone number. More important, the document is now organized in proper hierarchical fashion with each individual element easily identifiable, making it easy for a software program to process this information.

Some Rules to Follow

I strictly follow rules—
till they start getting in the way!

You need to observe some of the following rules in order to have an XML-compliant language:

Each starting tag must have an ending tag. In HTML you can get away by not specifying ending tags for some elements. Thus, <BR> works even if you don't specify a closing </BR>. However, XML is not so lenient. There can be only one root tag, and tags are case-sensitive. Therefore, <Name> is different from <NAME>.

Displaying an XML document

XML is oriented toward giving meaning to information. It does not deal with display aspects, which are left up to other languages. For example, you can use XSL with an XML document to describe how your document should be displayed. The great advantage of doing so is that you can create multiple stylesheets (XSL documents) that display the data contained in an XML document in different ways. In other words, you can provide different views of the same data without having to write the data in separate files. With HTML, if you want to present the address information in two formats—the first organized as shown earlier and the second organized in the form of a TABLE—you have to create two HTML files, containing the same data but different display tags. This approach doesn't work well if you want multiple presentations of the same data, as any change in data would have to be made in all the HTML files.

Data Interchange with an XML Document

An eye for an eye, a byte for a byte!

Data interchange is one area in which XML can and will play a very prominent role. As opposed to a database, in which data may be organized and stored in a proprietary format, an XML file is an ASCII representation of the data, a representation that has the advantage of hierarchical organization yet one that can be easily transmitted.

Revisiting the simple example shown earlier, let us assume there are two companies that do online registrations and keep track of names, addresses, and phone numbers. Now the first company's database could have the following fields:

FirstName, LastName, StreetLine1, StreetLine2, City, State, Zip, Country, Phone

The second could have the following fields:

Name, Street, City, State, Zip, Phone

If they want to exchange their membership information, both would have to write a program that understands the other's database. This also means that if someday the first company changes the field name from FirstName to First_Name, the software program of the second would suddenly stop working.

Also, in all probability neither company would be inclined to give the other direct access to its database. Instead, both would want to write out information from their database into an export file and have the other one read this. This means that they would each have to write a program that writes out their database and another that reads the database file from the other company and stores it in their own format.

But this is just the simplest scenario. Imagine having five different companies, five different databases with different schemas. Each company would have to write a program that reads the formats of all the others and then store it in their database. The complexity of the undertaking would require much time and effort not only to build these systems but also to maintain them.

One way of solving this problem would be to have all five companies implement their schemas in a consistent format. But this is easier said than done. In all likelihood the different companies would not be interested in spending resources for this effort. It would not only mean an overhaul of their database, it would also mean that they would have to change all software applications that use data from this database.

Fortunately, XML provides a solution to this fairly common problem. All that the five companies have to decide is a common way of publishing their information. Once they agree that they will all write out the information in a standard way, all that each company has to do is write a program that reads from this standard format and store this in its own database. This action grants them all complete independence of the others' databases.

Thus, each company could write a program that reads from its own database and writes out an XML file as shown above. Also, each could write a program that reads from this XML file and store data in the database. If their database schema changes, the other companies are not affected and don't have to change their systems; they just deal with the XML file.

Document Type Definitions (DTDs)

Definition: X.M.L.—Roman for 10.1000.50

When you design a database, you specify the datatypes of the different fields. For example, if you have defined a field as NUMERIC and try to insert character data into it, you will get an error. Similarly, XML allows you to define the structure of the document so that the validity of the data can be checked. This structure is defined in a document called the Document Type Definition document (DTD).

A DTD is like the table layout of an XML document. It describes the hierarchical organization as well as showing what type of data goes into the different fields, what data is optional, and so on.

A DTD for the XML document we created earlier would look like this:

```
<!ELEMENT People (Person)* >
<!ELEMENT Person (Name, Address, Phone) >
<!ELEMENT Name (First?, Last) >
<!ELEMENT Address (Street, City, Zip) >
<!Element First   (#PCDATA) >
<!Element Last    (#PCDATA) >
<!Element Street  (#PCDATA) >
<!Element City    (#PCDATA) >
<!Element Zip     (#PCDATA) >
<!Element Phone   (#PCDATA) >
```

This shows that People consist of 0 or more Person(s). Person consists of Name, Address, and Phone. Each Name has a Last name and an optional First. Each address has a Street, City, and Zip.

It is not necessary for an XML document to have a DTD, but having one can be helpful, especially in checking for erroneous data.

You can include the DTD inside the XML document itself, or you can include a reference to it in the XML file. If you've saved the above DTD in a file called People.dtd, your XML file would look like this:

```
<?xml
version="1.0"
?>
<!DOCTYPE People SYSTEM "People.dtd">
<People>
  .....
```

Parsers

Who needs parsers—
all they do is Komplane abaoot mi Sintaks!

In order to use an XML document, a software program needs to parse it so that it can extract the required data. A number of things can then be done with the data, from displaying it to performing calculations or transmitting the data for interchange with another system.

A number of parsers have evolved in the market that can be used for parsing XML documents. You can download parsers from the Web sites of a number of prominent Internet companies. There are parsers available for use with several languages, like C, C++, and Java.

These parsers read the XML document and help build a tree in which the data is organized as represented in the XML document. The parsers allow you to retrieve the data that you are interested in.

There are essentially two approaches being followed by parsers. One is to read the entire document, build a tree, and then allow a program to request any data element from the tree. Another approach is to provide a callback interface, so that you can invoke the parser and have predefined methods invoked whenever an element is encountered. This approach being interactive, is very useful if you are reading a large document.

The first approach is called DOM, the second is called SAX.

Using XML

Now we look at some ways in which XML can be used. As mentioned earlier, XML can be used in conjunction with stylesheets to provide customized look and feel without having to generate multiple HTML files containing the same data. Another area where XML can be used is for data manipulation on the client side. You can perform calculations or present a subset of the data based on user preference.

Parsers play a prominent role in data manipulation. We look at an example where a parser can be used for displaying different sets of data to the user by parsing an XML document on the client side.

Client-Side Usage

Using XML on the client side is heavily dependent on the client software. If the client software is such that it has an XML parser, you can easily use a language like Javascript (or a Java applet). Internet Explorer 5.0 contains XML support. There is a built-in

XML parser technology called msxml, which you can use to parse an XML document using Java or Javascript. To use it in Javascript, you can refer to the elements of the document through a Java applet called XMLDSO created by Microsoft. You can include this applet in your HTML page along with Javascript code that can access elements from the applet.

As an alternative, you could write your own applet that uses a parser to parse the XML document. You may then retrieve elements of the document by calling methods in this applet.

If you use the XMLDSO applet, your HTML file would look like this:

```
<HTML><HEAD></HEAD>
<BODY>
  <APPLET CODE =com.ms.xml.dso.XMLDSO.class ID=xmldso>
    <PARAM NAME='url' VALUE='people.xml'>
  </APPLET>
</BODY>
</HTML>
```

This applet reads up the file "people.xml" and parses it. Now you can write another applet or a Javascript program that retrieves parsed information and displays it in a particular way.

As an example, let's say we want to give users a filter option, allowing them to look at only those people whose last name is Sharma. For this, put a text field and a button in the HTML page above:

```
<FORM>
  <INPUT TYPE='text' NAME='last' VALUE=' '><BR>
  <INPUT TYPE='button' NAME='Search' VALUE='Search'
                        onClick='searchIt(this.form)'>
</FORM>
```

Then add Javascript code: a function called searchIt that reads the text field called "last," then searches for requested information, and displays the total number of people found with this last name.

The code would look as follows:

```
function searchIt(frm)
{
    last = frm.last.value;
    totalFound = 0;
```

```
// xmldso is the applet that we included in the HTML page. From this we're retrieving
//  the root of the XML document.
    var docRoot = xmldso.getDocument().root;
```

```
// This retrieves a list of all Person(s)
    var persons = docRoot.children.item("Person");
```

```
// This is the total number of persons in this document
    var len = persons.length;
```

/* Look at the record of each person. See if their last name matches the one typed in.
If so, add it to the output display list */

```
    for(i=0; i<len; i++)

    {
// Get a handle to one Person
        var aPerson = persons.item(i).children;
```

```
// Get the Name field of the person
        var name = aPerson.children.item("Name");
```

// Look at a particular name. "name" contains only one element, which is the
0th one

```
        var aName = name.item(0).children;
```

```
// Find the value of the "Last" field
        var aLastName = aName.item("Last").text;
```

// If value matches with the value typed by the user, increment the totalFound
counter

```
        if(aLastName == last)
            totalFound ++;
    }
    document.write("Total persons with last name: " + last +
                " is " + totalFound);
}
```

Similarly, you can write applications that allow display of only a subset of the data. If somebody is interested in looking at only those persons who are in zip code 44444, they can do so. In other words, data has been kept separate from display logic using XML.

Server-Side Usage

Eighty percent of our server software is based on standards.
The rest? Well, it works!

XML can be effectively used for data interchange. Looking at the example of companies exchanging registration information, if they come up with an XML as declared earlier, you can write programs that read from your database and render the information in that format. You can also write a program that reads the XML file and writes information into your database.

The part that involves writing to the XML file can be implemented using JDBC. It could look something like this:

```
public class WriteXml
{
    public static void main(String[] args)
    {
        PrintStream pos;

        /* Open an output file */

        out.println("<?xml\nversion=\"1.0\"\n?>");
        out.println("<People>");

    /* Establish JDBC connection */
    ....
        String querySQL =
                "SELECT first_name,last_name,street, city,
                 zip, phone FROM members";
        ResultSet rset = stmt.executeQuery(querySQL);
        while(rset.next())
        {
            out.println("<Person>");
            String first = rset.getString(1);
            String last = rset.getString(2);
            ....
            out.println("<Name>");
                out.println("<First>");
                    out.println(first);
                out.println("</First>");
                out.println("<Last>");
                    out.println(last);
                out.println("</Last>");
            out.println("</Name>");

            /* Similarly print out the other elements */
            ...
        }
        /* Close the root tag */
        out.println("</People>");
    }
}
```

This type of program would create an XML document similar to the one we created earlier.

The next step is to write a program that would read the XML document and store information in the database.

This program would need to import the parser as well as some other packages. A typical DOM-based program would look like this:

```
import java.io.*;
import java.net.*;
import org.w3c.dom.*;
import org.w3c.dom.Node;
import java.util.*;

public class ReadXml
{
    public static void main(String[] args)
    {
        try{
                XMLParser parser = new XMLParser();
                URL url = new URL(xmlFile);
                parser.setErrorStream(System.err);
                parser.setValidationMode(false);
                parser.showWarnings(false);
                parser.parse(url);

                // This gives you a handle to the document tree
                doc = parser.getDocument();
```

/* Now you can traverse through the list and get values of individual elements. Traversal would be similar to one shown in the Javascript example. You can use methods like **getChildNodes()**, **getNodeName()**, and **item()** to traverse through the list. You can read each record line by line and then retrieve each individual elements. These can then be stored in the database using JDBC */

```
        }catch(Exception e){}
    }

}
```

A combination of the two programs shown here can be used by your business to exchange information with other businesses. For instance, if you are selling a special line of clothing, you could sell information about your customer base to a more general clothing store. For this you would need to exchange your customer information with them.

Some Practical Examples

Now we look at some practical examples of how XML can be used. The first example shows how you can query data from your database using JDBC and generate XML file. The second shows how such an XML data can be read back into the database. You can develop programs like these for exchanging information with other companies or within departments of your own company. Both examples are based on the email_addresses table we presented in Chapter 6. The first example extracts data from this table and renders it in XML format. You could use this if you plan on selling your customers' email addresses to other companies. The second example reads data that is in this type of format and stores it in your database. You could use this type of program if you have bought customer information from another company that was rendered to you in XML.

In the third example, we revisit the StocksServlet example that was presented in Chapter 4.

Example 1: Generating XML from the Database

```java
import java.sql.*;
import java.io.*;
public class DatabaseRetriever
{
    String host = "HOST", port="PORT", sid = "SID";
    String login="LOGIN", password="PASSWORD";

    public static void main(String[] args)
    {
        if(args.length < 1)
        {
            System.out.println("Usage: java DatabaseRetriever
                <outputFileName>");
            System.exit(0);
        }
        DatabaseRetriever r = new DatabaseRetriever();
        r.start(args[0]);
    }
    public void start(String outFile)
    {
        PrintStream pos = createXmlFile(outFile);
        Connection conn = getConnection();
        try{
            Statement stmt = conn.createStatement();
            String query = "SELECT first_name, last_name, email
                    FROM email_addresses WHERE ok_to_send_email
                        = 1";
            ResultSet rset = stmt.executeQuery(query);
            String firstName, lastName, email;
            while(rset.next())
            {
```

```
                    firstName = rset.getString(1);
                    lastName = rset.getString(2);
                    email = rset.getString(3);
                    writeDataRecord(firstName, lastName, email,
                        pos);
            }
        }catch(Exception ex){}
        closeXmlFile(pos);
    }
    public PrintStream createXmlFile(String outputFileName)
    {
        PrintStream pos = null;
        try{
            DataOutputStream dos =
                new DataOutputStream(
                    new FileOutputStream(outputFileName));
            pos = new PrintStream(dos);

            pos.println("
                <?xml version=\"1.0\" encoding=\"ISO-8859-1\"
                    ?>");
            pos.println("<Document>");

        }catch(Exception ex){}
        return pos;
    }
    public void writeDataRecord(String f, String l,
                                String e, PrintStream pos)
    {
        try{
            pos.println("<Person>");
                pos.println("<FirstName>" + f + "</FirstName>");
                pos.println("<LastName>" + l + "</LastName>");
                pos.println("<Email>" + e + "</Email>");
            pos.println("</Person>");
        }catch(Exception ex){}
    }
    public void closeXmlFile(PrintStream pos)
    {
        try{
            pos.println("</Document>");
            pos.close();
        }catch(Exception ex){}
    }
    public Connection getConnection()
```

```
    {
        Connection conn = null;
        try{
                DriverManager.registerDriver(
                        new oracle.jdbc.driver.OracleDriver());
                String connectString = "jdbc:oracle:thin:@" +
                        host + ":" + port + ":" + sid;
                conn =  DriverManager.getConnection (
                                        connectString,
                                        login, password);
        }catch(SQLException sqlE){}
        return conn;
    }
}
```

This program takes the name of an output file as its command-line argument. It then queries the database table email_addresses and retrieves the name and email address of every customer who has elected to receive emails. An XML file is generated. The file looks as shown:

```
<?xml version="1.0" encoding="ISO-8859-1" ?>
<Document>
<Person>
<FirstName>John</FirstName>
<LastName>Doe</LastName>
<Email>john@doe.doe</Email>
</Person>
<Person>
<FirstName>Jill</FirstName>
<LastName>Doe</LastName>
<Email>jill@doe.doe</Email>
</Person>
</Document>
```

The top tag of this is <Document>, and there are multiple <Person> records in it. Each <Person> has a <FirstName>, a <LastName>, and an <Email>. Of course you can change the tag names if required.

One interesting aspect here is the encoding attribute in the first line, which indicates how this file is encoded. In this case we are saying that the file uses the ISO-8859-1 character set. You can specify other types of encoding as well, depending on your requirements. If your data is limited to alphanumeric and a few other common characters, you can get away with not providing an encoding attribute at all.

Now that the file is in XML format, it can be transmitted (to the company that wants to buy this information from you) using electronic means such as email. In fact you can use the email-sending utility we developed to send this file to multiple people at the same time!

Example 2: Reading XML Data into the Database

But what if you were at the receiving end, i.e., if you were to receive such an XML file and wanted to store it in your database. That is the topic of this example. Earlier in the chapter we briefly described how a DOM-based parser can be used for reading and parsing XML data. However, if file sizes are very large, DOM-based parsers are not the right choice. Instead you should use the SAX parser. This type of parser is implemented with a callback interface, which means you can intercept the parser as it is executing.

This step allows us to retrieve one record at a time from the XML file and do something with it rather than waiting for the parser to parse the entire document and build the complete tree.

In order to use this example, you would need to download an XML parser and include its **jar** file in your CLASSPATH. For example, if you've downloaded Oracle's XML Parser, you would include it in your CLASSPATH with a statement like the following:

setenv CLASSPATH

/home/vsharma/XML/ORACORE_MAIN_SOLARIS_990129_XML/lib/ xmlparser.jar

In this example we begin by creating a class called SAXReader, which invokes the SAX-based parser of Oracle. It extends the HandlerBase class and implements methods like **startDocument(), endDocument(), startElement()**, and **endElement()**—all of which will be called by the parser during the course of parsing an XML file. For instance, when the parser encounters a new tag, it will call the **startElement()** of this class. When it encounters the end of a tag, it will call **endElement()**. We can write whatever we want within these routines. Once the routines have completed their operation, control will return back to the parser. Now, when the parser encounters another element in the XML file, it will again call one of the methods in our class. This will go on till the file ends or until there is an Exception somewhere.

Our SAXReader is called by the class XmlRetriever. It retrieves data records using the SAX parser, and whenever one complete record has been read (a person's record in this case includes FirstName, LastName, and Email), it calls the **oneRecord()** method of XmlRetriever. This method can be used for writing the information in the database. In our version of the XmlRetriever, the method **oneRecord()** simply prints the retrieved values, but you can easily write a JDBC program that writes this data to the database instead of displaying it.

The **SAXReader** has been written in such a way that it looks for the elements between the <Person> and </Person> tags. Every tag and its value are collected and stored in a Hashtable, "currentRow." When the </Person> tag is reached, it calls the **oneRecord()** method of XmlRetriever.

For this we make use of the **startElement(), endElement()**, and **characters()** methods. We've set a variable called rowTag whose value is "Person." When the parser starts parsing, it calls **startElement()** for every start tag that is encountered. We compare the name of the tag with "rowTag" (whose value is "Person"). If they match, it means that a new <Person> row has started. For every tag that we encounter after this, we store its name in the **currentElement** variable. Now **characters()** will be called by the parser when it has retrieved the value of this **currentElement**. So in the characters element we put the name and value of the current tag in the Hashtable.

endElement() is called every time the parser encounters an ending tag. We compare the name of the tag with "Person." When a match is found, it means that this row has ended. Now our Hashtable should contain names and values of all tags for this person.

The contents of the Hashtable would look like this:

FirstName   John

LastName   Doe

Email   john@doe.doe

Now that we have all the information about one <Person>, it's time to call the **oneRecord()** method. The **oneRecord()** method can now do whatever it wants with this data. Once it finishes its execution, the parser will resume its operation.

SAXReader.java

```
import org.xml.sax.*;
import java.io.*;
import java.net.*;
import oracle.xml.parser.*;
import java.util.*;

public class SAXReader extends HandlerBase
{
    static Locator locator;
    static Hashtable currentRow = new Hashtable();
    static String rowTag = "Person";
    static String currentElement = "";
    static boolean rowStarted = false;
    static XmlRetriever xr = null;

  static boolean firstElementInRowFound = false;

  public SAXReader()
  {
  }
  public SAXReader(String xmlFile, XmlRetriever xmr)
    throws Exception
  {
```

```
         SAXReader sample = new SAXReader();
         xr = xmr;
         Parser parser = new XMLParser();

         parser.setDocumentHandler(sample);
         parser.setEntityResolver(sample);
         parser.setDTDHandler(sample);
         parser.setErrorHandler(sample);
         parser.parse(fileToURL(new File(xmlFile)).toString());
   }

   static URL fileToURL(File file)
   {
      String path = file.getAbsolutePath();
      String fSep = System.getProperty("file.separator");
      if (fSep != null && fSep.length() == 1)
         path = path.replace(fSep.charAt(0), '/');
      if (path.length() > 0 && path.charAt(0) != '/')
         path = '/' + path;
      try
      {
         return new URL("file", null, path);
      }
      catch (java.net.MalformedURLException e)
      {
         throw new Error("unexpected MalformedURLException");
      }
   }

   public void setDocumentLocator (Locator locator)
   {
      this.locator = locator;
   }

   public void startDocument()
   {
   }

   public void endDocument() throws SAXException
   {
      currentRow = new Hashtable();
      xr.oneRecord(currentRow);
   }
   public void startElement(String name, AttributeList atts)
                                                throws
                                                SAXException
```

```
{
    if(rowStarted == true)
        if(firstElementInRowFound == false)
            firstElementInRowFound = true;
    if(name.equals(rowTag))
    {
        currentRow = new Hashtable();
        rowStarted = true;
    }
    currentElement = name;
}
public void endElement(String name) throws SAXException
{
    currentElement = "";
    if(name.equals(rowTag))
    {
        rowStarted = false;
        firstElementInRowFound = false;
        Enumeration ex = currentRow.keys();
        while(ex.hasMoreElements())
        {
            String var = (String)ex.nextElement();
        }
        xr.oneRecord(currentRow);
    }
}

public void characters(char[] cbuf, int start, int len)
{
    if(firstElementInRowFound == true)
    {
        if(currentElement.equals("") == false)
            currentRow.put(currentElement, new String(cbuf));
    }
}

public void ignorableWhitespace(char[] cbuf, int start, int
    len)
{
}

public void processingInstruction(String target, String data)
            throws SAXException
{
}
```

```
    public InputSource resolveEntity (String publicId, String
        systemId) throws SAXException
    {
       return null;
    }
    public void notationDecl (String name, String publicId,
                                  String systemId)
    {
    }

    public void unparsedEntityDecl (String name, String publicId,
                           String systemId, String notationName)
    {
    }
    public void warning (SAXParseException e)
            throws SAXException
    {
    }

    public void error (SAXParseException e)
            throws SAXException
    {
       throw new SAXException(e.getMessage());
    }

    public void fatalError (SAXParseException e)
            throws SAXException
    {
       throw new SAXException(e.getMessage());
    }
}
```

XmlRetriever.java

This is the entry-point program. It accepts the name of an XML file as input. It creates an instance of SAXReader by passing the name of the XML file and a reference to itself (so that the method **oneRecord()** can be called).

The method **oneRecord()** is called each time the parser has returned all elements in a <Person> row. This method receives a Hashtable containing the names and values of all the elements. In this implementation it simply looks for the **FirstName** element and prints its value.

```
import java.util.*;
public class XmlRetriever
{
```

```
public static void main(String[] args)
{
        if(args.length != 1)
        {
                System.out.println("Usage: java XmlRetriever
                    <xmlFileName>");
                System.exit(0);
        }
        XmlRetriever x = new XmlRetriever();
        x.start(args[0]);
}
public void start(String fileName)
{
    try{
        SAXReader s = new SAXReader(fileName, this);
    }catch(Exception ex){ex.printStackTrace();}
}
public void oneRecord(Hashtable h)
{
        Enumeration e = h.keys();
        while(e.hasMoreElements())
        {
                String field = (String)e.nextElement();
                String value = (String)h.get(field);
                if(field.equals("FirstName"))
                        System.out.println("First Name: " + value);
        }
}
}
```

This is how the output of this program would look:

First Name: John
First Name: Jill
First Name: Vivek

Example 3: XML-Based Stock Analyzer

In Chapter 4, when we introduced a Stock Reader, we mentioned the problem associated with reading and parsing an HTML output. Since an HTML file is presentation-oriented, not data-oriented, instead of locating the data by a unique name, you have to locate it by its position—for example, the fourth column in the fifth row of the sixth table. And if for some reason the HTML generator changes the output even slightly (for example, presenting the seventh table before the sixth), all programs depending on the data will start giving wrong results. However, if the data was separated from the presentation logic using XML, this problem would be solved as long as the same tag names were used for representing the data. And that is exactly what we're doing in this example. The StocksServletXml returns XML data in response to a query instead of HTML data. The StocksReaderXml program parses this XML data and retrieves the value of the stock from it. In this case we're not using the XML parser just to illustrate that parsers are a convenience, not a necessity. We're doing the parsing ourselves. You may very well use the XML parser. However, don't forget to add the **jar** file of the parser in the **wrapper.classpath** parameter of your **jserv.properties**. Also, you will have to restart Apache for new CLASSPATH to become effective.

StocksServletXml.java

```
import java.io.*;
import javax.servlet.*;
import javax.servlet.http.*;
import java.util.*;
public class StocksServletXml extends HttpServlet
{
    public void doGet (HttpServletRequest req, HttpServletResponse
        res)
    {
        doPost(req, res);
    }
    public void doPost (HttpServletRequest req,
        HttpServletResponse res)
    {
        PrintWriter out = null;
        res.setContentType("text/html");
        try{
            out = res.getWriter();
        }catch(Exception ex){}

        Hashtable quotes = new Hashtable();
        quotes.put("MSFT", new Double(100.95));
        quotes.put("ORCL", new Double(55.95));

        Enumeration values = req.getParameterNames();
        Vector symbolVector = new Vector();
        while(values.hasMoreElements())
        {
            String name = (String)values.nextElement();
            String[] value = req.getParameterValues(name);
            if(name.equalsIgnoreCase("symbol"))
```

```
                {
                    int len = value.length;
                    for(int i=0; i<len; i++)
                        symbolVector.addElement(value[i]);
                }
            }

            int size = symbolVector.size();
            for(int i=0; i<size; i++)
            {
                String symbol = (String)symbolVector.elementAt(i);
                String value = "";
                Double val = (Double)quotes.get(symbol);
                if(val == null)
                    value = "Illegal symbol";
                else
                    value = val.toString();
                out.println("<SYMBOL>" + symbol +
                    "<SYMBOL><TIME>12:15pm</TIME><VALUE>" +
                    value + "</VALUE>");
            }
            out.close();
        }
}
```

StocksReaderXml.java

```
import java.net.*;
import java.io.*;

public class StocksReaderXml
{
    String theURL = "http://myServer.com/example/StocksServletXml";
    public static void main(String[] args)
    {
        String symbol = args[0];
        StocksReaderXml sr = new StocksReaderXml();
        sr.start(symbol);
    }
    public void start(String symbol)
    {
        try
        {
            URL myURL = new URL(theURL);
            URLConnection conn = myURL.openConnection();
```

```
                conn.setDefaultUseCaches(false);
                conn.setDoOutput(true);
                conn.setRequestProperty("Content-type",
                        "application/octet-stream");
                String message="symbol=" + symbol;
                conn.setRequestProperty("Content-length", "" +
                        message.length());
                OutputStreamWriter outStream =
                    new OutputStreamWriter(conn.getOutputStream());
                PrintWriter pout = new PrintWriter(outStream);
                pout.write(message);
                outStream.flush();
                outStream.close();
                InputStreamReader inpStream =
                        new InputStreamReader(conn.getInputStream());
                BufferedReader br = new BufferedReader(inpStream);

                String oneLine;

                while ((oneLine = br.readLine()) != null)
                {
                        parseIt(oneLine, symbol);
                }
                br.close();
        } catch (MalformedURLException mex)
          {
                mex.printStackTrace();
          } catch (IOException ioex)
            {
                ioex.printStackTrace();
            }
    }
    public void parseIt(String line, String symbol)
    {
        String symbolTag = "<SYMBOL>";
        String symbolEndTag = "</SYMBOL>";
        String valueTag = "<VALUE>";
        String valueEndTag = "</VALUE>";

        int index = line.indexOf(symbolTag);
        int index2 = line.indexOf(symbolEndTag);
        if(index != -1 && index2 != -1)
        {
            String sym =
                line.substring(index + symbolTag.length(),
```

```
                        index2);
            if(symbol.equalsIgnoreCase(sym))
            {
                    index = line.indexOf(valueTag);
                    index2 = line.indexOf(valueEndTag);
                    String val = line.substring(index +
                                        valueTag.length(),
                                        index2);
                    System.out.println("Value of " + symbol +
                                        " is " + val);
            }
        }
    }
}
```

Conclusion

The real explosion of XML will come when some standard XML-based languages have been defined. A language for the financial industry would allow different banks to exchange data easily. Similarly, an XML language for the health industry would enable hospitals using proprietary systems to exchange patient information easily. But till that time comes, you can still use XML by defining something that suits your needs as well as those of partners with whom you want to exchange information. And of course, you can use it along with XSL even today to provide customized views of your catalog.

References

You can get a lot of information about XML online. Try visiting the following sites:

http://www.xml.org

http://www.w3.org/XML

http://xml.com

To learn more about XSL and style sheets in general:

http://www.w3.org/Style/XSL/

http://www.oasis-open.org/cover/xsl.html

You may also visit Web sites of companies like Microsoft, IBM, and Oracle to get more information.

Part III

Chapter 8

Credit Card Verification

The last purchase on my credit card was a book called
How to Deal with Card Companies If You're Broke!

In order to sell goods over the Internet you need to be equipped to take payments in an efficient manner. While you could have customers call your toll-free phone number to provide their credit card information, that manual step is unnecessary. Instead, what you need is an online credit card authorization system that can do the job automatically. Setting up your business to handle credit cards is the subject of this short but important chapter.

First, let's look at just what is involved in using credit cards online. To do this we need to understand how credit cards work in a regular store. Just as a customer with a credit card has a credit card number, a merchant needs to obtain a merchant id. A merchant id is normally issued by a bank. Like a credit card number, a merchant id is associated with an account. When a person wants to purchase goods using a card, the merchant obtains an authorization, typically by swiping the card in a machine that transmits information to the bank that issued the credit card. The bank then verifies the validity of the card and sends back an acceptance or denial signal.

When the merchant swipes the credit card, the authorization request first goes to the merchant's bank (known as the acquirer). The acquirer forwards the request to the bank that issued the credit card. If the customer's bank authorizes the payment, the acquirer reserves the amount of the transaction for crediting to the merchant's account. The communication between the two banks occurs over an interchange network. These networks are maintained by credit card companies such as Visa and MasterCard.

If you want to start accepting credit cards, the first thing you need to do is obtain a merchant id, with which your bank will in all probability be able to provide you. If not, talk to some big banks like Bank of America, Wells Fargo, etc.

The next step is to choose a method for authorization. The easiest way to go about doing this is by working with a company that specializes in credit card authorizations. Several different companies provide this service, and there are several different ways of accessing their services. Some require your customers to download software. One such company is CyberCash. As a merchant, you would also have to install software on your server, and in order to buy something, your customers would have to download and install a wallet application. The customer's wallet application interacts with the merchant's software, which talks to the CyberCash gateway, which in turn uses credit card authorization networks to provide the authorization. You can get more information on CyberCash at *www.cybercash.com*.

Another method is one followed by First Virtual. In this system a customer establishes a PIN with First Virtual. Whenever he/she wishes to purchase something online, the customer gives his/her First Virtual PIN to the merchant. The merchant next sends this number for authorization to First Virtual, which then sends an email to the customer to confirm that (s)he intends to purchase the goods. Upon customer confirmation an acceptance is issued to the merchant. To learn more, go to *http://www.fv.com*.

We are going to look at two more methods in detail, neither of which requires customers to download software or establish an account with another party. Avoiding this step can be really useful if your target market includes people who just want to use a credit card as they do at the grocery store.

Both these methods work by having a merchant establish an account with a third party that provides card authorization service. The merchant then receives an id from the authorization company that would be used for any transactions between the two parties.

Card Authorization URLs

With this method the authorization company would provide you with a URL that the merchant can use to obtain authorizations. This URL is a CGI script (or a Servlet or something similar) that accepts certain parameters such as credit card number, expiration date, and so on. The backend application of this URL does the card authorization and returns a result to the (merchant's) calling program—or calls another URL that can be specified by the calling program. The result can then be evaluated by the merchant's URL and appropriate action taken.

Several companies provide this kind of service and have their own URLs that you can use from your applications. Most of these companies provide you with more than the authorization service; for instance, you can use them for capturing credit card information from the customer on a secure server.

Security is a big concern for e-commerce, and credit card information is thus very sensitive data. Customers need to be assured that when they provide their card number, it will be transmitted securely. The best thing to do is to set up a secure server (an HTTPS server running SSL) to ensure that any exchange of data over the network is encrypted. Any page or application that needs to capture or transmit credit card information should reside on a secure server.

However, depending on resources and expertise, you may not be able to support a secure server, and in that case you can use the services of these third parties to gather the customer's credit card number. Note that if you want to take the latter approach, your business model of interaction with the third party would change significantly. Unlike the case above where you sent a credit card number to this URL, here you just provide the amount of the transaction. The card authorization company then asks the customer for card information and uses the amount provided by you for authorization. Once the verification is complete, the credit card company invokes one of your URLs. This URL can be a Servlet that interprets the results and takes appropriate action.

Since the authorization company will call the same URL on your machine for all customers, how can you distinguish the customer whose card is valid from the one whose credit was denied? To solve this problem, you can generate a unique id before calling the third-party URL—let's call this an orderId. You can store details of the transaction such as the customer id, items purchased, and so on along with the orderId in a table.

Now, while calling the verification company's URL, you can pass on this orderId along with the amount that you want authorized. Once the verification process is over, this unique id can be passed back to your URL along with a success or failure code. Using the returned orderId, your URL can determine which customers' cards were approved.

Let's take a look at both approaches in turn. First, the case where you have your own secure server. Note that even if you have a secure server, you would want to maintain a nonsecure server for nonsensitive applications and pages. The reason for doing this is that security comes with a cost. Communication between the client and the server is significantly slower if you're using a secure server, because both ends need to do a handshake to verify each other's identity, and the data needs to be encrypted or decrypted by both parties.

The application that shows products being sold by your store can therefore be kept on a nonsecure server, as can the shopping cart. However, when customers want to check out, they should be transported to the secure server. In HTML terms, the checkout page would have a FORM with a Submit button (that works as the Checkout interface). This FORM would invoke an application or page on the secure server that would gather the credit card information. Here's how one would look:

```
<FORM  ACTION='https://mySecureServer.com/Checkout' METHOD='POST'>
    . . . . . . . .
```

Hidden variables contain information like the list of products the customer wants to purchase and the customer's username or unique id.

```
    . . . . . . .
        <INPUT TYPE='submit' NAME='submit' VALUE='Checkout'>
</FORM>
```

The Checkout application would reside on the secure server. It would read the list of items the customer wants to buy, calculate the price, and present a FORM to the customer, asking for the credit card information. This FORM would contain an orderId generated by the Checkout application, which would be used for further communication with the card verification company. Pressing the Submit button on this FORM would invoke the credit card verification company's URL.

Here's how this FORM might look:

```
<FORM ACTION='https://cardVerificationCompany.com/cardVerifyUrl'
    METHOD='POST'>

    ...... .
    Card number    <INPUT TYPE='text' NAME='ccardNumber'
                      SIZE='12'>
    Card expiration <INPUT TYPE='text' NAME='ccardExp'.........

    <INPUT TYPE='hidden' NAME='amount' VALUE='29.95'>
    <INPUT TYPE='hidden' NAME='orderId' VALUE='50001'>
    <INPUT TYPE='hidden' NAME='merchantNumber'  VALUE='2002'>
    <INPUT TYPE='hidden' NAME='returnURL'
                  VALUE='http://myServer.com/ProcessOrder'>

    <INPUT TYPE='submit' NAME='pay' VALUE='Make payment'>
</FORM>
```

When the customer presses the "Make Payment" button, the cardVerifyUrl of the verification company is invoked. This URL reads the credit card number and expiration date as provided by the customer. It also reads the amount and merchant number (this is the number established between the merchant and the third party). A verification of the credit card and amount takes place. The verification company then calls the URL specified by the merchant in the returnURL parameter (in this case Process Order on myServer.com). Process Order receives a confirmation or denial and the orderId. This orderId is important because in the Checkout page the user is going out of your system (into the third party's system). When he/she comes back to your site (automatically) after the card verification has been done, you have no way of knowing who this customer is. The checkout application can generate a unique orderId and store relevant information like customer id, list of items purchased, etc. in a database. When the verification process is complete, ProcessOrder can retrieve information from the database using the unique orderId, which is returned by the card verification company.

The other scenario is one in which you don't have a secure server. In this case your Checkout page looks like the one we used above, except that it does not ask for credit card information. It will still contain the orderId, merchantNumber, amount, and the returnURL. The returnURL also works as discussed above.

A quick search on the Web for such companies brought these two results:

http://anacom.com/
http://www.quakenet.com

Anacom has a product called WebCharge that can be used as discussed. Here's a sample FORM that Anacom provides as an example of how to use its service:

```
<form method=post
action="https://www.anacom.com/order/username/default.htm">
    <input type=hidden name=fulltotal value="payment_amount">
    <input type=hidden name=returnlink
            value="http://www.mysite.com/index.htm">
    <input type=submit value="Click Here for Secure Credit Card
Payment"></form>
```

You can talk to these companies to obtain more personalized service; for instance, some of them may allow your company logo to be displayed at the top of the page to give customers the impression that it is one of your own sites.

In Chapter 4 we looked at the stocks example, which demonstrated how you can invoke a FORM through a Servlet. You can use similar technology in the Checkout application if you want to do card verification in the background. The Ordering Management System (part of the complete example at the end of the book) uses this technology.

Third-Party APIs

Some companies provide programmatic authorization service through the use of APIs. One such company, Shielded Technologies, has a Java API that your applications can use. This API contains a method that connects to the verification URL of Shielded and comes back with a result. The advantage is that your applications can do authorization transparently without having to write any connection code at all. To use their API, you would create an instance of CardShieldAPI class that Shielded provides free. Then you would call the method SecureSale(), which accepts the credit card number, expiration date, etc. and returns a success or error code. A typical usage would look as shown:

```
public class Checkout
{
    doPost()
    {
        /*Read credit card number, expiration date, list of items being purchased, etc.
        Calculate total amount to be charged.*/
    }
    public void checkout()
    {
        /* Create  an instance of CardShieldAPI—the first argument is your card
            shield merchant id.
```

This id is established between you and Shielded before you can start using the service.

The second argument tells the class whether you're calling the verification URL through an applet or not; this is required because applets have different security restrictions from those of normal applications. We've set this to false, as we're using the API in an application. */

```
CardShieldAPI capi = new CardShieldAPI(cardShieldMerchantId,
                           false);
```

/* Now invoke the SecureSale method, which will do the verification */

```
String result =  capi.SecureSale(clerk, comment,
                                 cardNumber, caredExpiration,
                                 amount,  zip, address);
```

/* Compare the result with the Approved variable in the CardShieldAPI class—if the value of result is the same as Approved, the card has been approved, otherwise there's been an error */

```
if (  result.equals( capi.Approved ) )
{
        Display Success page
}
else
{
        Display failure page
}

    }
}
```

To get more information about credit card verification methods and companies that help your business accept payments online, you can visit the following URLs:

www.verifone.com

www.cybercash.com

www.fv.com

www.shielded.com

Chapter 9

Security and Performance

Security is naturally a big concern for any business on the Internet, since data is being transported over the network, making it possible for outsiders to snoop and derive critical information. Considering this, a number of measures can be taken to safeguard the data. In this chapter we are going to discuss some technologies that can be leveraged to enhance the security of your systems, but since our focus is from an application point of view, several areas related to this topic are not covered. We do, however, try to address the major ones and have provided pointers where you can find more information.

When an application is deployed in a production environment, its behavior can be quite different from the one observed on development machines. Performance deteriorates when a large number of users simultaneously try to execute the applications. Some steps can be taken to ensure that the degradation does not affect your business. We discuss some common pitfalls and resolutions in the second section of this chapter.

This chapter assumes knowledge of Java and some knowledge of the Internet.

Security

My computer is very secure—
I got a cell for it in Alcatraz!

Security is not limited to physical aspects. Machines need to be put behind a lock and key, no doubt, but if data is being transmitted over a public network, almost anybody can have access to it. This fact does not reduce the importance of physically securing your servers, however. If you don't have the bandwith to secure your systems, you can use services of companies specializing in this business. Several companies can host your computers for you and physically secure them by all possible means including 24-hour surveillance. One such company is AboveNet. You can find more information about this company at *www.abovenet.com*.

Firewalls

The funny thing about computers is that you don't have to be in the vicinity of one to do damage. As long as your computer is connected to the Internet, somebody could potentially log in remotely and create trouble. Consequently, some companies prefer to have an intranet—is a network that works like a mini-Internet, accessible by people within the company. None of the machines in an intranet is directly accessible from the outside world, and traffic routing is instead done through a separate machine called the firewall. This machine and its software work like a filtering system, preventing unauthorized machines from connecting to machines in the intranet. It can also work as a proxy server, which allows users inside the intranet to connect to the outside world (the Internet).

There are two types of firewalls: IP filtering firewalls, which restrict access from the outside world, and proxy servers, which allow users on the inside to access the Internet.

There is an excellent discussion about firewalls at the following site:

http://security.tsu.ru/info/fw/fwfaq/

You can also get information about IP routers from the Web sites of networking companies such as Cisco.

Database Security

Be sure to read the manuals that come along with the database you're using to understand what kind of security is built into the system. It should not be very easy for someone to read or write sensitive portions of your database. Most databases allow you to create schemas with restricted access, giving different sets of users different privileges.

SQL has a GRANT command that can be used for assigning or revoking privileges to certain schemas. This command can normally be issued only by database administrators. You would have to read documentation about the database system you're using to determine how you can use GRANT.

The GRANT command allows a good level of granularity. For instance, you can specify that a particular user can insert into a table but cannot delete from it. And you can even specify that this user can insert into specific columns of a table but be restricted from the rest. Here are examples for both the cases:

```
GRANT select, insert ON orders TO customer;
```

This means that anybody who's logged into the database's customer schema can issue a SELECT and INSERT statement in the orders table.

```
GRANT insert(name) ON profile TO customer;
```

This means that the "customer" can insert only into the name field of the profile table. There is an ALL shortcut that can be used for granting all priviliges to a user:

```
GRANT ALL ON products TO customer;
```

You can get more information on these in database manuals. For Oracle you can look up the "Oracle Server Administrator's Guide." You can also look for security information on your database system's Web site.

Software Patches

One of the potential security risk factors is the software you're using on the system. A number of security issues recur frequently with various softwares like Operating Systems, Java, and so on. In this ongoing fight with hackers, companies are trying to do as much as possible, since their business depends on providing security to users. You should regularly look for any published flaws and patches that can be installed.

You can obtain information from the Web sites of companies whose software you're using. Thus, Solaris security and patch information can be found at *www.sun.com,* while Windows NT information is available at *www.microsoft.com.*

Data Transmission Security

The most vulnerable place is the network over which data is being transmitted. Whenever a customer sends a credit card number, the data is transmitted over the Internet and may be accessed by somebody in between. To prevent this from happening, you need a mechanism by which users can encrypt the data so that only you can decrypt it. Another potential problem is that somebody else might pose as you, the merchant, and lure the customer into providing a credit card number. For this you need to provide a mechanism by which users can validate that they are indeed talking to you and not to some impostor. This brings us to the topic of Public and Private Keys.

Public and Private Keys

Data can be encrypted or decrypted using Public and Private Keys. These keys are just a unique pair of numbers that an encryption algorithm uses to change the visual appearance of data before transmission and to restore the data with a decryption algorithm. The keys come in the form of tightly coupled pairs—there is only one Public Key corresponding to a Private Key and vice versa. If you encrypt a piece of data using a Public Key, the data can be decrypted only if the decryption algorithm uses the corresponding Private Key.

Anybody can generate Public and Private Key pairs. The Private Key is kept confidential, whereas the Public Key can be sent to anybody. Even if it gets into wrong hands, it is not a problem.

So let's see how this can be applied to solve the problems of data transmission security. If you want to send encrypted data to somebody so that no snooper can gain access to this private information, you can request the Public Key of the party to whom you are sending data. You then encode the data using this Public Key before sending it. As a result, only the person who has the Private Key can decode the data. Since there is only one Private Key corresponding to a given Public Key, your information is safe even if the data is intercepted by somebody. Of course, this holds true only if the Private Key has been kept confidential. A Private Key is meant to be top secret and should never be transmitted over the Internet or left in a place where somebody can access it.

These measures ensure that your credit card number cannot be recovered by anybody else except the intended person. But what if some snooper changes the data before it reaches the intended receiver? This is a good possibility, especially because the hacker has access to the Public Key and can create a new set of data, encrypt it using the Public Key, and then send it without the original sender or receiver knowing that this is happening. The receiver must therefore have a way of knowing whether the data is coming from you or some other source.

The solution to this problem is surprisingly similar to the first solution, except that it works the other way round. You "sign" the data using your Private Key; in other words, you generate a signature based on the contents of your data with the Private Key. At the other end, the receiver validates your signature by trying to read this signature using your Public Key. If the receiver can validate it, it means that the data was not modified by somebody in between, because only you have the Private Key, and therefore only you could create a valid signature.

Certificates

Java allows us to generate Public and Private Key pairs. It also allows digital signing, which we will discuss in brief detail. The key is transmitted in the form of a certificate. A certificate is just another piece of data that contains the Public Key of an entity and additional information such as the entity's name. You can create your own certificate, but the general practice is to use certain companies, known as Certificate Authorities (CAs), which create these certificates. Client-side software knows about these trusted CAs, so they accept the certificates generated by one of them. If a certificate is received by the client, it first checks whether the certificate has been created by a CA. If so, it is accepted.

Ciphers

Ciphers are cryptographic algorithms that can be used for encrypting and decrypting data. Some cryptographic algorithms are RSA, SHA-1, DSA, DES, and MD5.

Secure Sockets Layer

Netscape has developed a solution for encrypted communication based on some of the principles we discussed above. The Secure Sockets Layer (SSL), as it is called, is essentially a protocol that lies between the low-level TCP/IP and the high-level HTTP. SSL allows encrypted communication between the client and the server, and it also allows each to authenticate the other.

An SSL session begins with a handshake between the client and the server, that is, an exchange of messages between the two machines so that authentication can take place. The process works in the following steps:

1. The client makes a connection to the secure port (an "https" connection instead of an "http" connection). Along with the request, it sends its SSL version and some other data.

2. When the server receives this information, it sends back its own SSL version and its certificate. It may also request the client's certificate if client authentication is required.

3. The client receives the certificate and checks its validity. It checks whether or not the certificate has expired and whether it was issued by a trusted CA. Clients maintain a list of trusted CA certificates to determine whether the received certificate should be trusted.

4. The client now creates a "premaster secret" to be used in this session. This secret is encrypted using the Public Key retrieved from the server's certificate and then sent to the server.

5. The server uses its Private Key to decrypt the premaster secret and then creates a master secret. The client also creates a master secret using the premaster secret.

6. The master secret is used by both to create keys for encrypting and decrypting information, as well as to detect any changes made by somebody during data transmission.

7. The client informs the server that it has been read and that it will encrypt messages using the Session Key. The server also sends a similar message to the client.

Once this is done, any data that is sent is encrypted before sending and decrypted before being used. The integrity of the data is also confirmed. For this the principles used are the same as those discussed above in the section on Public and Private Keys.

Servers and browsers have methods for enabling HTTPS (for using SSL communication) using the following steps:

1. Get a Private Key and a certificate containing the corresponding Public Key.

2. Install the certificate (your software should instruct you where the certificate is to be installed).

3. Enable SSL features and make the software aware of the files containing the certificate and your Private Key.

You can get more information about integrating SSL with your web server at *http://www.modssl.org/*

Message Digests

In addition to encryption provided by SSL, you can also take some programmatic measures to ensure data integrity, that is, detection of data altering along the way. One feature that can be of immense use here is a Message Digests. A Message Digest is a hash value generated from a piece of data. It is a unique value that has been derived from the data. To derive the hash value from a given piece of data, you can use algorithms that work in such a way that the same hash value is generated whenever the algorithm is applied on that data. The chances of obtaining the same hash value from two different sets of data are extremely remote.

Now let's look at an example that shows how you can derive a unique hash value from a given set of data. The class HashCreator has a String called sharedSecret, which contains a secret value that should be shared only with other parties who want to determine integrity of data sent by you.

We are using the **java.security package**. This contains a class called MessageDigest. We get an instance of the class using the static method **getInstance()**.

Our class contains a method **generate()**, which takes a String argument as input. It then generates a hash value based on this input String and sends the resulting hash as the output.

In the **generate()** method we are getting an instance of MessageDigest. We have specified that we want to use the MD5 algorithm for creating the hash. But before calculating the hash, we're appending our secret String to the input String. MessageDigest contains a method called **digest()**, which generates the Message Digest. Since this method takes a byte array as input, we create a byte array using the **getBytes()** method of String. This byte array is then fed to the Message Digest instance, and the resulting hash value is converted to a String before being returned.

```java
import java.security.*;
public class HashCreator
{
    private String sharedSecret = "mySharedSecret1999";
    public String generate(String s)
    {
        String theHash = "";
        try{
            MessageDigest md;
            md = MessageDigest.getInstance("MD5");
            String hashSeed = s + sharedSecret;
            byte[] seedBytes = hashSeed.getBytes();
            byte[] theHashBytes = md.digest(seedBytes);
            theHash = new String(theHashBytes);
        }catch(Exception ex){}
        return theHash;
    }
}
```

Now let us see how this type of functionality can be used. Let's say you are transmitting a piece of data to somebody and want to make sure that if anybody changes the data before it reaches the destination, the receiver should be able to detect this. In addition to sending the data itself, you can send the generated hash value as well.

At the receiver's end, the hash will again be computed based on the input data and the shared secret String (it is assumed that both the sender and the receiver have agreed to using a shared secret String that is not known to anybody else). The generated hash will be compared with the sent hash value. If they match, it means that nobody along the way tampered with the data. If they don't, some problem has been detected and appropriate action can be taken.

One situation in which you could use this system is when you're informing the credit card validation company about the amount that needs to be charged. When you call the company's URL, you can send this hash value as an additional parameter. The company can then confirm that the amount it has received is correct.

Password Security

In the software world, passwords play a big role. A password is the equivalent of a key. If somebody else gets hold of it, you can easily be taken for a ride. It is very important to choose cryptic passwords—your last name or birth date are poor choices. A combination of different types of characters is usually considered good. Also, you should not write down passwords where they can be accessed by others.

Since this system is to be used by customers who may not be very computer savvy, it is very important to let them know the importance of a password. It is equally important to put up a security page on your Web site that customers can read so that they can understand the security implications.

Some Hints on Making the Applications Secure

- You should not display passwords openly in your applications.

- You may want to avoid displaying the credit card numbers. This is a tricky user interface issue, though; credit card numbers are typically long, and if they are presented in a Password dialog box (as opposed to a text box), the chances of users error are higher.

- If you are storing confidential information, it is always a good idea to encrypt it. That way, even if a hacker breaks into your database containing customers' credit card numbers, (s)he would have to break your encryption to retrieve the numbers. You may even consider not storing credit card numbers at all.

- While it is a good idea to allow users to modify their data through an update profile system, you should think carefully about what data users should be able to modify directly. For instance, you may not want them to modify their shipping address without the intervention of your customer support. Or you may put some more authentication logic in the application that asks for additional questions like date of birth, etc,. to verify the identity of the person trying to modify sensitive data.

- Whenever an order is placed, you can check for the total amount and see if it exceeds a certain limit. In such cases you can put a hold on the shipping and contact the customer to confirm.

- Changing passwords, including database passwords, on a regular basis is a good idea. Note that you may have to change your applications accordingly to accommodate these password changes, but this step is very important.

- You can also write some software that monitors your systems for potential trouble-makers. Here's a simple Java program that runs every hour. It contains a **security-Check()** method that you can implement. With this method you can do things like monitoring the database to see how many people have placed an order in the last hour. If the number is much higher than average, the method should flag somebody who can attend to this potential problem. Depending on the severity of the problem, this method may also force a shutdown of the site or the database or take some such drastic steps.

```java
public class SecurityMonitor
{
    public static void main(String[] args)
    {
        try{
            while(true)
            {
                securityCheck();
                Thread.sleep(60*60*60);
            }
        }catch(Exception ex){ex.printStackTrace();}
    }
    public static void securityCheck()
    {
        // Perform security checks here and flag somebody if
        //  suspicious activity is discovered
    }
}
```

Performance

*A friend challenged me to improve the performance of his slow 386,
so I dropped it from the eighth floor—and it went really fast!*

As a developer of an e-commerce system, you will have to play a major role in making sure that the system works well in a production environment. The normal tendency while developing applications is to work in a stand-alone environment. However, the real test comes when you make your applications available to the world. Under heavy load conditions, the performance of an application can be significantly different from its performance on an internal test machine.

Tuning applications and systems is an art that is acquired over time. However, there are a few basic principles that you can adhere to right from the start. Before writing the applications you must identify the potential bottlenecks. Applications that do a lot of I/O (database accesses or file system read/writes) belong in this category. You should identify how these can be made more efficient and try to reduce the number of I/O accesses.

As the data in your database grows bigger, the database system itself may start becoming a bottleneck. Check your SQL statements to make sure they are optimized. Columns that are queried frequently should be indexed so that data retrieval is faster. It would be good to obtain the help of an experienced database administrator to tune your database.

The machines and other software you're using (like the Operating System) need to be tuned to achieve optimal performance. In this respect you need to configure your machines according to the purpose for which they are being used. For instance, the configuration for your mail server machine might be quite different from one running applications. The difference is because the two would require different resources. One might be memory-intensive, while the other might be CPU-intensive. A good system administrator can go a long way toward making the machine work in full gear.

Another area of concern is your connectivity to the Internet. If you want customers to have fast access to your servers, you should be using a good network connection. Two important items in determining the speed of your connection are the upload and download speeds. The download speed determines how quickly you can download material from the Internet, which is important if you want to use your machine for surfing the Net. But if you want your business to be accessed by others on the Net, you should be concerned instead about the upload speed (the speed with which a customer would be able to access your site). The companies that can provide you with an Internet connection should tell you both the upload and download speeds they're offering. Normally the upload speed is much lower than the download speed, but you can get good connectivity by paying a higher price. In deciding the speed you want to have, you should be guided by the network traffic you expect on your site. You can begin with a cheap option and upgrade as the need arises.

With this background in mind, let's now look at some concrete steps you can take. In most of these cases you may want to get help from a system administrator and/or database administrator.

Finding and Fixing Bottlenecks

Memory

Memory plays an important role in the performance of a system. If memory usage is 100 percent or even close, this will definitely be one of your bottlenecks. Memory may be consumed by your applications or by some other software (including your database). Make sure that all your applications are freeing up resources that are not required. Fortunately, Java does its own memory management. Unlike C, in which you have to deallocate memory yourself, the JVM takes care of garbage collection for you. However, this will not help if you have an application bug that is causing a Vector or Hashtable to grow infinitely. Another thing to check is your database parameters. Databases can end up eating a lot of memory if not configured properly.

It is quite possible that even after tuning other things, your memory utilization will not go down. This means you need to add more memory. Check the amount of swap space. On most systems the recommended swap space is at least twice the size of your regular memory.

CPU

The CPU (Central Processing Unit) is the brain of your machine. It is a good idea to monitor it every now and then to make sure it is not loaded. A general rule is that your CPUs should not have an idle time of zero. Idle time is the time that your CPU has in which it is capable of handling more instructions.

Memory bottlenecks and disk bottlenecks can be the cause of CPU overloading. Another problem area could be your applications that are performing CPU-intensive calculations. Bug-ridden applications can cause a CPU to spin off. You need to identify such applications and fix them.

If CPU use is very high even after these problems are fixed, chances are you will have to add more CPUs to your server.

Disk I/O

Disk manufacturers provide you with disk specifications, which include the maximum recommended I/O transactions per second. You should monitor the disks to see if this number is being exceeded. Another thing to look at is the distribution of load across the disks. If one of the disks is overloaded and another is not, the fault probably lies with your disk controller. Otherwise you need to add more disks. Also, you should look at your applications to see if you can somehow reduce the disk I/O. Databases do a lot of disk I/O. You should read the database manuals to see how you can configure multiple disks to get optimal performance from the database.

Some Unix Commands

Here are some Unix commands that can help you identify bottlenecks. Note that detailed description is beyond the scope of the book, but you can get more information by reading your system manuals and by looking at man pages.

mpstat—shows usage of each CPU ("idl" shows idle time for CPU—if this is near 0 you have a problem).

Example output:

CPU minf mjf xcal intr ithr csw icsw migr smtx srw syscl usr sys wt idl

  0   5 6   0 413 190 206 17   0   0   6 87   9 4 13 75

vmstat—shows virtual memory usage.

Example output:

procs   memory   page   disk   faults   cpu

r b w   swap free re mf pi po fr de sr s0 s1 s4 s6   in   sy   cs us sy id

0 0 37 2664 1312   3   5 138 160 193 0 42 1 0 18 0 313 87 206 9 4 88

swap -a to add swap space
swap -l to view swap space

   It will show you the total number of blocks allocated for swap space, as well as the number of free blocks still available. If this number is too low, you can add more swap space or more memory (or both).

iostat—"tps" tells us average number of disk transactions per second (for each disk)

Example output:

   tty   sd0   sd1   sd4   sd6   cpu

tin tout Kps tps serv Kps tps serv Kps tps serv Kps tps serv us sy wt id

  0   5 12 1 19   4 0 21 284 18 18   0 0 29 9 4 13 75

ps—shows what percentage of CPU is being used by each application (including the database), and also the memory usage of each application.

Some Suggestions

Network

- Move database closer to the application server. This will reduce the time it takes for an application to connect to the database.
- Get better Internet connectivity with high upload speed.
- Reduce network accesses by reducing I/O activity and database accesses.

- Use multiple servers with a network router that routes customers to different machines.
- Replicate the site on multiple servers—each site can cater to one or more regions.

Databases

If you expect a very high database usage, you can use distributed databases. Some database companies, such as Oracle, support distributed databases. In all probability you would not have to change your applications to make use of the distributed option. Use some analysis methods to see how SQL commands can be tuned. Look at the EXECUTION PLAN and ANALYZE commands that come with Oracle. Make good use of indexes; they can be a tremendous help in improving response time from SQL statements.

Applications

Use distributed technologies such as CORBA/RMI.

Have different applications on different machines to reduce overloading of one machine.

Look into using stored procedures if applications that require execution of a number of SQL statements can be grouped.

Stress Test Tools

Use stress test tools that can pound your applications at a fast rate, simulating a real-world environment.

A company called RSW Software makes an e-Test software that is easy to use and can be configured for heavy load testing. For more information, see *www.rswsoftware.com*.

Several other companies build similar tools, and it is a good idea to evaluate them.

Part IV

Chapter 10

System Design

Introduction

In previous chapters we looked at different technologies that can be used for building complex, Web-based systems. This section of the book uses those technologies to create several such systems.

In this chapter we look at the overall design of the system. Since this is a database-oriented system, the first thing that needs to be designed is the set of tables and sequences that will be used. After looking at some requirements, we will create the necessary tables and sequences, which will form the backbone of the system. The tables and sequences will be used by the systems that we develop in the following chapters. This chapter assumes you have working knowledge of SQL. If that is not the case, we recommend that you go back and read the relevant part of Chapter 6.

We are going to develop five different, interrelated systems. Some systems help in gathering and updating information, while others merely read the information. So what are these systems?

Inventory Management System

The first system is an Inventory Management System. This allows you to manage the products that your company sells. The system will be built so that all product information is stored in the database. The catalog that is presented to customers when they're looking for products will be dynamically generated from the latest contents in the database. The advantage here is that any changes you make to your product list will be effective immediately, thus giving customers immediate access to the latest information.

Let us look at a few goals of this system. First, it should allow you to specify a name and price for the product. The name is the one that is displayed to a customer; the price is used for internal calculations. You can store the unit price of each product here. However, you may want to display the price to your customers in a slightly different format. For example, you may be selling tomatoes at $4.80/5 lbs. Your unit price is thus $0.96/lb. This means that in the table for product information you need two columns for price, one for the display price and the other for the actual unit price.

While displaying the product, it is a good idea to provide a link to more detailed information about it. This link could be an HTML page containing information and/or pictures of the product, which would enable customers to analyze your products before they decide to buy them. If you are selling some software, this HTML page could actually be a virtual demo of the product and/or its technical specifications.

At the same time you need an internal description of the product. This information—perhaps special notes about the product or some other relevant information—can be used internally in the company.

When you make a product available for sale in your shop, you need to have an idea of the quantity you currently have. You therefore need a column for storing this information. Of course the whole system needs to be designed so that you can add or subtract from this quantity as your stock increases or decreases.

You may also want to be warned if the quantity falls below a certain level, so that you can reorder well in advance and not lose business due to lack of stock.

And who does the warning go to? You can store an email address along with the product information so that a warning email can be generated when the danger level is reached.

We will also develop a search subsystem as part of the ordering system. This would allow customers to look for specific items by typing in a search keyword. For this you need to have a column in your products table that can store these keywords.

In addition we can maintain some administrative data so that we know exactly who modified details about a product and when. This data can be used as a tracking tool.

But one very big element is missing in this design, namely, the ability to have specific categories of products. In most stores goods are organized in certain categories. Thus, if you go to a bookstore, there will be a magazines category, a books category and so on. These categories often have subcategories for more specific organization. For example, the magazines section may have a sports category, a fashion category, an arts category, etc. All these things are designed to make it easier for customers to find what they are looking for. Imagine going into a 4,000 square feet bookstore in which all magazines, books, and periodicals were stacked on top of each other in no particular order.

Similarly, we need to add the concept of categories to our system, for which we need a separate categories table. We will need to modify the products table so it can belong to a particular category. In the system presented a product can belong to only one category. However, you can extend it to belong to multiple categories. We will discuss that possibility briefly toward the end of this section.

Since some categories overlap (sports magazines belong to the magazines category), the categories table must be designed to accommodate this scenario. In a sense a category is like a product. It has a name and a description. You may also want it to contain the location of an HTML page that describes it and can be presented to a customer. A category should be searchable, which means you need to be able to store keywords associated with the category. Also, as you would with a product, you may want to track who modified the category last and when.

With this background we can look at the actual tables. First, take a look at SQL for creating the products table.

```
CREATE TABLE products
    (id                  NUMBER PRIMARY KEY,
    category_id          NUMBER CONSTRAINT cat_fkey REFERENCES
                            categories,
    name                 VARCHAR2(100),
    description_url      VARCHAR2(100),
    email                VARCHAR2(50), - email address for reporting
                            problems
    price                NUMBER(10, 2),
    display_price        VARCHAR2(20),
    quantity_in_stock   NUMBER,
    danger_level         NUMBER, - percentage of quantity_in_stock
    description          VARCHAR2(1000),
    search_keywords     VARCHAR2(200),
    last_modified_by    VARCHAR2(100),
    last_modification_date   DATE
    );
```

The first field is an id. As you will see, all tables that we create will contain an id field. This field is supposed to contain a unique number so that the row in the table can be uniquely identified. It can also be used for establishing foreign key relationships. In all cases this field has been defined as the primary key of the table, because a large number of queries will use the id, by making it a primary key, we can achieve optimization.

We will create a sequence called **products_seq** to be used for populating values for this field.

```
CREATE SEQUENCE products_seq START WITH 1;
```

The **category_id** field establishes the relationship each product has to a category. As mentioned above, we will assign each product to a category. **category_id** will contain the id of the category to which it belongs. So if you have a category called Fruits, which has an id of 200, then the product Grapes will have **category_id = 200**. Both id and **category_id** are of the type NUMBER. **category_id** has been declared a foreign key for the categories table.

name contains the name of the product. **description_url** contains the URL of an HTML page that contains description for customers. **email** contains the address to which an email should be sent when quantities fall below danger level. These three fields are of the type VARCHAR.

price contains the unit price of each product. It has been declared as NUMBER(10, 2), which means that the price will be a max of 10 digits and will have a precision of 2. Thus, if you try to store 99.057, the database will store it as 99.06.

display_price is the price that is displayed to customers. **quantity_in_stock**, which is a number, contains the available quantity. As people purchase products, this number will automatically be decremented. **danger_level** contains the danger mark for product quantity.

description is an internal description of the product. **search_keywords** contains keywords that you may enter. When a customer tries to do a search in your system, this field will be looked up.

last_modified_by will contain the username of the user who last modified the product. **last_modification_date**, which is a DATE field, will contain the date and time when the modification was made.

The categories table is as follows:

```
CREATE TABLE categories
   (id                  NUMBER PRIMARY KEY,
    category_id         NUMBER CONSTRAINT cat_cat_fkey
                        REFERENCES categories,
                -- a category can belong to another
                -- eg. Cans belong to Food which belongs to Grocery
                -- Cans would have Garbanzo beans as product
                -- Top levels have id = 0
    has_sub_categories NUMBER,
                -- 0 if it contains products, 1 if sub_categories
    name                VARCHAR2(100),
    description_url     VARCHAR2(100),
    description         VARCHAR2(1000),
    search_keywords     VARCHAR2(200),
    last_modified_by    VARCHAR2(100),
    last_modification_date  DATE
   );
```

Here id will be populated by a sequence called **categories_seq**, created as follows:

```
CREATE SEQUENCE categories_seq START WITH 1;
```

Since we are allowing a category to belong to another category, we have a field called **category_id** in this table. This field contains the id of the category to which a particular category belongs. If Magazines has an id of 500, then the **category_id** field of Sports Magazines would be 500.

At this point it is important to understand that categories can be either terminal or nonterminal. A terminal category is one with no subcategories. It can only contain products in it. Thus, Fruits might be a terminal category, as it can contain Oranges, Bananas, etc., which are the final products you are selling.

A nonterminal category, on the other hand, is one that does not contain any products, just other categories. Magazines, for example, is a nonterminal category, as it contains several subcategories.

Nonterminal categories are also of two types, though the distinction is minor. We have divided them into a set of categories that are at the top of the hierarchy and another set that belongs to a lower level. The top-level ones have a category_id of 0. This distinction is necessary, because when a person first comes to the site you may want to display only the top-level categories, rather than cluttering up the screen with all the different categories. So instead of finding an endless list consisting of Magazines, Books, Sports Magazines, Fiction, Nonfiction, Arts Magazines, and so on, you can present just Magazines and Books, and users then can drill down the paths they are interested in.

has_sub_categories is just a field of convenience. This field contains 0 if the category is a terminal category; otherwise, its value is 1. This will help us in optimizing our queries (since there would be quite a few queries in which we would want to look at only terminal categories).

The rest of the fields—name, description, etc.—are the same as required in the products table.

Things to Think About

These fields and sequences should be enough to develop a reasonably flexible inventory management system. Based on your needs, you can add or remove some fields. Here are some suggestions about things that can be done to meet some other needs.

If you want a product to belong to multiple categories, you can establish a many-to-many table relationship. One way of doing this is to create another table that contains the id of both the product and the category or categories to which it belongs. You don't need the **category_id** field in the products table any longer. The new table would look like this:

```
CREATE TABLE product_categories(
    product_id        NUMBER,
    categories_id     NUMBER);
```

Here "product_id" is the id of a product and "categories_id" is the id of the category to which it belongs. So, if you have a product A with id 22 that belongs to category C1 (id 100) and category C2 (id 101), the rows in the "product_categories" table would look like this:

product_id	categories_id
22	100
22	101

To find out categories to which your product belongs, your statement would be like this:

```
SELECT categories_id FROM product_categories WHERE product_id=22;
```

Depending on business requirements, another field you may want to add to products and categories tables is one that determines whether the product or category is available for customers. This may be a requirement if you want to keep all products in the database irrespective of whether they are available or not. For example, you may want to discontinue a product for a short period of time.

The system only tracks the person who last modified a product or category. If you want, you can create a history table that contains a history of all modifications made. Here is what this table would look like:

```
CREATE TABLE modification_history(
        product_or_category_id      NUMBER,
        modification_date           DATE,
        modified_by                 VARCHAR2(20));
```

Profile Management System

This system is customer-oriented. It allows customers to register themselves on your site and create a profile. Information that is typically required from a customer includes first name, last name, and address. If you want to have a credit card–based system, you may decide to store customers' credit card information so that they don't have to enter it every time they buy something. This system also needs to provide enough self-service utility to enable customers to manage their own profile. There would be times when they would like to change their address or use a new credit card. The system needs to provide an interface for allowing this.

Our ordering system is designed to allow customers to establish an identity with the store in form of a username and password. Every time they want to purchase something or browse around the site, they need to enter this username and password. These two elements thus need to be tracked along with other profile information.

Here is the SQL for creating a profile:

```
CREATE TABLE profiles
    (id                 NUMBER PRIMARY KEY,
     username           VARCHAR2(20) CONSTRAINT  uq_user UNIQUE,
     password           VARCHAR2(20),
     registration_date  DATE,
     first_name         VARCHAR2(30),
     last_name          VARCHAR2(30),
     phone              VARCHAR2(30),
     fax                VARCHAR2(30),
     email              VARCHAR2(30),
     ccard_num          VARCHAR2(20),
     ccard_exp_date     DATE,
     ccard_company      VARCHAR2(20),          -- Visa,Mastercard etc.
```

```
    status              VARCHAR2(20)    -- NEW_USER
    );
```

As always, we have an id field that gets its value from a sequence, in this case

```
CREATE SEQUENCE profiles_seq START WITH 1;
```

username and **password** fields contain the login information about the **customer. registration_date** is a DATE field that contains the date on which a person first registered on this site. New users begin by entering a username and password of their choice. As a result, a record is created in the profiles table. When a user tries to buy something, remaining information such as name, address, etc., is asked. But if users don't reach the buying stage, you could end up with a large number of profiles that are incomplete. You can use the registration date to purge these profiles periodically to recover some database space. The registration date can also help you track how many new users are coming in on a weekly or monthly basis.

first_name, **last_name**, **phone**, **fax**, and **email** contain the corresponding information. **ccard_num**, **ccard_exp_date**, and **ccard_company** contain information about the credit card.

status field contains the current status the user is in. When a new user comes in (the stage when the profile is incomplete), we're storing the value **NEW_USER** in this field. When the user has updated the records with other information, this field is updated to **UPDATED_USER**. This helps us distinguish between incomplete and complete records.

One thing missing here is the address. The reason for this is that we want to make the system flexible. A person can have multiple addresses—the shipping address could be different from the mailing address, for example. However, the structure of both addresses would be the same: a street name, a city, a state, and a zip code. As such, creating separate fields for each type of address would not be a good design. Instead, we've created a separate addresses table and have added a type field to it that contains the type of address a record contains. This could be SHIPPING or MAILING or anything else. Thus, if a new type of address needs to be added in the future, you won't have to modify your database.

This is how the addresses table is created:

```
CREATE TABLE addresses
    (id              NUMBER PRIMARY KEY,
    profile_id      NUMBER CONSTRAINT profile_fkey REFERENCES profiles,
    type            VARCHAR2(10),
    line1           VARCHAR2(100),
    line2           VARCHAR2(100),
    city            VARCHAR2(100),
    state           VARCHAR2(20),
    zip             VARCHAR2(20)
    );
```

The id gets its value from the **addresses_seq** sequence:

```
CREATE SEQUENCE addresses_seq START WITH 1;
```

profile_id provides the linkage between a profile and the corresponding addresses. **type** contains SHIPPING or MAILING depending on the type of address, so a person whose profile id is 21 would have two records in the addresses table that would look like this:

```
id      profile_id    type      line1 .......
10        21         SHIPPING        .....
11        21          MAILING        .....
```

Things to Think About

If you anticipate capturing other telecom information in the future—cell phone number, pager number, or any future communication device—you may consider putting phone, fax, and email in a separate table. This would be something similar to the concept we've applied to addresses. The new table could look like this:

```
CREATE TABLE telecom_address(
    id                  NUMBER,
    profile_id          NUMBER,
    value               VARCHAR2(100),
    type                VARCHAR2(20));
                        -- eg. PHONE, FAX, EMAIL, CELL
```

Just as we created a history table in the Inventory Management System, you may want to create a table for storing the history of modifications made by users to their profile.

Ordering Management System

This system allows customers to view your products/categories and purchase. It keeps track of all orders placed by customers and payments received. The system uses tables created in the systems above, in addition to having its own set of tables and sequences. Besides allowing orders to be placed, the Ordering System also allows some amount of personalization. For example, it permits customers to establish a list of regularly purchased items in a reusable shopping cart. Users can assign products that they buy regularly to a personal cart. Next time(s) they visit the site, they can retrieve items from the regular cart rather than having to browse all the categories and products, and thus get their shopping done at a fast pace.

For each order we need to store the total amount that was charged to the customer, the date the order was placed, and the status of the order (whether it has been shipped or not). In addition, we need to store the list of products that were purchased. Since prices of a product may vary over a period of time, we will store the price at which the product was purchased by the customer and the quantity that was purchased.

Here is the SQL for achieving all these things:

```
CREATE TABLE orders
   (id               NUMBER PRIMARY KEY,
    profile_id       NUMBER CONSTRAINT prof_key REFERENCES profiles,
    date_ordered     DATE,
    date_shipped     DATE,
    shipment_method  VARCHAR2(20),
    status           VARCHAR2(30),
                  -- WITH_SHIPPING_DEPARTMENT, SHIPPED,
                     INCORRECT_ADDRESS
    payment_received NUMBER,
    total_billed     NUMBER(10, 2)
   );
```

A record in this table represents one order made by a customer. Here id is a unique number that is generated from the following sequence:

```
CREATE SEQUENCE orders_seq START WITH 1;
```

profile_id links an order to a person. It contains the id of a record in the profiles table discussed under the Profile Management System.

date_ordered is the date on which the order was placed. **date_shipped** is initially NULL, but when the order has been shipped, this field is updated by the shipping system. The shipping system also updates the **shipment_method** field, which could contain values like UPS, FedEx, etc.

status contains the current status of the order. Initially, an order is listed as WITH_SHIPPING_DEPARTMENT, which means that the order has been accepted and has been forwarded to the shipping department of the company. Once the shipping department has shipped it, the field is updated to contain the value SHIPPED. You may enter any other status into this field to help track where the order is in the process. For instance, if the shipment is returned because of a wrong address, you could update the status field to reflect this.

A field **payment_received** has been placed. This is a number field in which you put the value 1 if payment has been received. For a credit card–based system you would create a record in the orders table after the credit card has been verified, so this field may in fact always show 1. However, if you want to switch to other systems such as accepting checks, the order may be in a state in which it is waiting to clear. In those cases this field can be of great use.

total_billed contains the total amount that the customer was charged.

To store information about each individual product that was purchased as part of this order, we use a table called **one_order**.

```
CREATE TABLE one_order   -- order is a reserved word
  (id            NUMBER PRIMARY KEY,
   orders_id     NUMBER CONSTRAINT ord_fkey REFERENCES orders,
   product_id    NUMBER CONSTRAINT prod_fkey REFERENCES products,
   quantity      NUMBER,
   price         NUMBER(10, 2));
```

The reason we've named it **one_order** and not simply "order" is that "order" is a reserved SQL word.

Once again, the value of id comes from a sequence:

```
CREATE SEQUENCE one_order_seq START WITH 1;
```

orders_id provides a linkage between a record in this table and the order to which it belongs; **product_id** contains the id of a particular product that was purchased; "quantity" is the quantity that was purchased; and "price" reflects the unit price at which it was bought.

An order thus consists of a record in the orders table and one or more records in the **one_order** table, each of which contains information about a particular product that was purchased.

The Ordering System also allows customers to maintain their own carts containing items that are ordered regularly. This capability saves them the hassle of selecting the same items every week (or whatever the buying frequency is). From the system's point of view, it requires a method of storing information about each user's regular cart. For this we have created a table called **regular_cart**.

```
CREATE TABLE regular_cart
  (id            NUMBER PRIMARY KEY,
   profile_id    NUMBER CONSTRAINT prf_fkey REFERENCES profiles,
   product_id    NUMBER CONSTRAINT prd_fkey REFERENCES products,
   quantity      NUMBER
  );
```

The value of id comes from the sequence:

```
CREATE SEQUENCE regular_cart_seq START WITH 1;
```

The **regular_cart** table contains zero, one, or more records for each profile. **profile_id** shows the profile to which this cart item belongs, **product_id** is the id of the product that belongs to the cart, and quantity is the quantity of this product that the person regularly buys. When customers request items from their regular cart, the records in this table are checked. All records that have the **profile_id** of the person logged into the system are retrieved and displayed.

Things to Think About

If your store is such that people don't buy items on a regular basis, you may want to get rid of the regular cart concept. On the other hand, if you have a store in which there are several different departments and people want to maintain separate carts for each department, you may want to add a **department_id** field to the regular cart, so that only relevant carts are displayed. This would provide further granularity for customers.

Other Systems

Other available systems are the Reporting and Shipping Systems. These systems don't really need to have tables of their own. The Shipping System is mainly concerned with the orders table that we defined in the Ordering System. People in your shipping department need to view pending orders and update them when an event like "shipped" or "invalid address" occurs.

The Reporting System creates reports based on records stored in the database. As such, it does not need to enter any information into the database. It just needs to retrieve the information and display it, using the tables created in the Profile Management System and the Ordering System.

Conclusion

This completes our discussion of the underlying database architecture of the system. This architecture acts as the foundation of all the systems, so you need to become thoroughly familiar with it in order to understand the implementation of the systems. Figure 10.1 provides a quick recap of the database for reference.

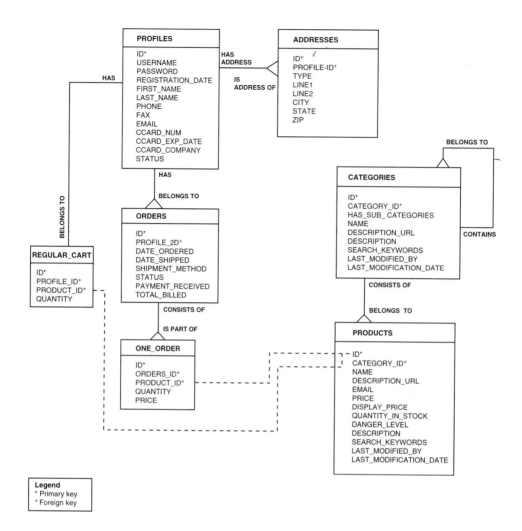

Figure 10.1

Chapter 11

Functionality

Introduction

This chapter looks at all the systems we are going to design from an end user's perspective. This chapter is like the functional specifications of a software system. We will see different screens that are presented to users and the functionality offered by the systems. We will walk through all the features of each of the five systems that will be built in the following chapters.

Note that for the sake of simplicity we have used a very rudimentary user interface. A fully finished system should look much more sophisticated than this. Appropriate use of graphics and coloring are required to make a site look professional. That topic, however, is beyond the scope of this book. You can refer to books on user interface designs for your site.

Inventory Management System

This system allows you to add all your products to the database and is used for maintaining your store's inventory in a database. It also enables you to organize the products in specific categories. You can add new categories and products. You may also modify and view them. In case you decide to discontinue some product or category, the system allows you to go in and delete it. All information is stored in the database and may be retrieved by other systems such as the Ordering System to build a catalog that is presented to customers.

Menu

This is a password-protected system that can be accessed only by users who have sufficient privileges. Figure 11.1 shows the entry point page of the system.

The figure shows the menu of the system. A Products menu allows you to add, modify, view, or delete products. The Categories menu enables you to add or delete categories. To make use of any of these features, you need to click on the appropriate link, but before that you need to provide a username and password so that validation can be implemented.

Adding a Category

Let us first take the path of **Categories->Add**. When you click on this link, you see the screen shown in Figure 11.2. This screen allows you to create a new category. A category is simply a way of organizing your products. Consider the case of a grocery store. Instead of haphazardly shelving different items, a grocery store arranges them in a specific order by creating appropriate aisles containing related items. The produce aisle contains fruits and vegetables, the poultry aisle contains chicken, and so on. You can think of Produce and Poultry as categories in which you want to put your products (apples and chicken, respectively).

In this screen you provide a name for the category, which also allows you to enter the path of a page that describes the category. This could be used to present details about your categories to customers. A category can belong to another category. So, Produce can contain a Fruits category and a Vegetables category, each of which would contain products (Bananas and Onions, respectively). The "Parent Category" section of the screen allows you to specify what category the current category falls under. There is one category present in the system by default. This is the TOP LEVEL category. All categories that have this as their parent are the ones that are displayed to customers when they first log into the Ordering Management System.

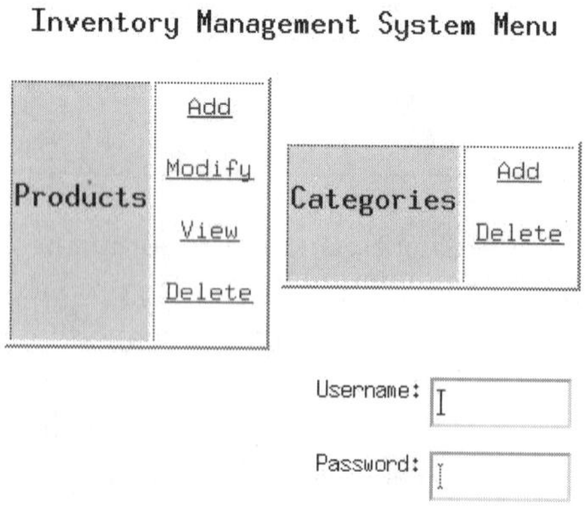

Figure   11.1

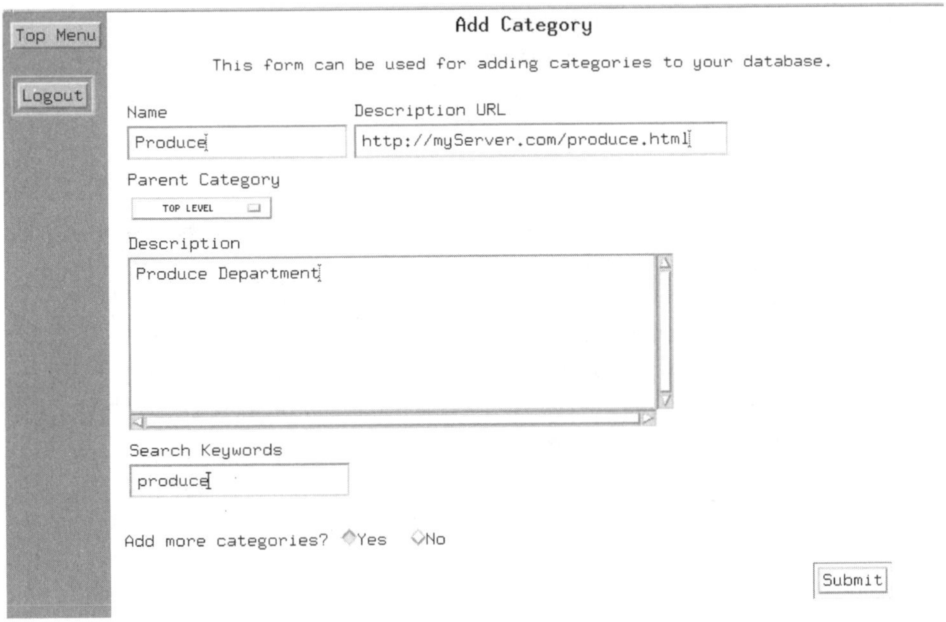

Figure 11.2

There is a text area called "description" in which you can store some internal information about the category. This is data that is never displayed to customers—it is for internal use only.

The Ordering Management System allows customers to search for specific items based on keywords they type in a search text box. The "Search Keywords" text field in this screen is where you enter the keywords against which searches will be performed for this category.

The "Add Category" link allows you to add more than one category in a session to save you the trouble of having to go back to the main menu and click on the link every time you want to add a new category. If you want to add more categories, you can check the Yes button when prompted, "Add more categories?"

After inputting all the information, you need to press the Submit button. If you opted to add more categories, another page, similar to this one, would appear and you could add more categories to the system.

Another thing to notice in this screen is the left portion. There are two buttons here: Top Menu and Logout. The first button takes you back to the main menu in Figure 11.1. The second logs you out of the system so that nobody can use the system from your machine without having to enter a username and password.

In the snapshot in Figure 11.2 we're adding a Produce category to the system that belongs to the top level. We've also checked the Yes button as we want to add more categories.

Once you have finished adding categories, you can check the No button and press Submit. A page similar to the one shown in Figure 11.3 will appear, confirming all the categories that you have added.

Adding a Subcategory

Now let us see how you would add a subcategory to an already existing category. For this, go to the main menu and click the "Add Category" link again. Now the "Parent Category" select list will offer Produce as one of the options (in addition to TOP LEVEL). So if you want to add a Vegetable subcategory, you can select its parent as Produce.

Figure 11.4 shows what the screen looks like.

Similarly, you can create any level of hierarchy consisting of categories and subcategories.

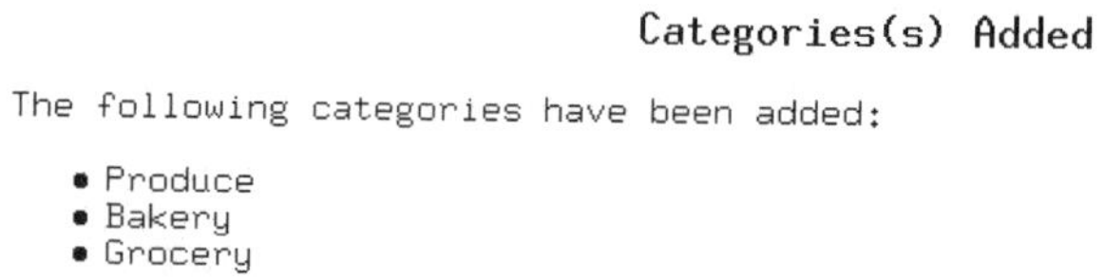

Categories(s) Added

The following categories have been added:

- Produce
- Bakery
- Grocery

Figure   11.3

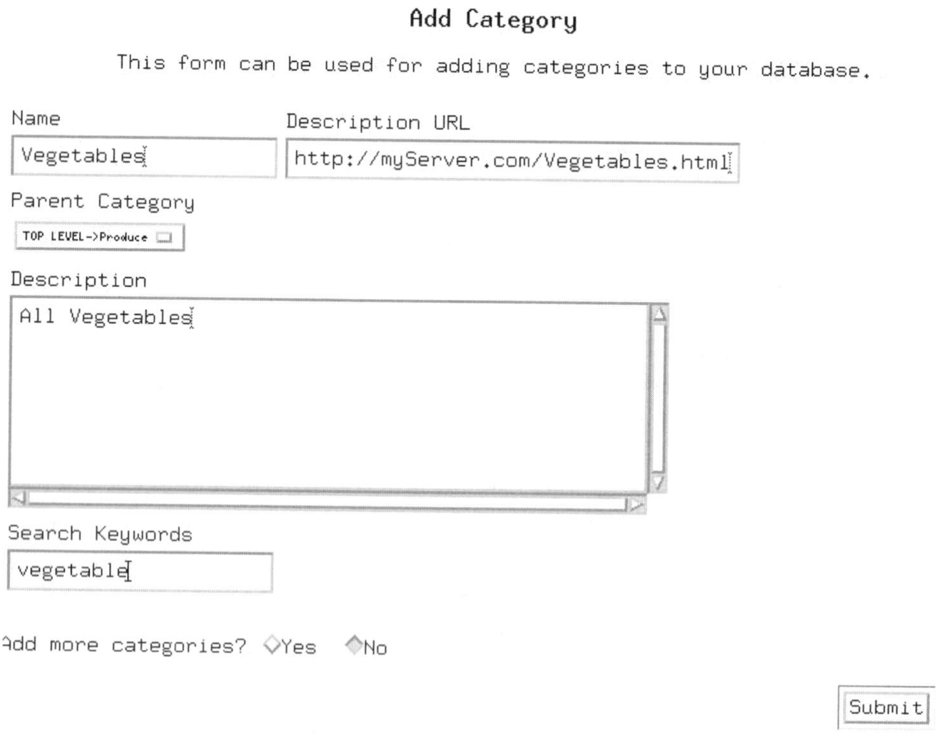

Add Category

This form can be used for adding categories to your database.

Name

Vegetables

Description URL

http://myServer.com/Vegetables.html

Parent Category

TOP LEVEL->Produce

Description

All Vegetables

Search Keywords

vegetable

Add more categories? ◇Yes   ◆No

Submit

Figure   11.4

Deleting Categories

You may also delete a category if it is no longer required. For this you need to click the **Categories->Delete** option.

On clicking this option you see the screen shown in Figure 11.5.

This list contains all the categories that you can delete. When you select the category and press the Submit button, the category will be removed from the system.

Note that the list contains only those categories that you can delete. If a category contains subcategories or products, you cannot delete it before the contents of the category are deleted. As a result, such categories will not be presented in the list.

Adding Products

Now that we have finished looking at the categories section, let's see how products can be added to the categories we have created. We begin by clicking the **Products->Add** link in the main menu. The page that comes up is shown in Figure 11.6.

A product has a name and a price. The price to be entered here is the unit price. However, this may be different from the price displayed to customers. You can also specify how many units of this product you have in stock in your warehouse. This is specified in the "Quantity in Stock" section of the page. The system also allows you to track whether the quantity of a product has fallen below a certain level, so that appropriate action can be taken in time. The "Danger Level" section of the form is where you specify the low-level mark. You can also specify the email address of a person or department to be informed about any problems with the product, such as falling quantities.

A product belongs to a category. In the example in Figure 11.6, we're adding the product Oranges to our system. The most appropriate category for it would be Fruits, which belongs to Produce, so we select this as the parent category. The Select list "Parent Category" contains all the categories to which products can be added.

The description URL field can be used for specifying a URL that describes the product. This can be presented as a link to customers who want more information.

Delete Category

Please select one category from the list below:

Figure   11.5

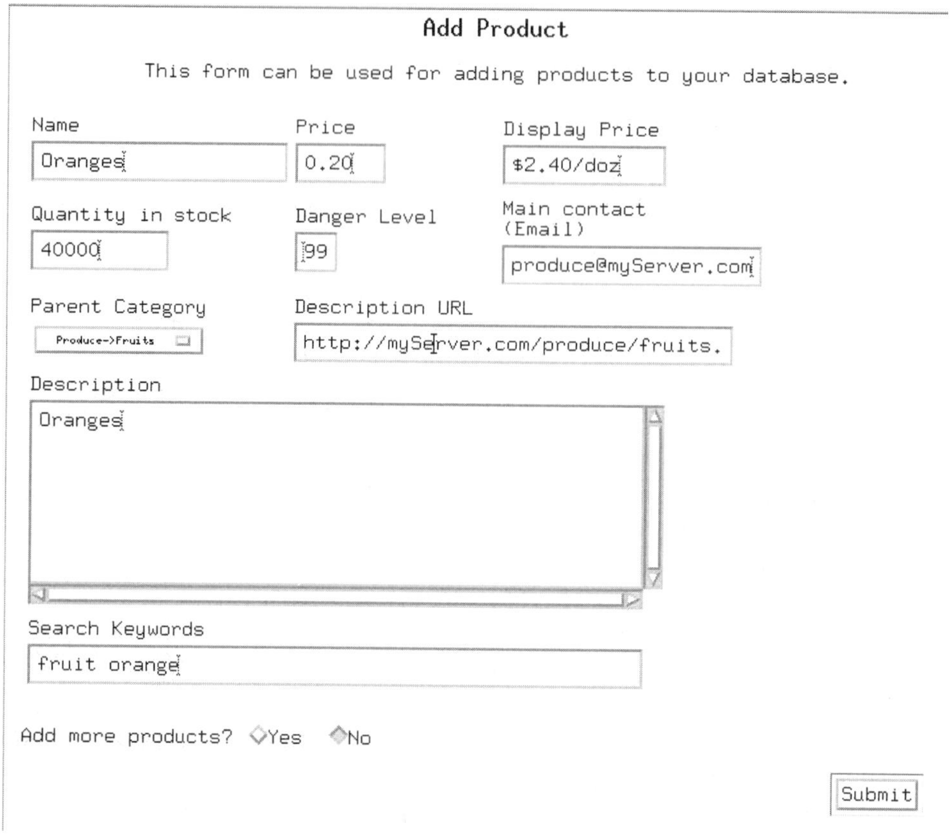

Add Product

This form can be used for adding products to your database.

Name | Price | Display Price
Oranges | 0.20 | $2.40/doz

Quantity in stock | Danger Level | Main contact (Email)
40000 | 99 | produce@myServer.com

Parent Category | Description URL
Produce->Fruits | http://myServer.com/produce/fruits.

Description

Oranges

Search Keywords

fruit orange

Add more products? ◇Yes ◆No

Submit

Figure 11.6

This link can be an HTML file containing, among other things, pictures of the product if applicable.

"Description" and "Search" keyword fields are as in the Categories section. Also, there is an "Add More" products checkbox that can be used for adding multiple products in one session.

Modifying Products

If you click on **Product->Modify**, **Product->Delete**, or **Product->View**, all the products in your system are displayed in a Select list. You can select one product at a time and view, modify, or delete it. A screen similar to the one shown in Figure 11.7 comes up when you select one of these options.

You need to select one product from this list. If you select Modify, hitting the Submit button will present details about the product. These details will be the ones you entered when you added the product (or when you modified it last). In addition they show who modified the product last and on what date it was modified (see Figure 11.8).

Modify Product

Please select one product from the list below:

Bananas
Oranges

Submit

Figure   11.7

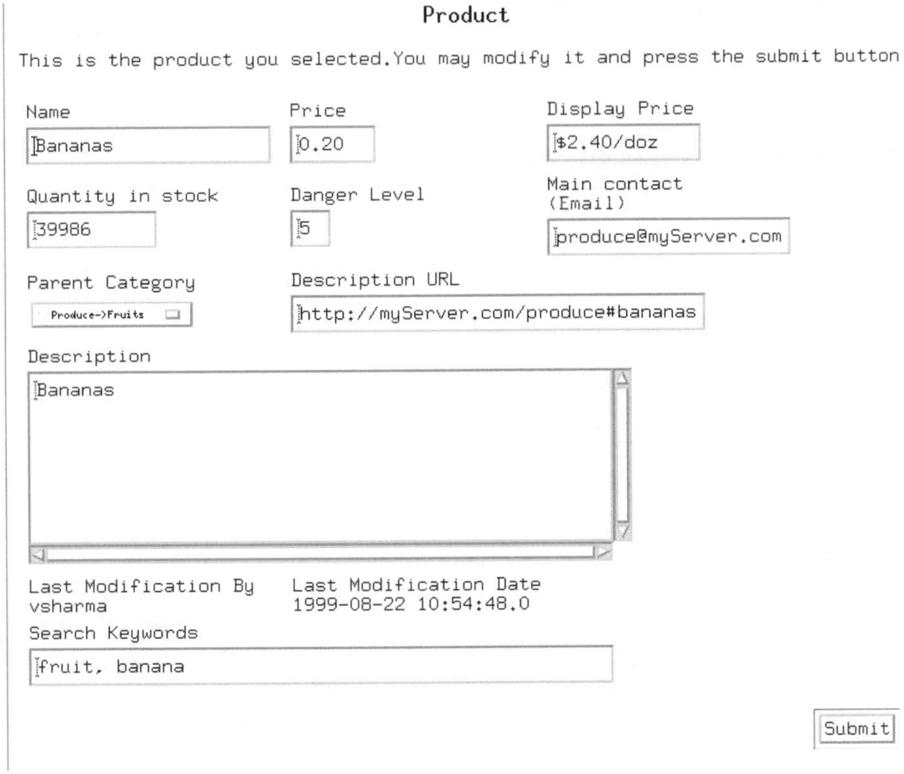

Product

This is the product you selected.You may modify it and press the submit button

Name   Price   Display Price

Bananas   0.20 $2.40/doz

Quantity in stock   Danger Level   Main contact
                                                       (Email)
39986   5   produce@myServer.com

Parent Category   Description URL

Produce->Fruits   http://myServer.com/produce#bananas

Description

Bananas

Last Modification By   Last Modification Date
vsharma   1999-08-22 10:54:48.0
Search Keywords

fruit, banana

Submit

Figure   11.8

You can change any of the values. When the Submit button is pressed, the database will be updated and new values will be stored. Next time you see this product, the updated values will be presented.

Once you've hit the Submit button, the following screen, shown in Figure 11.9, comes up, confirming the modification.

Here "Id" represents an internal id assigned to each product by the system.

```
                  Product Modified

The following product has been modified:

Id: 11
Name: Bananas
```

Figure   11.9

Viewing and Deleting Products

When you click on these options, a list of products appears (just as we saw when the
"Modify Product" option was clicked). You need to select one product. When you
press Submit, a Delete operation will delete the selected product from the system,
whereas View will display details about the product without letting you modify them.

Typical Usage Scenario

An authorized person selects the "Add Category" option and adds some categories.
That person can then add subcategories by coming back to the main menu and selecting "Add Category" again. Then the person comes back to the main menu and select
the "Add Product" option. One or more products are added to some categories, and
the person presses the Logout button to exit the system.

Another scenario could be one in which a person would come in and modify a
product or delete a product or category.

Ordering System

The Ordering System is a customer's view of your store, through which customers can
purchase products from you. Customers log in with a username and password, which
establishes the identity of each user. After the customers log in, a list of top-level categories is presented. Customers can then go down the aisles they are interested in and
look at products. They can add products they want to purchase to a shopping cart that
is displayed in a separate window. Every time a product is selected for purchase, it is
added to the checkout cart.

When they are done with their shopping, customers choose the checkout option,
which allows them to pay using a credit card.

The system also allows individual customers to maintain a personal cart containing
items that they buy on a regular basis. It also has a search option that allows customers
to look for specific products by typing in keywords.

Customers can also see a history of orders they have placed in the past using this
system.

Sign-In Page

This is the first page that customers see when they come to your ordering site (see Figure 11.10).

Users need to enter a username and password before they can see the ordering menu. Customers who have signed in before can enter the username and password they chose when they first signed in. This action helps bring up details about their regular cart and any ordering history they may have. First-time users can type in any username and password that they want to use. They also need to reenter the password in the confirm box as a precaution to ensure they have entered their password as intended (since characters are not displayed when a password is being entered, people can make mistakes).

Usernames are unique; no two users can have the same one. So if somebody types in a username that has already been selected, an error message needs to be thrown. Also, if a person types in the wrong password, (s)he needs to be informed. Figure 11.11 shows the screen that comes up if such an error occurs.

```
                              Welcome!

This is an example of an internet based shopping site.
Blah blah blah! In order to look at our catalog and to purchase items
you must sign in. If you have established a password with use
previousl you may enter your username and password below.
If you are a first time user, choose a username and a password easy
for you to remember. First time users will have to enter their
password twice (for confirmation).You may also enter a hint word that
would help you remember your password in case you forget.
```

All users		First time users	
Username	Ivsha		
		Confirm Password	I
Password	*		

```
                                          Ok
```

Figure   11.10

```
                       Error!

The following error occured:

Invalid username/password -
There is an account in the system with this username but with a
different password. If you are a new user, please select a different
username.
```

Figure   11.11

Ordering Menu

Upon signing in, a screen with two sections is presented (see Figure 11.12). The left frame shows the customer's options, whereas the right frame shows the top-level categories in your system.

Since we added Produce, Bakery, and Grocery as top-level categories in the Inventory Management System, these show up on the right screen. If you now add another top-level category, the next customer who logs in will see that additional category in the right frame.

If you click on any of these links, the system looks for any subcategories or products that belong to the category that was clicked. Those products and categories are displayed in this frame. We will look at this below.

All the options are present in the left frame. The first, "Categories," simply presents the top-level categories in the right frame, so if customers want to see the top-level categories in the right frame at any time, they should click the Categories button.

The contents of the customer's cart are displayed in a separate window. When the customer first logs in, the cart window comes up by itself. However, there is an option to dismiss it. The window can then be brought up later, by clicking the "Cart Contents" option.

The Checkout button takes the customer to where (s)he can pay. The "Personal Cart" option brings up the contents of the customer's personal cart, which you can be added to the checkout cart.

The Order History button helps customers view information about previous orders they have placed at this site.

The Search button allows them to look for specific products by typing in a keyword.

Now let's look at each of these options in more detail.

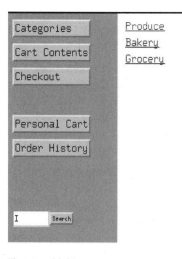

Figure 11.12

Adding Products to Checkout Cart

Let's say a customer wants to buy some fruit. First (s)he clicks on the Produce link to bring up the contents of the Produce category. In the Inventory Management System we added the Fruits and Vegetables subcategories to Produce, so these are displayed when the Produce link (see Figure 11.13) is clicked.

If the customer clicks on Fruits, the products in it (all fruits) are displayed (see Figure 11.14).

This screen shows Bananas and Oranges. Both the item names are presented as links. This is a link to the description URL that was specified when the product was

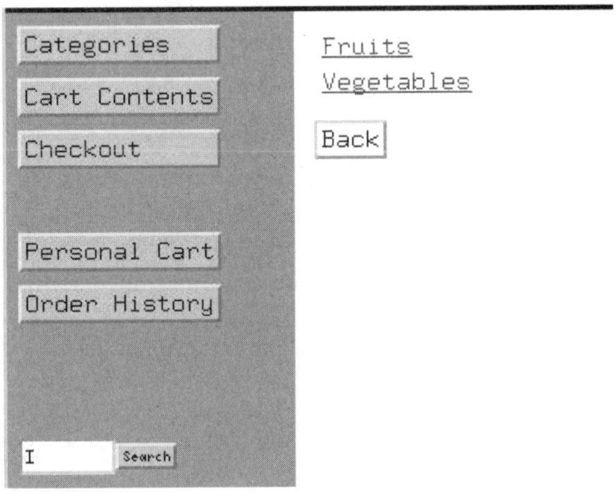

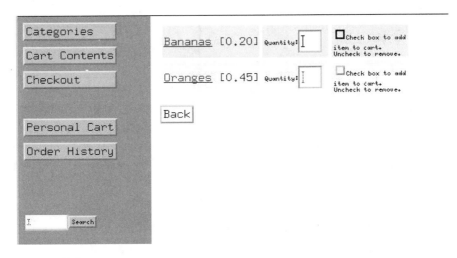

Figure   11.13

Figure   11.14

added using the Inventory Management System. If a user clicks on this link, the description URL is presented in a separate window.

The display price of the product is shown along with the name. Customers can specify the quantity they want to purchase by entering the amount in the text box. Once they have decided to buy the item, they can select the checkbox. Upon doing so, the contents of the cart are updated. To remove an item from the cart, they can uncheck this box.

The Back button allows the user to go back one screen.

Cart Contents

Items selected for purchase appear in a cart window. As shown in Figure 11.15, every time the customer adds or removes items, the cart is automatically updated.

The customer can press the Dismiss Window button if (s)he doesn't want the window to show, and can bring it back any time later on by pressing the Cart Contents button in the left frame menu.

Checkout

Once finished shopping, the customer can press the Checkout button. The next screen will show the items in the checkout cart and the total price. The customer may change the quantities of items at this stage and can also decide not to buy one or more of the items by setting the quantity to 0. Every time a change is made, the new total price appears when the Recalculate Total Price button is clicked.

Figure   11.15

There is a checkbox next to each item. If the product is not in the customer's regular cart, clicking on this checkbox will add it. If it already belongs in the regular cart, the customer can remove it by clicking on this checkbox.

Checkout for Existing Users

For existing users (customers whose profile was recorded by the system when they bought something from the site previously), the checkout screen looks as shown in Figure 11.16.

Since the system has already recorded their credit card information from the last time they purchased from this site, they have the option of using that credit card. Otherwise, they can select the "Another Card" option, which allows them to update their profile.

For new users, the checkout screen looks as shown in Figure 11.17—since we don't have their credit card number yet, the button says "Get Credit Card Info."

Once the credit card is processed, a thank-you page comes up containing the customer's username, order id, price billed, and list of items/prices purchased (see Figure 11.18). At the same time an email is sent to the shipping department informing it about the new order.

Personal Cart Option

If the customer clicks the "Personal Cart" option and has some items that were added to the regular cart earlier, those will now be displayed, and can be added to the checkout cart. The customer can also navigate and add more items to his or her checkout cart before checking out (see Figure 11.19).

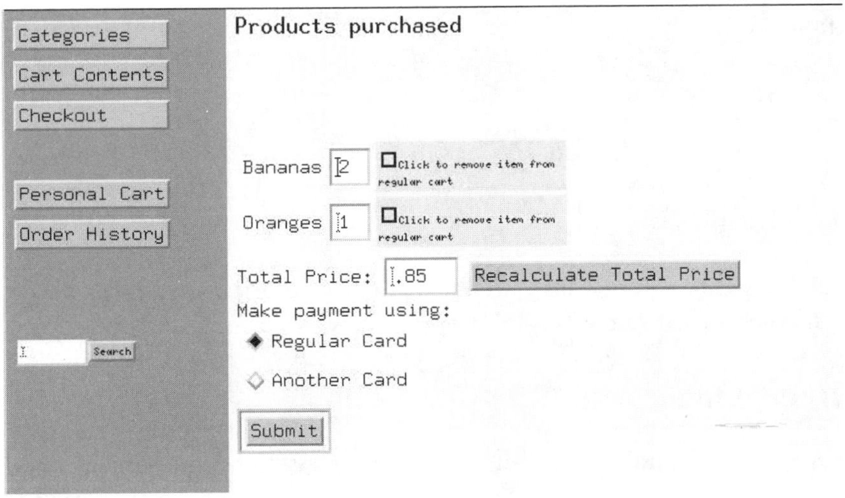

Figure   11.16

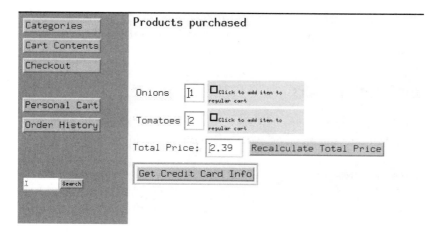

Figure 11.17

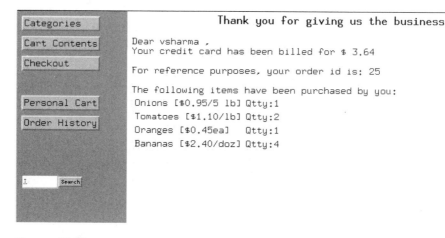

Figure 11.18

Categories Option

Clicking the "Categories" option calls up to the top-level categories page, shown in Figure 11.20, which looks like the sign-in page.

Order History Option

When the Order History button is clicked, a list of all the customer's orders is displayed as links. The list contains the id of each order and each date on which it was placed (see Figure 11.21).

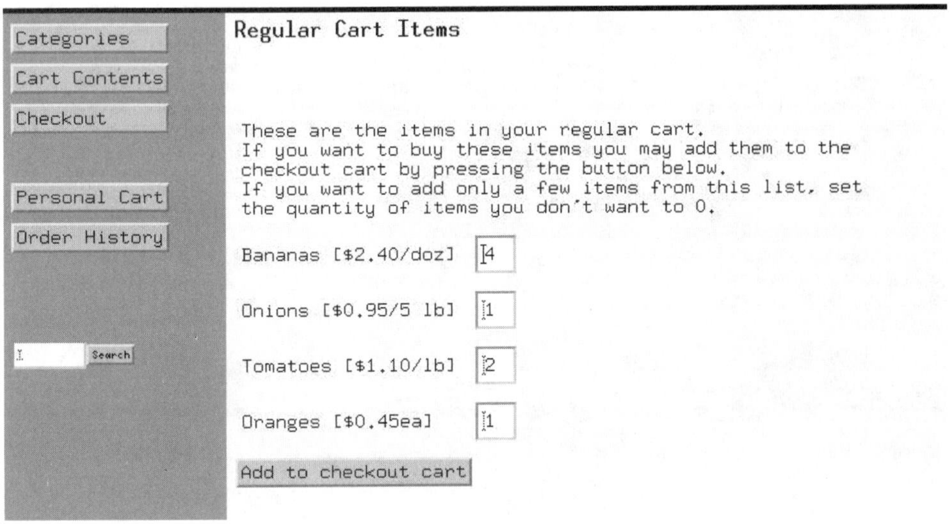

Figure   11.19

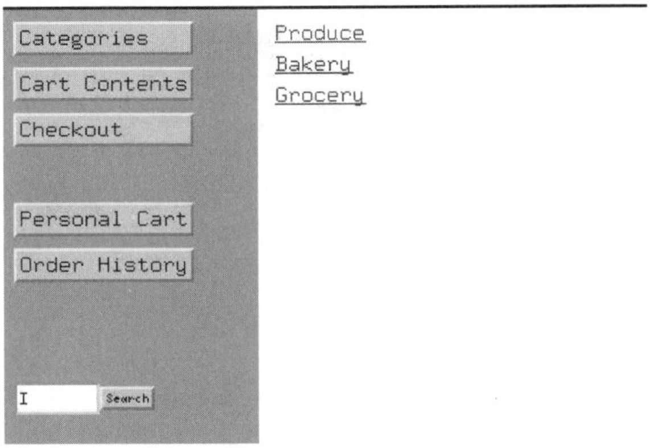

Figure   11.20

Clicking on one of these links (see Figure 11.22) calls up information about the order, such as what was ordered and whether it has been shipped or not.

Search Option

The search option consists of a text field in which one or more keywords can be typed and a Search button. When this button is pressed, the system looks for keywords typed in by the customer in Products. A match is done against keywords that were specified for each product in the Inventory Management System. All products for which a match is found are displayed on the screen.

Figure 11.23 shows the result of doing a search on "tomato."

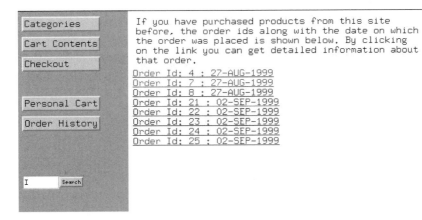

Figure 11.21

Figure 11.22

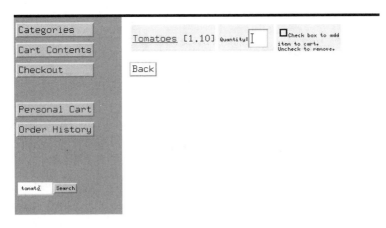

Figure 11.23

Typical Usage Scenario

A customer types in his or her username and password. He or she next selects the Personal Cart option and views all the contents of the personal cart, clicking the Add to Checkout Cart button to add items to the checkout cart. The customer then types in a search keyword, looking for another item to purchase. The results are displayed in the right frame, where the customer types in a quantity and clicks the checkbox to add the item to the checkout cart. The customer then presses the Checkout button and, finally, the Submit button, which charges the credit card and brings up the thank-you page.

Profile Management System

The Profile Management System helps you manage profiles of your customer base. It consists of a registration system whereby users enter their profile information—name, shipping address, phone, and credit card information. An "Update Profile" option allows them to modify information if it changes or if there are any errors. The system also consists of an option that helps users locate lost passwords as well as contact customer support in an organized way.

Top Menu

Addition of the Profile Management System changes the appearance of the ordering menu. It adds a menu bar at the top with a number of options: Registration, Contact us, Password finder, Login, and Update. Figure 11.24 shows how the entry page of the ordering system looks when the Profile Management System has been integrated.

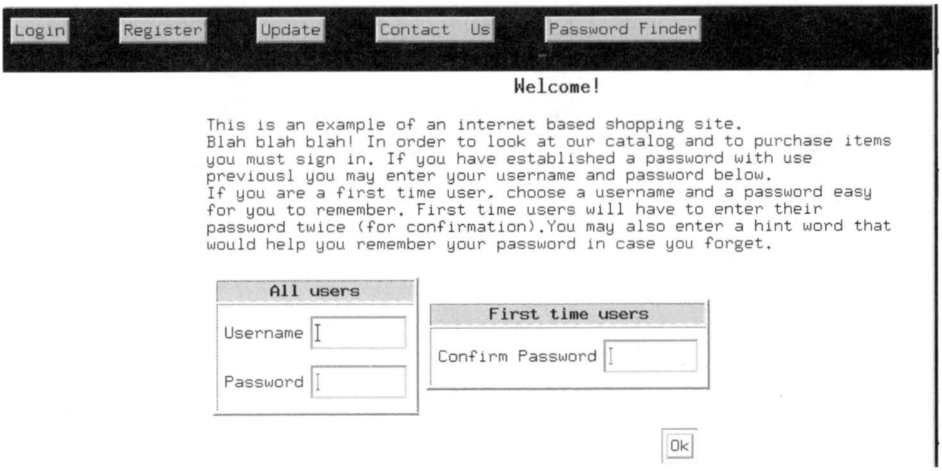

Figure 11.24

Registration

The Register option allows a user to register with your site. Customers either click the Register button initially or when they check out after adding items to their checkout cart. Figure 11.25 shows the screen that comes up for new users when they press the Get Credit Card Info button in the checkout screen.

The registration process consists of two parts. Both of these appear in one screen. The first part asks for profile information—name, shipping address, phone, fax, etc.

The second portion asks for payment-related information like credit card details and billing address (see Figure 11.26).

If the Copy from Shipping Address checkbox is clicked, the address that was entered as the shipping address is copied over automatically. This feature is very useful, as in a large number of cases the two addresses are the same.

The screen shown in Figure 11.27 comes up if the customer has successfully registered. A Pay button comes up if this page has been reached from the checkout screen. If users choose to register directly instead of first going through a shopping experience, the Pay button will not show.

Profile Update

To update their profile, customers are asked for their username and password. This page can be reached either by clicking on the "Update Profile" option or the Another Card button on the checkout page (see Figure 11.28).

The Update page looks like the Registration page except that it is prepopulated with information about this user (see Figures 11.29 and 11.30).

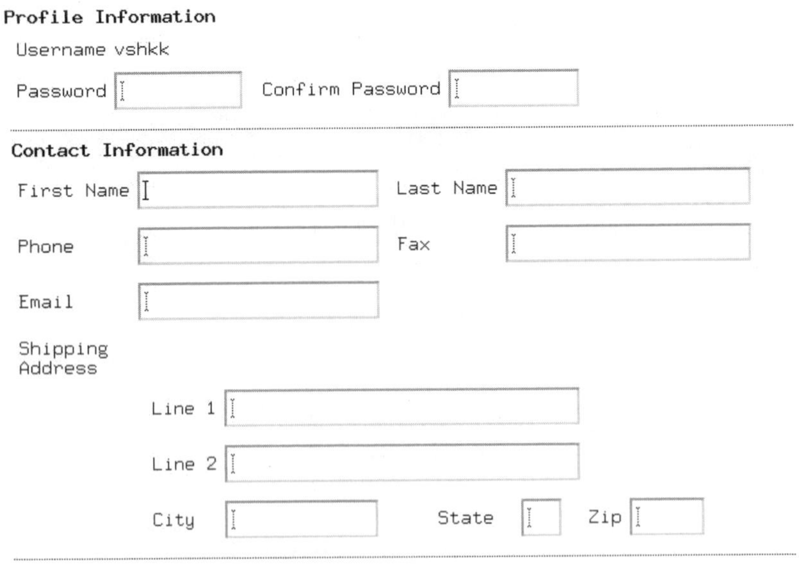

Profile Information

Username vshkk

Password [ ]   Confirm Password [ ]

Contact Information

First Name [ ]   Last Name [ ]

Phone [ ]   Fax [ ]

Email [ ]

Shipping
Address

Line 1 [ ]

Line 2 [ ]

City [ ]   State [ ]   Zip [ ]

Figure 11.25

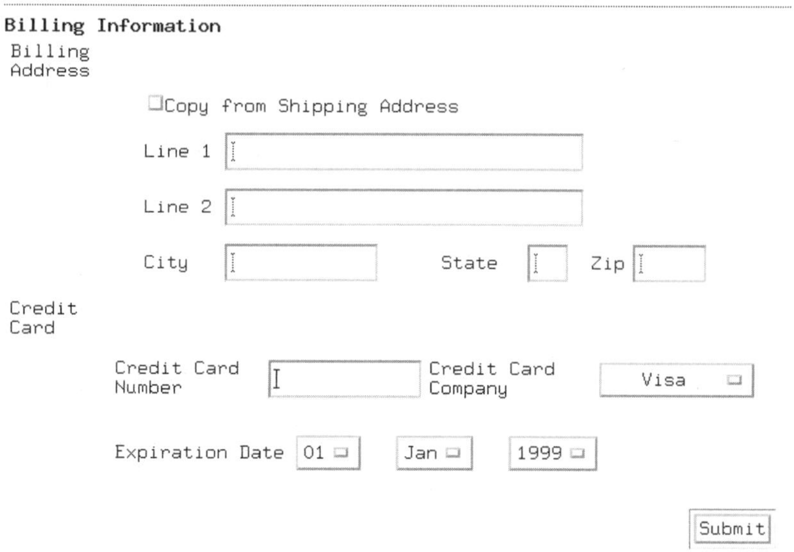

Billing Information

Billing
Address

☐Copy from Shipping Address

Line 1 [   ]

Line 2 [   ]

City [   ]   State [ ]   Zip [   ]

Credit
Card

Credit Card   [   ]   Credit Card   [Visa   ☐]
Number   Company

Expiration Date [01 ☐]   [Jan ☐]   [1999 ☐]

[Submit]

Figure   11.26

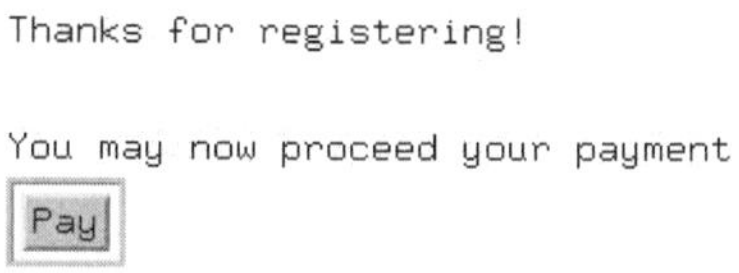

Thanks for registering!

You may now proceed your payment

[Pay]

Figure   11.27

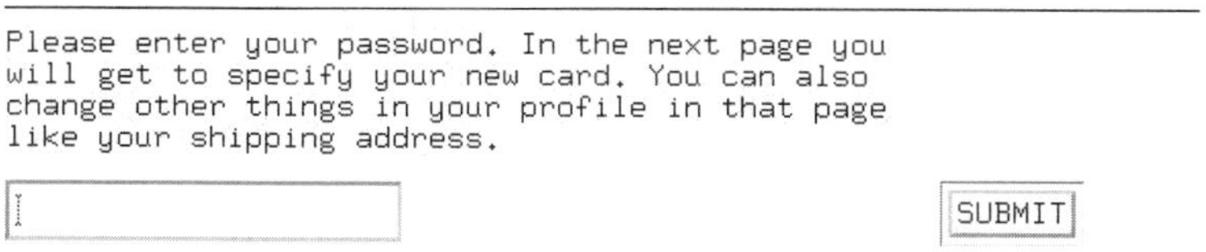

Please enter your password. In the next page you
will get to specify your new card. You can also
change other things in your profile in that page
like your shipping address.

[   ]   [SUBMIT]

Figure   11.28

Contact Us Option

This screen comes up to enable customers to contact those who maintain the store site. It presents a Frequently Asked Questions link first to save unnecessary traffic. Then it asks for username and an email address so that an adequate response can be sent. Problems are divided into categories to streamline the traffic. Email messages are sent to whichever customer support representative is appropriate based on the category chosen. A detailed description of the problem can be entered in the description box (see Figure 11.31).

Depending on what data is entered in the contactUs.html, a screen like the one shown in Figure 11.32 comes up.

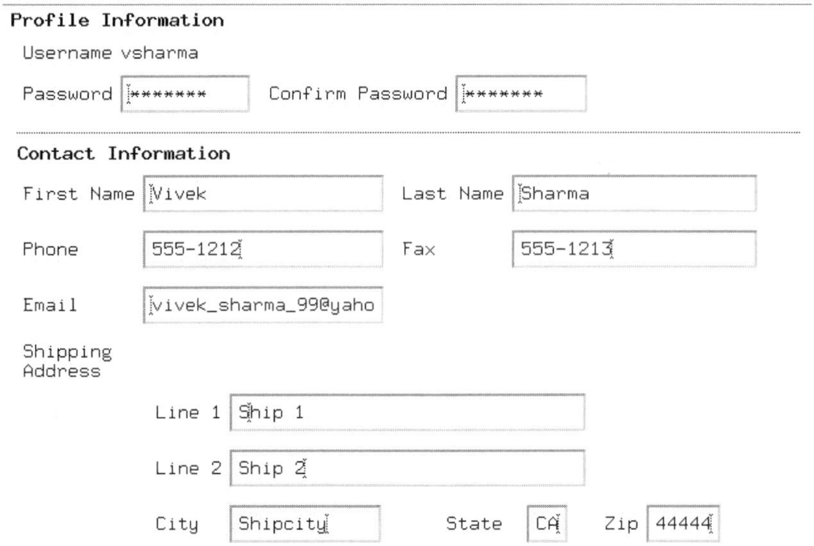

Profile Information

Username vsharma

Password [*******]   Confirm Password [*******]

Contact Information

First Name [Vivek]   Last Name [Sharma]

Phone [555-1212]   Fax [555-1213]

Email [vivek_sharma_99@yaho]

Shipping
Address

Line 1 [Ship 1]

Line 2 [Ship 2]

City [Shipcity]   State [CA]   Zip [44444]

Figure   11.29

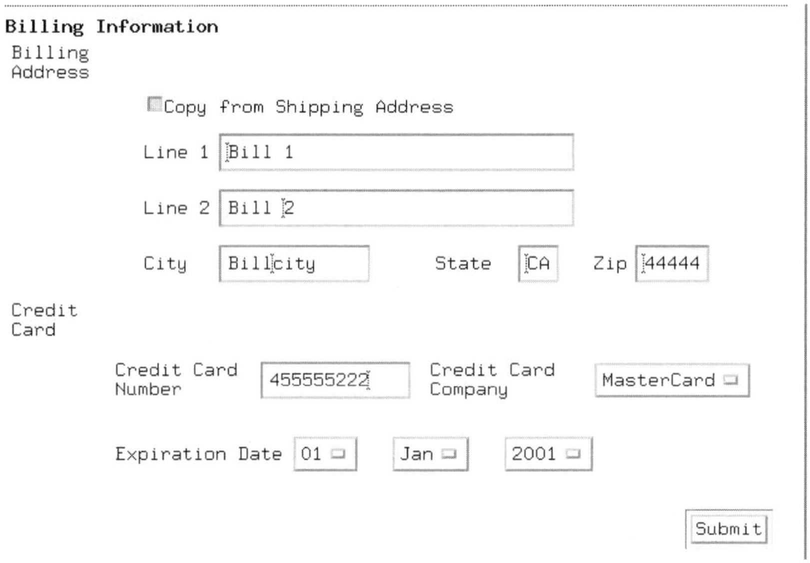

Billing Information

Billing
Address

☐Copy from Shipping Address

Line 1 [Bill 1]

Line 2 [Bill 2]

City [Billcity]   State [CA]   Zip [44444]

Credit
Card

Credit Card
Number [455555222]   Credit Card
Company [MasterCard ▾]

Expiration Date [01 ▾]   [Jan ▾]   [2001 ▾]

[Submit]

Figure   11.30

```
You can use this form to send us your queries. But before you
do so, it might be a good idea to read our list of
Frequently Asked Questions
```

```
Username [        ]
```

```
Email    [        ]
```

```
Category [Registration Problem ▭]
```

```
Brief description
┌────────────────────────────────────────────┐▲
│I                                           │
│                                            │
│                                            │
│                                            │
│                                            │
│◄                                          ▼│
└────────────────────────────────────────────┘
                                    [Submit]
```

Figure   11.31

```
The following mail message has been sent
from user vsharma at email address
vivek_sharma_99@yahoo.com to
helpOrder@myCompany.com :
```

```
I ordered on 07/99 but have not received
items so far.
```

```
Thanks for contacting us. We will try to get
back to you at the earliest.
```

Figure   11.32

Password Finder Option

This option helps customers retrieve their password in case they've forgotten it. It asks customers to type in their username, last name, and email. If a match is found, the password is displayed. For security purposes, if a username has not been supplied by the last name and email match, the username and password are sent to the email address instead of being displayed on the next page (see Figure 11.33).

If the customer entered all the data correctly, the response page will look like Figure 11.34.

If the customer did not enter username but the rest of the information was OK the screen shown in Figure 11.35 will come up.

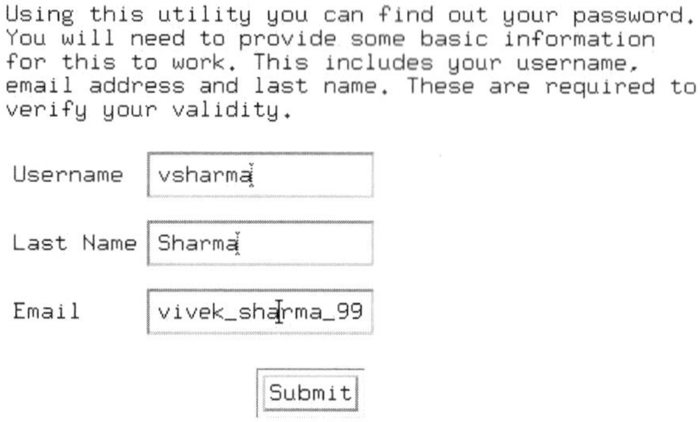

```
Using this utility you can find out your password.
You will need to provide some basic information
for this to work. This includes your username,
email address and last name. These are required to
verify your validity.
```

Username [vsharma]

Last Name [Sharma]

Email [vivek_sharma_99]

[Submit]

Figure   11.33

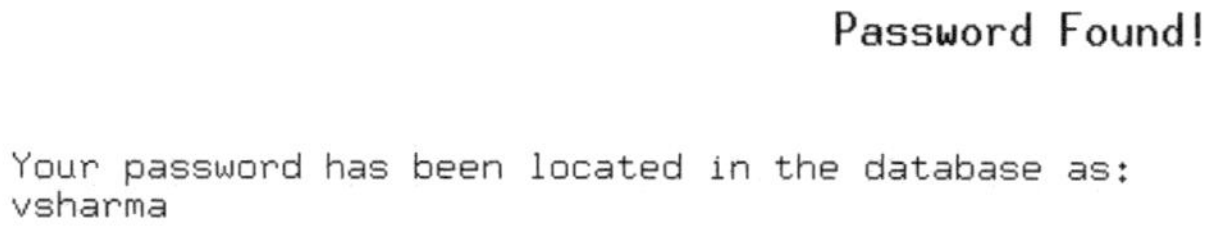

Password Found!

```
Your password has been located in the database as:
vsharma
```

Figure   11.34

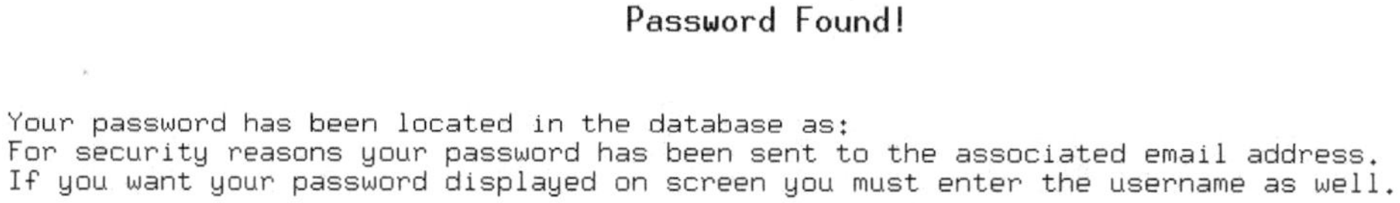

Password Found!

```
Your password has been located in the database as:
For security reasons your password has been sent to the associated email address.
If you want your password displayed on screen you must enter the username as well.
```

Figure   11.35

Shipping Management System

This system is the interface viewed by your shipping department. It allows the department to look at pending orders and to update an order when an event takes place. An event could refer to the fact that the order had been shipped, that it had been returned, that the address was invalid, and so on.

Sign-In Page

The sign-in page of the shipping system looks as shown in Figure 11.36. A username and password are needed to view this system.

Three options are available on logging in: (1) information about an order by its id, (2) a list of all orders, or (3) a list of orders that have not yet been shipped. Also, a logout button appears in the left frame (see Figure 11.37).

A customer who knows the id of an order can use the first option. Information about the order that is relevant to the shipping department, such as the products and

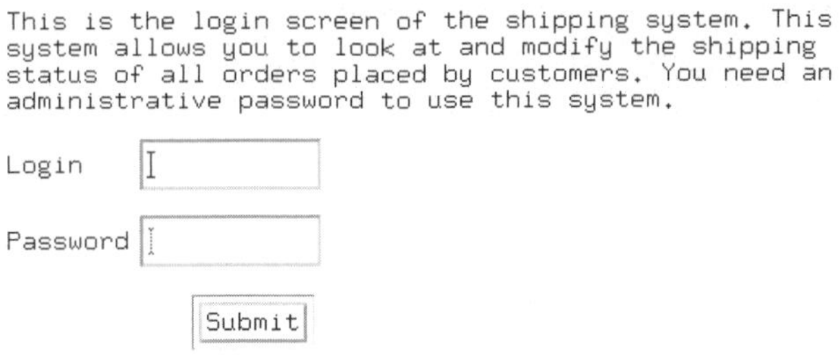

This is the login screen of the shipping system. This
system allows you to look at and modify the shipping
status of all orders placed by customers. You need an
administrative password to use this system.

Login   I

Password   I

     Submit

Figure   11.36

Logout

You can view/modify shipping orders using
this form. If you want to modify one order
at a time and know the id of the order you
can use the first option below. If you want
to do batch updates you can use the next two
options.

Get by order id: I   Go

Show all orders
Show orders not shipped so far

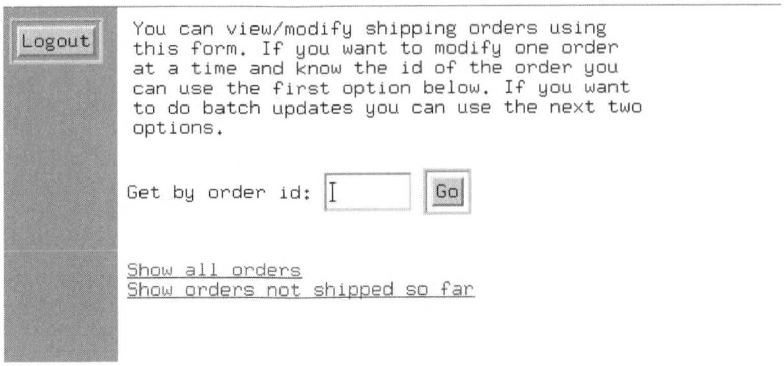

Figure   11.37

quantities to be shipped, is displayed. The current status of the order is also displayed
(see Figure 11.38).

Clicking on Show All Orders produces this screen. The shipping date, method and
status of one or more orders can be set, and the update will then be applied to all
orders selected in the Select list (see Figure 11.39).

Selecting "Show orders not shipped so far" will yield a similar screen, except that the
list will not contain orders that have been shipped.

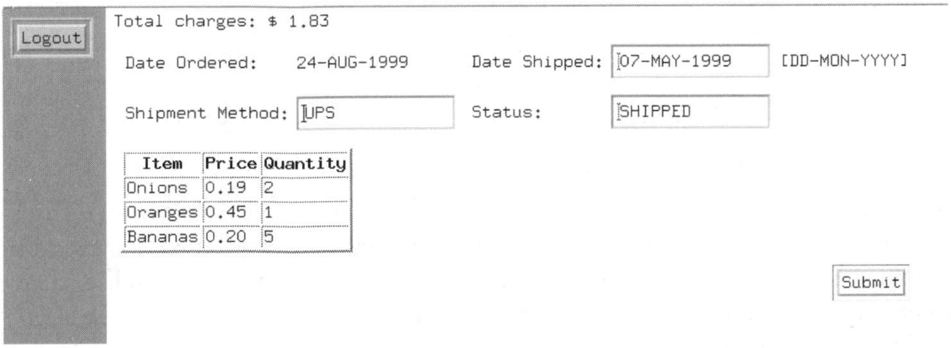

Logout

Total charges: $ 1.83

Date Ordered: 24-AUG-1999   Date Shipped: 07-MAY-1999   [DD-MON-YYYY]

Shipment Method: UPS   Status: SHIPPED

Item	Price	Quantity
Onions	0.19	2
Oranges	0.45	1
Bananas	0.20	5

     Submit

Figure   11.38

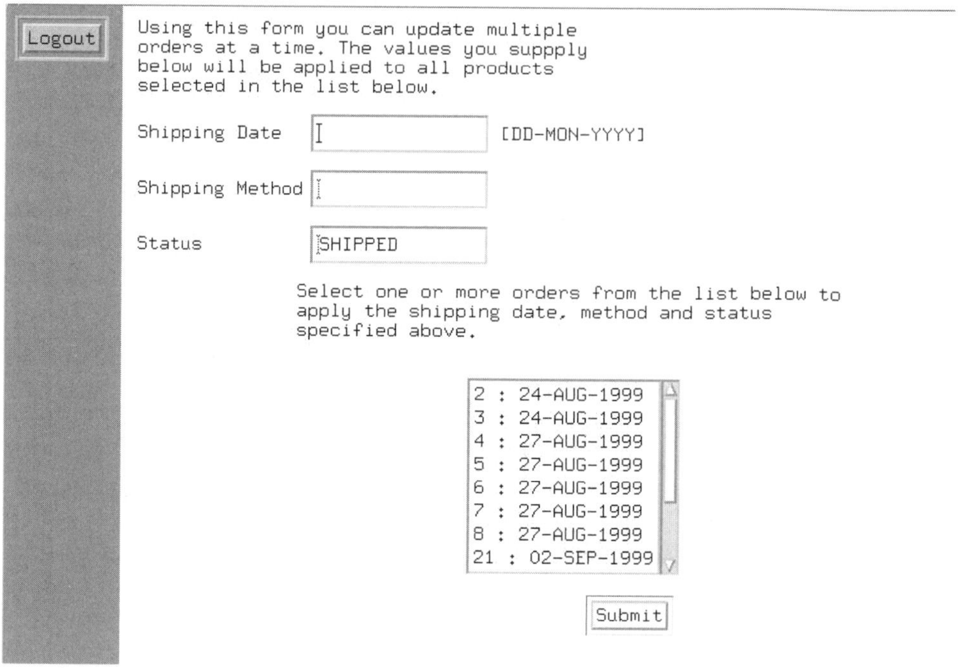

Figure 11.39

Reporting System

The reporting system allows you to analyze customer and sales trends, as well as helping you determine which products are generating the most revenues or where most customers are concentrated.

Sign-In Page

You sign in by typing a username and password authorizing you to view this information (see Figure 11.40).

Reporting Menu

Once you've logged in, you see four options: distribution analysis of both users and sales, and time and frequency analysis of both users and sales (see Figure 11.41). Distribution analysis allows you to see how your users and sales are distributed. The user distribution helps you find out how many customers are present in each zip code or state, while sales distribution helps you see how much revenue each product is generating.

The time and frequency analysis helps you compare total sales and user registrations on each day of a week, each week of a month, each month of a year, and so on.

```
This is the login screen of the reporting system. This
system allows you to analyze your user base and monitor
sales of your products. You need an administrative
account to use this system.

Login     [I              ]

Password  [I              ]

          [ Submit ]
```

Figure   11.40

```
[ Logout ]   Distribution analysis

                          User base
                                     This report allows you to see the
                                     distribution of your customers by
                                     geographical location. You can see how
                                     many customers have registered in each
                                     state or zip between given dates.

                          Sales
                                     This report allows you to see the
                                     distribution of your sales by
                                     products/categries. You can see total
                                     sales from each product or category
                                     between given dates.

             Time/Frequency analysis

                          User Registrations
                                     This report allows you to see the
                                     total number of registrations each
                                     week, each day, each month or each
                                     year between given dates.

                          Sales
                                     This report allows you to see the
                                     total sales each week, each day,
                                     each month or each year between
                                     given dates.
```

Figure   11.41

User Distribution

If you click on **Distribution Analysis->User**, you get to a screen asking you to decide whether you want to see distribution by state or by zip code. As shown in Figure 11.42, you can also specify two dates, and the system will then look for users registered between those dates only.

Figure 11.43 shows how a result screen looks.

Sales Distribution

If you click on **Distribution Analysis->Sales**, you reach a screen where you can decide whether you want to see distribution by product or by category. As shown in Figure 11.44, you can also specify two dates so that the system will look for sales between those dates only.

Figure 11.45 shows how a result screen looks.

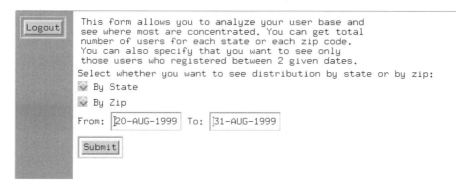

Figure   11.42

User distribution

state	Total Users
MA	1
TX	1
CA	1

Figure   11.43

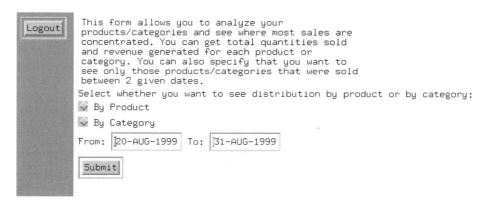

Figure   11.44

Sales distribution

Product Id	Product Name	Quantity	Revenue
17	Onions	6	$1.14
16	Tomatoes	4	$4.4
15	Oranges	4	$1.8
14	Bananas	19	$3.8

Figure   11.45

User Frequency

Figure 11.46 shows a screen that allows you to see total user registrations on a daily, weekly, monthly, or yearly basis between two given dates.

Figure 11.47 shows the screen you see if you choose the daily option.

Figure 11.48 shows the screen you see if you choose the weekly option.

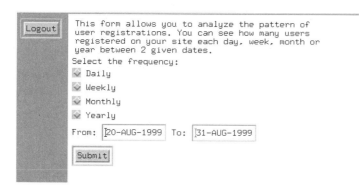

```
Logout   This form allows you to analyze the pattern of
         user registrations. You can see how many users
         registered on your site each day, week, month or
         year between 2 given dates.
         Select the frequency:
         ☑ Daily
         ☑ Weekly
         ☑ Monthly
         ☑ Yearly

         From: [20-AUG-1999   To: [31-AUG-1999

         [Submit]
```

Figure   11.46

User frequency

From	To	Total Registrations
20-AUG-1999	21-AUG-1999	0
21-AUG-1999	22-AUG-1999	0
22-AUG-1999	23-AUG-1999	0
23-AUG-1999	24-AUG-1999	0
24-AUG-1999	25-AUG-1999	0
25-AUG-1999	26-AUG-1999	0
26-AUG-1999	27-AUG-1999	0
27-AUG-1999	28-AUG-1999	3
28-AUG-1999	29-AUG-1999	0
29-AUG-1999	30-AUG-1999	0
30-AUG-1999	31-AUG-1999	0
31-AUG-1999	1-SEP-1999	0
1-SEP-1999	2-SEP-1999	0
2-SEP-1999	3-SEP-1999	1
3-SEP-1999	4-SEP-1999	0

Figure   11.47

User frequency

From	To	Total Registrations
20-AUG-1999	27-AUG-1999	0
27-AUG-1999	3-SEP-1999	4
3-SEP-1999	10-SEP-1999	0

Figure   11.48

Sales Frequency

Figure 11.49 shows the screen that allows you to see total sales on a daily, weekly, monthly, or yearly basis between two given dates.

Figure 11.50 shows the screen you see if you choose the daily option.

Figure 11.51 shows the screen you see if you choose the weekly option.

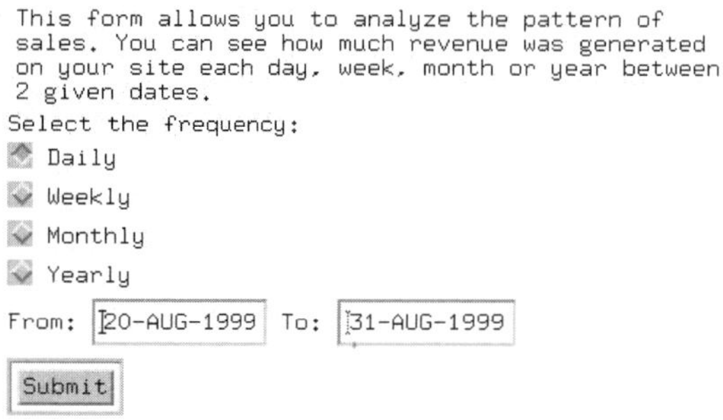

```
This form allows you to analyze the pattern of
sales. You can see how much revenue was generated
on your site each day, week, month or year between
2 given dates.
Select the frequency:
◉ Daily
◉ Weekly
◉ Monthly
◉ Yearly

From: [20-AUG-1999]  To: [31-AUG-1999]

[Submit]
```

Figure   11.49

Sales Frequency

From	To	Revenue
20-AUG-1999	21-AUG-1999	$0.0
21-AUG-1999	22-AUG-1999	$0.0
22-AUG-1999	23-AUG-1999	$0.0
23-AUG-1999	24-AUG-1999	$0.0
24-AUG-1999	25-AUG-1999	$3.66
25-AUG-1999	26-AUG-1999	$0.0
26-AUG-1999	27-AUG-1999	$0.0
27-AUG-1999	28-AUG-1999	$7.48
28-AUG-1999	29-AUG-1999	$0.0
29-AUG-1999	30-AUG-1999	$0.0
30-AUG-1999	31-AUG-1999	$0.0
31-AUG-1999	1-SEP-1999	$0.0
1-SEP-1999	2-SEP-1999	$0.0
2-SEP-1999	3-SEP-1999	$15.41
3-SEP-1999	4-SEP-1999	$0.0

Figure   11.50

Sales Frequency

From	To	Revenue
20-AUG-1999	27-AUG-1999	$3.66
27-AUG-1999	3-SEP-1999	$22.89
3-SEP-1999	10-SEP-1999	$0.0

Figure   11.51

Chapter 12

Utilities

Introduction

While each of the systems described in previous chapters does specific things and is different from others, there is some common ground. And that common ground is a set of utility classes that we describe in this chapter.

We could have easily built these utilities into each of the systems. However, that would mean a lot of code redundancy. An even bigger problem would be code maintenance. So we took the approach of keeping this common code separate and modular so that it can be easily plugged into a system that requires it.

Before you read this chapter or any of the subsequent chapters—except the index, of course—you should have gone through the previous sections of the book and should have at least a basic understanding of the technologies covered.

Description of the Utilities

Let's see what these utilities are and what they do. The systems we are going to build need to interact with the database. This means we need an efficient way of connecting to the database using JDBC. Whereas it is perfectly valid for each class that needs a connection to create its own connection and use it, the design of such a system would be very poor for several reasons. For one, if you change a JDBC driver, you have to make changes in every place that creates a connection. But the bigger disadvantage lies in the fact that it takes a considerable chunk of time to establish a connection. If your application had to create a connection every time a Web request came in, there would be a delay that would lead to a bad user experience. To solve this problem, we have built a utility that creates a number of connections to the database and keeps the connections open for use by any application that requires the connection.

While we are talking about databases, another important thing required by most applications is a method of authenticating users, that is, asking a user to enter a username and password in order to restrict access to the system. For this we have built a utility class that accepts a database connection, username, and password as input and returns a result confirming the validity or invalidity of a user.

Another thing required by most systems is the ability to send emails. These could be informational emails, promotions, or anything else. The mail utility uses the Javax Mail API to send emails.

A lot of the work we're doing will involve dynamic generation of HTML pages. We could write the HTML code in our Java servlets. However, that would make the look and feel heavily dependent on compiled code. So every time you want to change the background color of some pages, you would have to modify Java classes and compile them. Also, "look and feel" aspects are normally handled by a department different from development. It is always a good idea to keep the code as much isolated from these "look and feel" aspects as possible. For this purpose we develop a utility that allows you to create HTML templates containing tags that are replaced with dynamic data as it is retrieved.

Next we look at each of these utilities to see how they have been written and how they operate. We begin with the connection-pooling utility.

Connection-Pooling Utility

As mentioned above, this utility creates a pool of connections with the database at the time of initialization. It then hands over an available connection to any class that requests it. The utility has been written to work in conjunction with a multithreaded Servlet environment. As such, it needs to handle cases where multiple threads of a Servlet instance are trying to request a database connection simultaneously. It also has a mechanism for putting back connections no longer required by anyone into a pool so that the connections can be reused.

The code for this utility is in a file called "ConnectionPool.java." We can look at individual components of the code to see how it works. First we import all the required packages: **io, sql**, and **util**.

```
import java.io.*;
import java.sql.*;
import java.util.*;
```

Next we define a variable called MAX_CONNECTIONS. This represents the maximum number of connections that should be created and stored for future use in the pool. It has been initialized to 10. Depending on your requirements, you can modify this number before you compile the class. Also, there is a Vector called "connections" (initialized to null) in which we store the database connections.

Now we specify the parameters required to establish a JDBC connection such as hostname, port, etc., and we create a connect String using the same.

Finally we create a static variable called **instance** of the type "ConnectionPool." We do this because we are going to create just one instance of this class that will be used by any other Servlet to request a connection. This point is important, because we want to ensure that only MAX_CONNECTIONS number of connections are established (having a large number of open connections can cause performance degradation). And by having one instance of the class, we can allow synchronization among different threads of one or more Servlets so that they don't step on each other while getting and putting database connections. Thus, we will synchronize the methods of this class, which means that only one thread can be inside that method at any given time.

```
public class ConnectionPool
{
      static final int MAX_CONNECTIONS = 10;
      static Vector connections = null;
      String hostName = "myServer.com";
      String login = "test", password="test",
            sidName="TEST", port="1521";
      String connectString = "jdbc:oracle:thin:@" + hostName +
                              ":" + port + ":" + sidName;

      static ConnectionPool instance = null;
```

Now that we have defined the variables of this class, we can look at the bigger picture to see what the different methods are and how they are accessed by Servlets.

A Servlet would try to get an instance of the ConnectionPool class in order to request database connections. It would call the **getInstance()** method of ConnectionPool. This is a static, synchronized method, which can be invoked as follows:

```
ConnectionPool c = ConnectionPool.getInstance()
```

But since it is synchronized, only one Servlet thread can execute it at a given time. In this method we are creating an instance of ConnectionPool, provided the variable **instance** is null. This would be true only the very first time the method is being called by anyone. After that the variable **instance** will contain an instance of ConnectionPool. This method first checks to see if **instance** is null. If so, it creates an instance of the class and stores it in the variable; otherwise, it returns the **instance**.

```
      public static synchronized ConnectionPool getInstance()
      {
            if(instance == null)
                  instance = new ConnectionPool();
            return instance;
      }
```

Once an instance of the ConnectionPool has been created, we need to initialize it so that database connections can be created and stored in the "connections" Vector. Each Servlet that gets an instance of ConnectionPool first calls the method **initialize()**. This is an instance method that has been synchronized to ensure that initialization happens only once, the first time that the method is called. As in the case of **getInstance()**, we check whether "connections" is null. If so, we create MAX_CONNECTIONS number of connections and store them in the "connections" Vector. If the variable is not null, this means it has already been initialized by an earlier call to this method, so we do nothing and return.

```
public synchronized void initialize()
{
    if(connections == null)
    {
        try
        {
            DriverManager.registerDriver(
                new oracle.jdbc.driver.OracleDriver());
            connections = new Vector();
            int count = 0;
            while(count < MAX_CONNECTIONS)
            {
                Connection c =
                    DriverManager.getConnection (
                                connectString,
                                login, password);
                connections.addElement(c);
                count++;
            }
        }catch(SQLException sqlE){}
    }
}
```

Now comes the method that is most important from our point of view, **getConnection()**. This method looks for an available connection in the "connections" Vector and returns it. If it is not able to find a connection, it returns a null. This method is also synchronized. As a result, if two threads are requesting a connection, control of execution goes to one of them. The "connections" Vector is looked up, and an available connection is returned. The other thread then gets to execute the method and retrieve an available connection.

We are simply retrieving the first element in the "connections" Vector and returning that. If the size of the Vector is 0, it means that MAX_CONNECTIONS number of connections are being used by different threads and there is no more connection available. If you find that your applications reach this stage very frequently, you should increase the value of MAX_CONNECTIONS.

```
public synchronized Connection getConnection()
{
    Connection c = null;
    if(connections == null)
        return null;
    if(connections.size() > 0)
    {
        c = (Connection)connections.elementAt(0);
        connections.removeElementAt(0);
    }
    return c;
}
```

Each Servlet that requests a connection should return it so that the connection can be given to some other thread that can reuse it. That is the whole point of this system. We have therefore created a method called **putConnection()**, which takes a connection as input and stores it in the "connections" Vector. This method also needs to be synchronized. If it is not, we may run into a case where two threads are simultaneously trying to put a connection in the "connections" Vector, causing corruption.

```
public synchronized void putConnection(Connection c)
{
    connections.addElement(c);
    notifyAll();
}
```

We have defined another method, called **removeAllConnections()**, which can be used for cleaning up the "connections" Vector at a time of shutdown or other emergency.

```
public synchronized void removeAllConnections()
{
    try{
        if(connections == null)
            return;
        int sz = connections.size();
        for(int i=0; i<sz; i++)
        {
            Connection c = (Connection)connections.
                elementAt(i);
            c.close();
        }
        connections.removeAllElements();
        connections = null;
    }catch(SQLException sqlE){}
}
```

Any Servlet, therefore, can get an instance of the ConnectionPool class, initialize it, and then request an available database connection that can be used for issuing SQL statements against the database. The Servlet can return the connection when it no longer requires it.

Next we look at the authenticator utility, which contains methods for verifying validity of users.

Authenticator

This class contains two methods: **verifyPassword()** and **isValidAdmin()**. The first method checks for a user in the customer database and determines whether it is a new user or an existing user with a valid or invalid password. This method is used in the Ordering and Profile Management Systems.

The second method is used by all internal systems, such as Reporting and Shipping, to verify whether the person trying to access the system has sufficient privileges.

Both methods take a username and password input along with a database connection object. This connection object is used for validating the username and password against the values stored in the database.

To understand the SQL queries, you need to understand the structure of the corresponding tables. This topic is discussed in the following chapters. However, to give you a basic idea, there is a profiles table that contains information about a customer. Among other things it contains a username and password that the customer uses to access the system. Customers choose their username and password during their first visit to the site. In subsequent requests they can use this username and password combination to retrieve profile-specific data, such as credit card information and history of previously placed orders.

Similarly, there is an admin table that contains information about administrators who have privileges to access internal tools such as the Shipping and Reporting Systems.

The first method, **verifyPassword()**, is slightly complex and needs more explanation, because in addition to checking the validity of the username and password combination, it also checks whether it is a new user. We therefore need to introduce briefly the Profile Management System.

When users come to the site, they are asked to enter a username and a password. If the username they entered does not exist in the database, they are considered new users. The chosen username and password are then stored in the profiles table. This table also contains a field called "status." For first-time users this is set to "NEW_USER." When a user has purchased something and has supplied the credit card information and other profile-related information, this flag is set to "UPDATED_USER." The method **verifyPassword()** needs to tell us which of the following states apply to the user:

1. NEW_USER—a person whose username does not exist in the database.
2. NEW_USER_COMING_AGAIN—a person who came into the system but did not provide profile information and is trying to access the system again using that username/password.
3. VALID_PASSWORD—a user whose account and profile have been fully established.
4. INVALID_PASSWORD—a person trying to access the system with an invalid username and password combination.

```java
import java.sql.*;
public class Authenticator
{
    static int NEW_USER = 1;
    static int INVALID_PASSWORD = 2;
    static int VALID_PASSWORD = 3;
    static int NEW_USER_COMING_AGAIN = 4;
    public int verifyPassword(String username, String password,
                Connection conn)
    {
        try{
            Statement stmt = conn.createStatement();
            String querySQL = "SELECT password, status FROM
                profiles WHERE username='" + username + "'";
            ResultSet rset = stmt.executeQuery(querySQL);
            boolean foundUser = false;
            String dbPassword = "";
            String status = "";
            while(rset.next())
            {
                foundUser = true;
                dbPassword = rset.getString(1);
                status = rset.getString(2);
            }
            if(foundUser == false)
                return NEW_USER;
            if(password.equals(dbPassword))
            {
                if(status.equalsIgnoreCase("NEW_USER"))
                    return NEW_USER_COMING_AGAIN;
                else
                    return VALID_PASSWORD;
            }
            return INVALID_PASSWORD;
```

```
        }catch(SQLException ex){}
        return INVALID_PASSWORD;
    }
    public boolean isValidAdmin(String username, String password,
                Connection conn)
    {
        boolean isValid = false;
        try
        {
            Statement stmt = conn.createStatement();
            String toExec = "SELECT password FROM admins WHERE
                username='" + username + "'";
            ResultSet rset = stmt.executeQuery(toExec);
            rset.next();
            String pwd = rset.getString(1);
            if(pwd.equalsIgnoreCase(password))
                isValid = true;
        }catch(Exception ex){}
        return isValid;
    }
}
```

The next common utility is one for sending out emails.

Email-Sending Utility

This utility uses the Mail API, which is an extension of Java that allows you to send emails. We have written a class that takes a recipient address, the mail header, and the mail message as input and sends a message to the recipient.

A static variable called **smtphost** has been declared. In this you need to specify an SMTP host capable of sending emails. Talk to your system administrator to find out the appropriate host. The constructor of this class stores details about the mail and the recipient. The method **send()** can be invoked to send the mail out.

The utility uses classes in the Mail API, the Activation framework (also available at the Javasoft site), and some standard JDK classes.

```
import java.io.*;
import java.net.InetAddress;
import java.util.Properties;
import java.util.Date;

import javax.mail.*;
import javax.mail.internet.*;
import javax.activation.*;
```

```java
public class MailSender
{
    static String smtphost = "myMailServer.com";
    String from, to, mailHeader, mailBody;
    MailSender(String f, String t, String mh, String mb)
    {
        from = f;
        to = t;
        mailHeader = mh;
        mailBody = mb;
    }
    public void send()
        throws Exception
    {
        Properties props = new Properties();
        props.put("mail.smtp.host", smtphost);
        Session session = Session.getDefaultInstance(props, null);
        Message msg = new MimeMessage(session);
        msg.setFrom(new InternetAddress(from));
        InternetAddress[] address = {new InternetAddress(to)};
        msg.setRecipients(Message.RecipientType.TO, address);
        msg.setSubject(mailHeader);
        msg.setSentDate(new Date());
        msg.setText(mailBody);
        Transport.send(msg);
    }
}
```

HTML Template Utility

This utility allows us to create HTML templates, which means that we can write HTML pages containing certain tags, whose value will be replaced with data retrieved dynamically.

To use this utility, you would create an HTML template. This is like a regular HTML file, except that it contains some tags. If you want to display an HTML page to the user that contains some static text followed by the list of items that the user ordered, you could have a template that looks like this:

```
<HTML>
  <HEAD></HEAD>
  <BODY>
  <B>List of items you ordered</B>
```

```
          <SELECT NAME='items' SIZE='5'>
<VAR_ORDER_OPTIONS>
          </SELECT>
    </BODY>
</HTML>
```

Note that we've added a tag, <VAR_ORDER_OPTIONS>. You are not bound to use a particular tag name (as long as it is not an HTML-reserved word). An application that reads information about all the orders can supply this template page to PageUtil. Then it can read the database, retrieve information about the orders, and create a String that looks like this:

```
<OPTION>Order 1<OPTION>Order 2
```

Then it can call the **setReplaceItem()** method of PageUtil and specify that all occurrences of <VAR_ORDER_OPTIONS> should be replaced by this String.

The code would look like this:

```
PageUtil pu = new PageUtil(templateLocation, out);
String options ="<OPTION>Order 1<OPTION>Order 2";
pu.setReplaceItem("<VAR_ORDER_OPTIONS>", options);
pu.printPage();
```

As a result, when printPage is called, all occurrences of the variable (tag) will be replaced by the supplied value.

The class contains three variables: **fName** is the name of the HTML template page, **replaceItems** is a Hashtable that is initially null, and **out** is a PrintWriter object.

```
import java.util.*;
import java.io.*;
public class PageUtil
{
    public String fName;
    public Hashtable replaceItems = null;
    public PrintWriter out;
    public PageUtil(String fileName, PrintWriter o)
    {
        fName = fileName;
        replaceItems = new Hashtable();
        out = o;
    }
```

It contains a method called **setReplaceItem** which takes two arguments. The first is the name of the tag that is to be replaced, and the second is the value with which it should be replaced. These are stored in the Hashtable replaceItems.

```
public void setReplaceItem(String tag, String replaceWith)
{
    replaceItems.put(tag, replaceWith);
}
```

The method **printPage** does all the substitutions before printing the page. It opens the template file and reads it line by line. It looks in the Hashtable to see if this line is one of the variables that needs to be replaced. If so, the corresponding value is retrieved from the Hashtable and substituted before the page is printed out.

```
public void printPage()
{
    try
    {
        File f = new File(fName);
        FileReader fr = new FileReader(f);
        BufferedReader bis = new BufferedReader(fr);
        String inpu;
        while((inpu = bis.readLine()) != null)
        {
            String repVal;
            repVal = (String)replaceItems.get(inpu);
            if(repVal == null)
                    out.println(inpu);
            else
                    out.println(repVal);
        }
        bis.close();
    }catch(Exception e){
        out.println("<HTML><HEAD></HEAD><BODY>");
        e.printStackTrace();
        out.println("</BODY></HTML>");
    }
}
```

With these four utilities in place, it will be much easier for us to develop our systems. In the following chapters we look at several different systems, how they relate to each other, and how they use these utilities effectively.

Inventory Management System

Prerequisites

Before you read this chapter, or any of the subsequent chapters, you should have read all the previous chapters. You should have an understanding of Java, Javascript, Jdbc, Servlets, and HTML; and you should be familiar with the different systems described in Chapter 11. You should also be familiar with the database design discussed in Chapter 10.

High-Level Description

The Inventory Management System helps you maintain an inventory of products available in your Web store. It enables you to categorize your products, add and modify products, and delete products that are no longer available. You can create categories and specify that one or more products belong to a category. The system also allows you to delete any unwanted categories.

The flow begins with the entry point page, **inventory.html**. You can access it via:

http://myServer.com:myPort/inventory.html.

Here you have the option of adding, viewing, modifying, or deleting products. You may also add or delete categories.

Classes and Their Methods

BaseInventory.java

BaseInventory is a base class that is the parent of most other classes in this package. It contains some common methods that may be used by the child classes, such as methods for debugging.

1. validPassword()

Checks whether user is authorized to access the Inventory Management System. If so, returns a true value; otherwise, throws up an error page and returns a false value.

2. showErrorPage()

A method for displaying an error page. Uses an HTML template and substitutes the value of the <ERROR_MSG> variable with a supplied error name.

3. initializeDebugFile()

A method that opens a debug file and returns the PrintStream object that can write to this file.

4. debug()

A method for writing debug information.

AddCategory.java

AddCategory is the Servlet that takes care of adding new categories to the database. It is invoked when you select the **Categories->Add** option in the main menu. The class displays a FORM in which information about the category—name, description, etc.—can be entered. The FORM is cyclic, so when you press Submit, AddCategory is again invoked. In the FORM users get to choose whether they want to add more categories. If they decide to do so, the FORM is presented again so that information about a new category can be added. If they decide not to, AddCategory writes the information about all categories that has been gathered to the database.

1. doPost()

doPost is a Servlet method that is invoked when the servlet has been invoked as a result of a POST operation. With this method, AddCategory determines whether the invocation has been done from the main menu or not. If it has, it reads the username and password supplied by the user and determines the validity. If the user is valid, a session is created. This session will be used for storing certain variables. If the servlet has not been invoked from the main menu, the session established with the client is retrieved, and so are the variables stored in the session.

The servlet also reads the variables supplied by the FORM from which it was invoked. If it has been invoked from the main menu, only the username and password are relevant. However, if it has been invoked because the user chose to add more categories, information about the previous category, which is available as FORM variables, is read and stored in a session variable.

If the user has indicated that he or she wants to add more categories (or if the Servlet has been invoked from the main menu), **showAddCategoryPage()** is invoked.

When the user finally decides that (s)he doesn't want to add more categories, the **writeCategories()** method is invoked.

2. writeCategories()

This method creates records in the database for all categories that the user wants to add.

3. showAddCategoryPage()

This method shows the **addCategory.html** template. It populates <VAR_CATEGORY_OPTIONS>, which is a variable in the template with a list of categories that can be the parent of the category being added.

AddProduct.java

This one handles addition of products to the database. It is quite similar to the AddCategory Servlet and contains similar methods.

SelectProduct.java

Whenever you want to view, modify, or delete a product, the system displays a list of products you can choose from. This Servlet goes to the database, retrieves a list of products, and shows them in a table.

1. doPost()

This method calls **showSelectProductPage()** and passes a database connection to it so that the method can retrieve a list of products from the database.

2. showSelectProductPage()

This method displays the **selectProduct.html** template. A connection to the database is made to retrieve names and ids of all products. The variable <VAR_PRODUCT_LIST> is replaced with the list of products before the template is displayed.

ShowProduct.java

Details of the product that has been selected are shown by this class. A Submit button is available if the user wants to modify the product; otherwise, just the information is displayed.

1. doPost()

The **showProductPage()** is called, and a database connection is passed to it. The id of the product that the user wants to view or modify is also passed.

2. showProductPage()

This method retrieves information from the database about the product whose id comes in as an input parameter from **doPost()**. It then populates the variables in the **showProduct.html** template before displaying it.

ModifyProduct.java

This class writes any modifications made to a product to the database. It is invoked when the user clicks on the Submit button in the FORM generated by ShowProduct.

1. doPost()

In this method, variables of the Modify Product FORM are read. These contain new values for the product—name, description, and quantity as specified by the user in the FORM. This method then calls **modifyProduct()** and passes a database connection to it.

2. modifyProduct()

This method makes the actual modifications to the database. It updates the record corresponding to the product that is to be modified.

SelectCategory.java

This Servlet displays all the categories in the system that can be deleted. It is invoked when the user clicks the **Category->Delete** option in the main menu.

1. doPost()

It calls the **showSelectCategoryPage()** and passes a database connection to it.

2. showSelectCategoryPage()

This method goes into the database and retrieves a list of categories that can be deleted. These include categories that have no products in them and have no subcategories. It then displays the list using the **selectCategory.html** template.

DeleteCategory.java

This one is invoked when the user chooses a category in the template and presses the Submit button.

1. doPost()

This calls the **categoryDeletedPage()** method and passes a database connection to it as well as the id of the product that is to be deleted.

2. categoryDeletedPage()

The method deletes the specified category from the database and displays a success page.

DeleteProduct.java

This is similar to DeleteCategory; it deletes a product from the database.

CategoryOptions.java

This contains some code that is used by both AddProduct and ShowProduct, a method of retrieving names and hierarchies of all categories.

1. get()

This method retrieves names of all terminal categories from the database. It then finds the name of the parent, grandparent, and so on of each category. For each terminal category it goes all the way up to the top-level category, writing the name of the parents to a String so that it eventually looks something like this:

Appliances->Electric->Small

Here "Small" is the terminal category, "Electric" is its parent, and "Appliances" is the parent of "Electric." This type of hierarchical name is established for each terminal category, and a String is created that contains each of these as an OPTION of a select list. The method returns this String so that it can be used by other methods that need to present the hierarchical list in a SELECT tag.

Product.java and *Category.java*

Each product and category are represented as an object of the type Product and Category, respectively. The classes contain constructors for storing product and category information such as name, description, etc. They also contain methods like **getName()** and **getDescription()** for retrieving these values.

SignOff.java

This Servlet invalidates a session, so nobody can use the Inventory Management System without signing in.

Detailed Description

All the classes of the Inventory Management System are contained in a package called Inventory. Each class thus begins with a line:

package Inventory;

Most of the classes use a number of packages. These include the **java.sql, java.io**, and **java.util** packages. They also make use of our Utilities package, which contains utilities such as the connection-pooling utility, the mail-sending utility, and so on.

Also, most of the classes extend the BaseInventory class, which will be described shortly. All the classes work within a Session environment. Therefore, the first time you invoke one of the applications, a Session is created. The username and password are verified against the database and are stored.

We now take a look at the individual classes.

1. BaseInventory

```
public class BaseInventory extends HttpServlet
```

This class extends HttpServlet. Most of the classes in this package are Servlets that will extend the BaseInventory class, that is why this class extends HttpServlet.

It contains the following variables:

```
static String BasePath = "/home/me/TEST_HTML/";
static boolean debugOn = true;
```

Here BasePath is the directory in which HTML files used by the system (i.e., all the HTML templates and files except the ones that need to go into document root) reside. Before compilation you need to change the value of this variable so that it contains the directory where you want to store the HTML files on your server.

debugOn is a Boolean variable that is used by other methods to determine if debugging information should be written.

Methods in This Class

a. `public PrintStream initializeDebugFile(String s)`

This method creates a PrintStream object that can be used for writing debugging information to a file. The input argument, **s**, is the name of the debugging file.

b. `public void debug(String s, PrintStream pos)`

This method can be used for writing debugging information to the PrintStream created using initializeDebugFile. Here, String **s** is a debugging string you want to write to the debug file.

Both these methods depend on the value of the variable **debugOn**. If this Boolean is set to false, no debugging information is written.

Here's an example of how you can set up debugging in any of the Servlets that extend BaseInventory.

```
PrintStream pos = initializeDebugFile("/tmp/myDebug.log");
debug("Debug String", pos);
```

c. `public boolean validPassword(String username, String password, String errorHtml, ConnectionPool c, Connection conn, PrintWriter out)`

This method makes use of the Authenticator class in the Utilities package to validate a username and password. It returns a true value if the username and password combination belongs to an administrator having access to this system, otherwise, it returns a false value and shows an error page.

d. `public void showErrorPage(PrintWriter out, String pgName, String value)`

This method displays the error page whose location is specified in **pgName**. The error page is assumed to be a template containing a variable called <ERROR_MSG>. The value of this variable is replaced by the input parameter **value**.

2. Product

This class represents one product. It contains variables for storing the various properties of a product like its id, the **category_id** (id of the category to which it belongs), its name, description, price, and so on. It also contains methods for retrieving values of each of these properties.

3. Category

Much like the Product class, this one represents a category and contains methods for retrieving the properties of the category.

4. AddProduct

This class is invoked when a user chooses the "Add Product" option in the main menu. It may also be invoked if a user chooses Yes in answer to the prompt, "Want to add more products?" in the Add Product screen.

It is a Servlet that extends BaseInventory. We take a look at some basic principles that will be used by almost all the Servlets in the different systems.

Here are the first few lines of the class:

```
package Inventory;

import java.util.*;
import java.io.*;
import java.sql.*;
import javax.servlet.*;
import javax.servlet.http.*;
import Utilities.*;

public class AddProduct extends BaseInventory
{
    ConnectionPool c = null;
    static String addProductHtml = BasePath + "addProduct.html";
    static String errorHtml = BasePath + "inventoryError.html";
    static String productsAddedHtml = BasePath + "productsAdded.
        html";
```

As can be seen, it belongs to the package Inventory and imports several other packages, including our Utilities package. It extends BaseInventory.

It contains a ConnectionPool variable, **c**, which is initialized to null. Notice that this has been declared as a global variable. This means that **c** will be shared by all the threads of this Servlet. The location of a number of HTML files and templates that will be used by the Servlet is also defined. Notice how each path consists of a combination of BasePath (which was defined in BaseInventory) and a filename. Since the BasePath is defined in a centralized location, the code becomes easier to maintain. If you want to change your templates directory, all you need to do is change its value in the BaseInventory class (instead of having to change paths of all templates in different servlets).

The ConnectionPool variable is used for obtaining a database connection from the pool maintained by that class. For this, we need to get an instance of the ConnectionPool class and initialize it.

```
if(c == null)
{
    c = ConnectionPool.getInstance();
    c.initialize();
}
```

Since **getInstance()** is a static synchronized method in the ConnectionPool class, we are sure that only one instance of that class will be returned and stored in the variable **c**. Even if two threads of this Servlet begin execution at the same time and invoke **getInstance()** simultaneously upon finding that c is null, only one of them will actually cause a new instance of ConnectionPool to be created. The **initialize()** method will cause MAX_CONNECTIONS number of database connections to be established. These connections can now be used by different threads of this Servlet.

To obtain a connection we invoke the **getConnection()** method of ConnectionPool. This is an instance method that is synchronized too. As a result, we can be sure that each thread has a separate connection to the database, avoiding chances of one thread stepping on another's SQL statements.

```
conn = c.getConnection();
```

All this is happening in the **doPost()** method, a method that is invoked when a POST submission is done from a FORM. In this method we also define a variable session of the type HttpSession, which will be used for establishing a session with the client machine. By establishing a session, we can avoid validation of the username and password every time the user tries to invoke a Servlet that belongs to the inventory package.

The **validPassword()** method defined in **BaseInventory()** is used for validation against the database. If the user is found to be authorized, a session is established:

```
session = req.getSession(true);
```

The username and password are stored in this session so that they don't have to be transmitted every time:

```
session.putValue("Inventory.username", username);
session.putValue("Inventory.password", password);
```

The next time the user invokes this Servlet, provided the session has not expired, the username is retrieved from the session **variable Inventory.username**.

This class has a dual purpose. The first time it is invoked (from the main menu), it displays the product entry screen in which you can type information about a new product that you want to add to the database. However, the Submit button of this entry screen also points to the same class, so when you press Submit, AddProduct is invoked again, because the AddProduct contains a method for writing the product information to the database as well. And how does it distinguish whether it should write to the database or just display another product entry page? The answer is determined by the user selection in response to the question, "Do you want to add more products?" If the user chooses Yes, another product entry screen is presented; otherwise, all the products whose information was supplied by the user are added to the database.

Information about all products that need to be added is stored in the session variable **AddProduct.productVector**. This is initialized to an empty vector the first time AddProduct is invoked in a session:

```
session.putValue("AddProduct.productVector", new Vector());
```

The method **showAddProductPage()** simply shows the screen in which users can define the name, price, etc. of a product they want to add. This method needs a database connection, as some items—for example, names of categories to which the product can be added—are retrieved from the database.

The connection is then returned to the pool, as it is no longer required:

```
c.putConnection(conn);
```

Now if the user presses the Submit button, the AddProduct Servlet is invoked again. This time, however, there's a difference, because it has been invoked from the Add Product screen instead of the main menu and thus it has to read information about the product that the user entered before pressing the Submit button. This information can be extracted from the FORM variables of the Add Product form such as name, description_url, description, and so on.

This time the Servlet gets a handle to the session using:

```
session = req.getSession(false);
```

The false value is passed in the argument as we want to use the session that was established the first time (instead of creating a new session). An instance of Product is created using the values supplied by the user. This Product is then added to the Vector or products that need to be added in this session:

```
Product p = new Product(id, category_id, name,
                description_url,email,
                price, quantity_in_stock, danger_level,
                description, display_price,
                search_keywords);
```

```
Vector v =
    (Vector)session.getValue("AddProduct.productVector");
v.addElement(p);
session.putValue("AddProduct.productVector", v);
```

Next we examine whether the user chose to add more products in this session or not. If no more products were added, the method **writeProducts()** is invoked; otherwise, **showAddProductPage()** is invoked.

Next we look at these two methods. **showAddProductPage()** uses the CategoryOptions class to retrieve a list of all categories. It does this because it needs to present a list of categories in the Add Product screen so that the user can specify the parent category of the product. The method **get()** of CategoryOptions returns a list of all categories to which products can be added, namely, the terminal categories.

writeProducts() is used for adding one or more products to the database. One of the inputs to this method is the vector "AddProduct.productVector," which contains one or more Product objects. It loops through all the products in this vector and creates a record in the products table. Each product is given a unique id through the **products_seq** sequence.

Here's the relevant code:

```
Statement stmt = conn.createStatement();
int size = productVector.size();
String baseSQL = "INSERT INTO products(id, category_id,
        name, description_url, email, price,
        quantity_in_stock, danger_level, description,
        last_modified_by, last_modification_date,
        display_price, search_keywords) VALUES(";
String sequenceSQL =
    "SELECT products_seq.NEXTVAL FROM dual";
ResultSet rset;
for(int i=0; i<size; i++)
{
    Product p = (Product)productVector.elementAt(i);
    rset = stmt.executeQuery(sequenceSQL);
    rset.next();

    String id = rset.getString(1);

    String insertSQL = baseSQL + id + "," +
        p.getCategoryId() + ",'" + p.getName() + "','" +
        p.getDescriptionUrl() + "','" + p.getEmail() +
        "','" + p.getPrice() +
        "'," + p.getQuantityInStock() + "," +
        p.getDangerLevel() + ",'" + p.getDescription()
        + "','" + username + "', SYSDATE, '" +
        p.getDisplayPrice() + "', '" +
```

```
              p.getSearchKeywords() + "')";
          stmt.executeUpdate(insertSQL);
      }
```

5. AddCategory

This class is quite similar to AddProduct and follows similar principles. Of course some of the SQL is different, as it inserts into the categories table and retrieves the unique id from a different sequence.

6. CategoryOptions

This is a helper class containing a method that returns the list of terminal categories. It shows the hierarchy by linking a category to its parents with a "->." A list returned by it could contain elements like the following:

Produce->Vegetables

Produce->Fruits

Appliances->Electric->Small

The String that is returned is a set of HTML OPTION tags that can be inserted into a SELECT list. The **get()** method takes an argument that is the id of the category you want selected by default in the list of options.

This is how the code looks like:

```
/* Find out all the categories that have no subcategories, that is, the terminal
   categories */
    String querySQL = "SELECT id, category_id, name
                FROM categories
                WHERE has_sub_categories=0";
    ResultSet rset = stmt.executeQuery(querySQL);
    while(rset.next())
    {
        String finalId = rset.getString(1);
        String finalCategoryId = rset.getString(2);
        String finalName = rset.getString(3);
        finalIds.addElement(finalId);
        finalCategoryIds.addElement(finalCategoryId);
        finalNames.addElement(finalName);
    }

    int sz = finalIds.size();
/* Loop through all the categories retrieved. For each of these, find the parent
   category. Keep on searching the parent till you reach the top-level category,
   which has no parent. In the process, keep on appending the name of the
```

parent category so that in the end we have a string that looks like this:
Appliances->Electric->Small. The name finally derived is stored in the
finalNames Vector.
*/

```
        for(int i=0; i<sz; i++)
        {
                String catId = (String)finalCategoryIds.
                    elementAt(i);
                while(true)
                {
                        querySQL = "SELECT category_id, name FROM
                                categories WHERE id=" + catId;
                        rset = stmt.executeQuery(querySQL);
```

/* Break when no parent is found - this will happen when we're examining
    a category with id = 0—the TOP LEVEL category */

```
                        if(rset.next() == false)
                                break;
                        catId = rset.getString(1);
                        String nm = (String)finalNames.elementAt(i);
                        nm = rset.getString(2) + "->" + nm;
                        finalNames.setElementAt(nm, i);
                }
        }
```

Then this function simply puts an <OPTION> tag around each of the category
names and sends back the list of options.

7. SelectProduct

This class displays a list of products. It is invoked when a user chooses to modify,
delete, or view a product. It calls the method **showSelectProductPage()**, which
retrieves all products from the database and presents them in a select list. This method
uses the template **selectProduct.html**. The template looks as follows:

```
<BODY BGCOLOR='#FFFFFF'>
    <CENTER><H1><B>
<VAR_HEADER>
    </B></H1></CENTER>
<P>
    <CENTER>
        Please select one product from the list below<P>

<VAR_FORM_NAME>
```

```
                <TABLE><TR><TD>
                    <SELECT NAME='product' SIZE='5'>;
<VAR_PRODUCT_LIST>
                    </SELECT>
<VAR_ACTION>
                    </TD></TR>
                    <TR><TD> ALIGN='right'><INPUT TYPE='submit' NAME='
                        submit' VALUE='Submit'>
                    </TD></TR>
                </TABLE>
            </FORM>
        </CENTER>
</BODY>
```

It contains the following variables:

<VAR_HEADER>—depending on the action that the user wants to perform (view, modify, or delete), this variable will take values like **Modify Product, Delete Product**, etc.

<VAR_FORM_NAME>—depending on the user chosen action, this will contain a <FORM> tag with the appropriate ACTION; for deletes, the ACTION will be **Inventory.DeleteProduct**.

<VAR_PRODUCT_LIST>—this will contain names of all the products that can be viewed, modified, or deleted.

<VAR_ACTION>—this variable is of use for distinguishing between "view" and "modify." If the user chooses "view," this selection will result in a hidden variable whose value is "view." This is an indication to the ShowProduct Servlet that it should display product details, but without a Submit button, so that the user cannot change product information. In the case of "modify," however, the value will be "modify," which will instruct ShowProduct to display the Submit button.

As mentioned, this class needs to retrieve a list of products from the database. Here is the relevant code:

```
            String querySQL = "SELECT id, name FROM products";
            ResultSet rset = stmt.executeQuery(querySQL);
            while(rset.next())
            {
                productList += "<OPTION VALUE='" + rset.
                    getString(1) + "'>" + rset.getString(2);
            }
```

And this is how the **productList** variable is used to populate the value of the **<VAR_PRODUCT_LIST>** variable:

```
            PageUtil p = new PageUtil(pgName, out);
            p.setReplaceItem("<VAR_PRODUCT_LIST>", productList);
```

8. DeleteProduct

This servlet deletes the product selected by the user in the previous screen. The SQL looks like this:

```
String deleteSQL = "DELETE FROM products WHERE id="
    + id;
stmt.executeUpdate(deleteSQL);
stmt.close();
```

Here id is obtained as a FORM variable, and the value is determined by the product that the user selected from the list of products.

9. ShowProduct

This class retrieves information about the product (selected by the user) from the database and displays it in another FORM. It uses the **showProduct.html** template. Values of variables like <VAR_NAME>, <VAR_PRICE>, <VAR_DISPLAY_PRICE>, and so on are replaced by the values retrieved from the database.

Here are portions of the code that do this:

// SQL for retrieving information about a product with a given id

```
String querySQL = "SELECT category_id, name, description_
    url, price, quantity_in_stock, danger_level,
    description, email, last_modified_by,
    last_modification_date, display_price, search_key
    words FROM products WHERE id=" + id;

ResultSet rset = stmt.executeQuery(querySQL);
rset.next();
category_id = rset.getString(1);
name = rset.getString(2);
description_url = rset.getString(3);
.....
```

// Retrieve a list of categories using the **get()** method of CategoryOptions

```
CategoryOptions co = new CategoryOptions();
String options = co.get(category_id, conn);
```

// Create HTML elements with default values set to the ones retrieved from the database

```
name = "<INPUT TYPE='text' NAME='name' SIZE='20'
        VALUE='" + name + "'>";
description_url = "<INPUT TYPE='text'
    NAME='description_url' SIZE='35' VALUE=" +
    description_url + "'>";
```

// Substitute the variables in the template with the HTML elements created above

```
PageUtil p = new PageUtil(pgName, out);
p.setReplaceItem("<VAR_NAME>", name);
p.setReplaceItem("<VAR_DESCRIPTION_URL>",
    description_url);
```

This will result in the display of the product description page.

10. ModifyProduct

This class modifies information about a product in the database. It is invoked when a user chooses the **Modify Product** path. The product information is displayed by **ShowProduct** and now if the user presses the Submit button, this Servlet is invoked. It reads the FORM variables to determine values that should be applied to different fields of this product:

```
if(nm.equalsIgnoreCase("name"))
    name = v1;
if(nm.equalsIgnoreCase("description_url"))
    description_url = v1;
if(nm.equalsIgnoreCase("description"))
    description = v1;
if(nm.equalsIgnoreCase("email"))
    email = v1;
```

It then creates a Product instance using these values:

```
Product p = new Product(intId, intCategoryId, name,
            description_url,email,
            price, quantity_in_stock, danger_level,
            description, display_price,
            search_keywords);
```

Then the method **modifyProduct()**, which makes modifications to the product record in the database, is called.

Here's a look at **modifyProduct()**:

```
String updateSQL = "UPDATE products SET category_id="
        + p.getCategoryId() +
    ", name='" + p.getName() + "', description_url='" +
      p.getDescriptionUrl() + "', email ='" + p.getEmail() +
      "', price='" + p.getPrice() + "',quantity_in_Stock=" +
      p.getQuantityInStock() + ", danger_level=" +
      p.getDangerLevel() + ", description='" +
          p.getDescription()
```

```
            + "', last_modified_by='" + username + "',
            last_modification_date=SYSDATE, search_keywords='" +
            p.getSearchKeywords() + "', display_price='" +
            p.getDisplayPrice() + "' WHERE id=" + p.getId();
    stmt.executeUpdate(updateSQL);
```

11. SelectCategory

This class is similar to SelectProduct in that it shows a list of categories. However, there is one big difference. In SelectProduct we displayed all products in the database. In the case of categories, however, this is not the right thing to do, especially in the case of the Delete Category option, as we don't want to allow deletion of a nonterminal category or a category containing products unless all the children have been deleted first. To do this, we need to use two levels of queries, as shown below.

First we retrieve a list of parent categories of all products and store them in a vector called **allProdCatIds**.

```
querySQL = "SELECT category_id FROM products";
rset = stmt.executeQuery(querySQL);
while(rset.next())
{
        allProdCatIds.addElement(rset.
            getString(1));
}
```

Next we retrieve the parent category of each category in the system.

```
querySQL = "SELECT category_id FROM
        categories";
rset = stmt.executeQuery(querySQL);
while(rset.next())
{
        String catId = rset.getString(1);
        if(catId != null)
            allProdCatIds.addElement(catId);
}
```

Now we look at the id and name of each category. If this id exists in the **allProdCatIds** Vector, this category either has products in it or subcategories under it. Otherwise, it is a candidate for the Select list, and we add it to the list of options:

```
querySQL = "SELECT id, name FROM categories";
rset = stmt.executeQuery(querySQL);
while(rset.next())
{
        boolean hasProdsInIt = false;
```

```
String catId = rset.getString(1);
String catName = rset.getString(2);
if(action.equalsIgnoreCase("Delete"))
{
        for(int k=0; k<prodCatsSize; k++)
        {
            if(catId.equals(
                (String)allProdCatIds.
                    elementAt(k)))
            {
                hasProdsInIt = true;
                break;
            }
        }
}
if(hasProdsInIt)
    continue;
categoryList += "<OPTION VALUE='" + catId + "'>"
                + catName;
```

12. DeleteCategory

This uses the following code to delete a category selected by the user from the system.

```
String deleteSQL = "DELETE FROM categories
                    WHERE id=" + id;
stmt.executeUpdate(deleteSQL);
```

13. SignOff

This Servlet is invoked when you press the Logout button. It invalidates the current session. As a result, if somebody tries to invoke one of the Servlets from the machine where a logout was done, the system will throw up an error asking the user to log in with a username and password.

```
HttpSession session = req.getSession(false);
session.invalidate();
res.setContentType("text/html");
try{
    PrintWriter out = res.getWriter();
    out.println("<HTML><HEAD></HEAD><BODY
BGCOLOR='#FFFFFF'></BODY></HTML>");
    out.close();
}catch(Exception ex){}
```

HTML Files in Document Root

inventory.html

This is the entry-point HTML file. It defines a frameset that includes two frames: one that contains blank.html and another that contains inventoryOptions.html.

blank.html

An HTML file that just displays a blank white screen. Initially, the left part of the frameset contains this file. However, it is replaced when the user has logged in.

inventoryOptions.html

This displays all the options that a user has, such as **Products->Add** and **Categories->Delete**. Each of these options belongs to a separate FORM and appears as a link. When the link is clicked, the corresponding Servlet is invoked.

It contains a **doSubmit**() method that executes a form submission when the link is clicked. This is how it works:

The form looks like this:

```
<FORM NAME='noName1' ACTION='/newZone/Inventory.AddProduct'
                     METHOD='POST'>
 <CENTER><A HREF=' ' onClick='return doSubmit(0)'>Add</A></CENTER>
```

Due to the **onClick** directive, when the link "Add" is clicked, the Javascript function **doSubmit**() is invoked.

Since each of the Servlets needs to verify the username and password, it is important that each FORM contain the value of username and password. However, instead of putting a username text field and password field in each form, we have created another form that contains these. When the user clicks the link for a Servlet, values are retrieved from that FORM and placed in hidden variables inside the FORM that is being submitted before the actual submission is done.

Each form thus contains the hidden variables "username" and "password" as follows:

```
<INPUT TYPE='hidden' NAME='username' VALUE=' '>
<INPUT TYPE='hidden' NAME='password' VALUE=' '>
```

The form that contains the actual username and password fields looks like this:

```
<FORM NAME='passwordForm'>
             <TR><TD><B><H5>Username:</H5></B>
             </TD>
          <TD><INPUT TYPE='text' NAME=
             'username'
               VALUE=' ' SIZE='8'>
             </TD></TR>
```

```
<TR><TD><B><H5>Password:</H5></B></TD>
<TD><INPUT TYPE='password' N
    AME='password' VALUE=' '
        SIZE='8'></TD></TR>
</FORM>
```

We have defined the Javascript function **doSubmit()** as follows:

```
<SCRIPT>
  function doSubmit(pos)
  {
        if(document.passwordForm.username.value.length == 0 ||
            document.passwordForm.password.value.length == 0)
        {
            alert('Please supply a username/password');
            return false;
        }
        document.forms[pos].username.value =
                document.passwordForm.username.value;
        document.forms[pos].password.value =
                document.passwordForm.password.value;
        parent.left.location.replace('signoff.html');
        document.forms[pos].submit();
        return false;
  }
</SCRIPT>
```

It first checks whether the user has supplied a username and password. If not, an alert is thrown and the form is not submitted. However, if a username and password has been supplied, the values are retrieved from the passwordForm and stuffed into the hidden variables of the form that is going to be submitted.

```
document.forms[pos].username.value =
        document.passwordForm.username.value;
document.forms[pos].password.value =
        document.passwordForm.password.value;
```

Also, the location of the left frame is replaced to show **signoff.html**, which contains a Logout button that can log a person out of the system.

```
parent.left.location.replace('signoff.html');
```

Finally, the submission is done.

```
document.forms[pos].submit();
```

signoff.html

This contains two buttons: one that can be used for logging out of the system and another for going back to the Main Menu page where all the options like Products-> Add are displayed.

Other HTML Files and Templates

inventoryError.html

This is an error template that is used for displaying any errors that may have occurred. It contains a variable **<ERROR_MSG>**. Whenever a Servlet wants to throw an error, it uses this template and replaces the variable with a String that describes the error that has occurred.

addCategory.html

This is a template that users can use for adding a new category to the system. Most of the elements in this are static. However, there is a variable **<VAR_CATEGORY_OPTIONS>**, which is a list of categories retrieved from the database that could be potential parents of the category being added.

A Javascript function, **verify()**, has been defined. This function is being used to check whether the user has supplied values for the required fields. If the user has not entered a name or a **description_url** and has pressed the Submit button, an alert is thrown up.

categoryDeleted.html

This template is displayed to indicate that a category has been successfully deleted from the database.

productModified.html

This template is displayed to indicate that a product has been successfully modified in the database.

selectProduct.html

In this template all the products in the database are displayed as a Select list. The user can choose one of these to view, modify, or delete the product. It contains a Javascript function, **isSelected()**, which makes sure that the user has selected a product before pressing the Submit button. If not, an alert is thrown.

addProduct.html

This template is similar to the addCategory.html template. It can be used to add a new category to the system. Most of the elements in this are static. However, the variable **<VAR_CATEGORY_OPTIONS>**, which is a list of categories retrieved from the database, could be a potential parent of the product being added.

This one also contains a **verify()** function.

productsAdded.html

This template is displayed to indicate that one or more products have been successfully added to the database.

categoriesAdded.html

This template is displayed to indicate that one or more categories have been successfully added to the database.

productDeleted.html

This template is displayed to indicate that a product has been successfully deleted from the database.

showProduct.html

This template is used to display details of product that is present in the database. It contains variables like **<VAR_NAME>** and **<VAR_PRICE>**, which are populated with values like the name and the price of the product retrieved from the database.

selectCategory.html

In this template all the categories in the database that can be deleted are displayed as a select list. The user can choose one of these to delete it. It contains a Javascript function, **isSelected()**, which makes sure that the user has selected a category before pressing the Submit button. If not, an alert is thrown.

Profile Management System

High-Level Description

The profile management system helps maintain information about your customers in the database. It allows customers to register so that they can use your site and purchase products. It helps to maintain personal information like name, phone, and shipping and billing addresses. The system also allows maintenance of credit card information so that customers don't have to type their credit card every time they want to purchase something from your site. The system helps as well in providing self-service to users. For instance, it allows users to look up their password in case they've forgotten it. It also provides a channeled feedback system through which customers can ask specific questions that fall into particular categories. The system provides an interface that customers can use for updating information too. For instance, if the customer moves to a new address, he or she can directly update that in the system without having to call a customer support person in your company.

There is no single entry point for this system. Links to the various subsystems appear in the menu bar when the user visits the ordering section of your site. A bar appears at the top of the frame with links to registration, update, feedback, and password retrieval applications.

Classes and Their Methods

BaseProfile.java

This is the base class that is the parent of all Servlets that belong to the Profile package. It is similar to the base class of Inventory, BaseInventory.java, and it contains similar methods for debugging and verifying the username and password of customers.

1. showErrorPage()
A method that is used by all Servlets for throwing an error page.

2. initializeDebugFile()
A method for creating a new debug file.

3. debug()
A method for writing debug information.

RegistrationPage.java

This Servlet is invoked when a user tries to register. This could happen if the user has clicked the Register button in the menu, or if some other application like GetPayment has redirected the user. It displays a Registration page in which the user can supply information such as name, address, and credit card number.

1. doGet()
This method reads some FORM variables to determine where this Servlet was called from. It gets a database connection and calls **showRegistrationPage()**.

2. showRegistrationPage()
This displays the registration page, in which users can type information to be saved to the database.

Register.java

Once the user has filled out registration information, this Servlet is invoked and writes the information to the database.

1. doPost()
This method retrieves FORM variables to find out the name, address, etc. that the user has supplied in the registration page. It then calls a method **dataError()**, which checks some basic things. If the data does not have errors, the method **registerUser()** is called.

2. dataError()
This method checks for validity of the data the user has entered in the registration page. It makes sure, for example, that the username is at least four characters long and that both a first name and last name have been supplied. Depending on what your storefront wants to enforce, you can add or remove code from this method.

3. registerUser()
This method creates records for the customer in the profiles and addresses table. It then shows a thank you page confirming that the user has been registered in the system.

UpdatePage.java

This Servlet is invoked when a user clicks on the Update Profile button. It may also be invoked if an existing user wants to use a different credit card in the checkout screen.

The Servlet first checks the username and password supplied by the user to access the system. It proceeds only if this combination is found to be valid. Then it retrieves profile information about the user from the database and shows it in a format similar to the registration page. This allows users to update their information.

1. **doPost()**

   This method reads FORM variables to determine the username and password supplied by the user for accessing the system. It also determines where the application is being called from. It then calls **showUpdatePage()**.

2. **showUpdatePage()**

   This method retrieves profile information about the user from the database. It compares the supplied password with the password in the database. If they don't match, it calls **showErrorPage()** and returns. Otherwise, it retrieves address information as well and displays the Update page template.

UpdateProfile.java

This Servlet is invoked when the user presses the Submit button in the update page generated by UpdatePage. It writes a user's updated information to the database.

1. **doPost()**

   This method retrieves FORM variables to find out the updated name, address, and so on that the user has supplied in the update page. It then calls a method dataError(), which checks some basic things. If the data does not have errors, the method **updateUser()** is called.

2. **dataError()**

   This method checks for validity of the data the user has entered in the update page. It makes sure that information such as the first name, last name, and credit card number have been supplied. Depending on what your storefront wants to enforce, you can add or remove code from this method.

3. **updateUser()**

   This method updates records of the customer in the profiles and addresses tables. It then shows a thank-you page confirming that the user's information has been updated.

GetNewCard.java

If you look at the Ordering System, you will recall that for an existing user who wants to use a new credit card, the Servlet GetNewCard that resides in the Profile package is called. This simply creates a page in which users can type in their username and password so that they can access the UpdatePage Servlet, allowing them to update their information.

1. **doGet()**

   This method reads the FORM variables specifying the username of this person and the place from which the Servlet is being called. It then brings up a template in which it supplies the username and also stores the value of the **calledFrom** variable. The action of this new template calls UpdatePage.

ContactUs.java

This Servlet is invoked when a customer has filled out the Contact Us form and has pressed the Submit button. It determines the category under which the user feedback falls and sends mail to the corresponding department.

1. doPost()

This method reads the email address and username of the customer who is using the feedback form. It also reads the category under which the feedback falls and a detailed description of the same. Based on the category, it determines the email address to which the feedback should be sent. It then calls the method **sendMail()**.

2. sendMail()

This method sends email to the specified feedback address and brings up a page informing the user that the feedback information has been mailed.

PasswordFinder.java

This Servlet tries to retrieve the password associated with the user from the database and provides it to the user.

1. doPost()

This method reads the values supplied by the user, such as username, email, and last name. It then calls **showPasswordFinder()**.

2. showPasswordFinder()

This method tries to retrieve the password of this user. It then either emails the password or displays it in another screen. If no match is found, it calls **showErrorPage()**.

3. sendMail()

This method is called if the Servlet wants to send a email to the user.

Detailed Description

All the classes of the Ordering Management System are contained in a package called Profile. Thus, each class begins with this line:

package Profile;

Most of the classes use a number of packages. These include the **java.sql**, **java.io**, and **java.util** packages. They also use our Utilities package, which contains utilities like the connection-pooling utility, the mail-sending utility, and so on.

Also, most of the classes extend the BaseProfile class.

1. BaseProfile.java

This Servlet is the base class of all servlets in the Ordering package. Its methods are quite similar to the ones in BaseInventory. It contains a **BasePath** variable.

2. RegistrationPage.java

This Servlet brings up the registration page. Since it may be called from the Get-Payment Servlet, there are chances that the username will be presupplied. However, if a user tries to register using the Register button, there would be no presupplied username, and the customer would have to choose one in the page itself. The Servlet distinguishes between the two cases. In the **doGet()** method, it checks the following two-form variables: **username** and **calledFrom**. These tell the Servlet the presupplied username and where it is being called from. The **doPost()** method calls **showRegistrationPage()** with this information.

If a username has been supplied, the status associated with this profile is checked:

```
String querySQL = "SELECT status FROM profiles
         WHERE username = '" + username + "'";
```

If a record with this username is found and the status is not NEW_USER, it means that somebody is trying to reregister with the same username. Therefore, an error page is shown in which the user is advised to use the Update Profile page.

```
if(status.equalsIgnoreCase("NEW_USER") == false)
{
        PageUtil p = new PageUtil(errorHtml, out);
        String errorMsg = "You are already a
            registered user. To update your
            profile you need to visit the Update
                section";
```

The method then loads the **registrationPage.html** template, substitutes the supplied username (if any) into the page, and displays it. This brings up the registration page in which the user can type information.

3. Register.java

This Servlet is invoked when the user presses the Submit button in the **registrationPage.html** screen. It retrieves the name, address and card information supplied by the user in the **doPost()** method. Then the method **dataError()**, in which validity of the data is checked is called. If the data is found to be invalid, an error page is thrown and the Servlet returns:

```
if( dataError(out,
        username,password, pw_confirm,
```

```
                firstName, lastName, phone,
                fax, email, shipLine1, shipLine2,
                shipCity, shipState, shipZip,
                billLine1, billLine2, billCity, billState,
                    billZip,
                ccardNumber, ccardCompany, date, month, year,
                calledFrom,
                errorHtml
                ) == true)
        {
            c.putConnection(conn);
            out.close();
            return;
        }
```

The method **dataError()** makes sure that, for example, the username is at least four characters:

```
public boolean dataError(PrintWriter out,
                String username, String password,  String
                    pw_confirm,
                String firstName,  String lastName,  String
                    phone,
                String fax,  String email,  String shipLine1,
                String shipLine2, String shipCity,
                String shipState,
                String shipZip, String billLine1,  String
                    billLine2,
                String billCity,  String billState,  String
                    billZip,
                String ccardNumber,  String ccardCompany,
                String date,
                String month,  String year,  String called
                    From,
            String pgName)
```

It returns a false value if any error is found. It also shows the error page before returning. Since there may be more than one error condition, it collects all the errors before displaying the error message. For this a String **errorMsg** is initialized to empty:

```
String errorMsg = "";
```

As errors are encountered, information is appended to this string, so if the username is less than four characters, a corresponding error message is appended. The Boolean error, which is initialized to false, is set to true to indicate that an error has occurred.

```
if(username.length() < 4)
{
```

```
        error = true;
        errorMsg += "<LI>Username should be at least 4
                      characters";
}
if(password.equals(pw_confirm) == false)
{
        error = true;
        errorMsg += "<LI>Password does not match confirm";
}
```

After all the checks have been performed, it checks whether error is true. If so, the error page is shown. Then it returns the Boolean error:

```
if(error == true)
{
        showErrorPage(out, pgName, errorMsg);
}
return error;
```

On the other hand, if the user data is valid, the method **registerUser()**, which writes information to the database, is called.

First, autoCommit is set to off, because we are going to add information to multiple tables in this routine. We want either all or none of the SQL statements to take effect.

```
        conn.setAutoCommit(false);
```

It first checks whether this user's username and password exist in the system. If so, profile information needs to be updated, as opposed to just being inserted.

```
String querySQL = "SELECT id,password FROM profiles
                WHERE username='" + username + "'";
```

If no record is found, an insert statement is issued. Before that, a unique profile id is obtained from the **profiles_seq** sequence:

```
            querySQL = "SELECT profiles_seq.NEXTVAL FROM
                dual";
            rset = stmt.executeQuery(querySQL);
            while(rset.next())
            {
                    id = rset.getString(1);
            }
            String insertSQL = "INSERT INTO profiles(id,
                username, password, first_name,
                last_name, phone, fax, email, ccard_num,
                ccard_exp_date, ccard_company,
                status) VALUES (" + id + ",'" + username +
```

```
                          "','" + password + "','" +
                          firstName + "','" + lastName + "','"
                             + phone
                          + "','" + fax + "','" + email
                          + "','" + ccardNumber + "', TO_DATE('"
                             + date
                          + "-" + month + "-" + year
                          + "', 'DD-MON-YYYY'), '" + ccardCompany
                             + "',
                          'UPDATED_USER')";

             stmt.executeUpdate(insertSQL);
```

On the other hand, if a record with this username exists in the database, the password supplied is matched with the corresponding password in the database. This situation arises if the Servlet has been called from GetPayment for a person who is using the payment module for the first time. This step is taken to prevent somebody from invoking the Servlet using just the username and without knowing the password.

It then updates the profile with all the new information and also updates the status in the profiles table to UPDATED_USER.

```
String updateSQL = "UPDATE profiles SET password='" +
    password +
    "', first_name='" +
    firstName + "', last_name='" + lastName + "', phone='" +
    phone + "', fax='" + fax + "',
    email= '" + email + "', ccard_num='" + ccardNumber + "',
    ccard_exp_date=TO_DATE('" + date + "-" + month + "-" +
        year
    + "', 'DD-MON-YYYY'),
    ccard_company='" + ccardCompany + "', status='UPDATED_
        USER'
                WHERE id = " + id;
```

Then it creates two entries in the addresses table: one for the SHIPPING address and another for the billing address. The id for both is retrieved from **addresses_seq**.

```
querySQL = "SELECT addresses_seq.NEXTVAL FROM
    dual";
String addId = "";
rset = stmt.executeQuery(querySQL);
while(rset.next())
{
    addId = rset.getString(1);
}
```

```
String insertSQL = "INSERT INTO addresses(id,
    profile_id, type, line1, line2,
    city, state, zip) VALUES (" + addId + ","
        + id +
    ",'SHIPPING', '" +
    shipLine1 + "', '" + shipLine2 + "', '" +
    shipCity + "', '" + shipState +
    "','" + shipZip + "')";
stmt.executeUpdate(insertSQL);

addId = "";
rset = stmt.executeQuery(querySQL);
while(rset.next())
{
    addId = rset.getString(1);
}
insertSQL = "INSERT INTO addresses(id, profile_id,
    type, line1, line2, city,
    state, zip) VALUES (" + addId + "," + id +
    ",'BILLING', '" + billLine1 +
    "', '" + billLine2 + "', '" + billCity +
        "', '"
    + billState + "','"
    + billZip + "')";
stmt.executeUpdate(insertSQL);
```

Now that we have been successful in adding all the records, we can commit the transaction and reset the **autoCommit** for this connection:

```
conn.commit();
stmt.close();
conn.setAutoCommit(true);
```

4. UpdatePage.java

This Servlet retrieves the profile information of the person from the database and presents it in an editable FORM. The template used is **updatePage.html**.

The bulk of the work is done in **showUpdatePage()**.

```
public void showUpdatePage(PrintWriter out, String username,
                           String password,
                           String calledFrom, String
                               pgName,
                           String errorHtml, Connection
                               conn)

    throws Exception
```

It begins with a declaration of four String arrays that contain possible values for credit card company names, dates, months, and years. These will be displayed as options to the user so that they can update their credit card information. We had these statically written in the registration template. However, in this case we need to have the original information entered by the user as preselected, so we can't have a static value for any of these fields.

The Servlet retrieves profile information about the user from the database:

```
String querySQL = "SELECT id, password,
    first_name,
  last_name, phone, fax,
  email, ccard_num, TO_CHAR(ccard_exp_date,
  'DD-MON-YYYY'), ccard_company, status
FROM profiles WHERE username = '" + username
    + "'";
```

It compares the retrieved password with the one entered by the user. If they don't match, an error page is shown:

```
if(password.equals(dbPassword) == false)
{
    showErrorPage(out, errorHtml,
    "Invalid Username/Password");
    return;
}
```

The date is retrieved in the DD-MON-YYYY format from the database. A StringTokenizer is used to split this into day, month, and year so that we can set the appropriate defaults when the user information is displayed. Also, SQL statements are issued for retrieving the SHIPPING and BILLING addresses of this user:

```
String baseQuerySQL = "SELECT line1, line2, city,
    state, zip FROM addresses
    WHERE profile_id=" + id + " AND type='";
querySQL = baseQuerySQL + "SHIPPING'";
rset = stmt.executeQuery(querySQL);
......
......
querySQL = baseQuerySQL + "BILLING'";
rset = stmt.executeQuery(querySQL);
```

Values thus obtained are used to substitute variables in the template, and the page is then displayed. Now users can make changes to their information and press the Submit button, which will invoke the UpdateProfile servlet.

5. UpdateProfile.java

This Servlet also checks for data validity using a **dataError()** method. It then calls **updateUser()** if the data is valid. Also in this method, initially autoCommit is set to false. It first updates the profiles table:

```
String updateSQL = "UPDATE profiles SET password='" +
    password + "', first_name='" +
    firstName + "', last_name='" + lastName + "', phone='" +
     phone + "', fax='" + fax + "',
    email= '" + email + "', ccard_num='" + ccardNumber + "',
    ccard_exp_date=
    TO_DATE('" + date + "-" + month + "-" + year + "',
    'DD-MON-YYYY'), ccard_company='" +
    ccardCompany + "', status='UPDATED_USER' WHERE id = "
        + id;
```

Then it tries to update the addresses table:

```
String updateSQL = "UPDATE addresses SET line1='" +
    shipLine1
    + "', line2='" + shipLine2
    + "', city='" + shipCity + "', state='" + shipState +
    "', zip='" + shipZip + "'
    WHERE profile_id=" + id + " AND type='SHIPPING'";
stmt.executeUpdate(updateSQL);

updateSQL = "UPDATE addresses SET line1='" + billLine1 +
    "', line2='" + billLine2  +
    "', city='" + billCity + "', state='" + billState + "',
    zip='" + billZip + "'
    WHERE profile_id=" + id + " AND type='BILLING'";
stmt.executeUpdate(updateSQL);
```

autoCommit is then set to true, and a commit is performed. This updates the record in the database.

6. GetNewCard.java

This Servlet brings up a page where users can type in a password and access the Servlets for updating their profiles. It retrieves the values of **username** and **calledFrom** FORM variables and substitutes them in the **getNewCard.html** template before displaying the template.

7. ContactUs.java

This Servlet directs a user feedback to an email address that's responsible for the processing category in which the feedback falls. If you look at Chapter 11, you will see that feedback can be organized into categories. You can modify these categories to whichever are appropriate for your store. The ContactUs Servlet stores a list of categories and the email addresses of persons responsible for these categories.

Here's how the default categories are stored:

```
String[] mailCategories = {"registrationProblem",
                           "orderingProblem",
                           "generalQuestion"};
String[] mailAddresses = {"helpReg@myCompany.com",
                          "helpOrder@myCompany.com",
                          "helpGeneral@myCompany.com"};
```

It then reads the values of the FORM variables category and description, which indicate in what category the user has classified his or her feedback and the detailed description of the feedback.

It traverses the **mailCategories** array till it finds a category whose name matches the one chosen by the user. The corresponding email address from the **mailAddresses** array is chosen as the address to which mail should be sent.

```
int len = mailCategories.length;
String mailTo = "";
for(int i=0; i<len; i++)
{
    if(mailCategories[i].equals(category))
    {
        mailTo = mailAddresses[i];
        break;
    }
}
```

The **sendMail()** method is then called. This method sends a mail and also shows a confirmation page to the user. The confirmation page is based on the **contactMailSent.html** template.

8. PasswordFinder.java

The PasswordFinder Servlet tries to find the password of a registered user based on some seed data supplied by the user. Seed data includes last name and email address of the user. If the user also supplies username as the seed data, the password is displayed in an HTML page. However, if you think this is a security risk, you may eliminate this option. If the username is not supplied, the password and username are sent to the email address to which the profile belongs.

In the **doPost()** method the username, email, and last name supplied by the user are read. Then the method **showPasswordFinder()** is called.

```
public void showPasswordFinder(PrintWriter out, String username,
                String email, String lastName,
                String showPasswordHtml, String errorHtml,
                Connection conn)
        throws Exception
```

This method first makes sure that the user has supplied an email address and a last name. If neither of these has been entered, it calls **showErrorPage()** and returns.

If the username has been supplied, it retrieves the password, email, and last name from the profiles table.

```
querySQL = "SELECT password FROM profiles WHERE NLS_UPPER
    (email)
        = '" + email.toUpperCase() +
        "' AND NLS_UPPER(last_name) = '" + lastName.
            toUpperCase() +
        "' AND username='" + username + "'";
```

If no record is found, this means the user supplied a wrong username. An error page is thrown to reflect this.

If a record is found, the last name and email retrieved from the database are matched with those supplied by the user. If a match is found, the password is displayed to the user using the **showPassword.html** template.

However, if the user did not specify a username, the username, password, and email are derived from the database for a user whose email address is the same as the one typed by the user.

```
querySQL = "SELECT username, password FROM profiles
    WHERE NLS_UPPER(email) = '" +
    email.toUpperCase() + "' AND NLS_UPPER(last_name) = '"
    + lastName.toUpperCase() + "'";
```

The last name entered by the user is matched against the database value. If a match is found, the username and password are sent by mail.

Document Root HTML Files

ordering.html

The Profile Management System is linked to the Ordering Management System. The introduction of this system makes changes in the main page of the Ordering System.

Instead of the two frames that **ordering.html** had originally, the Profile Management System adds another frame that contains the **profileOptions.html** file:

```
<FRAMESET ROWS='60,*' BORDER='0'>
    <FRAME NAME='top' SRC='profileOptions.html'>
    <FRAMESET COLS='180, *' BORDER='0'>
        <FRAME NAME='left' SRC='blank.html'>
        <FRAME NAME='right' SRC='mainOrdering.html'>
    </FRAMESET>
</FRAMESET>
```

This frame appears as a bar at the top.

profileOptions.html

This file contains options provided by the Profile Management System. It adds buttons that allow users to register, update their profiles, contact site administrators, and locate lost passwords.

contactUs.html

This is the page users see if they click on the Contact Us button in the profile options bar. It contains a FORM whose action is the Profile.ContactUs Servlet. One of the fields in the form, category, contains names of categories in which you want to break up user feedback. The more categories you have, the more granularity you can provide. You can modify this FORM to add or remove categories. Corresponding changes will have to be made in the Profile.ContactUs servlet. By default there are three categories:

```
<SELECT NAME='category'>
    <OPTION VALUE='registrationProblem'>
                                    Registration Problem
    <OPTION VALUE='orderingProblem'>Ordering Problem
    <OPTION VALUE='generalQuestion'>General Question
</SELECT>
```

passwordFinder.html

This is the FORM users see if they click the Password Finder button. It asks for user-name, last name and email. On pressing the Submit button, Profile.PasswordFinder is invoked.

updateProfile.html

This FORM leads to the Profile.UpdatePage page. It asks for username and password so that the user can be validated before information is presented for update.

Other HTML Files and Templates

registrationPage.html

This is the registration page in which users can supply information such as username, password, name, address, and credit card information. It contains a Javascript function **verify**(), which is invoked when users press the Submit button. This checks for any data errors like a username of length less than four characters. The ACTION of this FORM is the Profile.Register Servlet.

The address is divided into two sections. In the first section the shipping address is asked for, while in the second section the billing address is requested. For a number of cases these addresses may be the same. We have therefore placed a checkbox next to the second address. If users click this, the address information that they typed for the shipping address is copied over. All this is done in Javascript. The checkbox is defined as follows:

```
<INPUT TYPE='checkbox' NAME='copy' VALUE=' '
      onClick='copyBillingAddress(this.form);'>
                     Copy from Shipping Address
```

The function **copyBillingAddress**() reads the address typed in the shipping address area and applies the same to the billing address area.

Here is the code for this:

```
function copyBillingAddress(frm)
{
    if(frm.copy.checked == true)
    {
            frm.billLine1.value = frm.shipLine1.value;
            frm.billLine2.value = frm.shipLine2.value;
            frm.billCity.value = frm.shipCity.value;
            frm.billState.value = frm.shipState.value;
            frm.billZip.value = frm.shipZip.value;
    }
}
```

registered.html

Once the user has been registered in the database, this template is shown. It contains a variable, **<VAR_SUBMIT>**. If the registration process was initiated from the GetPayment Servlet, this variable is replaced by a Submit button that takes the user back to the GetPayment Servlet so that the Ordering System can charge the customer against the credit card specified during registration.

updatePage.html

This template is used for displaying user information that can be updated. It contains a number of variables whose value is retrieved from the database.

updated.html

This page comes up when a user's information has been successfully updated in the database. This template also contains a **<VAR_SUBMIT>** variable that behaves like the one in **registered.html**.

getNewCard.html

This is the entry-point page to the Update Profile subsystem for existing customers who want to use a new credit card.

contactMailSent.html

This template informs the user that an email has been sent to the appropriate department based on the feedback supplied through the contact us page.

showPassword.html

In this template a user's password is shown if a match is found by the Password Finder.

profileError.html

All Servlets in the package use this template for displaying error messages.

Chapter 15

Ordering Management System

High-Level Description

The Ordering Management System is the system customers used to view your products and then to purchase them. This system is the front end of the store, where customers can place orders. It displays products and categories that have been added using the Inventory Management System. Users can walk down aisles of their choice and add products to a shopping cart. In the end they can go to a checkout counter and pay. The system is password-protected. Customers log in with a username and password.

Customers can choose to maintain a regular cart. This option is useful for stores where customers typically buy the same things quite frequently. A perfect example is the grocery store. The system also allows customers to view the history of their previous orders to obtain details such as what they purchased, at what price, on what date, and when the order was been shipped.

The flow begins with the entry point page, ordering.html. You would access it like this:

http://myServer.com:myPort/ordering.html

The first thing users need to do is supply a username and password to log in. First time customers can establish a new username and password on this page.

Classes and Their Methods

BaseOrdering.java

This is the base class that is the parent of all Servlets that belong to the ordering package. Similar to the base class of Inventory, BaseInventory.java, it contains similar methods for debugging and for verifying the customer's username and password.

Another method that this class contains is **sendTheMail()**, which can be used for sending mails. The method uses one of the classes in the Utilities package.

SignIn.java

This Servlet is invoked when a person signs in. It checks whether the username and password is valid, and whether this person is a new user trying to access the system. It establishes a session with the client machine and creates a database connection. It then shows a screen consisting of two frames. The left frame shows the customer's options—viewing contents of the checkout cart, doing a search, checking out. The right frame shows the top-level categories in which products are organized in your Web store. Users can then drill down these categories to purchase the products they want.

1. **doPost()**
   This method determines the validity of a user. For an incorrect username and password combination, it throws up an error page. For new users it calls the **addNewUser()** method. Finally, it calls the **showSignInPage()** method.

2. **addNewUser()**
   This method is used for creating a new record in the Profiles table. At this point the only things known about this user are the username and password, so a record is created with just these values. Later on, when the user buys something, the Profile Management System kicks in and records the name, address and so on.

3. **showSignInPage()**
   This method retrieves the names of all the top-level categories and displays them in the right frame. It also retrieves the ids of products that belong to the regular cart of this person (if any) and stores them in the parent frame so that the values can be used by other pages.

GetCategories.java

This class retrieves all the top-level categories and displays them in the right frame. It is invoked when the customer presses the Categories button in the left frame.

1. **doPost()**
   This method calls the **showGetCategoriesPage()** method

2. **showGetCategoriesPage()**
   This method retrieves the top-level categories from the database.

GetProduct.java

This Servlet is invoked when a customer clicks on a category link in the right frame. It either displays a list of products or a list of subcategories that belong to the selected category.

1. **doPost()**

   This method finds out whether the link that resulted in this Servlet being invoked belongs to a terminal category or not. If it belongs to a terminal category, this Servlet should display all products in that category. For this, **showGetProductsPage()** method is called. On the other hand, if the link pointed to a nonterminal category, **showGetCategoriesPage()** method is invoked.

2. **showGetProductsPage()**

   This method retrieves details about the products that belong to the given category. The name, display, price, and so on of each product are displayed. It uses the DisplayProduct class's **display()** method to write out the HTML.

3. **showGetCategoriesPage()**

   Subcategories of the given category are retrieved by this method and displayed as links. Customers can click these links to drill down. All link clicks will result in this Servlet being invoked again.

DisplayProducts.java

This helper class is used to display all products belonging to a selected category. It brings up an HTML page in which users can select the products and add them to their shopping cart.

1. **display()**

   This method takes as input ids, names, prices, display prices, and URLs of one or more products. Each product is then displayed in a line of its own. The name is provided with a link to the URL that describes it. Next to that is the display price, followed by a text box in which the customer can type in the quantity he or she wants to purchase. A checkbox next to that can be used for adding the item to the shopping cart.

SearchProducts.java

This Servlet provides another method by which customers can view a list of products they want to purchase. It is invoked when the user presses the Search button. It looks through the search keywords of all products to find those that have the value typed in by the user. All the products are displayed in a screen similar to the one shown by DisplayProducts.

1. **doPost()**

   This reads the keyword(s) supplied by the user and calls **showSearchResults()**.

2. **showSearchResults()**

   This method searches for the keywords in the products database and prepares a list of products that match. It then uses the DisplayProducts class to display all these products.

GetPayment.java

This Servlet is invoked when the user has reviewed items at the checkout counter and has agreed to pay by pressing the Submit button. The Submit button looks different for first-time users and regular users. First-time users see a button that says "Get Credit Card Info," whereas regular users see a pair of radio buttons followed by a Submit button. The radio button asks if they want to use the credit card stored in the database or a new card. GetPayment takes different actions based on these scenarios. It may either call a card-verifying routine, redirect the customer to a registration page where credit card information can be supplied, or refer the customer to an update page where credit card information can be updated.

1. **doPost()**
   In this method the products selected for purchase are identified based on FORM values. Also, any products that the customer wants to add to or remove from the regular cart are determined. It also checks whether the request is for a new user, who then has to supply a credit card number, or for an existing user who wants to use a new or existing credit card. For new users, the **showNewUserPage()** method is called. If it is a regular customer who wants to use a different credit card, **showGetNewCardPage()** is called. For regular customers who want to use their regular credit card, **callPaymentModule()** is called. It also calls **addToRegularCart()** and **removeFromRegularCart()** to add or remove products to the regular cart of this user.

2. **removeFromRegularCart()**
   This method removes the given product ids from the list of product ids that belong to the regular cart of this user.

3. **addToRegularCart()**
   This method adds the given product ids to the list of product ids that belong to the regular cart of this user.

4. **callPaymentModule()**
   This method retrieves the credit card information about the customer and calculates the total amount the customer should be charged. It then calls **verify()** method of CardVerifier to charge the customer's credit card. Once an approval has been retrieved, it calls **storeProdsInOrderTable()** to write to the orders and one_order tables. Then it calls the **showThankYouPage()** method. If the **verify()** method returns a value indicating that the credit card for some reason couldn't be used, it calls **printErrorPage()**. The method also invalidates the session.

5. **storeProdsInOrderTable()**
   This method creates an entry for the order placed by the customer. It records all the items bought, including the quantities and the prices at which they were bought. It also subtracts from the available quantity of each product as these items are considered to be consumed from the inventory database.

6. showThankYouPage()

Once the order has been recorded, this method is called to show a thank you page. It displays the total amount that was charged, the items that were bought, and the order id. The customer can then use this id to get information about the order in the future. In the end it calls **sendMailToShipping()**.

7. sendMailToShipping()

This method generates an email to be sent to the shipping department, informing them about what has been ordered and to which address the items should be sent.

8. showGetNewCardPage()

This method simply redirects the user to the update profile page.

9. showNewUserPage()

This method redirects the user to the registration page.

CardVerifier.java

This class just shows how a typical credit card verification process would happen. It contains a method that contacts a credit card agency and tries to validate card information. You will need to modify it for use with your credit card verification company.

1. verify()

This method invokes a CGI/Servlet and passes the credit card information and amount to be charged to it, and returning the result from that CGI back to the calling method.

SelectOrder.java

This Servlet retrieves ids and dates of all orders ever placed by the customer. It is invoked when a user presses the Order History button.

1. doPost()

This calls **showSelectOrdersPage()**, which retrieves the orders list from the database.

2. showSelectOrdersPage()

This method looks up the orders database and prepares a list of orders. These are then presented as a set of links. Clicking on any of the links, the customer can get detailed information about that order.

ShowOrderDetails.java

This Servlet is invoked when a user clicks on one of the order links generated by SelectOrder.

1. doGet()

Here the order id is determined; it is read from one of the FORM variables. The method **showOrderDetailsPage()** is then called.

2. showOrderDetailsPage()

The method goes to the database and retrieves information about the order. This is then displayed in a separate page.

Detailed Description

All the classes of the Ordering Management System are contained in a package called Ordering, so each class begins with a line:

package Ordering;

Most of the classes use a number of packages. These include the **java.sql, java.io**, and **java.util** packages. They also use our Utilities package, which contains utilities like the connection-pooling utility, the mail-sending utility, and so on.

Also, most of the classes extend the BaseOrdering class.

1. BaseOrdering.java

This is the base class of all Servlets in the ordering package. The methods in this are quite similar to the ones in BaseInventory. This Servlet contains a BasePath variable. In addition, it contains the variables **orderDepartmentEmail** and **shipDepartmentEmail** which contain email addresses of your ordering and shipping departments. These email addresses will be used for sending emails to the shipping department every time a customer places an order.

public void sendTheMail(String f, String t, String h, String b)

This method is used for sending email. The input arguments are the "from" address, the "to" address, the header of the mail, and the body of the mail. It uses the **send()** method of the MailSender class defined in Utilities.

2. SignIn.java

This Servlet establishes a session with the user and verifies username and password. It adds new users to the system and retrieves regular cart information about existing ones.

```
public boolean addNewUser(String username, String password,
                String pw_confirm, String errorHtml,
                PrintWriter out, Connection conn)
```

This method inserts the username and password of the user into the database. It sets the status of the user to "NEW_USER", meaning that there is no credit card information and shipping information for this user at this point. The user is assigned a unique id that is obtained from the **profiles_seq** sequence.

```
         String querySQL = "SELECT profiles_seq.NEXTVAL FROM
             dual";
         ResultSet rset = stmt.executeQuery(querySQL);
         String id="";
         while(rset.next())
             id = rset.getString(1);
         String insertSQL = "INSERT INTO profiles(id, username,
password, registration_date, status) VALUES (" + id + ",'" +
username + "','" + password + "',SYSDATE, 'NEW_USER')";
         stmt.executeUpdate(insertSQL);

     public void showSignInPage(PrintWriter out, String pgName,
                 int userType, String username, Connection conn)
         throws Exception
```

This method retrieves names and ids of all categories that belong to the top level
(i.e., those that have **category_id** = 0).

```
         String querySQL = "SELECT id, has_sub_categories, name
             FROM categories WHERE category_id = 0";
         ResultSet rset = stmt.executeQuery(querySQL);
```

Each record that is returned by the query constitutes one row in the table that is
presented to the user. For each category we create a link whose name is the name of the
category. The HREF attribute of this is set to the GetProduct Servlet, and the id of the
category is one of the parts of the query string of this link. We also add the variable
has_sub_categories to the query string, which indicates whether this is a terminal category or not. This is because GetProduct treats the two cases differently.

```
         tableRows += "<TR><TD>
     <A HREF='Ordering.GetProduct?id=" + rset.getString(1) +
     "&has_sub_categories=" + rset.getString(2) + "'>";
         tableRows += rset.getString(3) + "</A></TD>
             </TR>";
```

Next we retrieve ids of the products that belong to this customer's regular cart. To do
this, first the profile id of the customer is derived from the profiles table using the username. All the product ids and quantities are then retrieved from the **regular_cart** table:

```
     querySQL = "SELECT product_id, quantity FROM
         regular_cart
             WHERE profile_id=" + profileId;
```

The name, price, and display_price of these products is retrieved from the products
table for each of the products. Then we add some Javascript code, which will store the
values of these in arrays maintained in the parent frame (**ordering.html**).

```
         regularCartValues += "parent.regularCartIds[" +
             k + "]=\"" +
```

```
                    (String)productId.elementAt(k) +
               "\";parent.regularCartNames[" + k +
               "]=\"" + (String)productName.elementAt(k) +
               " [" +  (String)productDisplayPrice.
                  elementAt(k)
             + "] \";parent.regularCartPrices["
              + k + "]=\"" + (String)productPrice.
                  elementAt(k)
             + "\";
             parent.regularCartQuantities[" + k + "]=\""
             + (String)quantity.elementAt(k)
             + "\";";
```

This rather cryptic looking code is actually a Javascript statement we're creating. This statement adds the id, name/display price, actual price, and quantity of each regular cart item to several arrays—**regularCartIds**, **regularCartNames**, **regularCartPrices**, and **regularCartQuantities**—all of which are arrays defined in **ordering.html**. Recall from Chapter 5 that a statement like

```
parent.regularCartIds[0]=1;
```

adds an element to the **regularCartIds** array present in the parent frame of this page.

The Javascript code generated above is added to the **<VAR_REGULAR_CART_VALUES>** variable in the template.

3. GetCategories.java

This Servlet retrieves the top-level categories in the database. This is the SQL for the same:

```
String querySQL = "SELECT id, has_sub_categories, name
        FROM categories
        WHERE category_id = 0";
```

4. GetProduct.java

This Servlet retrieves the subcategories or products that belong to a category.

```
public void showGetCategoriesPage(PrintWriter out, String
   pgName,
                                  String id, Connection conn)
      throws Exception
```

This method displays the subcategories belonging to this category. This is the SQL used:

```
String querySQL = "SELECT id, has_sub_categories, name
        FROM categories
        WHERE category_id = " + id;
```

```
public void showGetProductsPage(PrintWriter out, String pgName,
                                String id, Connection conn)
    throws Exception
```

This method retrieves the products that belong to the category.

```
String querySQL = "SELECT id,category_id, name, price,
        description_url, display_price
        FROM products WHERE category_id = " + id;
```

It then calls **DisplayProducts.display**() to display these products.

5. DisplayProducts.java

This is a helper class that accepts one or products as input. It then generates an HTML page in which the products with their prices are displayed, along with a checkbox so that users can add the product(s) to their shopping cart.

```
public void display(PrintWriter out, Vector productIds,
    Vector productNames, Vector productPrices,
    Vector productDescURLs,
    Vector productDisplayPrices)
    throws Exception
```

It accepts five vectors, containing the id, name, price, description URL, and display price of all products that are to be shown. Each product is shown on a separate line. The lines have alternating colors of yellow and blue.

Here's the code that generates each line of the output table:

```
tableRows += "<FORM><TR BGCOLOR='" + color + "'>
        <TD><A HREF='" + description_url + "'>" + name +
        "</A> [" +  display_price + "]</TD>";
tableRows += "<TD><FONT size='-2' face='Arial, Helvetica,
            San Serif'>Quantity:</FONT>
            <INPUT TYPE='text' SIZE='2' NAME='quantity'>
            </TD>
            <TD WIDTH='100'><INPUT TYPE='checkbox'
              NAME='" + prodId + "'
            VALUE = ' ' onClick='addToCart(this.
              form, \""
              + prodId + "\"," +
              prodId + ",\"" + name + "\", " + price +
              ");'>
            <FONT size='-2' face='Arial, Helvetical,
                San Serif'>
```

```
            <B>Check box to add item to cart.
                Uncheck to remove.</B></TD></TR></FORM>";
```

Each line belongs to a FORM. The first cell in this row is a link that points to a URL describing the product. The name is presented as a combination of the product name and its display price.

The second cell contains a textbox of size 2 named quantity in which the customer can specify the quantity that he or she wants to purchase. The third cell contains a checkbox; the name of this variable is the id of the product being shown in this row. If the user clicks this checkbox, the Javascript function **addToCart()** is invoked. This function will update arrays in the parent frame that contain information about products that the user has added to the cart. The id, name, and price of the product are passed to the function.

To see how the screen looks, see Chapter 11.

6. GetPayment.java

This Servlet either redirects customers to a registration or update page or validates the credit card and generates an order in the database. It also adds or removes entries in the regular cart of the user.

doPost()

This Servlet reads the ids and quantities of products that the user wants to purchase from FORM variables (Variable in the checkout form). To understand these, we need to see what the checkout form looks like.

The checkout form contains variables whose names begin with "ID_" corresponding to each product in the user's shopping cart. The format of these variables is **ID_<Product_Id>**. Here **<Product_Id>** is the database id of the product. The value of the variable is equal to the quantity of this product that the user wants to purchase. If, for example, a customer wants to buy three onions (let's say product id 500) and two oranges (product id 550), there would be two variables in thi form:

ID_500 with value 3 and ID_550 with value 2

A similar concept is followed for products a user may want to add or remove from the regular cart. For this, the variable name has this format:

regCart_<Product_Id>

The value is "Add" or "Remove."

In the **doPost()** method we retrieve the ids of all these products and put them in vectors, which will be used later.

Here's the code that retrieves the id and quantitiy of all products that the user wants to purchase:

```
Enumeration paramNames = req.getParameterNames();
while(paramNames.hasMoreElements())
{
        String nm = (String)paramNames.nextElement();
        String vl = req.getParameterValues(nm)[0];

        if(nm.indexOf("ID_") != -1)
        {
                String id = nm.substring(3);
                String qtty = vl;
                if((new Integer(qtty)).intValue() != 0)
                {
                        productIds.addElement(id);
                        productQuantities.addElement(qtty);
                }
        }
        .....
}
public void addToRegularCart(Vector addIds, Vector allIds,
            Vector allQuantities, String username, Connection
                conn)
        throws Exception
```

This method is called for adding certain product ids to the regular cart of this person. It determines the profile id of this person. Then it loops through the addIds Vector and adds all the product ids to the **regular_cart** table for this person.

```
String querySQL = "SELECT id FROM profiles
        WHERE username='" + username + "'";
ResultSet rset = stmt.executeQuery(querySQL);
while(rset.next())
    profileId = rset.getString(1);
String updateSQL = "INSERT INTO
    regular_cart(id, profile_id, product_id, quantity)
    VALUES (" + cartId + "," + profileId + "," + idToAdd
    + "," + qtty + ")";
stmt.executeUpdate(updateSQL);
```

The method **removeFromRegularCart()** works similarly, except that it removes records from the **regular_cart** table.

```
public void callPaymentModule(PrintWriter out, Vector
    productIds,
            Vector  productQuantities, String username,
            Connection conn, HttpSession session)
        throws Exception
```

This method is called if credit card verification is to be done, that is, when the user has indicated (s)he is ready to pay. This would happen if the Servlet had been invoked from the checkout form for a regular user in which the user wanted to use a regular card. It could also happen if the user had filled out the credit card information in the registration or update page.

It first retrieves credit card information about this customer from the database:

```
String querySQL = "SELECT ccard_num,
         TO_CHAR(ccard_exp_date, 'DD-MON-YYYY'),
         ccard_company, first_name, last_name, id
         FROM profiles
         WHERE username='" + username + "'";
```

For each product that the customer wants to purchase, the price, display_price, and name are retrieved from the database:

```
querySQL = "SELECT price, display_price,name
                 FROM products WHERE id=" + id;
```

Total price is calculated as the retrieval is being done:

```
double price = 0.0;
while(rset.next())
{
    double d = rset.getDouble(1);
    .....
    price += d*qtty;
    .....
```

Now the credit card verification routine is called. It is passed the price to be charged, the credit card number, company, and expiration date:

```
CardVerifier cv = new CardVerifier(price, ccardNum,
                        ccardCompany, ccardExpDate);
String result = cv.verify();
```

If the card is charged ok, **storeProdsInOrderTable()** is called followed by a call to **showThankYouPage()**.

```
public String storeProdsInOrderTable(Vector productIds,
         Vector productQuantities, Vector productPrices,
         String totalPrice, String profileId,
         Connection conn)
     throws Exception
```

This method creates one record in the orders table and one or more in the **one_order** table. The order id is obtained from a sequence:

```
String querySQL = "SELECT orders_seq.NEXTVAL FROM dual";
```

A record is created in the orders table:

```
String insertSQL = "INSERT INTO orders(id, profile_id,
                        date_ordered, date_shipped,
                        status, payment_received, total_
                            billed)
                VALUES(" + ordersId + "," + profileId + ",
                        SYSDATE,
                        NULL,
                        'WITH_SHIPPING_DEPARTMENT', 1," +
                        totalPrice + ")";
```

It sets the status of the order to "WITH_SHIPPING_DEPARTMENT," because at this stage the order has not been shipped; only the shipping department is being notified.

For each product in the order, a record is created in the **one_order** table:

```
insertSQL = "INSERT INTO one_order(id, orders_id,
                product_id,
            quantity, price)
            VALUES(" + oneOrderId + "," + ordersId + ","
            + prodId + ","
                        + prodQtty + "," + prodPrice + ")";
```

The **quantity_in_stock** field for each product is updated, and the quantity consumed by the user in this order is subtracted:

```
insertSQL = "UPDATE products SET quantity_in_stock
                    = quantity_in_stock-"
                    + prodQtty + " WHERE id=" + prodId;
public void showThankYouPage(Vector productNames,
                        Vector productQuantities,
                        Vector displayPrices, String
                            orderId,
                        String price, String username,
                        String pgName, Connection conn,
                        PrintWriter out)
            throws Exception
```

This method shows a thank-you page. In this page the order id is shown. Also, it displays the products that were purchased, the quantities and prices, and the total amount charged to the customer's card. It uses the template **orderingThankYou.html** for the purpose. It also calls the method **sendMailToShipping**(), which sends an email to the shipping department informing them about the items ordered and the address to which they should be shipped.

```
public void sendMailToShipping(String itemList, String orderId,
            String username, Connection conn)
    throws Exception
```

This method sends an email to the shipping department. It knows the list of items that the user has ordered, but it has to obtain the shipping address of the person from the database:

```
String querySQL = "SELECT id, email, phone, fax,
            first_name, last_name FROM profiles
        WHERE username='" + username + "'";
    ....
        profileId = rset.getString(1);
```

Now that the profileId is known, it can be used for obtaining the mailing address of this person:

```
querySQL = "SELECT line1, line2, city, state, zip
    FROM addresses
    WHERE type='SHIPPING' AND profile_id=" + profileId;
```

It then invokes the **sendTheMail()**, defined in BaseOrdering, to send the mail.

7. SearchProducts.java

This Servlet is invoked when a user is searching for a product based on a keyword. It retrieves the search keywords typed by the user (which are present in a FORM variable called **searchList**). Then the method **showSearchResults()** is called:

```
public void showSearchResults(PrintWriter out, String
    searchList,

                    Connection conn)
```

This method searches the database for those keywords and displays the results using DisplayProducts. Since a user may have typed more than one keyword separated by a space, it uses the StringTokenizer class to split into a Vector, with each element being one keyword.

```
StringTokenizer st = new StringTokenizer(searchList);
Vector searchItems = new Vector();
while(st.hasMoreTokens())
    searchItems.addElement((st.nextToken()).
        toUpperCase());
```

Then a search is done for each keyword in the database. A query statement is created that contains all the keywords in the WHERE clause, separated by an OR. Further, we've converted all the keywords to uppercase so that we can do a case-insensitive search by using the **NLS_UPPER()** database function.

```
String querySQL = "SELECT id,category_id, name,
        price, description_url, display_price
        FROM products WHERE ";

int size = searchItems.size();
for(int i=0; i<size; i++)
{
    if(i != 0)
        querySQL += " OR ";
    querySQL += "NLS_UPPER(search_keywords) LIKE '%" +
                (String)searchItems.elementAt(i) +
                    "%'";
}
```

All the products that are returned by this query are displayed using the
DisplayProducts.display() method.

8. CardVerifier.java

This class shows how one Servlet can invoke another Servlet or CGI and get results
back from it. It is a demonstration of one way you could call the URL of a credit card
verification company to charge a customer's credit card. Some companies may have
their own API, so you may need to rewrite this module. In any case, this module
assumes names of some CGI variables that are passed to the URL, which will have to
be mutually decided between you and the credit card verifier. In other words, this class
is just a reference, and more work needs to be done before it can be used.

```
public String verify()
```

This method creates a connection with the URL of the credit card–verifying company. This URL is expected to be some CGI or Servlet that will accept the following
FORM variables:

ccardNum—credit card number

ccardExpDate—credit card expiration date

ccardCompany—name of the credit card company

price—the amount that should be charged

The method opens a URLConnection with the URL:

```
URL myURL = new URL(cardVerifyingCompany);
URLConnection conn = myURL.openConnection();
```

It sets the request property indicating that a CGI request is being placed:

```
conn.setRequestProperty("Content-type", "application/
octet-stream");
```

The message body thus created is the query string that will be passed in the request. It contains the four variables discussed above:

```
String message = "ccardNum=" + URLEncoder.
    encode(ccardNum) +
        "&ccardExpDate=" + URLEncoder.
            encode(ccardExpDate) +
        "&ccardCompany=" +
        URLEncoder.encode(ccardCompany) + "&price=" +
            URLEncoder.encode(price);
```

The queryString is then sent to the URL:

```
PrintWriter pout = new PrintWriter(outStream);
pout.write(message);
```

Now it opens an input stream with the URL to receive results. Once again, you will have to set a protocol for the result with your credit card verifier. For example, if they send a result string of ALL_OK, you could interpret this to mean that the card has been charged, and if they send CARD_INVALID, it would mean the card is invalid. Likewise, you can decide codes that can be parsed so that you know the exact outcome of this transaction.

```
InputStreamReader inpStream =
        new InputStreamReader(conn.getInputStream());
BufferedReader br = new BufferedReader(inpStream);
String tmp = "";
while((tmp = br.readLine()) != null)
{
    result += tmp;
}
```

The result is then returned to the calling method for analysis.

9. SelectOrder.java

This Servlet displays a list of all orders placed by a customer at this site.

```
public void showSelectOrdersPage(String username, String pgName,
        Connection conn, PrintWriter out)
    throws Exception
```

This method retrieves id and date of all orders placed by the customer and writes them to an HTML page:

```
querySQL = "SELECT id, TO_CHAR(date_ordered,
    'DD-MON-YYYY')
```

```
                    FROM orders WHERE profile_id='" + profileId
                        + "'";
```

A link is created for each order:

```
    orderIdOptions +=
        "<A HREF='Ordering.ShowOrderDetails?orderId=" +
            orderId +
                "'>Order Id : " + orderId + " : " +
                    date_ordered + "</A><BR>";
```

All the links are written to the template **selectOrder.html**. The variable
<VAR_ORDER_OPTIONS> is substituted with this list of links.

10. ShowOrderDetails.java

As we saw earlier, the page generated by SelectOrder contains links that cause the execution of this Servlet. The order id is sent as a query string variable of the name orderId. This servlet obtains detailed information about the order and displays it using the **orderDetails.html** template.

```
    public void showOrderDetailsPage(String orderId, String pgName,
            Connection conn, PrintWriter out)
        throws Exception
```

This method goes to the database and retrieves details about the given order id. It first obtains the **profile_id** of the person who ordered, the date the order was placed, total charges, shipment method, and status from the orders table for this order:

```
    String querySQL = "SELECT profile_id, TO_CHAR(date_ordered,
        'DD-MON-YYYY'),
        TO_CHAR(date_shipped, 'DD-MON-YYYY'),
        total_billed, shipment_method, status
        FROM orders WHERE id=" + orderId;
```

Then it retrieves all the records from the **one_order** table that belongs to this order, that is, those records that have an **orders_id** equal to the id of this order:

```
    querySQL = "SELECT product_id, quantity, price
                FROM one_order WHERE orders_id=" + orderId;
```

We're storing the product id of the purchased product, not its name, in the **one_order** table. This name is obtained from the products table for each product for display purposes:

```
    String baseQuerySQL = "SELECT name FROM products WHERE
        id=";
```

Variables in the template are substituted with the values thus obtained.

Document Root HTML Files

In this system, a lot of work has been done in Javascript, because Javascript code executes on the client side and thus gives the users a better response time.

ordering.html

Our initial HTML file is **ordering.html**. This is actually a parent file containing two frames. We are also using this to store some global variables that are used by the child frames. For instance, the file stores a list of products that the user has selected for purchase. It also stores a list of products that belong to the regular shopping cart of the user.

The following variable is defined in this:

```
var newUser = false;
```

The following variable tells if this is a new user or an existing customer:

```
var windowUp = false;
```

This is true if the checkout cart window is being displayed. The checkout cart window is the window showing products the customer has selected for purchase so far.

```
regularCartIds = new Array();
regularCartQuantities = new Array();
regularCartNames = new Array();
regularCartPrices = new Array();
```

The id, quantity, name, and price of all products that belong to this customer's regular cart. Their value is obtained from the database by the SignIn Servlet.

```
purchasedIds = new Array();
 purchasedQuantities = new Array();
 purchasedNames = new Array();
 purchasedPrices = new Array();
```

The id, quantity, name, and price of products added to the checkout cart by the user. Values are updated as a user adds or removes items for purchase. So if you want to see how much of a particular product the user is purchasing and at what price, you would first locate the element in the purchasedIds array that contains this product's id. Let's say it is at position 5. Now you can find the amount the user wants to purchase by looking at **purchasedQuantities[5]**. The name of the product would be **purchasedNames[5]** and its price would be **purchasedPrices[5]**.

var cw;

A placeholder for the checkout cart window that displays products selected by the user for buying.

It contains a number of functions that do things then, like invoking the SearchProducts Servlet, the SelectOrder Servlet, and so on.

It divides the screen into two frames; the left portion is initally blank, and the right portion contains **mainOrdering.html**.

signIn.html

This is the template that is used by the sign-in process, in which top-level categories are displayed. The variable **<VAR_REGULAR_CART_VALUES>** is substituted with Javascript code that adds information about the regular cart items of this user. Upon loading, it calls the function **showMenuAndCart()**. This function brings up the **orderingMenu.html** page and also calls the **showCart()** function in **ordering.html**, which pops up a window displaying contents of the user's checkout cart.

mainOrdering.html

This is the form that you see when you visit the ordering site. It asks for a username and password, when the Submit button is pressed, it invokes the SignIn Servlet.

showCart.html

This HTML file uses Javascript to retrieve the name, price, and so on of products that the user has selected for purchase and dynamically builds a page displaying the same. In other words, it shows the current contents of the checkout shopping cart of the user.

Here's the code:

```
<SCRIPT>
        for(i = 0; i<window.opener.purchasedIds.length; i++)
        {
            q = new Number(window.opener.purchasedQuantities[i]);
            if(q == 0)
                continue;
            document.write("<TR BGCOLOR='#FFFFCC'><TD>"
                        + window.opener.purchasedNames[i] +
                    "</TD><TD>     Quantity:
                        " +
                    window.opener.purchasedQuantities[i]  +
                    "</TD></TR>");
        }
</SCRIPT>
```

Here **window.opener** refers to the parent of this frame, **ordering.html**. It retrieves the ids, names, and so on of the products selected by the customer from the corresponding arrays where the values are stored. It loops through each product and looks at the quantity the user wants to purchase. If the quantity is not 0, the product name and quantity are displayed as one row of a table.

regularCart.html

This HTML file uses Javascript to retrieve the name, price, and so on of products that belong to the regular cart of the user and dynamically builds a page displaying the same. The code is somewhat similar to the one we saw for **showCart.html**:

```
for(i=0; i<len; i++)
{
    q = new Number(parent.regularCartQuantities[i]);
    if(q <= 0)
        continue;
    document.write("<TR><TD>" + parent.regularCartNames[i] +
                "</TD><TD>");
    document.write("<INPUT TYPE='text' NAME='" +
                parent.regularCartIds[i] +
            "' SIZE='2' VALUE='" +
            parent.regularCartQuantities[i] +
            "'></TD><TD></TD></TR>");
}
```

The table thus generated contains the name of the product, followed by a text field in which users can type in the quantity they want to purchase. Each text field's name is the same as the product id.

It contains a button named "Add to checkout cart." If the customer clicks this, the function **addToCheckoutCart()** is invoked, adding the products to the list of products the user wants to purchase.

```
function addToCheckoutCart(frm)
```

This function goes through all the form variables except the last one—the only variables in this FORM are the text fields whose name is the id of the product and value is the quantity that the user wants to purchase. For all the fields where the value is not 0 or less, the function calls the function **add()** which adds the product to the purchasedIds array maintained in **ordering.html**.

```
function add(id, quantity)
```

The function **add** is called by **addToCheckoutCart()** for each product that needs to be purchased. It first checks whether this product id is already present in the purchasedIds array. If so, only the total quantity to be purchased is updated.

This is because in the purchasedIds array we are maintaining only one entry per product id.

```
purchasedLen = parent.purchasedIds.length;
foundItem = false;
for(m=0; m<purchasedLen; m++)
{
    pId = parent.purchasedIds[m];
    if(pId == id)
    {
        foundItem = true;
        pQtty = new Number(parent.purchasedQuantities[m]);
        pQtty += quantity;
        parent.purchasedQuantities[m] = pQtty;
        break;
    }
}
```

If the item has not been purchased so far, though, its name and price are obtained from the **regularCartNames** and **regularCartPrices** arrays and new elements are created in the **purchasedNames, purchasedPrices, purchasedQuantities**, and **purchasedIds** arrays.

```
parent.purchasedIds[purchasedLen] = id;
parent.purchasedQuantities[purchasedLen] = quantity;
var name="";
var regCartLen = parent.regularCartIds.length;
for(z=0; z<regCartLen; z++)
{
    if(parent.regularCartIds[z] == id)
    {
        name = parent.regularCartNames[z];
    }
}
price = getProductPrice(id);
parent.purchasedNames[purchasedLen] = name;
parent.purchasedPrices[purchasedLen] = price;
parent.lastCount++;
```

checkout.html

This HTML file is presented when the user presses the Checkout button. Its purpose is to display all the products the user added to the checkout cart and to give the user a chance to add or remove these from the regular cart. It also presents the interface that customers can use for paying for the products. However, there's a difference between the interface that is presented to new users from that presented to existing customers, because for first-time customers the system does not have payment information or the shipping address. And for existing customers, it needs to give the customers a chance to either change their credit card or to use the one stored in the database.

Let us see how all this is achieved in the code:

The body of this HTML file contains a FORM tag, whose ACTION is the GetPayment Servlet in the ordering package. When a customer presses the Submit button, first a Javascript function **clearGlobals**() is called and then GetPayment is invoked.

```
<FORM ACTION='/newZone/Ordering.GetPayment' METHOD='POST'
onSubmit='return clearGlobals();'>
```

After this there is Javascript code that generates HTML dynamically based on whether this is a new user or an existing user. The part common to both is the table that lists products the customer wants to purchase. We thus go through the arrays maintained in **ordering.html** and display all products for which the user has selected a quantity greater than 0.

```
len = parent.purchasedIds.length;
document.write("<H1>Products purchased</H1><BR><BR><BR>
    <TABLE>");
var price = 0.0;
for(i=0; i<len; i++)
{
    q = new Number(parent.purchasedQuantities[i]);
    if(q <= 0)
        continue;
    document.write("<TR><TD>" + parent.purchasedNames[i] +
            "</TD><TD>");
    document.write("<INPUT TYPE='text' NAME='ID_" +
        parent.purchasedIds[i] +
        "' SIZE='2' VALUE='" + parent.purchasedQuantities[i] +
        "'></TD>");
}
```

As we saw in GetPayment, there is a text field corresponding to each product that the user wants to purchase. Its name begins with an "ID_," followed by the id of the product. The code above creates these text boxes.

In the checkout screen we also allow users to specify whether they want to add or remove an item from the regular cart. For each product displayed in the checkout screen, the code checks whether it belongs to the regular cart of this user. If so, a checkbox is created, and if the user clicks this checkbox, the item will be removed from the regular cart. On the other hand, if the item does not belong to the user's regular cart, clicking the checkbox will add it to the regular cart. So next time this customer comes to the site and wants to use the regular cart, this item will be present (along with other items that he or she added to the regular cart using the procedure described).

```
if(belongsToRegularCart(parent.purchasedIds[i]))
{
     document.write("<TD WIDTH='150' BGCOLOR='#CCFFCC'>
          <INPUT TYPE='checkbox'
          NAME='regCart_" + parent.purchasedIds[i] +
          "' VALUE='Remove'>
       <FONT size='-2' face='Arial, Helvetical, San Serif'>
          Click to remove item from regular cart
          </FONT></TD></TR>");
}
else
{
     document.write("<TD WIDTH='150' BGCOLOR='#FFCCCC'>
          <INPUT TYPE='checkbox'
          NAME='regCart_" + parent.purchasedIds[i] +
          "' VALUE='Add'>
          <FONT size='-2' face='Arial, Helvetical, San
             Serif'>
             Click to add item to regular cart
          </FONT></TD></TR>");
}
```

As we saw in GetPayment, a FORM variable **regCart_<Product_ID>** along with its value (Add or Remove) determines whether a product should be removed or added to the regular cart. The code shown above generates this FORM variable for each product in the user's checkout cart.

Another feature common to new and existing users is a display of the total amount that is being charged. Calculations are done, and the total amount is presented in a text box, so that customers are able to change the quantities they want to purchase in the checkout screen. They can then press the Recalculate button to get the new total price.

```
document.write("Total Price: <INPUT TYPE='text' NAME = 'price'
SIZE='5' VALUE='" + prc + "'>
     <INPUT TYPE='button' NAME='recalculate'
        VALUE='Recalculate Total Price'
        onClick='calculateTotalPrice(this.form)'>");
```

If the button is clicked, the function **calculateTotalPrice()** is called. This updates the text box with the newly calculated total price.

Next comes the code that distinguishes between a new user and an existing user. The decision is made on the basis of the variable newUser, which is set during SignIn. (In the SignIn process, the authentication routine finds out if this is a new user or an existing user, based on the status of the profile, and sets the Javascript variable **newUser** in **ordering.html** to true or false accordingly).

We give existing users the option of using either their regular credit card or another card. New users, are presented with a Get Credit Card Info button. In both cases the Submit button invokes GetPayment. This Servlet determines the action to be taken based on the FORM variable **paymentFrom**, which may take one of the following values, **regularCard** or **newCard** and the variable **userType**, which may take the value "new."

```
if(parent.newUser == false)
{
    document.write("<BR>Make payment using:");
    document.write("<TABLE><TR><TD><INPUT TYPE='radio'
                NAME='paymentFrom'
        VALUE='regularCard' CHECKED></TD>
            <TD>Regular Card</TD></TR>");
    document.write("<TR><TD><INPUT TYPE='radio'
        NAME='paymentFrom' VALUE='newCard'></TD>
        <TD>Another Card</TD></TR></TABLE>");
    document.write("<INPUT TYPE='submit'
                NAME=''ubmit' VALUE='Submit'>");
}
else
{
    document.write("<INPUT TYPE='hidden'
            NAME='paymentFrom' VALUE='newCard'>");
    document.write("<INPUT TYPE='hidden'
            NAME='userType' VALUE='new'>");
    document.write("<BR><INPUT TYPE='submit'
            NAME='submit' VALUE='Get Credit Card Info'>");
}
```

It also sets a hidden variable called **calledFrom** with a value **Checkout**. GetPayment may be called from this FORM or from a registration and update page in the Profile Management System. This variable tells GetPayment where it is being called from so that it can take appropriate action.

```
function belongsToRegularCart(id)
```

This function checks whether the given product id is present in **parent. regularCartIds**. If so, it returns a true value; otherwise, it returns a false.

```
function calculateTotalPrice(frm)
```

This function looks at all products that the user wants to purchase, multiplies their price with the quantity, and returns a sum total.

```
function clearGlobals()
```

This function resets all the arrays in **ordering.html**. This is done when the user presses the Submit button in the checkout page. It is a sort of safeguard to prevent customers from ordering the same items twice unintentionally. This could happen if the user presses the Submit button, next presses the browser's back button, and then accidentally presses the Submit button again.

orderingMenu.html

This is the HTML that appears in the left portion of the screen. It displays a number of buttons, including the Cart Contents, Search, Order History and Checkout. Each button has an onClick event that invokes a function in **ordering.html**.

Other HTML Files and Templates

getCategories.html

This template is used for displaying categories.

getProducts.html

This template is used for displaying products that a user may add to the checkout cart. As we saw in the description of DisplayProducts, when a user clicks on a checkbox next to a product in this page, the item is added to the checkout cart by a call to the function **addToCart()**. The function is defined in this template.

It first locates the checkbox that was clicked and determines whether it is checked or unchecked. For this it goes through all elements in the form until it finds one that has the name "cbName." The position is recorded in the variable **checkboxPos**.

```
function addToCart(frm, cbName, id, name, price)
{
    el = frm.elements;
    ln = el.length;
    checked = false;
    for(i=0; i<ln; i++)
    {
        if(el[i].name == cbName)
        {
            if(el[i].checked == true)
            {
                checked = true;
            }
```

```
        break;
    }
  }
  checkboxPos = i;
```

If the box is checked, it means the item needs to be added to the checkout cart; otherwise, it needs to be removed. For adding, the function also needs to see if this item has been added before. If so, it just adds the new quantity to the existing one in the **purchasedQuantities** array. The function also checks things like whether a quantity has been specified or not and whether the value specified is a number between 0 and 9.

Finally it calls **parent.cartRefresh()**, which updates the popup window to reflect the latest contents of the user's cart.

orderingError.html

This is the error template used by any Servlet in the ordering package that wants to throw an error message.

selectOrder.html

A list of orders the customer has placed in previous sessions is displayed using this template.

orderDetails.html

Details of a particular order that the user chose from the **selectOrder.html** page are displayed using this template.

orderingThankYou.html

This template is used for displaying a thank-you note along with order details to a customer when the payment has been made.

Part V

Shipping Management System

High-Level Description

The Shipping Management System is a system that is used internally by your shipping department to schedule and manage shipment of customer orders. Using this system, your shipping department can view pending orders and obtain details about each ones. As you may recall from the Ordering Management System, every time a customer places an order, an email is sent to the shipping department. This mail contains the order id. Using the order id, the department can look up details about the order in the database. The shipping department can also use a Servlet that shows just those orders that haven't been shipped so far. The shipping department can also append comments about a particular shipment, allowing customers to get a clear idea of whether the order has been shipped or what its status is.

The flow begins with the entry-point page, **shipping.html**. You would access it like this:

http://myServer.com:myPort/shipping.html

The first thing users need to do is supply a username and password to log in.

Classes and Their Methods

BaseShipping.java

This base class is the parent of all Servlets that belong to the shipping package. It is similar to the base class of Inventory, BaseInventory.java, and contains similar methods for debugging and verifying the username and password of administrators allowed to use the system.

ShippingLogin.java

This Servlet checks the validity of the password of a user. Valid users are presented with a set of options they can choose from.

1. **doPost()**
   The username and password are checked. The method **validPassword()** is used for this. If the user is found to be valid, the method **showShippingOptionsPage()** is called.

2. **showShippingOptionsPage()**
   This method simply shows the options a shipping administrator has.

ShippingOrderDetails.java

This Servlet is invoked if the user wants to see the details of a shipment by its order id. This is the first option on the shipping options page.

1. **doPost()**
   The order id entered by the user is read in this method. It then calls **showShippingOrderDetailsPage()** to show details of the order.

2. **showShippingOrderDetailsPage()**
   This method retrieves detailed information about the order and displays it in a page where modifications can be made.

ModifyShippingOrder.java

This Servlet is called if the user viewed details using the ShippingOrderDetails Servlet described above and pressed the Submit button. The user-supplied changes are applied to the database. Thus it allows a shipping administrator to make changes—like changing the status of an order from WITH_SHIPPING_DEPARTMENT to SHIPPED—and to supply a shipment method and date.

1. **doPost()**
   The order id, status, shipment method, and shipment date are read so that they can be applied. The method **updateShipOrder()** is then called.

2. **updateShipOrder()**
   This method writes the updated information to the database.

SelectShippingOrders.java

This Servlet is invoked if the user chooses the second or the third option in the main menu. It displays a page in which the user can apply changes to the shipment data of a number of orders at one go. So, if you know that there are 20 order ids that have been shipped today, instead of using the first option to apply the changes to each record individually, you can use the second or third option to apply the changes in a batch mode.

1. **doGet()**

   This method reads the "type" variable that determines whether the user wants to see all orders or only those that have not been shipped so far. It then calls **showSelectShippingOrdersPage()**.

2. **showSelectShippingOrdersPage()**

   This method shows the page in which order information can be changed. It retrieves ids of all relevant orders and displays them in a table so that the user can select the orders to which changes need to be applied.

ModifyOrders.java

This Servlet applies changes specified by the user in the screen above.

1. **doPost()**

   This method reads the ids of all orders to which changes need to be applied. It then calls **updateShipOrder()**.

2. **updateShipOrder()**

   This method applies all changes to the specified orders in the database.

Detailed Description

All the classes of the Shipping Management System are contained in a package called Shipping. Each class begins with a line:

package Shipping;

Most of the classes extend BaseShipping.

1. BaseShipping.java

This is the base class of all Servlets in the Shipping package. The methods in this are quite similar to the ones in BaseInventory. It contains a **BasePath** variable, which determines where the HTML templates used by the system reside.

2. ShippingLogin.java

This is the login Servlet where username and password are verified. It reads the username and password from the CGI parameters. The method **validPassword()** is called to check the validity, and a session is then established. It then calls **showShippingOptionsPage()**.

This method displays the template **shippingOptions.html**.

3. ShippingOrderDetails.java

If the user chooses to view details by order id, this Servlet is invoked. In the **doPost()** method, the value of orderId is retrieved. This is the order number entered by the user. After checking the validity of the session, it calls **showShippingOrderDetailsPage()**.

```
public void showShippingOrderDetailsPage(PrintWriter out,
        String pgName, String orderId, Connection conn)
    throws Exception
```

In this method detailed information about the order is retrieved from the database and is displayed using the template **shippingOrderDetails.html**.

It first retrieves the **profile_id**, date of ordering, and a few other things from the orders table. Information is then retrieved for the record whose order id is the one entered by the user.

```
String querySQL = "SELECT profile_id,
        TO_CHAR(date_ordered, 'DD-MON-YYYY'),
        TO_CHAR(date_s hipped, 'DD-MON-YYYY'),
            total_billed,
        shipment_method, status FROM orders
        WHERE id=" + orderId;
....
        profileId = rset.getString(1);
```

Next it retrieves information from the **one_order** table about each product that was purchased as part of this order:

```
querySQL = "SELECT product_id, quantity, price
        FROM one_order
        WHERE orders_id =" + orderId;
```

For each product id thus retrieved, the name of the product is retrieved from the products table:

```
String baseQuerySQL = "SELECT name FROM products WHERE
        id=";
```

A variable called **tableRows**, which contains information about each product, its price, and its quantity, is created:

```
tableRows += "<TR><TD>" + name + "</TD><TD>" +price +
        "</TD><TD>" + qtty + "</TD></TR>";
```

The values retrieved are put in the **shippingOrderDetails.html** template, which has a Submit button in this template. If the user presses this, any changes made are applied to the database using the ModifyShippingOrder Servlet.

4. ModifyShippingOrder.java

This Servlet is invoked if the Submit button is pressed in the **shippingOrderDetails. html** template. It reads the id of the order to which changes need to be applied. It also reads the shipment method, date, and status if the user has entered these values. It retrieves a database connection and calls **updateShipOrder()** with these values:

```
public void updateShipOrder(PrintWriter out, String orderId,
        String dateShipped, String shipMethod, String
            status,
        String pgName, Connection conn)
    throws Exception
```

This method applies the changes to the database:

```
String querySQL = "UPDATE orders SET
    date_shipped=TO_DATE('" + dateShipped + "',
    'DD-MON-YYYY'), shipment_method='" +
    shipMethod + "', status='" +
    status + "' WHERE id=" + orderId;
```

5. SelectShippingOrders.java

This Servlet is invoked when the second or third option in the main menu is clicked. It uses the **type** variable to determine if the user wants to see all orders or only those that have not been shipped so far. The value of **type** is retrieved in the **doGet()** method. After determining the validity of the session, the **showSelectShippingOrdersPage()** method is called.

In this method, ids and dates of all orders matching the criteria are retrieved. Here's the SQL for this:

```
String querySQL = "SELECT id, TO_CHAR(date_ordered, 'DD-MON-YYYY')
                FROM orders";
```

If the user wants to see only those orders that have not been shipped, the **type** variable will have the value **unshipped**. In this case, a WHERE condition needs to be added to the SQL statement. The new statement looks like this:

```
if(type.equalsIgnoreCase("unshipped"))
        querySQL = querySQL + " WHERE date_shipped IS
            NULL";
```

The values retrieved are put as options of the select list variable **<VAR_ORDER_OPTIONS>** in the **selectShippingOrders.html** template.

6. ModifyOrders.java

If the user selects one or more orders in the select list of **selectShippingOrders.html**, changes are applied to those orders using this Servlet. In the **doPost()** method, all order ids to which changes need to be applied are read and added to an orderIds vector.

```
Enumeration paramNames = req.getParameterNames();
while(paramNames.hasMoreElements())
{
        String nm = (String)paramNames.nextElement();
        if(nm.equalsIgnoreCase("orderIds"))
        {
            String[] allVals = req.getParameterValues(nm);
            int len = allVals.length;
            for(int k=0; k<len; k++)
                orderIds.addElement(allVals[k]);
        }
}
```

The shipment method, status, and date that the user wants to apply are also read. The method **updateShipOrder()** is called to apply the changes.

```
public void updateShipOrder(PrintWriter out, Vector orderIds,
        String dateShipped, String shipMethod, String
            status,
        String pgName, Connection conn)
    throws Exception
```

This method loops through all the elements in the orderIds Vector and applies changes to them:

```
String querySQLbase = "UPDATE orders SET
        date_shipped=TO_DATE('" + dateShipped + "',
        'DD-MON-YYYY'),
        shipment_method='" + shipMethod + "', status='"
        + status +
        "' WHERE id=";
int len = orderIds.size();
String querySQL;
for(int i=0; i<len; i++)
{
        querySQL = querySQLbase +
                    (String)orderIds.elementAt(i);
        stmt.executeUpdate(querySQL);
```

Document Root HTML Files

shipping.html

This is the entry-point HTML file. It contains a FRAMESET consisting of two frames. Initially, a blank page is displayed in the left frame, and the login page is presented in the second.

```
<FRAMESET COLS='100, *' BORDER='0'>
   <FRAME NAME='left' SRC='blank.html'>
   <FRAME NAME='right' SRC='shippingLogin.html'>
</FRAMESET>
```

shippingLogin.html

This is the login page. It contains a username and a password field. When the user presses the Submit button, the Servlet ShippingLogin is invoked.

shippingSignoff.html

This displays a button that can be clicked for signing out of the shipping system.

Other HTML Files and Templates

shippingError.html

This is the error file used by all Servlets for showing an error message.

shippingOptions.html

This page shows the options a shipping administrator has. These include the ability to see order details by order id or for applying batch updates to multiple orders.

When this page loads up, it calls the method **showSignOff()**, which brings up the **shippingSignoff.html** in the left frame.

shippingOrderDetails.html

This is a template in which details of a particular order are displayed.

selectShippingOrders.html

This template displays a list of orders to which a user can apply updates.

shippingOrderUpdated.html

This file indicates success in applying an update to one or more orders.

Reporting System

High-Level Description

The Reporting System allows you to monitor activity on your site in terms of user registrations and product sales. Authorized users can log in and get different types of reports that can help determine how well the Web store is doing.

The flow begins with the entry point page, **reporting.html**. You would access it like this:

http://myServer.com:myPort/reporting.html.

Classes and Their Methods

BaseReporting.java

This base class is the parent of all Servlets that belong to the Reporting package. It is similar to the base class of Inventory and contains similar methods for debugging and to verify username and password of administrators allowed to use the system.

ReportingLogin.java

This Servlet checks the validity of the password of a user. Valid users are presented with a set of options they can choose from.

1. doPost()

The username and password are checked. The method **validPassword**() is used for this. If the user is found to be valid, the method **showReportingOptionsPage**() is called.

2. showReportingOptionsPage()

This method simply shows the options a reporting administrator has.

DistributionReporting.java

This Servlet is invoked if the user chooses one of the first two options, namely, those that fall under the distribution analysis category. Based on which of the two options the user has selected, it displays another form in which the user can give details about the type of report that is required.

1. doGet()

This method determines whether the user wants a sales distribution report or a customer distribution report. It then calls **showDistributionReportingPage()**, which takes care of the display.

2. showDistributionReportingPage()

This method either displays the user distribution analysis form or the sales distribution analysis form, depending on the link in the options page that the user clicked.

FrequencyReporting.java

This Servlet is invoked if the user chooses one of the last two options, namely, those that fall under the Time/Frequency Analysis category. Based on whichever one of the two options the user has selected, it displays another form in which the user can give details about the type of report that is required.

1. doGet()

This method determines whether the user wants a sales distribution report or a customer distribution report. It then calls **showFrequencyReportingPage()**, which takes care of the display.

2. showFrequencyReportingPage()

This method either displays the user frequency analysis form or the sales frequency analysis form, depending on the link in the options page that the user clicked.

UserDistribution.java

This Servlet calculates the distribution of users across states or zip codes and displays the results in an HTML page.

1. doGet()

It reads form variables to determine whether the user wants to see distribution of customers by state or by zip code. It also reads variables to find the two dates between which reporting should be done. It then calls **showUserDistributionPage()**, which does the calculations.

2. showUserDistributionPage()

This method builds a query based on the user's input and retrieves data from the database. It then formats the data and displays it.

SalesDistribution.java

This Servlet calculates the distribution of sales across products and displays the results in an HTML page. Note that the provided implementation does not contain code for calculating distribution of sales across categories. This has been left as an exercise to the reader, as doing this would give you a hands-on opportunity to understand the database and how the other Servlets interact with it.

1. **doGet()**
   It reads form variables to determine whether the user wants to see distribution of sales by products or by categories. It also reads variables to find the two dates between which reporting should be done. It then calls **showUserDistributionPage()**, which does the calculations.

2. **showSalesDistributionPage()**
   This method determines whether the user wants to see distribution by products or by categories. It then calls **showProductSalesDistributionPage()** or **showCategorySalesDistributionPage()**.

3. **showProductSalesDistributionPage()**
   This method builds a query based on the user's input and retrieves data from the database. It then formats the data and displays it.

4. **showCategorySalesDistributionPage()**
   This code has not been implemented in the distribution. It is left as a reader exercise.

UserFrequency.java

This Servlet displays frequency of customer registrations on a daily, weekly, monthly, or yearly basis.

1. **doGet()**
   This method reads the form values supplied by the user. It then calls the method **showUserFrequencyPage()** with these values and a database connection that can be used for retrieving data from the database.

2. **showUserFrequencyPage()**
   This method loops through all dates between the start and end dates given by the user and calls the method **getFrequency()**, which calculates the number of registrations between those dates. It then displays the results using a template.

3. **getFrequency()**
   This method calculates the number of user registrations between the two dates that it receives as input parameters. The results are returned to the calling method.

4. **getNextDate()**
   This method receives as input a particular date and the type of frequency the user wants. It then calculates the next date using the frequency type.

5. **getDate()**
   There are two forms of this method. The first receives int values for a day, month,

and year—it converts the information to a String representation of the date. The second method creates a date representation from a String representation.

6. getMonth()

This method also has two implementations. The first gets an **int** value and returns the String representation of the month it represents. The other receives the name of a month and returns the int value of the same.

SalesFrequency.java

This Servlet displays frequency of sales on a daily, weekly, monthly, or yearly basis.

1. doGet()

This method reads the form values supplied by the user. It then calls the method **showSalesFrequencyPage()** with these values and a database connection that can be used for retrieving data from the database.

2. showSalesFrequencyPage()

This method loops through all dates between the start and end dates given by the user and calls the method **getFrequency()**, which calculates the number of sales between those dates. It then displays the results using a template.

This Servlet also contains methods **getNextDate()**, **getDate()**, and **getMonth()**.

Detailed Description

All the classes of the Reporting Management System are contained in a package called Reporting. So, each class begins with a line:

package Reporting;

Most of the classes extend BaseReporting.

1. BaseReporting.java

This is the base class of all Servlets in the Reporting package. The methods in this are quite similar to the ones in BaseReporting. It contains a **BasePath** variable that determines where the HTML templates used by the system reside.

2. ReportingLogin.java

This is the login Servlet where username and password are verified. It reads the username and password from the CGI parameters. The method **validPassword()** is called to check the validity, and a session is then established. It then calls **showReportingOptionsPage()**. It displays the template **reportingOptions.html**.

3. DistributionReporting.java

This Servlet reads the type of distribution reporting the user wants, whether customer distribution or sales distribution. This is determined using the CGI variable **type**:

```
Enumeration paramNames = req.getParameterNames();
while(paramNames.hasMoreElements())
{
        String nm = (String)paramNames.nextElement();
        String vl = req.getParameterValues(nm)[0];
        if(nm.equalsIgnoreCase("type"))
            type = vl;
}
```

It contains names of the templates for customer distribution and sales distribution.

```
    static String userDistReportingPage = BasePath +
"userDistReporting.html";
    static String salesDistReportingPage = BasePath +
"salesDistReporting.html";
```

Depending on the type the user has selected, the appropriate template is displayed:

```
if(type.equalsIgnoreCase("sales"))
    pgName = salesDistPage;
if(type.equalsIgnoreCase("user"))
    pgName = userDistPage;
PageUtil pu = new PageUtil(pgName, out);
pu.printPage();
```

4. FrequencyReporting.java

This Servlet reads the type of distribution reporting the user wants, whether customer distribution or sales distribution. This is determined using the CGI variable **type**:

```
Enumeration paramNames = req.getParameterNames();
while(paramNames.hasMoreElements())
{
        String nm = (String)paramNames.nextElement();
        String vl = req.getParameterValues(nm)[0];
        if(nm.equalsIgnoreCase("type"))
            type = vl;
}
```

It contains names of the templates for customer distribution and sales distribution.

```
        static String userFreqReportingPage = BasePath +
    "userFreqReporting.html";
        static String salesFreqReportingPage = BasePath +
    "salesFreqReporting.html";
```

Depending on the type the user has selected, the appropriate template is displayed.

5. UserDistribution.java

This Servlet reads the CGI variables **type, from**, and **to** to see what kind of user distribution reporting is required (that is, by state or by zip) and the dates between which calculations should be performed. Since the address of each user is contained in a separate table from the profiles table (which contains registration date), we will have to perform queries on both tables. We do this as follows:

First we retrieve the ids of all users who registered between the given dates and store these in a Hashtable, **allIds**:

```
querySQL = "SELECT id FROM profiles WHERE
    registration_date
    BETWEEN TO_DATE(' " + from + "', 'DD-MON-YYYY')
    AND TO_DATE('" + to + "','DD-MON-YYYY')";
rset = stmt.executeQuery(querySQL);
while(rset.next())
{
    allIds.put(rset.getString(1), "NO_VAL");
}
```

Then we query the addresses table to see the state or zip code of each user's SHIPPING address. For each resulting row we see if the profile id of this user is present in the **allIds** table (to see if the user is one of those who have registered between the given dates). It also maintains the Hashtable **ht**, which contains the name of a state or zip and the number of customers in that zip. For each user who has a profile id in the **allIds** table, the counter for the corresponding state or zip is increased in the **ht** table.

```
querySQL = "SELECT profile_id, " + type + "
    FROM addresses WHERE type='SHIPPING'";
rset = stmt.executeQuery(querySQL);
while(rset.next())
{
    String profId = rset.getString(1);
    String stateOrZip = rset.getString(2);
    /* If profileId is not in list of people
        who registered between given
        dates, don't count it. */
```

```
        if(allIds.get(profId) == null)
            continue;
        Integer total = (Integer)ht.get(stateOrZip);
        if(total == null)
            total = new Integer(1);
        else
            total = new Integer(total.intValue() + 1);
        ht.put(stateOrZip, total);
    }
```

In the end **ht** contains the names of each state and zip code and the total customers in them. These values are then retrieved from **ht** and added to a String called tableRows:

```
Enumeration e = ht.keys();
while(e.hasMoreElements())
{
    String key = (String)e.nextElement();
    Integer val = (Integer)ht.get(key);
    tableRows += "<TR><TD>" + key + "</TD><TD ALIGN=
        'right'>"
        + val + "</TD></TR>";
}
```

The resulting string is then used to replace the variable **<VAR_TABLE_ROWS>** in the **userDistribution.html** template.

```
PageUtil pu = new PageUtil(pgName, out);
pu.setReplaceItem("<VAR_TABLE_ROWS>", tableRows);
```

6. SalesDistribution.java

The implementation of this is similar to that of UserDistribution. First the id and name of each product are retrieved from the products table and stored in the Hashtable **productNames**.

```
querySQL = "SELECT id, name FROM products";
rset = stmt.executeQuery(querySQL);
while(rset.next())
{
    productNames.put(rset.getString(1), rset.
        getString(2));
}
```

The table orders are then queried to retrieve the id of all orders placed between the given two dates:

```
querySQL = "SELECT id FROM orders
        WHERE date_ordered BETWEEN TO_DATE('" + from +
        "', 'DD-MON-YYYY')
        AND TO_DATE('" + to + "', 'DD-MON-YYYY')";
rset = stmt.executeQuery(querySQL);
while(rset.next())
{
    orderIds.addElement(rset.getString(1));
}
```

The **one_order** table is then queried for each order id in the orderIds Vector.

```
querySQL = "SELECT product_id, quantity, price
        FROM one_order WHERE orders_id=" + orderId;
```

Quantity for each product is stored in the **productQuantities** Hashtable, and the revenue generated by each is stored in the **productRevenues** Hashtable. Revenue generated by a product from an order is calculated by multiplying the quantity purchased with the price it was purchased at.

The resulting values are then displayed by replacing the **<VAR_TABLE_ROWS>** variable in the **salesDistribution.html** template.

7. UserFrequency.java

This Servlet reads values of the CGI variables **type, from**, and **to**. Based on the **type**—which could be daily, weekly, monthly, or yearly—it calculates the number of registrations between the two dates with the specified frequency and displays them in a tabular form. It contains a method **showUserFrequency()**, which calls the method **getFrequency()** to get the total registrations for each of the frequency periods between the given dates. To get the frequency periods, it calls the method **getNextDate()**.

Since "from" and "to" are dates in String format, these are first converted to **java.util.Date** format with the method **getDate()**.

```
startDate = getDate(from);
endDate = getDate(to);
```

Then it loops through these two dates. It uses the **before()** method of **java.util.Date** to check whether the first date is before the second date; the loop ends when the second date is greater than the first. The next date for the period is derived by calling **getNextDate()**.

```
while(nextDate.before(endDate))
{
    nextDate = getNextDate(curDate, type);
```

Total registrations are stored in the variable count. The result is stored in **tableRows**, which contains all rows of the table that are displayed using the template **userFrequency.html**.

```
int count = getFrequency(fromDate, toDate, conn);
tableRows += "<TR><TD>" + fromDate + "</TD><TD>" +
        toDate + "</TD><TD ALIGN='right'>" +
        count + "</TD></TR>";
```

getFrequency() uses the following query to retrieve data:

```
querySQL = "SELECT count(*) FROM profiles
        WHERE registration_date BETWEEN
        TO_DATE('" + from + "', 'DD-MON-YYYY') AND
        TO_DATE('" + to + "','DD-MON-YYYY')";
```

The method **getNextDate()** returns the next date in the frequency period. For this it creates an instance of GregorianCalendar using the input parameter date.

```
int month = curDate.getMonth();
int date = curDate.getDate();
int year = curDate.getYear() + 1900;
Calendar cal;
cal = new GregorianCalendar(year, month, date, 0, 0,
        0);
```

Then it retrieves the next date according to the frequency. So if the frequency is weekly, this is how the next date is derived:

```
if(type.equalsIgnoreCase("weekly"))
    cal.add(Calendar.DATE, 7);
```

Then a **java.util.Date** object is created using these values and returned:

```
month = cal.get(Calendar.MONTH);
date = cal.get(Calendar.DATE);
year = cal.get(Calendar.YEAR)-1900;
java.util.Date toRet =
        new java.util.Date(year, month, date);
return toRet;
```

8. SalesFrequency.java

In this Servlet also there is a method that loops through all the frequency periods and calculates the total sales for that period. A table is built using these and is displayed using the template **salesFrequency.html**.

The **getFrequency()** method uses the following SQL for retrieving the total amount of sales:

```
querySQL = "SELECT SUM(total_billed)
        FROM orders WHERE date_ordered BETWEEN
        TO_DATE('" + from + "', 'DD-MON-YYYY') AND
        TO_DATE('" + to + "','DD-MON-YYYY')";
```

Document Root HTML Files

reporting.html

This is the entry point of the Reporting System. This HTML file contains a FRAMESET consisting of two frames. The left one is initially blank, and the right one contains the login HTML file, **reportingLogin.html**.

reportingLogin.html

This contains a username and a password field.

reportingSignoff.html

This contains a Logout button. If the user presses it, he or she is logged out of the system.

Other HTML Files and Templates

reportingError.html

This error template is used by most of the Servlets in the Reporting package for reporting errors.

reportingOptions.html

This contains all the options a user has after logging into the reporting system. Each option is a link to a Servlet. The first two options, which allow distribution reporting, invoke the DistributionReporting Servlet. For user base reporting, the parameter type with the value user is supplied. For the sales distribution reporting, the parameter type has the value **sales**.

```
<A HREF='/newZone/Reporting.DistributionReporting?type=user'>User
    base</A>
<A HREF='/newZone/Reporting.DistributionReporting?type=sales'>
    Sales</A>
```

For time/frequency analysis, it contains links that invoke the Servlet FrequencyReporting.

userDistReporting.html

This contains a FORM that invokes UserDistribution. It allows users to supply values for the **type, from** and **to** variables.

salesDistReporting.html

This contains a FORM that invokes SalesDistribution. It allows users to supply values for the **type, from** and **to** variables.

userDistribution.html

This template is used for displaying distribution of user registrations between given dates for all states and zip codes.

salesDistribution.html

This template is used for displaying total sales between given dates for all products and categories.

userFreqReporting.html

This FORM allows users to supply values for the "from" and "to" dates. It also allows them to select the frequency with which reporting should be done—daily, weekly, monthly, or yearly.

salesFreqReporting.html

This FORM allows users to supply values for the "from" and "to" dates. It also allows them to select frequency with which reporting should be done—daily, weekly, monthly, or yearly.

userFrequency.html

This template is used for displaying total user registrations between given dates on a daily, weekly, monthly, or yearly basis.

salesFrequency.html

This template is used for displaying total sales between given dates on a daily, weekly, monthly, or yearly basis.

Appendix A

Installation and Configuration Instructions

This appendix contains installation and configuration instructions for the various tools/technologies used in the book. It covers the following: Apache, JServ, JDBC, mSQL, Oracle, and JavaMail.

Apache

Apache is probably the most popular Web server in the world. It is an open-source software project developed and maintained by the Apache Software Foundation, a nonprofit corporation.

Installation

You can download Apache from the following site:

http://www.apache.org

The download section for the server contains compiled binaries for different platforms. Alternatively, you could download the source and compile it in your own environment. You would need an ANSI C compiler like **gcc** in order to compile the source. An executable called "httpd" would be produced as a result; this is the main executable for the HTTP Daemon.

If you want to compile yourself, you can find excellent instructions in the INSTALL file that comes as part of the distribution.

Let's see what needs to be done for installing Apache 1.3.6 for Solaris:

1. Download apache_1.3.6.tar.gz.

2. Unzip it using "gunzip":
gunzip apache_1.3.6.tar.gz

3. Untar the resulting tar file:
tar xf apache_1.3.6.tar

4. Go to the apache_1.3.6 directory:
cd apache_1.3.6

5. Set up the configuration script that will create the Makefiles. For this you need to run "configure," which comes with the distribution. You can specify an argument, "—prefix=<where you want to install>." So you could say:
./configure —prefix=/local/vsharma/APACHE/apache_1.3.6

6. Execute make:
make

7. Install the resulting executables/files:
make install

This is really all you need to do to install Apache.

Troubleshooting

Apache needs an ANSI C compiler for installation. It first tries to look for **gcc**, the GNU C compiler. However, if you don't have it, but have another ANSI C compiler like **/opt/SUNWspro/bin/cc**, you can do the following:

1. Set the path so that the directory containing **cc** is the first thing in your path:
set path=(/opt/SUNWspro/bin:$path)

2. Change src/Configure so that it looks for **cc** instead of **gcc**.
In this file there is a line that looks like this:
for compilers in **gcc cc acc c89**
Change it to look like this:
for compilers in **cc acc c89**

An executable called "apachectl" will also be installed as a result of the installation. You can use this to start or shut down the Web server. Installation will be done in the directory you specified in the prefix argument of configure. To start Apache, go to the directory where it is installed and run:

bin/apachectl start

To shut down run:

bin/apachectl stop

But before you run you might want to update a few configuration files.

Configuration

Apache has three main configuration files: **httpd.conf**, **access.conf**, and **srm.conf**. However, Apache recommends that all directives be put in **httpd.conf**. The configuration files reside in **<directoryWhereYouInstalled>/conf**.

These directives control a number of features, for example, which directory should act as the root directory for your documents, which directories need to be secured, what your CGI directory is, and so on. The configuration file that comes with the distribution is adequately commented. Nevertheless, we look at some of the directives.

ServerRoot <directory>

Here **<directory>** refers to the top of the directory tree where the configuration, error, and log files are placed.

Port <Number>

This determines the port on which Apache listens for new Web requests. If you want to assign a number less than 1023, you will need to start Apache as root. A port is a part of the URL, so if you're running Apache on the machine www.myMachine.com at port 2000, URLs to your site will look like this:

http://www.myMachine.com:2000/<HtmlFile>

DocumentRoot <directory>

<directory> is the root directory where your HTML files/documents are present. You could create subdirectories under this to categorize your documents. If somebody tries to access the URL *http://www.myMachine.com:2000/doc.html,* the file **doc.html** that exists in <directory> will be returned. If the person tries to access *http://www.myMachine.com:2000/docs/doc.html,* the file in <directory>/docs will be returned.

> **AuthType Basic**
> **AuthName myName**
> **require valid-user**

These directives can be used in conjunction with some other directives to make a directory secure. In other words, if you want to restrict access to a directory on the basis of a username and password, you need to specify the above directives. Examples for this would be present in the default configuration files.

The traditional system of maintaining usernames and passwords is through a utility called htpasswd. You can look at this utility's documentation to find out more on how you can secure access to your Web site.

Another configuration file of importance is **mime.types**. This file associates file extensions with the Internet media types they represent. Before a document is sent back by the Web server, it sends the MIME type of the document. This is an indication to the client concerning the kind of data it should expect and how it is to be displayed and executed. A Web server serves not only HTML documents but also several other types, ranging from plain text to PDF files to audio files. The first piece of information that is sent when an HTML file is being returned is Content-type:text/html. Similarly, if an MS Word file is being sent, the appropriate information (MIME Type) that should be sent is Content-type:application/msword.

Naturally, you would want that this be done automatically, so if one of your links points to a Word file (whose extension is .doc), you would want the Web server to recognize this as a Word file (based on the extension) and send the appropriate MIME type so that the file is displayed properly on the client side. These directives are present in the **mime.types** file. In most cases you won't need to touch this file. However, if you want to add a new MIME type or change the extension associated with some MIME type, you will need to look at this file in detail.

JServ

Apache JServ is a 100 percent pure Java Servlet engine. It allows you to execute Servlets in an Apache Web server environment. The engine works as a server application that listens for requests following the Apache JServ Protocol. An Apache Jserv module, mod_jserv, can be integrated with Apache so that Servlet requests are sent by the Web server to the Servlet engine.

Installation

Before you begin the installation of Apache JServ, you should download and install the Java Servlet Development Kit. For JServ 1.0b3 you will need JSDK version 2.0.

Download this from *http://java.sun.com/products/servlet/index.html*.
You need the following file:

jsdk20-solaris2-sparc.tar.Z

This is a compressed tar file. You need to complete the following steps:

uncompress jsdk20-solaris2-sparc.tar.Z

tar xf jsdk20-solaris2-sparc.tar

Let's say you installed this in the following directory:

/local/vsharma/SERVLETS/JSDK

Upon uncompressing, you will see a directory JSDK2.0. This contains a "lib" directory, which contains a jar file, jsdk.jar. This contains the Servlet API provided by Javasoft, which will be used by the Servlet engine. You will also need to include this in your CLASSPATH in order to compile your Servlets. To put this in the CLASSPATH:

setenv CLASSPATH /local/vsharma/SERVLETS/JSDK/JSDK2.0/lib/jsdk.jar: $CLASSPATH

Now you are ready to get and install JServ. You can download Apache JServ from this site: *http://java.apache.org*.

For the 1.0 Beta 3 version, you can download Apache-JServ-1.0b3.tar.gz. This is a GNU zip file that needs to be unzipped. To do this you need gunzip:

gunzip Apache-JServ-1.0b3.tar.gz

The resulting tar file needs to be untarred:

tar xf Apache-JServ-1.0b3.tar

This will create a directory: Apache-JServ-1.0b3
Assuming you want to install JServ in: /local/vsharma/SERVLETS/JSERV/ Apache-JServ-1.0b3
Go to the Apache-JServ-1.0b3 directory:

cd Apache-JServ-1.0b3

Run configure with the following two options:

—with-apache-src=<directory_where_your_Apache_source_exists>

—prefix=<where_you_want_install_JServ)

configure —with-apache-src=/local/vsharma/APACHE/apache_1.3.6 — prefix=/local/vsharma/SERVLETS/JSERV/Apache-JServ-1.0b3

make

make install

Now you will need to go back to the Apache source directory and reconfigure it so that the JServ module is included in Apache.
Go to the directory where Apache source is:

cd /local/vsharma/APACHE/apache_1.3.6

Run configure with the —activate-module option in addition to the —prefix option:

configure —prefix=/local/vsharma/APACHE/apache_1.3.6 —activate-module=src/modules/jserv/mod_jserv.c

make

make install

This is all the installation that is required. As a result of this installation, Jserv has been integrated with Apache. When you start Apache, JServ will automatically be started. It listens for requests on a particular port. Next we look at some configuration that needs to be done before we finally start up Apache and JServ.

Configuration

The topmost configuration file is **jserv.conf**. By default it is installed in the "example" directory that is created under "Apache-JServ-1.0b3." You need to put a directive in Apache's "httpd.conf" file so that it knows where this file exists. The directive looks like this:

Include /local/vsharma/SERVLETS/JSERV/Apache-JServ-1.0b3/example/jserv.conf

JServ has a concept of Servlet zones. Each Servlet can reside in one of the zones, which can be viewed as distinct areas that allow you to put Servlets of one kind in a separate place from Servlets of another kind. You may want to have your production Servlets in a different directory from your test Servlets, which you can do by creating two separate zones for the purpose. Zones have an alias, and when a request for a Servlet comes in, JServ first identifies what zone it belongs to using this alias so that the appropriate Servlet can be executed.

Zones are declared in **jserv.conf**. For each zone, there is a properties file. The location of this file is specified in jserv.properties, which is another "top" level configuration file.

We first explore **jserv.conf** to see what directives it contains.

ApJServManual off

This directive decides whether JVM should be started by Apache by default when it starts or not. "off" means Apache starts it; "on" means you will have to do it manually.

ApJServProperties <location_of_jserv.properties>

Here you put the location of the jserv.properties file. Usually, it is in the same directory as **jserv.conf**.

ApJServLogFile <fileName>

JServ logs error cases and other things. Using this directive, you can specify where the logs should go.

ApJServMount [name] [jserv-url]

This directive indicates the Servlet zones. There is one such line for each zone, so if you have a zone called testZone on this machine, you would specify it like this:

ApJServMount /testZone /testZone

jserv.properties

This file contains some other "top-level" directives.

wrapper.bin=/jdk1.1.4/bin/java

This directive tells which JVM is to be used for execution of the Servlets.

wrapper.classpath=/local/vsharma/SERVLETS/JSERV/Apache-JServ-1.0b3/src/java/Apache-JServ.jar

This directive can be specified multiple times—whatever directories you specify here will be included in the CLASSPATH of the JVM that is going to execute the Servlets.

zones=<servlet zone>,<servlet zone>...

This lists all the zones in current configuration. If you add a new zone, you will not only add an entry in the **jserv.conf** file, you will also have to add it to the "zones" list. If you have two zones, "example" and "testZone," this line will look like this:

    zones=example,testZone

<zoneName>.properties=<locationOfPropertiesFile>

As mentioned earlier, each zone has a properties file. This directive specifies the properties file for each zone. For testZone it will look like this:

    testZone.properties=/local/vsharma/SERVLETS/JSERV/Apache-JServ-1.0b3/
    testZone/testZone.properties

<zoneName>.properties

This file contains directives specific to each zone.

repositories=[repository],[repository]...

This directive shows the directories that contain the Servlets belonging to this zone. So, if you have your Servlets in /local/vsharma/SERVLETS/JSERV/Apache-JServ-1.0b3/testZone, it will look like this:

    repositories=/local/vsharma/SERVLETS/JSERV/Apache-JServ-1.0b3/testZone

session.timeout=(long)>0

This directive specifies how long a session is allowed to last. If you want sessions to be finished 30 minutes after last usage, you can say this:

    session.timeout=1800000

Once you have set these parameters, you are ready to start up JServ. For this, start up Apache:

apachectl start

Assuming you are running Apache at Port 3000 in myMachine.com, you can access the Hello servlet in the example zone by accessing *http://myMachine.com:3000/example/Hello*.

Steps to add a new zone

Here's how to create a zone named finalZone.

1. Add an ApJServMount directive in jserv.conf:
   ApJServMount /finalZone /finalZone

2. Add finalZone to the zones directive in jserv.properties:
   zones=example,finalZone

3. Add a finalZone.properties line jserv.properties on the line of example.properties:
   finalZone.properties=/local/vsharma/SERVLETS/JSERV/Apache-JServ-1.0b3/finalZone/finalZone.properties

4. Create finalZone directory in your Apache-Jserv-1.0b3 directory"
   mkdir /local/vsharma/SERVLETS/JSERV/Apache-JServ-1.0b1/finalZone

5. Create finalZone.properties in this directory (copy from ../example/example.properties):
   cp ../example/example.properties finalZone.properties

6. Change the repositories directive in finalZone.properties to reflect the physical directory in which servlets of this zone will reside:
   repositories=/local/vsharma/SERVLETS/JSERV/Apache-JServ-1.0b3/finalZone
   You may also change other parameters according to your needs.

7. Restart Apache, and the new zone will be in effect.

Oracle

Oracle is the most popular and widely installed database in the world. It comes with an installer that you can use for doing installation and configuration. For more information about Oracle, visit *www.oracle.com*.

Utilities

You can get a number of utilities with Oracle. A popular tool for inserting and reading table data is SQL*Plus.

There are specialized tools like the Designer for creating tables and Discoverer for generating reports.

mSQL

mSQL is another database management system. This can be downloaded from *http://www.hughes.com.au/software/msql1/current.htm*.

To get the 1.0.16 version you will need to download msql-1.0.16.tar.gz. Then you can gunzip it, extract the tar file, and do this:

    gunzip *.gz

    tar xf *.tar

    cd msql-1.0.16

    make target

Now a directory targets would be created. In this there would be a directory for your platform. Go to this directory:

    cd targets/Solaris-2.4-Sparc

Here you need to run a script called "setup":

    ./setup

This will ask a few questions. Here are some typical answers:

Top of install tree ?   /home/vsharma/MSQL

Will this installation be running as root ? n

What username will it run under ? vsharma

Directory for pid file ? /home/vsharma/MSQL

Defines for directory stuff? -DHAVE_SYS_DIRENT_H -DHAVE_DIRENT -DHAVE_DIRENT_H

Now you can run:

    make

    make install

This will install mSQL in the directory you specified as the "Top of the install tree."

Troubleshooting

Installation uses "bison"—if you don't have it but have yacc on your system, in site.mm change "bison -y" to "yacc."

If you don't have gcc, change "gcc" to "cc" in site.mm.

You may want to change the LDLIBS line depending on which libraries you have:

    LDLIBS= -L$(TOP)/lib $(EXTRA_LIB) -lsocket -lnsl

If you're facing some compile errors

In msql/msql.c:

  Add

    #include "netdb.h"

  after

    #include "msql.h"

Once these changes are applied, you will need to run make and make install again.

Utilities

After installation you can start the mSQL daemon as follows:

/home/vsharma/MSQL/bin/msqld&

You will need to run the msqladmin tool to create a new database:

msqladmin create test

The mSQL monitor can be used to create tables, add/modify/remove records, etc. To start this:

msql <database name>

If you have a database called test (created with msqladmin), you can connect to it using the monitor as follows:

msql test

Once you're connected, you can issue SQL statements. To execute a statement, you would have to type in "\g."

Here's an example of how you would create a table called mytable:

  ./msql test

  > create table mytable

    -> (a char(24))

    -> \g

Here's an example of how you would insert into this table:

  mSQL > insert into mytable values('Test')

    -> \g

Here's an example of how you would retrieve from this table:

  mSQL > select * from mytable

    -> \g

To quit you can use "\q."

You can find more information on mSQL and the monitor at the site from which it can be downloaded.

JDBC Drivers

You would need to download a driver depending on the database that you installed. For Oracle you can get the driver from *www.oracle.com*. It comes as a zip file (classess111.zip for JDK1.1). You can place this zip file anywhere. It needs to be included in the CLASSPATH.

For mSQL you can get a driver from the following site: *ftp://ftp.imaginary.com/pub/Java/database/mSQL-JDBC.tar.gz*.

If you gunzip and untar this, you will get a zip file that contains the driver. There are examples that show how you can make connections. Typically your JDBC code will look like this:

Class.forName("com.imaginary.sql.msql.MsqlDriver");

String url = "jdbc:msql://myServer.com:4333/test";

Connection con = DriverManager.getConnection(url);

Statement stmt = con.createStatement();

Here myServer.com is the machine on which the mSQL database exists, and 4333 is the port on which it is running. "test" is the name of the database to which we are connecting.

Troubleshooting

If you are getting a connection-refused error:
Check /home/vsharma/MSQL/msql. conf.
    Check the value of RemoteAccess. If it is false, set it to true.
    Whichever driver you use will have to be included in the CLASSPATH for your classes to be able to use it. So if you want to use it in your servlets, you would have to add a "wrapper.classpath" line to your **jserv.properties** file.

JavaMail

The JavaMail API is an extension to Java that models a mail system. You can use the API to build mail applications like an email-sending system. You need to download the API from *www.javasoft.com*. You will also need to download the JavaBeans Activation

Framework package in order to use the API. This package can also be downloaded from the Java Web site.

Download the zip file for the JavaMail API. Unzip this file. Also download the Java Activation Framework. Add the following files to your CLASSPATH (both are required for you to successfully compile and execute a program that uses the JavaMail API):

mail.jar (from the JavaMail API download)

activation.jar (from the Java Activation Framework download)

Appendix B

Complete Code Listing

Installation

Code Organization

PLEASE SPECIFY WHERE THE TAR FILE EXISTS

Code for the five systems and the utilities can be extracted from the tar file. Upon untarring, the following six directories will be created: Inventory,Ordering, Profile, Shipping, Reporting, and Utilities.

The directories contain Java files and some HTML files/templates. All directories except Utilities contain a DOC_ROOT directory, which contains HTML files that need to be moved to the DocumentRoot directory on your system.

Prerequisites

The system is designed using Apache with JServ. You need to install these. Instructions for installation and configuration can be found in Appendix A of this book. It is assumed that installation will be done in a Servlet zone whose name is "newZone."

See instructions in Appendix A for creating/configuring Servlet zones, and create a zone with this name.

You also need to install/configure a database (like Oracle/mSQL, etc.) and get the corresponding JDBC driver.

Modifications to Be Made

You will need to make some modifications in order to use the systems. The values of a few variables in the Java and HTML files need to be replaced with those relevant to your environment. These include things like database connection information (login, password, etc.) and Web server information (Document Root, host name, and port).

The values of following variables need to be replaced:

HTML_DIRECTORY—replace this with the name of a directory in which you want to keep the HTML files and templates (except those in the DOC_ROOT directory).

Important note: Assuming you are installing on a Unix machine, you should put a trailing "/" with the directory name. Here's an example of a value: /home/vsharma/HTML/

HTTP_VALUE— replace this with a value that looks like this: http://<server_machine>:<port>

Here <server_machine> is the machine on which your Web server is running, and <port> is the port on which it is listening. You can find the port by looking at the value of the "Port" directive in the httpd.conf file. Here's an example of what this would look like: http://myServer.com:8080

SHIP_DEPARTMENT_EMAIL—replace this with the email address of your shipping department.

HTTP_CARD_COMPANY_VALUE—replace this with the URL at which credit card verification is done.

LOGIN—replace this with the login of your database schema.

PASSWORD—replace this with the password of your database schema.

SID—replace this with the sid of your database schema.

PORT—replace this with the port of your database schema.

HOST—replace this with the host of your database schema (check with a database administrator if you are unsure of these values).

SMTPHOST—replace this with the name of the machine that is your SMTP host (check with a system administrator if you are unsure of this value).

If you are using a database other than Oracle, you will need to change the JDBC connection information. You may also need to change some SQL statements if they are not compatible with your database.

Here's a complete list of files in which replacements need to be made.

Inventory Management System

Directory: Inventory

Files in which changes need to be made:

1. BaseInventory.java
   Replace HTML_DIRECTORY
   (Don't forget to put a trailing "/"—an example value would be :
   /home/vsharma/HTML/)

Ordering Management System

Directory: Ordering

Files in which changes need to be made:

1. **BaseOrdering.java**
   Replace HTML_DIRECTORY.
   Replace HTTP_VALUE.
   Replace SHIP_DEPARTMENT_EMAIL.
2. **CardVerifier.java**
   Replace HTTP_CARD_COMPANY_VALUE with http address of credit card
   verifier.
3. **signIn.html**
   Replace HTTP_VALUE

Profile Management System

Directory: Profile

Files in which changes need to be made:

1. **BaseProfile.java**
   Replace HTML_DIRECTORY
2. **ContactUs.java**
   Replace helpReg@myCompany.com, helpOrder@myCompany.com,
   helpGeneral@myCompany.com.
3. **registered.html**
   Replace HTTP_VALUE.
4. **updated.html**
   Replace HTTP_VALUE.
5. **DOC_ROOT/ordering.html**
   Replace HTTP_VALUE.
   (occurs in several places)

Shipping Management System

Directory: Shipping

Files in which changes need to be made:

1. **BaseShipping.java**
   Replace HTML_DIRECTORY.

2. **shippingOptions.html**
   Replace HTTP_VALUE.

Reporting System

Directory: Reporting

Files in which changes need to be made:

1. **BaseReporting.java**
   Replace HTML_DIRECTORY.

2. **reportingOptions.html**
   Replace HTTP_VALUE.

Utilities

Directory: Utilities

Files in which changes need to be made:

1. **ConnectionPool.java**
   MAX_CONNECTIONS (optional)
   LOGIN
   PASSWORD
   SID
   PORT
   HOST

   You may also need to change the connect String here if you want to use some other database like mSQL.

2. **MailSender.java**
   SMTPHOST

Compilation

Once you've made the changes, you will have to compile the Java files. In order for the classes to compile, you will need to have the following in your CLASSPATH:

1. The zip file of your Jdbc driver.
2. activation.jar and mail.jar (for the Java mail API stuff).
3. jsdk.jar (the JSDK kit for Servlets).
4. The directory that contains the Utilities directory (required because all systems use the Utilities package).

Go to each directory and compile the Java files.

cd Inventory;

javac *.java;

cd ../Ordering;

javac *.java;

cd ../Profile;

javac *.java;

cd ../Shipping;

javac *.java;

cd ../Reporting;

javac *.java;

cd ../Utilities;

javac *.java;

(It may be a good idea to create a Makefile if you expect to make a lot of changes.)

Creating Database Elements

The CODE directory contains a file called SQL. This is an SQL script that needs to be executed on your database to create the required tables and sequences. You need to do this before you can start using the system. For this you can use any interface to your database—for instance, with mSQL you can use the mSQL monitor, and with Oracle you can use SQL*Plus.

Moving Files to the Appropriate Directories

Copy *.class from each directory to the corresponding directory in the zones area.

Let's say your "newZone" maps to the physical directory: /home/me/SERVLETS/ newZone. Create the following directories in this:

Inventory

Ordering

Profile

Shipping

Reporting

Utilities

Now do the following:

cp Inventory/*.class /home/me/SERVLETS/newZone/Inventory

cp Ordering/*.class /home/me/SERVLETS/newZone/Ordering

cp Profile/*.class /home/me/SERVLETS/newZone/Profile

cp Shipping/*.class /home/me/SERVLETS/newZone/Shipping

cp Reporting/*.class /home/me/SERVLETS/newZone/Reporting

cp Utilities/*.class /home/me/SERVLETS/newZone/Utilities

Copy *.html from each directory to your HTML_DIRECTORY.
Let's say your HTML_DIRECTORY is /home/me/HTML.

cp Inventory/*.html /home/me/HTML_DIRECTORY

cp Ordering/*.html /home/me/HTML_DIRECTORY

cp Profile/*.html /home/me/HTML_DIRECTORY

cp Shipping/*.html /home/me/HTML_DIRECTORY

cp Reporting/*.html /home/me/HTML_DIRECTORY

Copy *.html from each DOC_ROOT to the Document Root directory.
Let's say your DocumentRoot is /home/me/DOC_ROOT.

cp Inventory/DOC_ROOT/*.html /home/me/DOC_ROOT

cp Ordering/DOC_ROOT/*.html /home/me/DOC_ROOT

cp Profile/DOC_ROOT/*.html /home/me/DOC_ROOT

cp Shipping/DOC_ROOT/*.html /home/me/DOC_ROOT

cp Reporting/DOC_ROOT/*.html /home/me/DOC_ROOT

Assuming server is myServer.com, port is 8080, you can access the five systems thus:

http://myServer.com:8080/inventory.html

http://myServer.com:8080/ordering.html

http://myServer.com:8080/profile.html

http://myServer.com:8080/shipping.html

http://myServer.com:8080/reporting.html

Inventory Management System

Java Files

AddCategory.java

```java
package Inventory;

import java.util.*;
import java.io.*;
import java.sql.*;
import javax.servlet.*;
import javax.servlet.http.*;
import Utilities.*;

public class AddCategory extends BaseInventory
{
    ConnectionPool c = null;
    static String addCategoryHtml = BasePath + "addCategory.html";
    static String errorHtml = BasePath + "inventoryError.html";
    static String categoriesAddedHtml = BasePath + "categoriesAdded.html";
    public void doPost (HttpServletRequest req,
                        HttpServletResponse res)
    {
      Connection conn = null;
      PrintWriter out = null;
      try{
          HttpSession session;

          String username="", password="";
          String name="", description_url="", description="";
          String search_keywords = "";
          int category_id=0; // cat_id = 0 ==> top level category
          boolean addMore = false;
          int id = -1;

          boolean firstTime = false;

          if(c == null)
          {
              c = ConnectionPool.getInstance();
              c.initialize();
          }
          conn = c.getConnection();
          Enumeration paramNames = req.getParameterNames();
          while(paramNames.hasMoreElements())
```

```
{
    String nm = (String)paramNames.nextElement();
    String vl = req.getParameterValues(nm)[0];
    if(nm.equalsIgnoreCase("username"))
        username = vl;
    if(nm.equalsIgnoreCase("password"))
        password = vl;
    if(nm.equalsIgnoreCase("name"))
        name = vl;
    if(nm.equalsIgnoreCase("description_url"))
        description_url = vl;
    if(nm.equalsIgnoreCase("description"))
        description= vl;
    if(nm.equalsIgnoreCase("category_id"))
        category_id= (new Integer(vl)).intValue();
    if(nm.equalsIgnoreCase("addMore"))
        if(vl.equalsIgnoreCase("Yes"))
            addMore = true;
        else
            addMore = false;
    if(nm.equalsIgnoreCase("firstTime"))
        firstTime = true;
}
out = res.getWriter();
res.setContentType("text/html");
if(firstTime == true)
{
    if(validPassword(username, password, errorHtml, c,
                    conn, out) == false)
        return;
    session = req.getSession(true);
    session.putValue("Inventory.username", username);
    session.putValue("Inventory.password", password);
    session.putValue("AddCategory.categoryVector", new Vector());
    showAddCategoryPage(out, addCategoryHtml, conn);
    c.putConnection(conn);
    return;
}
else
{
    session = req.getSession(false);
    if(session == null)
    {
        username = null;
```

```
                password = null;
            }
            else
            {
                username = (String)session.getValue("Inventory.username");
                password = (String)session.getValue("Inventory.password");
            }
            if(validPassword(username, password, errorHtml, c,
                             conn, out) == false)
                return;
        }
        String has_sub_categories = "0";
        Category p = new Category(id, category_id, name, description_url,
                description, has_sub_categories, search_keywords);
        Vector v = (Vector)session.getValue("AddCategory.categoryVector");
        v.addElement(p);
        session.putValue("AddCategory.categoryVector", v);
        if(addMore)
            showAddCategoryPage(out, addCategoryHtml, conn);
        else
        {
            writeCategories(out, v, username, categoriesAddedHtml,
            session, conn);
        }
        c.putConnection(conn);
        out.close();
    }catch(Exception ex){
            if(c != null && conn != null)
            {
                c.putConnection(conn);
                showErrorPage(out, errorHtml, ex.getMessage());
            }
        }
    }
}


public void writeCategories(PrintWriter out, Vector categoryVector,
                    String username, String pgName,
                    HttpSession session, Connection conn)
        throws Exception
{
        String has_sub_categories = "0";
        Statement stmt = conn.createStatement();
        String names = "<UL>";
        int size = categoryVector.size();
```

```
            String baseSQL = "INSERT INTO categories(id, category_id,
                name, description_url, description, has_sub_categories,
                last_modified_by, last_modification_date,
                search_keywords) VALUES(";
            String sequenceSQL = "SELECT categories_seq.NEXTVAL FROM dual";
            ResultSet rset;
            for(int i=0; i<size; i++)
            {
                Category p = (Category)categoryVector.elementAt(i);
                rset = stmt.executeQuery(sequenceSQL);
                rset.next();

                String id = rset.getString(1);

                String insertSQL = baseSQL + id + "," + p.getCategoryId() +
                    ",'" + p.getName() + "','" +  p.getDescriptionUrl() +
                    "','" + p.getDescription() + "'," + has_sub_categories
                    + ",'" + username + "', SYSDATE, '" +
                    p.getSearchKeywords() + "')";

                stmt.executeUpdate(insertSQL);

                /* If this is not the top level category, then we
                    will update its parent
                    to indicate that the parent has subcategories in it */

                String updateSQL = "UPDATE categories SET
                    has_sub_categories=1 WHERE id=" + p.getCategoryId();
                if(p.getCategoryId() != 0)
                        stmt.executeUpdate(updateSQL);

                names += "<LI>" + p.getName();
            }
            stmt.close();
            names += "</UL>";
            PageUtil p = new PageUtil(pgName, out);
            p.setReplaceItem("<CATEGORIES_ADDED>", names);
            p.printPage();
            session.removeValue("AddCategory.categoryVector");
            Vector v = new Vector();
            session.putValue("AddCategory.categoryVector", v);
    }

    public void showAddCategoryPage(PrintWriter out, String pgName,
                                    Connection conn)
            throws Exception
```

```
{
        Vector finalIds = new Vector();
        Vector finalNames = new Vector();
        Vector tempIds = new Vector();
        Vector tempNames = new Vector();
        Vector tempIds2 = new Vector();
        Vector tempNames2 = new Vector();

        finalIds.addElement("0");
        finalNames.addElement("TOP LEVEL");

        tempIds.addElement("0");
        tempNames.addElement("TOP LEVEL");

        // Cans can belong to Grocery as well as cat food—these should
        // be displayed as Grocery -> cans and Cat Food -> cans
        while (true)
        {
            int sz = tempIds.size();
            if(sz == 0)
                break;
            for(int i=0; i<sz; i++)
            {
                /* We want to show only those categories as possible
                   parents of this category which have no products in
                   them. This is because we distinguish between leaf
                   categories and non-leaf categories Leaf categories can
                   have only products in them, not other categories */

                String querySQL = "SELECT category_id FROM products";
                Statement stmt = conn.createStatement();
                ResultSet rset = stmt.executeQuery(querySQL);
                Vector allProdCatIds = new Vector();
                while(rset.next())
                {
                    allProdCatIds.addElement(rset.getString(1));
                }
                int prodCatsSize = allProdCatIds.size();

                String name = (String)tempNames.elementAt(i);

                querySQL = "SELECT id, name FROM categories
                    WHERE category_id=" + (String)tempIds.elementAt(i);
                rset = stmt.executeQuery(querySQL);
                while(rset.next())
                {
```

```java
            boolean hasProdsInIt = false;
            String finalId = rset.getString(1);
            for(int k=0; k<prodCatsSize; k++)
            {
                if(finalId.equals(
                    (String)allProdCatIds.elementAt(k)))
                {
                    hasProdsInIt = true;
                    break;
                }
            }
            if(hasProdsInIt)
                continue;
            String finalName = name + "->" + rset.getString(2);
            finalIds.addElement(finalId);
            finalNames.addElement(finalName);
            tempIds2.addElement(finalId);
            tempNames2.addElement(finalName);
        }
        stmt.close();
    }
    tempIds = tempIds2;
    tempNames = tempNames2;
    tempIds2 = new Vector();
    tempNames2 = new Vector();
}

String options = "";
int sz = finalIds.size();

for(int i=0; i<sz; i++)
{
    options += "<OPTION VALUE='" +
        (String)finalIds.elementAt(i) + "'>" +
        (String)finalNames.elementAt(i);
}
PageUtil p = new PageUtil(pgName, out);
p.setReplaceItem("<VAR_CATEGORY_OPTIONS>", options);
p.printPage();
    }
}

AddProduct.java

package Inventory;
```

```java
import java.util.*;
import java.io.*;
import java.sql.*;
import javax.servlet.*;
import javax.servlet.http.*;
import Utilities.*;

public class AddProduct extends BaseInventory
{
    ConnectionPool c = null;
    static String addProductHtml = BasePath + "addProduct.html";
    static String errorHtml = BasePath + "inventoryError.html";
    static String productsAddedHtml = BasePath + "productsAdded.html";
    public void doPost (HttpServletRequest req,
                        HttpServletResponse res)
    {
      Connection conn = null;
      PrintWriter out=null;
      try{
          HttpSession session;

          String username="", password="";
          String name="", description_url="", email="", price="",
                 quantity_in_stock="";
          String danger_level="", description="";
          String display_price="", search_keywords="";
          boolean addMore = false;
          int id = -1, category_id = -1;

          boolean firstTime = false;

          if(c == null)
          {
              c = ConnectionPool.getInstance();
              c.initialize();
          }
          conn = c.getConnection();
          Enumeration paramNames = req.getParameterNames();
          while(paramNames.hasMoreElements())
          {
              String nm = (String)paramNames.nextElement();
              String vl = req.getParameterValues(nm)[0];
              if(nm.equalsIgnoreCase("username"))
                  username = vl;
              if(nm.equalsIgnoreCase("password"))
```

```
                    password = v1;
            if(nm.equalsIgnoreCase("name"))
                name = v1;
            if(nm.equalsIgnoreCase("description_url"))
                description_url = v1;
            if(nm.equalsIgnoreCase("description"))
                description= v1;
            if(nm.equalsIgnoreCase("email"))
                email = v1;
            if(nm.equalsIgnoreCase("price"))
                price = v1;
            if(nm.equalsIgnoreCase("display_price"))
                display_price = v1;
            if(nm.equalsIgnoreCase("search_keywords"))
                search_keywords = v1;
            if(nm.equalsIgnoreCase("quantity_in_stock"))
                quantity_in_stock = v1;
            if(nm.equalsIgnoreCase("category_id"))
                category_id = (new Integer(v1)).intValue();
            if(nm.equalsIgnoreCase("danger_level"))
                danger_level = v1;
            if(nm.equalsIgnoreCase("addMore"))
                if(v1.equalsIgnoreCase("Yes"))
                    addMore = true;
                else
                    addMore = false;
            if(nm.equalsIgnoreCase("firstTime"))
                firstTime = true;
        }
        out = res.getWriter();
        res.setContentType("text/html");
        if(firstTime == true)
        {
            if(validPassword(username, password, errorHtml, c,
                            conn, out) == false)
                return;
            session = req.getSession(true);
            session.putValue("Inventory.username", username);
            session.putValue("Inventory.password", password);
            session.putValue("AddProduct.productVector", new Vector());
            showAddProductPage(out, addProductHtml, conn);
            c.putConnection(conn);
            return;
        }
```

```
    else
    {
        session = req.getSession(false);
        if(session == null)
        {
            username = null;
            password = null;
        }
        else
        {
            username = (String)session.getValue("Inventory.username");
            password = (String)session.getValue("Inventory.password");
        }
        if(validPassword(username, password, errorHtml, c,
                        conn, out) == false)
            return;
    }
    Product p = new Product(id, category_id, name, description_url,email,
            price, quantity_in_stock, danger_level, description,
            display_price,
            search_keywords);
    Vector v = (Vector)session.getValue("AddProduct.productVector");
    v.addElement(p);
    session.putValue("AddProduct.productVector", v);
    if(addMore)
        showAddProductPage(out, addProductHtml, conn);
    else
    {
        writeProducts(out, v, username, productsAddedHtml,
                    session, conn);
    }
    c.putConnection(conn);
    out.close();
}catch(Exception ex){
        if(c != null && conn != null)
        {
            c.putConnection(conn);
            showErrorPage(out, errorHtml, ex.getMessage());
        }
    }
}


public void writeProducts(PrintWriter out, Vector productVector,
                String username, String pgName,
```

```
                        HttpSession session, Connection conn)
            throws Exception
{
        Statement stmt = conn.createStatement();
        String names = "<UL>";
        int size = productVector.size();
        String baseSQL = "INSERT INTO products(id, category_id, name,
            description_url, email, price, quantity_in_stock,
            danger_level, description, last_modified_by,
            last_modification_date, display_price,
            search_keywords) VALUES(";
        String sequenceSQL = "SELECT products_seq.NEXTVAL FROM dual";
        ResultSet rset;
        for(int i=0; i<size; i++)
        {
            Product p = (Product)productVector.elementAt(i);
            rset = stmt.executeQuery(sequenceSQL);
            rset.next();

            String id = rset.getString(1);

            String insertSQL = baseSQL + id + "," + p.getCategoryId() +
                ",'" + p.getName() + "','" + p.getDescriptionUrl() +
                "','" + p.getEmail() + "','" + p.getPrice() + "'," +
                p.getQuantityInStock() + "," + p.getDangerLevel() +
                ",'" + p.getDescription() + "','" + username + "',
                SYSDATE, '" + p.getDisplayPrice() + "', '" +
                p.getSearchKeywords() + "')";

            stmt.executeUpdate(insertSQL);

            names += "<LI>" + p.getName();
        }
        stmt.close();
        names += "</UL>";
        PageUtil p = new PageUtil(pgName, out);
        p.setReplaceItem("<PRODUCTS_ADDED>", names);
        p.printPage();
        session.removeValue("AddProduct.productVector");
        Vector v = new Vector();
        session.putValue("AddProduct.productVector", v);
}

public void showAddProductPage(PrintWriter out, String pgName,
        Connection conn)
        throws Exception
{
```

```
                CategoryOptions co = new CategoryOptions();
                String options = co.get("0", conn);
                PageUtil p = new PageUtil(pgName, out);
                p.setReplaceItem("<VAR_CATEGORY_OPTIONS>", options);
                p.printPage();
        }
}

BaseInventory.java

package Inventory;

import java.util.*;
import java.io.*;
import java.sql.*;
import javax.servlet.*;
import javax.servlet.http.*;
import Utilities.*;

public class BaseInventory extends HttpServlet
{
    static String BasePath = "HTML_DIRECTORY";
    static boolean debugOn = true;

    public boolean validPassword(String username, String password,
                String errorHtml, ConnectionPool c, Connection conn,
                PrintWriter out)
    {
        boolean isValid = true;
        if(username == null || password == null)
            isValid = false;
        Authenticator a = new Authenticator();
        if(a.isValidAdmin(username, password, conn) == false)
            isValid = false;
        if(isValid == false)
        {
            c.putConnection(conn);
            showErrorPage(out, errorHtml, "Invalid Username/Password");
            return false;
        }
        else
            return true;
    }

    public void showErrorPage(PrintWriter out, String pgName, String value)
    {
        PageUtil p = new PageUtil(pgName, out);
```

```
            p.setReplaceItem("<ERROR_MSG>", value);
            p.printPage();
    }

    public PrintStream initializeDebugFile(String s)
    {
        PrintStream pos = null;
        try
        {
            if(debugOn == false)
                return null;
            pos = new PrintStream(new FileOutputStream(new File(s)));
        }catch(Exception ex){}
        return pos;
    }
    public void debug(String s, PrintStream pos)
    {
        try
        {
            if(debugOn == false)
                return;
            pos.println(s);
        }catch(Exception ex){}
    }
}
```

Category.java

```
package Inventory;
import Utilities.*;

public class Category
{
    int id;
    int category_id;
    String name;
    String description_url;
    String description;
    String has_sub_categories;
    String searchKeywords;

    public Category(int i, int c, String n, String d_u,
                    String d, String hs, String sk)
    {
        id = i;
        category_id = c;
```

```java
            name = n;
            description_url = d_u;
            description = d;
            has_sub_categories = hs;
            searchKeywords = sk;
        }
    public int getId()
    {
            return id;
    }
    public int getCategoryId()
    {
            return category_id;
    }
    public String getSearchKeywords()
    {
            return searchKeywords;
    }
    public String getName()
    {
            return name;
    }
    public String getDescriptionUrl()
    {
            return description_url;
    }
    public String getHasSubCategories()
    {
            return has_sub_categories;
    }
    public String getDescription()
    {
            return description;
    }
}

CategoryOptions.java

package Inventory;

import java.util.*;
import java.io.*;
import java.sql.*;
import Utilities.*;
```

```
public class CategoryOptions
{
    public String get(String selectedId, Connection conn)
    {
        String options = "";
        try{
            Vector finalIds = new Vector();
            Vector finalCategoryIds = new Vector();
            Vector finalNames = new Vector();

            Statement stmt = conn.createStatement();

            String querySQL = "SELECT id, category_id, name
                    FROM categories WHERE has_sub_categories=0";
            ResultSet rset = stmt.executeQuery(querySQL);

            while(rset.next())
            {
                String finalId = rset.getString(1);
                String finalCategoryId = rset.getString(2);
                String finalName = rset.getString(3);
                finalIds.addElement(finalId);
                finalCategoryIds.addElement(finalCategoryId);
                finalNames.addElement(finalName);
            }

            // Cans can belong to Grocery as well as cat food—these should
            // be displayed as Grocery -> cans and Cat Food -> cans
            int sz = finalIds.size();
            for(int i=0; i<sz; i++)
            {
                String catId = (String)finalCategoryIds.elementAt(i);
                while(true)
                {
                    querySQL = "SELECT category_id, name
                        FROM categories WHERE id=" + catId;
                    rset = stmt.executeQuery(querySQL);
                    if(rset.next() == false)
                        break;
                    catId = rset.getString(1);
                    String nm = (String)finalNames.elementAt(i);
                    nm = rset.getString(2) + "->" + nm;
                    finalNames.setElementAt(nm, i);
                }
            }
        }
```

```
            stmt.close();

            sz = finalIds.size();

            for(int i=0; i<sz; i++)
            {
                    String name = (String)finalNames.elementAt(i);
                    String id = (String)finalIds.elementAt(i);
                    String selected = "";
                    if(id.equalsIgnoreCase(selectedId))
                        selected = "SELECTED";
                    else
                        selected = "";
                    options += "<OPTION VALUE='" + id + "' " + selected +
                               ">" + name;

            }
        }catch(Exception ex){}
        return options;
    }
}

DeleteCategory.java

package Inventory;

import java.util.*;
import java.io.*;
import java.sql.*;
import javax.servlet.*;
import javax.servlet.http.*;
import Utilities.*;

public class DeleteCategory extends BaseInventory
{
    ConnectionPool c = null;
    static String categoryDeletedHtml = BasePath + "categoryDeleted.html";
    static String errorHtml = BasePath + "inventoryError.html";

    public void doPost (HttpServletRequest req,
                        HttpServletResponse res)
    {
      Connection conn = null;
      PrintWriter out=null;
      try{
          HttpSession session;

          String username="", password="", action="";
```

```
        String id = "";

        if(c == null)
        {
            c = ConnectionPool.getInstance();
            c.initialize();
        }
        conn = c.getConnection();
        Enumeration paramNames = req.getParameterNames();
        while(paramNames.hasMoreElements())
        {
            String nm = (String)paramNames.nextElement();
            String vl = req.getParameterValues(nm)[0];
            if(nm.equalsIgnoreCase("category"))
                id = vl;
        }
        out = res.getWriter();
        res.setContentType("text/html");
        session = req.getSession(false);
        if(session == null)
        {
            username = null;
            password = null;
        }
        else
        {
            username = (String)session.getValue("Inventory.username");
            password = (String)session.getValue("Inventory.password");
        }
        if(validPassword(username, password, errorHtml, c,
                    conn, out) == false)
            return;

    categoryDeletedPage(out, id, categoryDeletedHtml, conn);
    c.putConnection(conn);
    out.close();
}catch(Exception ex)
    {
        if(c != null && conn != null)
        {
            c.putConnection(conn);
            showErrorPage(out, errorHtml, ex.getMessage());
        }
    }
```

```
        }

        public void categoryDeletedPage(PrintWriter out, String id,
                                String pgName, Connection conn)
            throws Exception
        {
                Statement stmt = conn.createStatement();
                String deleteSQL = "DELETE FROM categories WHERE id=" + id;
                stmt.executeUpdate(deleteSQL);
                stmt.close();
                PageUtil p = new PageUtil(pgName, out);
                p.setReplaceItem("<VAR_CATEGORY_ID>", id);
                p.printPage();
        }

}

DeleteProduct.java

package Inventory;

import java.util.*;
import java.io.*;
import java.sql.*;
import javax.servlet.*;
import javax.servlet.http.*;
import Utilities.*;

public class DeleteProduct extends BaseInventory
{
    ConnectionPool c = null;
    static String productDeletedHtml = BasePath + "productDeleted.html";
    static String errorHtml = BasePath + "inventoryError.html";

    public void doPost (HttpServletRequest req,
                    HttpServletResponse res)
    {
      Connection conn = null;
      PrintWriter out=null;
      try{
          HttpSession session;

          String username="", password="", action="";

          String id = "";

          if(c == null)
          {
```

```
                    c = ConnectionPool.getInstance();
                    c.initialize();
            }
            conn = c.getConnection();
            Enumeration paramNames = req.getParameterNames();
            while(paramNames.hasMoreElements())
            {
                    String nm = (String)paramNames.nextElement();
                    String vl = req.getParameterValues(nm)[0];
                    if(nm.equalsIgnoreCase("product"))
                        id = vl;
            }
            out = res.getWriter();
            res.setContentType("text/html");
            session = req.getSession(false);
            if(session == null)
            {
                    username = null;
                    password = null;
            }
            else
            {
                    username = (String)session.getValue("Inventory.username");
                    password = (String)session.getValue("Inventory.password");
            }
            if(validPassword(username, password, errorHtml, c,
                            conn, out) == false)
                    return;

            productDeletedPage(out, id, productDeletedHtml, conn);
            c.putConnection(conn);
            out.close();
        }catch(Exception ex)
            {
                    if(c != null && conn != null)
                    {
                        c.putConnection(conn);
                        showErrorPage(out, errorHtml, ex.getMessage());
                    }
            }
    }

    public void productDeletedPage(PrintWriter out, String id,
                            String pgName, Connection conn)
            throws Exception
```

```
            {
                  Statement stmt = conn.createStatement();
                  String deleteSQL = "DELETE FROM products WHERE id=" + id;
                  stmt.executeUpdate(deleteSQL);
                  stmt.close();
                  PageUtil p = new PageUtil(pgName, out);
                  p.setReplaceItem("<VAR_PRODUCT_ID>", id);
                  p.printPage();

            }

}

ModifyProduct.java

package Inventory;

import java.util.*;
import java.io.*;
import java.sql.*;
import javax.servlet.*;
import javax.servlet.http.*;
import Utilities.*;

public class ModifyProduct extends BaseInventory
{
    ConnectionPool c = null;
    static String errorHtml = BasePath + "inventoryError.html";
    static String productModifiedHtml = BasePath + "productModified.html";

    public void doPost (HttpServletRequest req,
                        HttpServletResponse res)
    {
      Connection conn = null;
      PrintWriter out=null;
      try{
          HttpSession session;

          String username="", password="";
          String name="", description_url="", email="", price="",
                 quantity_in_stock="";
          String danger_level="", description="";
          String search_keywords="", display_price="";
          boolean addMore = false;
          String id ="", category_id = "-1";

          boolean firstTime = false;

          if(c == null)
```

```
{
    c = ConnectionPool.getInstance();
    c.initialize();
}
conn = c.getConnection();
Enumeration paramNames = req.getParameterNames();
while(paramNames.hasMoreElements())
{
    String nm = (String)paramNames.nextElement();
    String vl = req.getParameterValues(nm)[0];
    if(nm.equalsIgnoreCase("username"))
        username = vl;
    if(nm.equalsIgnoreCase("password"))
        password = vl;
    if(nm.equalsIgnoreCase("name"))
        name = vl;
    if(nm.equalsIgnoreCase("description_url"))
        description_url = vl;
    if(nm.equalsIgnoreCase("description"))
        description = vl;
    if(nm.equalsIgnoreCase("email"))
        email = vl;
    if(nm.equalsIgnoreCase("price"))
        price = vl;
    if(nm.equalsIgnoreCase("display_price"))
        display_price = vl;
    if(nm.equalsIgnoreCase("search_keywords"))
        search_keywords = vl;
    if(nm.equalsIgnoreCase("quantity_in_stock"))
        quantity_in_stock = vl;
    if(nm.equalsIgnoreCase("danger_level"))
        danger_level = vl;
    if(nm.equalsIgnoreCase("id"))
        id = vl;
    if(nm.equalsIgnoreCase("category_id"))
        category_id = vl;
}
out = res.getWriter();
res.setContentType("text/html");
session = req.getSession(false);
if(session == null)
{
    username = null;
    password = null;
```

```
            }
            else
            {
                    username = (String)session.getValue("Inventory.username");
                    password = (String)session.getValue("Inventory.password");
            }
            if(validPassword(username, password, errorHtml, c,
                            conn, out) == false)
                    return;

            int intId = (new Integer(id)).intValue();
            int intCategoryId = (new Integer(category_id)).intValue();

            Product p = new Product(intId, intCategoryId, name,
                    description_url,email, price, quantity_in_stock,
                    danger_level, description, display_price,
                    search_keywords);

            modifyProduct(out, p, username, productModifiedHtml, conn);
            c.putConnection(conn);
            out.close();
        }catch(Exception ex)
            {
                    if(c != null && conn != null)
                    {
                        c.putConnection(conn);
                        showErrorPage(out, errorHtml, ex.getMessage());
                    }
            }
    }

    public void modifyProduct(PrintWriter out, Product p,
                String username,String pgName, Connection conn)
            throws Exception
    {
            Statement stmt = conn.createStatement();
            String updateSQL = "UPDATE products SET category_id=" +
                p.getCategoryId() + ", name='" + p.getName() + "',
                description_url='" + p.getDescriptionUrl() + "',
                email='" + p.getEmail() + "', price='" + p.getPrice() +
                "',quantity_in_Stock=" + p.getQuantityInStock() + ",
                danger_level=" + p.getDangerLevel() + ", description='" +
                p.getDescription() + "', last_modified_by='" + username +
                "', last_modification_date=SYSDATE, search_keywords='" +
                p.getSearchKeywords() + "', display_price='" +
                p.getDisplayPrice() + "' WHERE id=" + p.getId();
```

```java
                stmt.executeUpdate(updateSQL);
                stmt.close();
                String pm = "<B>Id: " + p.getId() + "<BR>Name: " +
                            p.getName() + "</B>";
                PageUtil pu = new PageUtil(pgName, out);
                pu.setReplaceItem("<VAR_PRODUCT_MODIFIED>", pm);
                pu.printPage();
        }
}


Product.java

package Inventory;
import Utilities.*;

public class Product
{
    int id;
    int category_id;
    String name;
    String description_url;
    String email;
    String price;
    String quantity_in_stock;
    String danger_level;
    String description;
    String displayPrice;
    String searchKeywords;
    public Product(int i, int c, String n, String d_u,
                   String e, String p, String q, String dl,
                   String d, String dp, String sk)
    {
        id = i;
        category_id = c;
        name = n;
        description_url = d_u;
        email = e;
        price = p;
        quantity_in_stock = q;
        danger_level = dl;
        description = d;
        displayPrice = dp;
        searchKeywords = sk;
    }
    public int getId()
```

```java
    {
        return id;
    }
    public int getCategoryId()
    {
        return category_id;
    }
    public String getDisplayPrice()
    {
        return displayPrice;
    }
    public String getSearchKeywords()
    {
        return searchKeywords;
    }
    public String getName()
    {
        return name;
    }
    public String getDescriptionUrl()
    {
        return description_url;
    }
    public String getEmail()
    {
        return email;
    }
    public String getPrice()
    {
        return price;
    }
    public String getQuantityInStock()
    {
        return quantity_in_stock;
    }
    public String getDangerLevel()
    {
        return danger_level;
    }
    public String getDescription()
    {
        return description;
    }
}
```

```
SelectCategory.java

package Inventory;

import java.util.*;
import java.io.*;
import java.sql.*;
import javax.servlet.*;
import javax.servlet.http.*;
import Utilities.*;

public class SelectCategory extends BaseInventory
{
    ConnectionPool c = null;
    static String selectCategoryHtml = BasePath + "selectCategory.html";
    static String errorHtml = BasePath + "inventoryError.html";

    public void doPost (HttpServletRequest req,
                        HttpServletResponse res)
    {
      Connection conn = null;
      PrintWriter out=null;
      try{
          HttpSession session;

          String username="", password="", action="";
          boolean firstTime = false;

          if(c == null)
          {
              c = ConnectionPool.getInstance();
              c.initialize();
          }
          conn = c.getConnection();
          Enumeration paramNames = req.getParameterNames();
          while(paramNames.hasMoreElements())
          {
              String nm = (String)paramNames.nextElement();
              String vl = req.getParameterValues(nm)[0];
              if(nm.equalsIgnoreCase("username"))
                  username = vl;
              if(nm.equalsIgnoreCase("password"))
                  password = vl;
              if(nm.equalsIgnoreCase("firstTime"))
                  firstTime = true;
              if(nm.equalsIgnoreCase("action"))
                  action = vl;
```

```
    }
    out = res.getWriter();
    res.setContentType("text/html");
    if(firstTime == true)
    {
        if(validPassword(username, password, errorHtml, c,
                         conn, out) == false)
            return;
        session = req.getSession(true);
        session.putValue("Inventory.username", username);
        session.putValue("Inventory.password", password);
    }
    else
    {
        session = req.getSession(false);
        if(session == null)
        {
            username = null;
            password = null;
        }
        else
        {
            username = (String)session.getValue("Inventory.username");
            password = (String)session.getValue("Inventory.password");
        }
        if(validPassword(username, password, errorHtml, c,
                         conn, out) == false)
            return;
    }
    showSelectCategoryPage(out, action, selectCategoryHtml, conn);
    c.putConnection(conn);
    out.close();
}catch(Exception ex)
    {
        if(c != null && conn != null)
        {
            c.putConnection(conn);
            showErrorPage(out, errorHtml, ex.getMessage());
        }
    }
}

public void showSelectCategoryPage(PrintWriter out, String action,
                            String pgName, Connection conn)
```

```
{
    String header = "";
    String formName = "<FORM NAME=''
        onSubmit='return isSelected(this);' METHOD='POST' ACTION='";
    String categoryList = "";
    String id="", name="";
    try{
        Statement stmt = conn.createStatement();
        ResultSet rset;
        String querySQL="";
        Vector allProdCatIds = new Vector();
        int prodCatsSize=0;

        if(action.equalsIgnoreCase("Delete"))
        {
            querySQL = "SELECT category_id FROM products";
            rset = stmt.executeQuery(querySQL);
            while(rset.next())
            {
                allProdCatIds.addElement(rset.getString(1));
            }
            querySQL = "SELECT category_id FROM categories";
            rset = stmt.executeQuery(querySQL);
            while(rset.next())
            {
                String catId = rset.getString(1);
                if(catId != null)
                    allProdCatIds.addElement(catId);
            }
            prodCatsSize = allProdCatIds.size();
        }
        querySQL = "SELECT id, name FROM categories";
        rset = stmt.executeQuery(querySQL);
        while(rset.next())
        {
            boolean hasProdsInIt = false;
            String catId = rset.getString(1);
            String catName = rset.getString(2);
            if(action.equalsIgnoreCase("Delete"))
            {
                for(int k=0; k<prodCatsSize; k++)
                {
                    if(catId.equals(
                        (String)allProdCatIds.elementAt(k)))
```

```java
                        {
                            hasProdsInIt = true;
                            break;
                        }
                    }
                }
                if(hasProdsInIt)
                    continue;
                categoryList += "<OPTION VALUE='" + catId + "'>" + catName;
            }
            stmt.close();
        }catch(SQLException e){}

        if(action.equalsIgnoreCase("Modify"))
        {
            header = "Modify Category";
            formName += "Inventory.ShowCategory'>";
        }

        if(action.equalsIgnoreCase("Delete"))
        {
            header = "Delete Category";
            formName += "Inventory.DeleteCategory'>";
        }
        if(action.equalsIgnoreCase("View"))
        {
            header = "View Category";
            formName += "Inventory.ShowCategory'>";
        }

        action = "<INPUT TYPE='hidden' NAME='action'
                VALUE='" + action + "'>";

        PageUtil p = new PageUtil(pgName, out);
        p.setReplaceItem("<VAR_HEADER>", header);
        p.setReplaceItem("<VAR_CATEGORY_LIST>", categoryList);
        p.setReplaceItem("<VAR_ACTION>", action);
        p.setReplaceItem("<VAR_FORM_NAME>", formName);

        p.printPage();
    }
}

SelectProduct.java

package Inventory;
```

```java
import java.util.*;
import java.io.*;
import java.sql.*;
import javax.servlet.*;
import javax.servlet.http.*;
import Utilities.*;

public class SelectProduct extends BaseInventory
{
    ConnectionPool c = null;
    static String selectProductHtml = BasePath + "selectProduct.html";
    static String errorHtml = BasePath + "inventoryError.html";

    public void doPost (HttpServletRequest req,
                        HttpServletResponse res)
    {
      Connection conn = null;
      PrintWriter out=null;
      try{
          HttpSession session;

          String username="", password="", action="";
          boolean firstTime = false;

          if(c == null)
          {
              c = ConnectionPool.getInstance();
              c.initialize();
          }
          conn = c.getConnection();
          Enumeration paramNames = req.getParameterNames();
          while(paramNames.hasMoreElements())
          {
              String nm = (String)paramNames.nextElement();
              String vl = req.getParameterValues(nm)[0];
              if(nm.equalsIgnoreCase("username"))
                  username = vl;
              if(nm.equalsIgnoreCase("password"))
                  password = vl;
              if(nm.equalsIgnoreCase("firstTime"))
                  firstTime = true;
              if(nm.equalsIgnoreCase("action"))
                  action = vl;
          }
          out = res.getWriter();
          res.setContentType("text/html");
```

```
        if(firstTime == true)
        {
            if(validPassword(username, password, errorHtml, c,
                            conn, out) == false)
                return;
            session = req.getSession(true);
            session.putValue("Inventory.username", username);
            session.putValue("Inventory.password", password);
        }
        else
        {
            session = req.getSession(false);
            if(session == null)
            {
                username = null;
                password = null;
            }
            else
            {
                username = (String)session.getValue("Inventory.username");
                password = (String)session.getValue("Inventory.password");
            }
            if(validPassword(username, password, errorHtml, c,
                            conn, out) == false)
                return;
        }
        showSelectProductPage(out, action, selectProductHtml, conn);
        c.putConnection(conn);
        out.close();
    }catch(Exception ex)
        {
            if(c != null && conn != null)
            {
                c.putConnection(conn);
                showErrorPage(out, errorHtml, ex.getMessage());
            }
        }
}


public void showSelectProductPage(PrintWriter out, String action,
                                String pgName, Connection conn)
{
    String header = "";
    String formName = "<FORM NAME=''
```

```
            onSubmit='return isSelected(this);' METHOD='POST' ACTION='"';

    String productList = "";
    String id="", name="";
    try{
        Statement stmt = conn.createStatement();
        String querySQL = "SELECT id, name FROM products";
        ResultSet rset = stmt.executeQuery(querySQL);
        while(rset.next())
        {
            productList += "<OPTION VALUE='" + rset.getString(1) +
                "'>" + rset.getString(2);
        }
        stmt.close();
    }catch(SQLException e){}

    if(action.equalsIgnoreCase("Modify"))
    {
        header = "Modify Product";
        formName += "Inventory.ShowProduct'>";
    }

    if(action.equalsIgnoreCase("Delete"))
    {
        header = "Delete Product";
        formName += "Inventory.DeleteProduct'>";
    }
    if(action.equalsIgnoreCase("View"))
    {
        header = "View Product";
        formName += "Inventory.ShowProduct'>";
    }

    action = "<INPUT TYPE='hidden' NAME='action'
            VALUE='" + action + "'>";

    PageUtil p = new PageUtil(pgName, out);
    p.setReplaceItem("<VAR_HEADER>", header);
    p.setReplaceItem("<VAR_PRODUCT_LIST>", productList);
    p.setReplaceItem("<VAR_ACTION>", action);
    p.setReplaceItem("<VAR_FORM_NAME>", formName);

    p.printPage();
    }
}
```

```
ShowProduct.java

package Inventory;

import java.util.*;
import java.io.*;
import java.sql.*;
import javax.servlet.*;
import javax.servlet.http.*;
import Utilities.*;

public class ShowProduct extends BaseInventory
{
    ConnectionPool c = null;
    static String showProductHtml = BasePath + "showProduct.html";
    static String errorHtml = BasePath + "inventoryError.html";
    PrintStream pos;

    public void doPost (HttpServletRequest req,
                        HttpServletResponse res)
    {
      Connection conn = null;
      PrintWriter out=null;
      try{
          HttpSession session;

          String username="", password="", action="";

          String id = "";

          if(c == null)
          {
              c = ConnectionPool.getInstance();
              c.initialize();
          }
          conn = c.getConnection();
          Enumeration paramNames = req.getParameterNames();
          while(paramNames.hasMoreElements())
          {
              String nm = (String)paramNames.nextElement();
              String vl = req.getParameterValues(nm)[0];
              if(nm.equalsIgnoreCase("product"))
                  id = vl;
              if(nm.equalsIgnoreCase("action"))
                  action = vl;
          }
```

```
        out = res.getWriter();
        res.setContentType("text/html");
        session = req.getSession(false);
        if(session == null)
        {
                username = null;
                password = null;
        }
        else
        {
                username = (String)session.getValue("Inventory.username");
                password = (String)session.getValue("Inventory.password");
        }
        if(validPassword(username, password, errorHtml, c,
                        conn, out) == false)
                return;

        showProductPage(out, id, action, showProductHtml, conn);
        c.putConnection(conn);
        out.close();
    }catch(Exception ex)
      {
                if(c != null && conn != null)
                {
                    c.putConnection(conn);
                    showErrorPage(out, errorHtml, ex.getMessage());
                }
        }

}

public void showProductPage(PrintWriter out, String id, String action,
                        String pgName, Connection conn)
{
      String header = "", category_id="";

      String name="", description_url="", email="", price="",
              quantity_in_stock="";
      String danger_level="", description="", last_modified_by="";
      String search_keywords="", display_price="",
              last_modification_date="";
      String submit = "";

      try{
          Statement stmt = conn.createStatement();
          String querySQL = "SELECT category_id, name, description_url,
```

```
                    price, quantity_in_stock, danger_level, description,
                    email, last_modified_by, last_modification_date,
                    display_price, search_keywords
                    FROM products WHERE id=" + id;
        ResultSet rset = stmt.executeQuery(querySQL);
        rset.next();
        category_id = rset.getString(1);
        name = rset.getString(2);
        description_url = rset.getString(3);
        price = rset.getString(4);
        quantity_in_stock = rset.getString(5);
        danger_level = rset.getString(6);
        description = rset.getString(7);
        email = rset.getString(8);
        last_modified_by = rset.getString(9);
        last_modification_date = rset.getString(10);
        display_price = rset.getString(11);
        search_keywords = rset.getString(12);
        stmt.close();
}catch(SQLException e){}

if(action.equalsIgnoreCase("Modify"))
{
        header = "This is the product you selected.You may modify it
                    and press the submit button";
        submit = "<INPUT TYPE='submit' NAME='submit' VALUE='Submit'>";
}
CategoryOptions co = new CategoryOptions();
String options = co.get(category_id, conn);

name =
    "<INPUT TYPE='text' NAME='name' SIZE='20' VALUE='" + name + "'>";
description_url = "<INPUT TYPE='text' NAME='description_url'
        SIZE='35' VALUE='" + description_url + "'>";
email = "<INPUT TYPE='text' NAME='email' SIZE='20' VALUE='" +
        email + "'>";
display_price = "<INPUT TYPE='text' NAME='display_price' SIZE='12'
        VALUE='" + display_price + "'>";
search_keywords = "<INPUT TYPE='text' NAME='search_keywords'
        SIZE='50' VALUE='" + search_keywords + "'>";
price = "<INPUT TYPE='text' NAME='price' SIZE='6' VALUE='" +
        price + "'>";
quantity_in_stock = "<INPUT TYPE='text' NAME='quantity_in_stock'
        SIZE='10' VALUE='" + quantity_in_stock + "'>";
danger_level = "<INPUT TYPE='text' NAME='danger_level' SIZE='2'
```

```
                    VALUE='" + danger_level + "'>";
        id = "<INPUT TYPE='hidden' NAME='id' VALUE='" + id + "'>";
        category_id = "<INPUT TYPE='hidden' NAME='category_id'
                VALUE='" + category_id + "'>";

        PageUtil p = new PageUtil(pgName, out);
        p.setReplaceItem("<VAR_HEADER>", header);
        p.setReplaceItem("<VAR_SUBMIT>", submit);
        p.setReplaceItem("<VAR_NAME>", name);
        p.setReplaceItem("<VAR_DESCRIPTION_URL>", description_url);
        p.setReplaceItem("<VAR_EMAIL>", email);
        p.setReplaceItem("<VAR_PRICE>", price);
        p.setReplaceItem("<VAR_QUANTITY_IN_STOCK>", quantity_in_stock);
        p.setReplaceItem("<VAR_DANGER_LEVEL>", danger_level);
        p.setReplaceItem("<VAR_DESCRIPTION>", description);
        p.setReplaceItem("<VAR_LAST_MODIFIED_BY>", last_modified_by);
        p.setReplaceItem("<VAR_LAST_MODIFICATION_DATE>",
                         last_modification_date);
        p.setReplaceItem("<VAR_DISPLAY_PRICE>", display_price);
        p.setReplaceItem("<VAR_SEARCH_KEYWORDS>", search_keywords);
        p.setReplaceItem("<VAR_ID>", id);
        p.setReplaceItem("<VAR_CATEGORY_ID>", category_id);
        p.setReplaceItem("<VAR_CATEGORY_OPTIONS>", options);

        p.printPage();
    }
}


SignOff.java

package Inventory;

import java.io.*;
import java.util.Enumeration;

import javax.servlet.*;
import javax.servlet.http.*;
import java.util.*;
import java.sql.*;
import Utilities.*;

public class  SignOff  extends HttpServlet
{
    public void doGet (HttpServletRequest req, HttpServletResponse res)
    {
        HttpSession session = req.getSession(false);
        session.invalidate();
```

```
            res.setContentType("text/html");
            try{
                PrintWriter out = res.getWriter();
                out.println("<HTML><HEAD></HEAD><BODY BGCOLOR='#FFFFFF'>
                    </BODY></HTML>");
                out.close();
            }catch(Exception ex){}
    }
}
```

Document Root Html Files

inventory.html

```
<HTML>
<FRAMESET COLS='100, *' BORDER='0'>
    <FRAME NAME='left' SRC='blank.html'>
    <FRAME NAME='right' SRC='inventoryOptions.html'>
</FRAMESET>
<BODY>
</BODY>
</HTML>
```

inventoryOptions.html

```
<HTML>
<HEAD> <TITLE>Inventory Management System Menu</TITLE></HEAD>
<SCRIPT>
    function doSubmit(pos)
    {
        if(document.passwordForm.username.value.length == 0 ||
            document.passwordForm.password.value.length == 0)
        {
            alert('Please supply a username/password');
            return false;
        }
        document.forms[pos].username.value = document.passwordForm.username.value;
        document.forms[pos].password.value = document.passwordForm.password.value;
        parent.left.location.replace('signoff.html');
        document.forms[pos].submit();
        return false;
    }
</SCRIPT>
<BODY BGCOLOR='#FFFFFF'>
    <CENTER><H1>Inventory Management System Menu</CENTER></H1>
    <P>
```

```
<CENTER>
    <TABLE>
            <TR><TD>
            <TABLE BORDER='2'>
                        <TR><TD ALIGN='CENTER'
BGCOLOR='#CCCCCC'><H2><B>Products</B></H2><H2></TD>
                        <TD>
                    <TABLE>
                            <TR><TD>
                        <FORM NAME='noName1'
                ACTION='/newZone/Inventory.AddProduct' METHOD='POST'>
                            <CENTER><A HREF=''
onClick='return doSubmit(0)'>Add</A></CENTER>
                                <INPUT TYPE='hidden' NAME='username' VALUE=''>
                                <INPUT TYPE='hidden' NAME='password' VALUE=''>
                                <INPUT TYPE='hidden' NAME='firstTime' VALUE='True'>
                        </FORM>
                        </TD></TR>
                        <TR><TD>
                        <FORM NAME='noName1'
ACTION='/newZone/Inventory.SelectProduct' METHOD='POST'>
                            <CENTER><A HREF=''
onClick='return doSubmit(1)'>Modify</A></CENTER>
                                <INPUT TYPE='hidden' NAME='username' VALUE=''>
                                <INPUT TYPE='hidden' NAME='password' VALUE=''>
                                <INPUT TYPE='hidden' NAME='firstTime' VALUE='True'>
                                <INPUT TYPE='hidden' NAME='action' VALUE='Modify'>
                        </FORM>
                        </TD></TR>
                        <TR><TD>
                        <FORM NAME='noName1'
ACTION='/newZone/Inventory.SelectProduct' METHOD='POST'>
                            <CENTER><A HREF=''
onClick='return doSubmit(2)'>View</A></CENTER>
                                <INPUT TYPE='hidden' NAME='username' VALUE=''>
                                <INPUT TYPE='hidden' NAME='password' VALUE=''>
                                <INPUT TYPE='hidden' NAME='firstTime' VALUE='True'>
                                <INPUT TYPE='hidden' NAME='action' VALUE='View'>
                        </FORM>
                        </TD></TR>
                        <TR><TD>
                        <FORM NAME='noName1'
ACTION='/newZone/Inventory.SelectProduct' METHOD='POST'>
                            <CENTER><A HREF=''
```

```
                                     onClick='return doSubmit(3)'>Delete</A></CENTER>
                                          <INPUT TYPE='hidden' NAME='username' VALUE=''>
                                          <INPUT TYPE='hidden' NAME='password' VALUE=''>
                                          <INPUT TYPE='hidden' NAME='firstTime' VALUE='True'>
                                          <INPUT TYPE='hidden' NAME='action' VALUE='Delete'>
                                          </FORM>
                                     </TD></TR>
                             </TABLE>
                             </TD></TR>
                     </TABLE>
                     </TD><TD>
                     <TABLE BORDER='2'>
                             <TR><TD ALIGN='CENTER'
BGCOLOR='#CCCCCC'><H2><B>Categories</B></H2></TD>
                                     <TD>
                             <TABLE>
                                     <TR><TD>
                                     <FORM NAME='noName1'
ACTION='/newZone/Inventory.AddCategory' METHOD='POST'>
                                             <CENTER><A HREF=''
onClick='return doSubmit(4)'>Add</A></CENTER>
                                                 <INPUT TYPE='hidden' NAME='username' VALUE=''>
                                                 <INPUT TYPE='hidden' NAME='password' VALUE=''>
                                         <INPUT TYPE='hidden' NAME='firstTime' VALUE='True'>
                                         </FORM>
                                     </TD></TR>
                                     <TR><TD>
                                         <FORM NAME='noName1'
ACTION='/newZone/Inventory.SelectCategory' METHOD='POST'>
                                             <CENTER><A HREF=''
onClick='return doSubmit(5)'>Delete</A></CENTER>
                                                 <INPUT TYPE='hidden' NAME='username' VALUE=''>
                                                 <INPUT TYPE='hidden' NAME='password' VALUE=''>
                                             <INPUT TYPE='hidden' NAME='firstTime' VALUE='True'>
                                                 <INPUT TYPE='hidden' NAME='action' VALUE='Delete'>
                                         </FORM>
                                     </TD></TR>
                             </TABLE>
                     </TD></TR>
             </TABLE>
             </TD></TR>
         <TR><TD></TD><TD ALIGN='right'>
             <TABLE>
                 <FORM NAME='passwordForm'>
```

```
                              <TR><TD><B><H5>Username:</H5></B></TD>
                                  <TD><INPUT TYPE='text' NAME='username' VALUE=''
SIZE='8'></TD></TR>
                              <TR><TD><B><H5>Password:</H5></B></TD>
                                  <TD><INPUT TYPE='password' NAME='password' VALUE=''
SIZE='8'></TD></TR>
                    </FORM>
                      </TABLE>
        </TD></TR>
        </TABLE>
    </CENTER>
</BODY>
</HTML>
```

signoff.html

```
<HTML><HEAD></HEAD>
<SCRIPT>
    function showTopMenu()
    {
        parent.right.location.replace('inventoryOptions.html');
    }
</SCRIPT>
<BODY BGCOLOR='#6699CC'>
    <FORM>
        <INPUT TYPE='button' NAME='button' VALUE='Top Menu' onClick='showTopMenu();'>
    </FORM>
    <FORM ACTION='/newZone/Inventory.SignOff'>
      <INPUT TYPE='submit' NAME='submit' VALUE='Logout'>
    </FORM>
</BODY>
</HTML>
```

Other Html Files and Templates

addCategory.html

```
<HTML><HEAD><TITLE>Add Category</TITLE></HEAD>
<SCRIPT>
    function verify(frm)
    {
        for(i=0; i<5; i++)
        {
            if(i == 2)
                continue;
            if(frm.elements[i].value.length == 0)
```

```
                    {
                        alert('You have not specified anything in field:\n' +
                                frm.elements[i].name);
                        return false;
                    }
                }
                return true;
        }
</SCRIPT>
<BODY BGCOLOR='#FFFFFF'>
        <CENTER><H1>Add Category</H1></CENTER>
        <P>
        <CENTER>This form can be used for adding categories to your database.
         </CENTER>
        <P>
        <FORM ACTION='Inventory.AddCategory' METHOD='POST'
                onSubmit='return verify(this)'>
        <TABLE>
                <TR><TD>
                        <TABLE>
                                <TR><TD>Name<BR><TD><INPUT TYPE='text'
                                        NAME='name' SIZE='20'></TD>
                                <TD>Description URL<BR><INPUT TYPE='text'
                                    NAME='description_url' SIZE='35'></TD></TR>
                                <TR><TD>Parent Category<BR> <FONT size="-4"
                                    face="Arial, Helvetica, San Serif">
                                 <SELECT NAME='category_id' SIZE='1'>
<VAR_CATEGORY_OPTIONS>
                                 </SELECT>
                                 </FONT>
                                  </TD><TD></TD></TR>
                                <TR><TD COLSPAN='4'>Description<BR>
<TEXTAREA NAME='description' ROWS='8' COLS='50'></TEXTAREA></TD></TR>
                                  <TR><TD COLSPAN='4'>Search Keywords<BR>
                        <INPUT TYPE='text' NAME='search_keywords SIZE='50'>
                                  </TD></TR>
                        </TABLE>
                        <P>
                        Add more categories? <INPUT TYPE='radio'
                            NAME='addMore' VALUE='Yes'>Yes  
                            <INPUT TYPE='radio' NAME='addMore' VALUE='No'
                            CHECKED>No
                </TD></TR>
                <TR><TD ALIGN='right'>
```

```
                          <INPUT TYPE='submit' NAME='submit' VALUE='Submit'>
              </TD></TR>
        </TABLE>
        </FORM>
</BODY>
</HTML>

addProduct.html

<HTML><HEAD><TITLE>Add Product</TITLE></HEAD>
<SCRIPT>
    function verify(frm)
    {
        for(i=0; i<8; i++)
        {
            if(i == 6)
                continue;
            if(frm.elements[i].value.length == 0)
            {
                alert('You have not specified anything in field:\n' +
                        frm.elements[i].name);
                return false;
            }
        }
        return true;
    }
</SCRIPT>
<BODY BGCOLOR='#FFFFFF'>
        <CENTER><H1>Add Product</H1></CENTER>
        <P>
        <CENTER>This form can be used for adding products to your database.
         </CENTER>
        <P>
        <FORM ACTION='Inventory.AddProduct' METHOD='POST'
              onSubmit='return verify(this)'>
        <TABLE>
                <TR><TD>
                        <TABLE>
                                <TR><TD>Name<BR><INPUT TYPE='text'
                                        NAME='name' SIZE='20'></TD>
                                        <TD>Price<BR><TD><INPUT TYPE='text'
NAME='price' SIZE='6'></TD>
                                        <TD>Display Price</BBR>
<INPUT TYPE='text' NAME='display_price' SIZE='12'></TD></TR>
```

```
                            <TR><TD>Quantity in stock<BR>
<INPUT TYPE='text' NAME='quantity_in_stock' SIZE='10'></TD>
                                    <TD WIDTH='150'>Danger Level<BR>
<INPUT TYPE='text' NAME='danger_level' VALUE='99' SIZE='2'></TD>
                                <TD>Main contact<BR>(Email)</BBR>
<INPUT TYPE='text' NAME='email' SIZE='20'></TD></TR>
                            <TR><TD>Parent Category<BR><FONT
size="-4" face="Arial, Helvetica, San Serif"><SELECT NAME='category_id'
SIZE='1'>
<VAR_CATEGORY_OPTIONS>
</SELECT>
</FONT>
                                </TD>
                                <TD COLSPAN='2'>Description URL<BR>
<INPUT TYPE='text' NAME='description_url' SIZE='35'></TD></TR>

                            <TR><TD COLSPAN='4'>Description<BR>
<TEXTAREA NAME='description' ROWS='8' COLS='50'></TEXTAREA></TD></TR>
                            <TR><TD COLSPAN='5'>Search Keywords<BR>
<INPUT TYPE='text' SIZE='50' NAME='search_keywords'></TD></TR>
                    </TABLE>
                    <P>
                    Add more products? <INPUT TYPE='radio' NAME='addMore'
VALUE='Yes'>Yes  <INPUT TYPE='radio' NAME='addMore'
VALUE='No' CHECKED>No
                </TD></TR>
                <TR><TD ALIGN='right'>
                        <INPUT TYPE='submit' NAME='submit' VALUE='Submit'>
                </TD></TR>
        </TABLE>
        </FORM>
</BODY>
</HTML>


categoriesAdded.html

<HTML><HEAD></HEAD>
<BODY BGCOLOR='#FFFFFF'>
<H1><CENTER><B>Categories(s) Added</B></CENTER></H1>
<P>
The following categories have been added:
<P>
<CATEGORIES_ADDED>
</BODY>
</HTML>
```

categoryDeleted.html

```
<HTML> <HEAD></HEAD>
<BODY BGCOLOR='#FFFFFF'>
    <H1><B><CENTER>Category Deleted</CENTER></B></H1>
    <P>
<VAR_CATEGORY_ID>
</BODY>
</HTML>
```

inventoryError.html

```
<HTML><HEAD></HEAD>
<BODY BGCOLOR='#FFFFFF'>
<H1><CENTER><B>Error!</B></CENTER></H1>
<P>
The following error occured:
<P>
<ERROR_MSG>
<P>
This may have happened because of one of the following reasons:
<P>
<UL>
  <LI> You typed in a wrong username/password
  <LI> You have disabled cookies in your browser
  <LI> It's been a while since you initially logged in
  <LI> You have logged out explicitly
</UL>
To Login again, you need to go back to: <A HREF='/inventoryOptions.html'>
Inventory Options</A>
</BODY>
</HTML>
```

productDeleted.html

```
<HTML> <HEAD></HEAD>
<BODY BGCOLOR='#FFFFFF'>
    <H1><B><CENTER>Product Deleted</CENTER></B></H1>
    <P>
<VAR_PRODUCT_ID>
</BODY>
</HTML>
```

productModified.html

```
<HTML><HEAD></HEAD>
<BODY BGCOLOR='#FFFFFF'>
```

```
    <CENTER><H1><B>Product Modified</H1></B></CENTER>
<P>
The following product has been modified:<P>
<VAR_PRODUCT_MODIFIED>
</BODY>
</HTML>

productsAdded.html

<HTML><HEAD></HEAD>
<BODY BGCOLOR='#FFFFFF'>
<H1><CENTER><B>Product(s) Added</B></CENTER></H1>
<P>
The following products have been added:
<P>
<PRODUCTS_ADDED>
</BODY>
</HTML>

selectCategory.html

<HTML><HEAD></HEAD>
<SCRIPT>
    function isSelected(frm)
    {
        if(frm.elements[0].selectedIndex == -1)
        {
            alert('You need to select one product');
            return false;
        }
        else
            return true;
    }
</SCRIPT>
<BODY BGCOLOR='#FFFFFF'>
    <CENTER><H1><B>
<VAR_HEADER>
    </B></H1></CENTER>
<P>
    <CENTER>
      Please select one category from the list below<P>
<VAR_FORM_NAME>
        <TABLE><TR><TD>
            <SELECT NAME='category' SIZE='5'>;
<VAR_CATEGORY_LIST>
```

```
                    </SELECT>
<VAR_ACTION>
                </TD></TR>
                <TR><TD ALIGN='right'><INPUT TYPE='submit' NAME='submit' VALUE='Submit'>
                </TD></TR>
            </TABLE>
        </FORM>
    </CENTER>
</BODY>
</HTML>
```

selectProduct.html

```
<HTML><HEAD></HEAD>
<SCRIPT>
    function isSelected(frm)
    {
        if(frm.elements[0].selectedIndex == -1)
        {
            alert('You need to select one product');
            return false;
        }
        else
            return true;
    }
</SCRIPT>
<BODY BGCOLOR='#FFFFFF'>
    <CENTER><H1><B>
<VAR_HEADER>
    </B></H1></CENTER>
<P>
    <CENTER>
        Please select one product from the list below<P>

<VAR_FORM_NAME>
        <TABLE><TR><TD>
            <SELECT NAME='product' SIZE='5'>;
<VAR_PRODUCT_LIST>
            </SELECT>
<VAR_ACTION>
            </TD></TR>
            <TR><TD ALIGN='right'><INPUT TYPE='submit' NAME='submit' VALUE='Submit'>
            </TD></TR>
        </TABLE>
    </FORM>
```

```
                        </CENTER>
</BODY>
</HTML>


showProduct.html

<HTML><HEAD><TITLE></TITLE></HEAD>
<BODY BGCOLOR='#FFFFFF'>
        <CENTER><H1><B>Product</B></H1></CENTER>
        <P>
        <CENTER>
<VAR_HEADER>
         </CENTER>
        <P>
        <FORM ACTION='Inventory.ModifyProduct' METHOD='POST'>
        <TABLE>
                <TR><TD>
                        <TABLE>
                                <TR><TD>Name<BR>
<VAR_NAME>
                                </TD><TD>Price<BR><TD>
<VAR_PRICE>
                                </TD><TD>Display Price</BBR>
<VAR_DISPLAY_PRICE>
                                </TD></TR>
                          <TR><TD>Quantity in stock<BR>
<VAR_QUANTITY_IN_STOCK>
                                </TD><TD WIDTH='150'>Danger Level<BR>
<VAR_DANGER_LEVEL>
                                </TD><TD>Main contact<BR>(Email)</BBR>
<VAR_EMAIL>
                                </TD></TR>
                          <TR><TD>Parent Category<BR><FONT size="-4" face="Arial,
Helvetica, San Serif"><SELECT NAME='category_id' SIZE='1'>
<VAR_CATEGORY_OPTIONS>
</SELECT>
</FONT>
                                </TD><TD COLSPAN='2'>Description URL<BR>
<VAR_DESCRIPTION_URL>
                                </TD></TR>

                          <TR><TD COLSPAN='4'>Description<BR>
<TEXTAREA NAME='description' ROWS='8' COLS='50'>
<VAR_DESCRIPTION>
</TEXTAREA></TD></TR>
```

```
                                    <TR><TD>Last Modification By<BR>
<VAR_LAST_MODIFIED_BY>
                                            </TD><TD>Last Modification Date<BR>
<VAR_LAST_MODIFICATION_DATE>
                                        </TD><TD></TD></TR>
                                    <TR><TD COLSPAN='5'>Search Keywords<BR>
<VAR_SEARCH_KEYWORDS>
                                            </TD></TR>
                            </TABLE>
                            <P>
                    </TD></TR>
                    <TR><TD ALIGN='right'>
<VAR_SUBMIT>
<VAR_ID>
                        </TD></TR>
            </TABLE>
            </FORM>
</BODY>
</HTML>
```

Ordering Management System

Java Files

BaseOrdering.java

```java
package Ordering;

import java.util.*;
import java.io.*;
import java.sql.*;
import javax.servlet.*;
import javax.servlet.http.*;
import Utilities.*;

public class BaseOrdering extends HttpServlet
{
    static String BasePath = "HTML_DIRECTORY";
    static String BaseHttpsPath = "HTTP_VALUE/newZone/";
    static String orderDepartmentEmail = "ordering";
    static String shipDepartmentEmail = "SHIP_DEPARTMENT_EMAIL";
    static boolean debugOn = true;
```

```java
    public void sendTheMail(String f, String t, String h, String b)
        throws Exception
    {
        MailSender ms = new MailSender();
        ms.send(f,t,h,b);
    }

    public int verifyPassword(String username, String password,
                Connection conn)
    {
        boolean isValid = true;
        if(username == null || password == null)
            isValid = false;
        Authenticator a = new Authenticator();
        return a.verifyPassword(username, password, conn);
    }

    public void showErrorPage(PrintWriter out, String pgName, String value)
    {
        PageUtil p = new PageUtil(pgName, out);
        p.setReplaceItem("<ERROR_MSG>", value);
        p.printPage();
    }

    public PrintStream initializeDebugFile(String s)
    {
        PrintStream pos = null;
        try
        {
            if(debugOn == false)
                return null;
            pos = new PrintStream(new FileOutputStream(new File(s)));
        }catch(Exception ex){}
        return pos;
    }
    public void debug(String s, PrintStream pos)
    {
        try
        {
            if(debugOn == false)
                return;
            pos.println(s);
        }catch(Exception ex){}
    }
}
```

```
CardVerifier.java

package Ordering;

import java.io.*;
import java.net.*;
import Utilities.*;

public class CardVerifier
{
    String cardVerifyingCompany = "HTTP_CARD_COMPANY_VALUE/Verify";
    String price, ccardNum, ccardCompany, ccardExpDate;
    public CardVerifier(String p, String cn, String cCom, String cExp)
    {
        price = p;
        ccardNum = cn;
        ccardCompany = cCom;
        ccardExpDate = cExp;
    }
    public String verify()
    {
      String result = "";
      try
      {
        URL myURL = new URL(cardVerifyingCompany);
        URLConnection conn = myURL.openConnection();
        conn.setDefaultUseCaches(false);
        conn.setDoOutput(true);
        conn.setRequestProperty("Content-type", "application/octet-stream");
        String message = "ccardNum=" + URLEncoder.encode(ccardNum) +
          "&ccardExpDate=" + URLEncoder.encode(ccardExpDate) +
          "&ccardCompany=" + URLEncoder.encode(ccardCompany) +
          "&price=" + URLEncoder.encode(price);
        conn.setRequestProperty("Content-length", "" + message.length());
        OutputStreamWriter outStream =
            new OutputStreamWriter(conn.getOutputStream());
        PrintWriter pout = new PrintWriter(outStream);
        pout.write(message);
        outStream.flush();
        outStream.close();
        InputStreamReader inpStream =
                new InputStreamReader(conn.getInputStream());
        BufferedReader br = new BufferedReader(inpStream);
        String tmp = "";
        while((tmp = br.readLine()) != null)
```

```
                {
                    result += tmp;
                }
        }catch(Exception ex){}
        return result;
    }
}

DisplayProducts.java

package Ordering;

import java.util.*;
import java.io.*;
import java.sql.*;
import Utilities.*;

public class DisplayProducts extends BaseOrdering
{

    static String errorHtml = BasePath + "orderingError.html";
    static String getProductsHtml = BasePath + "getProducts.html";

    public void display(PrintWriter out, Vector productIds,
            Vector productNames, Vector productPrices, Vector productDescURLs,
            Vector productDisplayPrices)
            throws Exception
    {
            String tableRows = "";
            boolean yellowColor = false;
            String color = "";
            int size = productIds.size();
            for(int i=0; i<size; i++)
            {
                    if(yellowColor == false)
                    {
                        yellowColor = true;
                        color = "#CCFFFF";
                    }
                    else
                    {
                        yellowColor = false;
                        color = "#FFFFCC";
                    }
                    String prodId = (String)productIds.elementAt(i);
                    String name = (String)productNames.elementAt(i);
                    String price = (String)productPrices.elementAt(i);
```

```
                    String description_url = (String)productDescURLs.elementAt(i);
                    String display_price = (String)productDisplayPrices.elementAt(i);

                    tableRows += "<FORM><TR BGCOLOR='" + color + "'><TD>
<A HREF='" + description_url + "'>" + name + "</A> [" +  display_price +
"]</TD>";
                        tableRows += "<TD><FONT size='-2' face='Arial, Helvetica,
San Serif'>Quantity:</FONT><INPUT TYPE='text' SIZE='2' NAME='quantity'> </TD>
<TD WIDTH='100'><INPUT TYPE='checkbox' NAME='" + prodId + "'
VALUE = '' onClick='addToCart(this.form, \"" + prodId + "\"," + prodId +
",\"" + name + "\", " + price + ");'><FONT size='-2'
face='Arial, Helvetical, San Serif'><B>Check box to add item to cart.
Uncheck to remove.</B></TD></TR></FORM>";
                }
                PageUtil p = new PageUtil(getProductsHtml, out);
                p.setReplaceItem("<VAR_TABLE_ROWS>", tableRows);
                p.printPage();
        }
}

GetCategories.java

package Ordering;

import java.util.*;
import java.io.*;
import java.sql.*;
import javax.servlet.*;
import javax.servlet.http.*;
import Utilities.*;

public class GetCategories extends BaseOrdering
{
    ConnectionPool c = null;

    static String errorHtml = BasePath + "orderingError.html";
    static String getCategoriesHtml = BasePath + "getCatgories.html";
    public void doGet (HttpServletRequest req,
                        HttpServletResponse res)
    {
      Connection conn = null;
      PrintWriter out = null;
      try{
          HttpSession session;

          if(c == null)
          {
```

```
                    c = ConnectionPool.getInstance();
                    c.initialize();
            }
        conn = c.getConnection();
        out = res.getWriter();
        res.setContentType("text/html");
        showGetCategoriesPage(out, getCategoriesHtml, conn);
        c.putConnection(conn);
        out.close();
    }catch(Exception ex)
        {
            if(c != null && conn != null)
                c.putConnection(conn);
            showErrorPage(out, errorHtml, ex.getMessage());
        }
    }

    public void showGetCategoriesPage(PrintWriter out, String pgName,
                Connection conn)
        throws Exception
    {
            Statement stmt = conn.createStatement();
            String querySQL = "SELECT id, has_sub_categories, name
                    FROM categories WHERE category_id = 0";
            ResultSet rset = stmt.executeQuery(querySQL);
            String tableRows = "";
            while(rset.next())
            {
                    tableRows += "<TR><TD><A HREF='Ordering.GetProduct?id="
                      + rset.getString(1) + "&has_sub_categories=" +
                      rset.getString(2) + "'>";
                    tableRows += rset.getString(3) + "</A></TD></TR>";
            }
            PageUtil p = new PageUtil(pgName, out);
            p.setReplaceItem("<VAR_TABLE_ROWS>", tableRows);
            p.printPage();
    }
}

GetPayment.java

package Ordering;

import java.util.*;
import java.io.*;
import java.sql.*;
```

```
import javax.servlet.*;
import javax.servlet.http.*;
import Utilities.*;

public class GetPayment extends BaseOrdering
{
    ConnectionPool c = null;

    static String errorHtml = BasePath + "orderingError.html";
    static String thankYouPageHtml = BasePath + "orderingThankYou.html";

    static String getNewCardHtml = BaseHttpsPath + "Profile.GetNewCard";
    static String registerUserHtml = BaseHttpsPath + "Profile.RegistrationPage";

    /* Results of credit card verification analysis */
    static int ALL_OK = 1;
    public void doPost (HttpServletRequest req,
                        HttpServletResponse res)
    {
      Connection conn = null;
      PrintWriter out = null;
      try{
          HttpSession session;
          String calledFrom = "";
          String paymentFrom = "";
          boolean newUser = false;
          Vector productIds = new Vector();
          Vector productQuantities = new Vector();
          Vector addToCartIds = new Vector();
          Vector removeFromCartIds = new Vector();

          if(c == null)
          {
              c = ConnectionPool.getInstance();
              c.initialize();
          }
          conn = c.getConnection();
          Enumeration paramNames = req.getParameterNames();
          while(paramNames.hasMoreElements())
          {
              String nm = (String)paramNames.nextElement();
              String vl = req.getParameterValues(nm)[0];
              if(nm.equalsIgnoreCase("calledFrom"))
                  calledFrom = vl;
              if(nm.equalsIgnoreCase("userType"))
                  if(vl.equalsIgnoreCase("new"))
```

```
                    newUser = true;
            if(nm.equalsIgnoreCase("paymentFrom"))
                paymentFrom = vl;
            if(nm.indexOf("ID_") != -1)
            {
                    String id = nm.substring(3);
                    String qtty = vl;
                    if((new Integer(qtty)).intValue() != 0)
                    {
                            productIds.addElement(id);
                            productQuantities.addElement(qtty);
                    }
            }
            if(nm.indexOf("regCart_") != -1)
            {
                    String id = nm.substring(8);
                    String action = vl;
                    if(action.equalsIgnoreCase("Add"))
                            addToCartIds.addElement(id);
                    else
                            removeFromCartIds.addElement(id);
            }
    }
    out = res.getWriter();
    res.setContentType("text/html");
    session = req.getSession(false);
    if(session == null)
    {
            showErrorPage(out, errorHtml, "Invalid Session");
            return;
    }
    String username = (String)session.getValue("Ordering.username");
    if(calledFrom.equals("Checkout"))
    {
        session.putValue("Ordering.productIds", productIds);
        session.putValue("Ordering.productQuantities",
                            productQuantities);
        addToRegularCart(addToCartIds, productIds,
                    productQuantities, username, conn);
        removeFromRegularCart(removeFromCartIds, username, conn);
    }
    if(newUser)
    {
            c.putConnection(conn);
```

```java
            showNewUserPage(res, username, registerUserHtml);
        }
        else
        {
            if(paymentFrom.equals("newCard"))
            {
                c.putConnection(conn);
                showGetNewCardPage(res, username, getNewCardHtml);
            }
            else
            {
                productIds = (Vector)session.getValue("Ordering.productIds");
                productQuantities =
                    (Vector)session.getValue("Ordering.productQuantities");
                callPaymentModule(out, productIds, productQuantities,
                        username, conn, session);
            }
        }
        c.putConnection(conn);
        out.close();
    }catch(Exception ex)
    {
        if(c != null && conn != null)
            c.putConnection(conn);
        showErrorPage(out, errorHtml, ex.getMessage());
    }
}
public void removeFromRegularCart(Vector ids, String username,
        Connection conn)
    throws Exception
{
    Statement stmt = conn.createStatement();
    String profileId = "";
    String querySQL = "SELECT id FROM profiles
                    WHERE username='" + username + "'";
    ResultSet rset = stmt.executeQuery(querySQL);
    while(rset.next())
        profileId = rset.getString(1);

    int sz = ids.size();
    for(int i=0; i<sz; i++)
    {
        String id = (String)ids.elementAt(i);
        String updateSQL = "DELETE FROM regular_cart
```

```
                   WHERE profile_id=" + profileId + " AND product_id=" + id;
            stmt.executeUpdate(updateSQL);
        }
        stmt.close();
    }
    public void addToRegularCart(Vector addIds, Vector allIds,
            Vector allQuantities, String username, Connection conn)
        throws Exception
    {
        Statement stmt = conn.createStatement();
        String profileId = "";
        String querySQL = "SELECT id FROM profiles WHERE username='"
                          + username + "'";
        ResultSet rset = stmt.executeQuery(querySQL);
        while(rset.next())
            profileId = rset.getString(1);

        int sz = addIds.size();
        for(int i=0; i<sz; i++)
        {
            String idToAdd = (String)addIds.elementAt(i);
            String qtty = getQuantity(idToAdd, allIds, allQuantities);
            String cartId = "";
            querySQL = "SELECT regular_cart_seq.NEXTVAL FROM dual";

            rset = stmt.executeQuery(querySQL);
            while(rset.next())
                cartId = rset.getString(1);
            String updateSQL = "INSERT INTO regular_cart(id, profile_id,
                product_id, quantity) VALUES (" + cartId + "," +
                profileId + "," + idToAdd + "," + qtty + ")";
            stmt.executeUpdate(updateSQL);
        }
        stmt.close();
    }
    public String getQuantity(String id, Vector allIds,
            Vector allQuantities)
    {
        String qtty = "0";
        int sz = allIds.size();
        for(int i=0; i<sz; i++)
        {
            String theId = (String)allIds.elementAt(i);
            if(theId.equals(id))
            {
```

```
                qtty = (String)allQuantities.elementAt(i);
                return qtty;
            }
        }
        return qtty;
    }
    public void callPaymentModule(PrintWriter out, Vector productIds,
                Vector  productQuantities, String username, Connection conn,
                HttpSession session)
            throws Exception
    {
            Statement stmt = conn.createStatement();

            String querySQL = "SELECT ccard_num, TO_CHAR(ccard_exp_date,
                    'DD-MON-YYYY'), ccard_company, first_name, last_name,
                    id FROM profiles
                    WHERE username='" + username + "'";
            String ccardNum="", ccardExpDate="", ccardCompany="";
            String firstName = "", lastName = "", profileId="";
            Vector displayPrices = new Vector();
            Vector productNames = new Vector();
            Vector productPrices = new Vector();
            ResultSet rset = stmt.executeQuery(querySQL);
            while(rset.next())
            {
                ccardNum = rset.getString(1);
                ccardExpDate = rset.getString(2);
                ccardCompany = rset.getString(3);
                firstName = rset.getString(4);
                lastName = rset.getString(5);
                profileId = rset.getString(6);
            }
            double price = 0.0;
            int size = productIds.size();
            for(int i=0; i<size; i++)
            {
                String id = (String)productIds.elementAt(i);
                String quantity = (String)productQuantities.elementAt(i);
                int qtty = (new Integer(quantity)).intValue();
                querySQL = "SELECT price, display_price,name
                            FROM products WHERE id=" + id;
                rset = stmt.executeQuery(querySQL);
                while(rset.next())
                {
```

```
                        double d = rset.getDouble(1);
                        String dp = rset.getString(2);
                        String nm = rset.getString(3);
                        displayPrices.addElement(dp);
                        productNames.addElement(nm);
                        productPrices.addElement((new Float(d)).toString());
                        price += d*qtty;
                    }
                }
                stmt.close();
                int resultAnalysis = ALL_OK;
/*

                CardVerifier cv = new CardVerifier(price, ccardNum,
                                    ccardCompany, ccardExpDate);
                String result = cv.verify();
                resultAnalysis = analyzeResult(result);
*/

                if(resultAnalysis == ALL_OK)
                {
                    String orderId;
                    orderId = storeProdsInOrderTable(productIds,
                                    productQuantities,
                                    productPrices,
                                    (new Float(price)).toString(),
                                    profileId, conn);
                    showThankYouPage(productNames, productQuantities,
                                    displayPrices, orderId,
                                    (new Float(price)).toString(),
                                    username, thankYouPageHtml, conn, out);
                }
                else
                    printErrorPage(resultAnalysis, errorHtml, out);
                session.invalidate();
    }
    public int analyzeResult(String r)
    {
        return ALL_OK;
    }
    public String storeProdsInOrderTable(Vector productIds,
                Vector productQuantities, Vector productPrices,
                String totalPrice, String profileId,
                Connection conn)
            throws Exception
    {
```

```
        String ordersId = "UNDEFINED";
        Statement stmt = conn.createStatement();
        String querySQL = "SELECT orders_seq.NEXTVAL FROM dual";
        ResultSet rset = stmt.executeQuery(querySQL);
        while(rset.next())
        {
            ordersId = rset.getString(1);
        }
        String insertSQL = "INSERT INTO orders(id, profile_id,
            date_ordered, date_shipped, status, payment_received,
            total_billed)
            VALUES(" + ordersId + "," + profileId + ", SYSDATE, NULL,
                    'WITH_SHIPPING_DEPARTMENT', 1," + totalPrice + ")";
        stmt.executeUpdate(insertSQL);
        int size = productIds.size();
        for(int i=0; i<size; i++)
        {
            String prodId = (String)productIds.elementAt(i);
            String prodQtty = (String)productQuantities.elementAt(i);
            String prodPrice = (String)productPrices.elementAt(i);
            querySQL = "SELECT one_order_seq.NEXTVAL FROM dual";
            String oneOrderId = "";
            rset = stmt.executeQuery(querySQL);
            while(rset.next())
                oneOrderId = rset.getString(1);
            insertSQL = "INSERT INTO one_order(id, orders_id, product_id,
             quantity, price) VALUES(" + oneOrderId + "," + ordersId + "," +
               prodId + "," + prodQtty + "," + prodPrice + ")";
            stmt.executeUpdate(insertSQL);
            insertSQL = "UPDATE products SET
                quantity_in_stock = quantity_in_stock-" + prodQtty +
                " WHERE id=" + prodId;
            stmt.executeUpdate(insertSQL);
        }
        stmt.close();
        return ordersId;
    }
    public void printErrorPage(int r, String pgName, PrintWriter out)
    {
    }
    public void showThankYouPage(Vector productNames,
                                 Vector productQuantities,
                                 Vector displayPrices, String orderId,
                                 String price, String username,
```

```
                        String pgName, Connection conn,
                        PrintWriter out)
        throws Exception
{
        int size = productQuantities.size();
        String purchaseList = "";
        String itemList = "";
        for(int i=0; i<size; i++)
        {
                String quantity = (String)productQuantities.elementAt(i);
                String dp = (String)displayPrices.elementAt(i);
                String nm = (String)productNames.elementAt(i);
                purchaseList += "<TR><TD>" + nm + " [" + dp + "]</TD>
                        <TD>Qtty:" + quantity + "</TD></TR>";
                itemList += nm + " " + quantity + "\n";
        }
        PageUtil pu = new PageUtil(pgName, out);
        pu.setReplaceItem("<VAR_PURCHASE_LIST>", purchaseList);
        pu.setReplaceItem("<VAR_PRICE>", price);
        pu.setReplaceItem("<VAR_USERNAME>", username);
        pu.setReplaceItem("<VAR_ORDER_ID>", orderId);
        pu.printPage();
        sendMailToShipping(itemList, orderId, username, conn);
}
public void sendMailToShipping(String itemList, String orderId,
            String username, Connection conn)
        throws Exception
{
        Statement stmt = conn.createStatement();
        String querySQL = "SELECT id, email, phone, fax, first_name,
            last_name FROM profiles WHERE username='" + username + "'";
        String profileId="", email="", phone="", fax="";
        String firstName="", lastName="";
        ResultSet rset = stmt.executeQuery(querySQL);
        while(rset.next())
        {
                profileId = rset.getString(1);
                email = rset.getString(2);
                phone = rset.getString(3);
                fax = rset.getString(4);
                firstName = rset.getString(5);
                lastName = rset.getString(6);
        }
        querySQL = "SELECT line1, line2, city, state, zip FROM addresses
```

```
                        WHERE type='SHIPPING' AND profile_id=" + profileId;
        String line1="", line2="", city="", state="", zip="";
        rset = stmt.executeQuery(querySQL);
        while(rset.next())
        {
                line1 = rset.getString(1);
                line2 = rset.getString(2);
                city = rset.getString(3);
                state = rset.getString(4);
                zip = rset.getString(5);
        }
        String mailBody = "Order Id: " + orderId + "\nItem List:\n" +
                itemList + "\nAddress:\n" + firstName + " " + lastName +
                "\n" + line1 + "\n"
                + line2 + "\n" + city + " " + state + " " + zip + "\n";

        String mailHeader = "Order id: " + orderId;
        sendTheMail(orderDepartmentEmail, shipDepartmentEmail, mailHeader,
                        mailBody);
    }

    public void showGetNewCardPage(HttpServletResponse res,
                String username, String pg)
        throws Exception
    {
        res.sendRedirect(pg + "?username=" + username + "&calledFrom=GetPayment");
    }
    public void showNewUserPage(HttpServletResponse res,
                String username, String pg)
        throws Exception
    {
        res.sendRedirect(pg + "?username=" + username + "&calledFrom=GetPayment");
    }

}

GetProduct.java

package Ordering;

import java.util.*;
import java.io.*;
import java.sql.*;
import javax.servlet.*;
import javax.servlet.http.*;
import Utilities.*;
```

```
public class GetProduct extends BaseOrdering
{
    ConnectionPool c = null;

    static String errorHtml = BasePath + "orderingError.html";
    static String getCategoriesHtml = BasePath + "getCategories.html";
    static String getProductsHtml = BasePath + "getProducts.html";
    public void doGet (HttpServletRequest req,
                       HttpServletResponse res)
    {
      Connection conn = null;
      PrintWriter out = null;
      try{
          HttpSession session;

          String has_sub_categories="", id="";

          boolean firstTime = false;

          if(c == null)
          {
              c = ConnectionPool.getInstance();
              c.initialize();
          }
          conn = c.getConnection();
          Enumeration paramNames = req.getParameterNames();
          while(paramNames.hasMoreElements())
          {
              String nm = (String)paramNames.nextElement();
              String vl = req.getParameterValues(nm)[0];
              if(nm.equalsIgnoreCase("id"))
                  id = vl;
              if(nm.equalsIgnoreCase("has_sub_categories"))
                  has_sub_categories = vl;
          }
          out = res.getWriter();
          res.setContentType("text/html");
          session = req.getSession(false);
          if(session == null)
          {
              showErrorPage(out,  errorHtml, "Invalid session");
          }
          if(has_sub_categories.equals("1"))
             showGetCategoriesPage(out, getCategoriesHtml, id, conn);
          else
```

```
            showGetProductsPage(out, getProductsHtml, id, conn);
        c.putConnection(conn);
        out.close();
    }catch(Exception ex)
      {
          if(c != null && conn != null)
              c.putConnection(conn);
          showErrorPage(out, errorHtml, ex.getMessage());
      }
  }

  public void showGetProductsPage(PrintWriter out, String pgName,
                                  String id, Connection conn)
      throws Exception
  {
        Vector productIds = new Vector();
        Vector productNames = new Vector();
        Vector productPrices = new Vector();
        Vector productDescURLs = new Vector();
        Vector productDisplayPrices = new Vector();

        Statement stmt = conn.createStatement();
        String querySQL = "SELECT id,category_id, name, price,
description_url, display_price FROM products WHERE category_id = " + id;
        ResultSet rset = stmt.executeQuery(querySQL);
        while(rset.next())
        {
              String prodId = rset.getString(1);
              String category_id = rset.getString(2);
              String name = rset.getString(3);
              String price = rset.getString(4);
              String description_url = rset.getString(5);
              String display_price = rset.getString(6);
              productIds.addElement(prodId);
              productNames.addElement(name);
              productPrices.addElement(price);
              productDescURLs.addElement(description_url);
              productDisplayPrices.addElement(price);
        }
        stmt.close();
        DisplayProducts dp = new DisplayProducts();
        dp.display(out, productIds, productNames, productPrices,
              productDescURLs, productDisplayPrices);
  }
  public void showGetCategoriesPage(PrintWriter out, String pgName,
```

```
                            String id, Connection conn)
        throws Exception
    {
            Statement stmt = conn.createStatement();
            String querySQL = "SELECT id, has_sub_categories, name
                    FROM categories WHERE category_id = " + id;
            ResultSet rset = stmt.executeQuery(querySQL);
            String tableRows = "";
            while(rset.next())
            {
                    tableRows += "<TR><TD><A HREF='Ordering.GetProduct?id=" +
rset.getString(1) + "&has_sub_categories=" + rset.getString(2) + "'>";
                    tableRows += rset.getString(3) + "</A></TD></TR>";
            }
            stmt.close();
            PageUtil p = new PageUtil(pgName, out);
            p.setReplaceItem("<VAR_TABLE_ROWS>", tableRows);
            p.printPage();
    }
}

SearchProducts.java

package Ordering;

import java.util.*;
import java.io.*;
import java.sql.*;
import javax.servlet.*;
import javax.servlet.http.*;
import Utilities.*;

public class SearchProducts extends BaseOrdering
{
    ConnectionPool c = null;

    static String errorHtml = BasePath + "orderingError.html";
    public void doGet (HttpServletRequest req,
                    HttpServletResponse res)
    {
      Connection conn = null;
      PrintWriter out = null;
      try{
          HttpSession session;

          String searchList = "";
```

```
            boolean firstTime = false;

            if(c == null)
            {
                c = ConnectionPool.getInstance();
                c.initialize();
            }
            conn = c.getConnection();
            Enumeration paramNames = req.getParameterNames();
            while(paramNames.hasMoreElements())
            {
                String nm = (String)paramNames.nextElement();
                String vl = req.getParameterValues(nm)[0];
                if(nm.equalsIgnoreCase("searchList"))
                    searchList = vl;
            }
            out = res.getWriter();
            res.setContentType("text/html");
            session = req.getSession(false);
            if(session == null)
            {
                showErrorPage(out,  errorHtml, "Invalid session");
            }
            showSearchResults(out, searchList, conn);
            c.putConnection(conn);
            out.close();
    }catch(Exception ex)
        {
            if(c != null && conn != null)
                c.putConnection(conn);
            showErrorPage(out, errorHtml, ex.getMessage());
        }
}

public void showSearchResults(PrintWriter out, String searchList,
                              Connection conn)
    throws Exception
{
        StringTokenizer st = new StringTokenizer(searchList);
        Vector searchItems = new Vector();
        while(st.hasMoreTokens())
            searchItems.addElement((st.nextToken()).toUpperCase());

        String querySQL = "SELECT id,category_id, name, price,
            description_url, display_price FROM products WHERE ";
```

```java
            int size = searchItems.size();
            for(int i=0; i<size; i++)
            {
                if(i != 0)
                    querySQL += " OR ";
                querySQL += "NLS_UPPER(search_keywords) LIKE '%" +
                            (String)searchItems.elementAt(i) + "%'";
            }

            Vector productIds = new Vector();
            Vector productNames = new Vector();
            Vector productPrices = new Vector();
            Vector productDescURLs = new Vector();
            Vector productDisplayPrices = new Vector();

            Statement stmt = conn.createStatement();
            ResultSet rset = stmt.executeQuery(querySQL);
            while(rset.next())
            {
                    String prodId = rset.getString(1);
                    String category_id = rset.getString(2);
                    String name = rset.getString(3);
                    String price = rset.getString(4);
                    String description_url = rset.getString(5);
                    String display_price = rset.getString(6);
                    productIds.addElement(prodId);
                    productNames.addElement(name);
                    productPrices.addElement(price);
                    productDescURLs.addElement(description_url);
                    productDisplayPrices.addElement(price);
            }
            stmt.close();
            DisplayProducts dp = new DisplayProducts();
            dp.display(out, productIds, productNames, productPrices,
                productDescURLs, productDisplayPrices);
        }
}

SelectOrder.java

package Ordering;

import java.util.*;
import java.io.*;
import java.sql.*;
import javax.servlet.*;
```

```
import javax.servlet.http.*;
import Utilities.*;

public class SelectOrder extends BaseOrdering
{
    ConnectionPool c = null;

    static String errorHtml = BasePath + "orderingError.html";
    static String selectOrderPage = BasePath + "selectOrder.html";

    public void doGet (HttpServletRequest req,
                        HttpServletResponse res)
    {
      Connection conn = null;
      PrintWriter out = null;
      try{
          HttpSession session;

          if(c == null)
          {
              c = ConnectionPool.getInstance();
              c.initialize();
          }
          conn = c.getConnection();
          Enumeration paramNames = req.getParameterNames();
          out = res.getWriter();
          res.setContentType("text/html");
          session = req.getSession(false);
          if(session == null)
          {
              showErrorPage(out, errorHtml, "Invalid Session");
              return;
          }
          String username = (String)session.getValue("Ordering.username");
          showSelectOrdersPage(username, selectOrderPage, conn, out);
          c.putConnection(conn);
          out.close();
      }catch(Exception ex)
          {
              if(c != null && conn != null)
                  c.putConnection(conn);
              showErrorPage(out, errorHtml, ex.getMessage());
          }
    }
    public void showSelectOrdersPage(String username, String pgName,
            Connection conn, PrintWriter out)
```

```
            throws Exception
    {
            Statement stmt = conn.createStatement();
            String profileId = "";
            String querySQL = "SELECT id FROM profiles WHERE username='" + username + "'";
            ResultSet rset = stmt.executeQuery(querySQL);
            while(rset.next())
                profileId = rset.getString(1);

            querySQL = "SELECT id, TO_CHAR(date_ordered, 'DD-MON-YYYY')
                        FROM orders WHERE profile_id='" + profileId + "'";
            rset = stmt.executeQuery(querySQL);
            String orderIdOptions = "";
            while(rset.next())
            {
                String orderId = rset.getString(1);
                String date_ordered = rset.getString(2);
                orderIdOptions += "<A HREF='Ordering.ShowOrderDetails?orderId=" + orderId
+ "'>Order Id: " + orderId + " : " + date_ordered + "</ABR>";
            }
            stmt.close();
            PageUtil pu = new PageUtil(pgName, out);
            pu.setReplaceItem("<VAR_ORDER_OPTIONS>", orderIdOptions);
            pu.printPage();
        }
}

ShowOrderDetails.java

package Ordering;

import java.util.*;
import java.io.*;
import java.sql.*;
import javax.servlet.*;
import javax.servlet.http.*;
import Utilities.*;

public class ShowOrderDetails extends BaseOrdering
{
    ConnectionPool c = null;

    static String errorHtml = BasePath + "orderingError.html";
    static String orderDetailsPage = BasePath + "orderDetails.html";

    public void doGet (HttpServletRequest req,
                       HttpServletResponse res)
```

```
{
   Connection conn = null;
   PrintWriter out = null;
   try{
       HttpSession session;
       String orderId = "";

       if(c == null)
       {
           c = ConnectionPool.getInstance();
           c.initialize();
       }
       conn = c.getConnection();
       Enumeration paramNames = req.getParameterNames();
       while(paramNames.hasMoreElements())
       {
           String nm = (String)paramNames.nextElement();
           String vl = req.getParameterValues(nm)[0];
           if(nm.equalsIgnoreCase("orderId"))
               orderId = vl;
       }
       out = res.getWriter();
       res.setContentType("text/html");
       session = req.getSession(false);
       if(session == null)
       {
           showErrorPage(out, errorHtml, "Invalid Session");
           return;
       }
       showOrderDetailsPage(orderId, orderDetailsPage, conn, out);
       c.putConnection(conn);
       out.close();
   }catch(Exception ex)
     {
         if(c != null && conn != null)
             c.putConnection(conn);
         showErrorPage(out, errorHtml, ex.getMessage());
     }
}
public void showOrderDetailsPage(String orderId, String pgName,
         Connection conn, PrintWriter out)
     throws Exception
{
     Statement stmt = conn.createStatement();
```

```
String profileId = "", dateOrdered="", dateShipped="";
String totalBilled = "", shipMethod="", status="";
String querySQL = "SELECT profile_id, TO_CHAR(date_ordered,
        'DD-MON-YYYY'), TO_CHAR(date_shipped, 'DD-MON-YYYY'),
        total_billed, shipment_method, status FROM orders
        WHERE id=" + orderId;
ResultSet rset = stmt.executeQuery(querySQL);
while(rset.next())
{
    profileId = rset.getString(1);
    dateOrdered = rset.getString(2);
    dateShipped = rset.getString(3);
    totalBilled = rset.getString(4);
    shipMethod = rset.getString(5);
    status = rset.getString(6);
}
if(dateShipped == null)
    dateShipped = "Yet to be shipped";

Vector prodIds = new Vector();
Vector prodNames = new Vector();
Vector prodQuantities = new Vector();
Vector prodPrices = new Vector();

querySQL = "SELECT product_id, quantity, price FROM one_order
            WHERE orders_id=" + orderId;
rset = stmt.executeQuery(querySQL);
while(rset.next())
{
    prodIds.addElement(rset.getString(1));
    prodQuantities.addElement(rset.getString(2));
    prodPrices.addElement(rset.getString(3));
}
String baseQuerySQL = "SELECT name FROM products WHERE id=";
int size = prodIds.size();
for(int i=0; i<size; i++)
{
    querySQL = baseQuerySQL + (String)prodIds.elementAt(i);
    rset = stmt.executeQuery(querySQL);
    while(rset.next())
    {
        prodNames.addElement(rset.getString(1));
    }
}
String tableRows = "";
```

```
                    for(int i=0; i<size; i++)
                    {
                            String name = (String)prodNames.elementAt(i);
                            String price = (String)prodPrices.elementAt(i);
                            String qtty = (String)prodQuantities.elementAt(i);
                            tableRows += "<TR><TD>" + name + "</TD><TD>" +price +
"</TD><TD>" + qtty + "</TD></TR>";
                    }
                    stmt.close();
                    PageUtil pu = new PageUtil(pgName, out);
                    pu.setReplaceItem("<VAR_TABLE_ROWS>", tableRows);
                    pu.setReplaceItem("<VAR_TOTAL_BILLED>", totalBilled);
                    pu.setReplaceItem("<VAR_DATE_ORDERED>", dateOrdered);
                    pu.setReplaceItem("<VAR_DATE_SHIPPED>", dateShipped);
                    pu.setReplaceItem("<VAR_ORDER_ID>", orderId);
                    if(shipMethod == null)
                        shipMethod = "";

                    pu.setReplaceItem("<VAR_SHIP_METHOD>", shipMethod);
                    pu.setReplaceItem("<VAR_STATUS>", status);
                    pu.printPage();
        }
}

SignIn.java

package Ordering;

import java.util.*;
import java.io.*;
import java.sql.*;
import javax.servlet.*;
import javax.servlet.http.*;
import Utilities.*;

public class SignIn extends BaseOrdering
{
    ConnectionPool c = null;

    static String errorHtml = BasePath + "orderingError.html";
    static String signInHtml = BasePath + "signIn.html";
    public void doPost (HttpServletRequest req,
                        HttpServletResponse res)
    {
      Connection conn = null;
      PrintWriter out = null;
      try{
```

```
        HttpSession session;

        String username="", password="";
        String pw_confirm="";

        boolean firstTime = false;

        if(c == null)
        {
            c = ConnectionPool.getInstance();
            c.initialize();
        }
        conn = c.getConnection();
        Enumeration paramNames = req.getParameterNames();
        while(paramNames.hasMoreElements())
        {
            String nm = (String)paramNames.nextElement();
            String vl = req.getParameterValues(nm)[0];
            if(nm.equalsIgnoreCase("username"))
                username = vl;
            if(nm.equalsIgnoreCase("password"))
                password = vl;
            if(nm.equalsIgnoreCase("pw_confirm"))
                pw_confirm = vl;
        }
        out = res.getWriter();
        res.setContentType("text/html");
        int userType = verifyPassword(username, password, conn);
        int showError = 0;

        if(userType == 2) // INVALID_PASSWORD
        {
            showErrorPage(out, errorHtml, "Invalid username/password-<BR>There is an
account in the system with this username but with a <BR>different password. If you are a
new user, please select a different username.");
            c.putConnection(conn);
            return;
        }
        if(userType == 1) // NEW_USER
        {
            boolean addedOk = true;
            if(password.equalsIgnoreCase(pw_confirm) == false)
            {
                showErrorPage(out, errorHtml, "Password and confirm do not match");
                c.putConnection(conn);
                return;
```

```
        }
        addedOk = addNewUser(username, password,
                             pw_confirm, errorHtml, out, conn);
        if(addedOk == false)
        {
            c.putConnection(conn);
            return;
        }
    }
    session = req.getSession(true);
    session.putValue("Ordering.username", username);
    session.putValue("Ordering.password", password);
    showSignInPage(out, signInHtml, userType, username, conn);
    c.putConnection(conn);
    out.close();
  }catch(Exception ex)
    {
        if(c != null && conn != null)
            c.putConnection(conn);
        showErrorPage(out, errorHtml, ex.getMessage());
    }
}


public boolean addNewUser(String username, String password,
            String pw_confirm, String errorHtml,
            PrintWriter out, Connection conn)
{
    boolean addedOk = true;
    String errorMsg = "";
    try{
        Statement stmt = conn.createStatement();
        String querySQL = "SELECT profiles_seq.NEXTVAL FROM dual";
        ResultSet rset = stmt.executeQuery(querySQL);
        String id="";
        while(rset.next())
            id = rset.getString(1);
        String insertSQL = "INSERT INTO profiles(id, username, password,
                registration_date, status) VALUES (" + id + ",'" +
                username + "','" + password + "',SYSDATE, 'NEW_USER')";
        stmt.executeUpdate(insertSQL);
    }catch(SQLException ex){addedOk=false; errorMsg=ex.getMessage();}
    if(addedOk == false)
    {
        PageUtil p = new PageUtil(errorHtml, out);
```

```
                p.setReplaceItem("<ERROR_MSG>", errorMsg);
                p.printPage();
            }
            return addedOk;
        }
        public void showSignInPage(PrintWriter out, String pgName,
                    int userType, String username, Connection conn)
            throws Exception
        {
            Statement stmt = conn.createStatement();
            String querySQL = "SELECT id, has_sub_categories, name
                            FROM categories WHERE category_id = 0";
            ResultSet rset = stmt.executeQuery(querySQL);
            String tableRows = "";
            while(rset.next())
            {
                    tableRows += "<TR><TD><A HREF='Ordering.GetProduct?id=" +
rset.getString(1) + "&has_sub_categories=" + rset.getString(2) + "'>";
                    tableRows += rset.getString(3) + "</A></TD></TR>";
            }
            querySQL = "SELECT id FROM profiles WHERE username='" + username + "'";
            rset = stmt.executeQuery(querySQL);
            String profileId = "";
            while(rset.next())
            {
                    profileId = rset.getString(1);
            }
            querySQL = "SELECT product_id, quantity FROM regular_cart
                        WHERE profile_id=" + profileId;
            Vector productId = new Vector();
            Vector quantity = new Vector();
            Vector productName = new Vector();
            Vector productPrice = new Vector();
            Vector productDisplayPrice = new Vector();

            rset = stmt.executeQuery(querySQL);
            while(rset.next())
            {
                    productId.addElement(rset.getString(1));
                    quantity.addElement(rset.getString(2));
            }

            int sz = productId.size();
            for(int k=0; k<sz; k++)
            {
```

```
                         querySQL = "SELECT name, price, display_price FROM products
                                    WHERE id = " + (String)productId.elementAt(k);
                         rset = stmt.executeQuery(querySQL);
                         while(rset.next())
                         {
                                 productName.addElement(rset.getString(1));
                                 productPrice.addElement(rset.getString(2));
                                 productDisplayPrice.addElement(rset.getString(3));
                         }
                 }
                 String regularCartValues = "var cartTotal=0;";
                 for(int k=0; k<sz; k++)
                 {
                         regularCartValues += "parent.regularCartIds[" + k + "]=\"" +
(String)productId.elementAt(k) + "\";parent.regularCartNames[" + k + "]=\"" +
(String)productName.elementAt(k) + " [" +
(String)productDisplayPrice.elementAt(k) + "] \";parent.regularCartPrices[" + k +
"]=\"" + (String)productPrice.elementAt(k) + "\";parent.regularCartQuantities[" +
k + "]=\"" + (String)quantity.elementAt(k) + "\";";
                 }
                 PageUtil p = new PageUtil(pgName, out);
                 p.setReplaceItem("<VAR_TABLE_ROWS>", tableRows);
                 String value = "";
                 if(userType == 1 || userType == 4)
                         /* NEW_USER or NEW_USER_COMING_AGAIN */
                     value = "parent.newUser = true;";
                 p.setReplaceItem("<VAR_SET_NEW_USER>", value);
                 p.setReplaceItem("<VAR_REGULAR_CART_VALUES>", regularCartValues);
                 p.printPage();
         }
}

Document Root Html Files

checkout.html

<META HTTP-EQUIV="Pragma" CONTENT="no-cache">
<HTML><HEAD></HEAD>
<SCRIPT>
    function belongsToRegularCart(id)
    {
        regCartLen = parent.regularCartIds.length;
        for(j=0; j<regCartLen; j++)
        {
            if(parent.regularCartIds[j] == id)
```

```
                    return true;
        }
        return false;
}
function calculateTotalPrice(frm)
{
        len = frm.elements.length;
        purchasedLen = parent.purchasedIds.length;
        // For each purchased item
        for(j=0; j<purchasedLen; j++)
        {
            for(i=0; i<len; i++)
            {
                nm = "ID_" + parent.purchasedIds[j];
                if(frm.elements[i].name ==  nm)
                {
                    newQ = frm.elements[i].value;
                    parent.purchasedQuantities[j] = newQ;
                    break;
                }
            }
        }
        len = parent.purchasedQuantities.length;
        var price = 0.0;
        for(i =0; i<len; i++)
        {
            q = new Number(parent.purchasedQuantities[i]);
            if(q <= 0)
                continue;
            price = price + q*(new Number(parent.purchasedPrices[i]));
        }
        prc = new String(price);
        indx = prc.indexOf(".");
        prc = prc.substring(0, indx + 3);
        frm.price.value = prc;
}
function clearGlobals()
{
        parent.lastCount = 0;
        parent.regularCartIds = new Array();
        parent.regularCartQuantities = new Array();
        parent.regularCartNames = new Array();
        parent.regularCartPrices = new Array();
```

```
            parent.purchasedIds = new Array();
            parent.purchasedQuantities = new Array();
            parent.purchasedNames = new Array();
            parent.purchasedPrices = new Array();
        }
</SCRIPT>
<BODY BGCOLOR='#FFFFCC'>
<FORM ACTION='/newZone/Ordering.GetPayment'
        METHOD='POST' onSubmit='return clearGlobals();'>
<SCRIPT>
    len = parent.purchasedIds.length;
    document.write("<H1>Products purchased</H1><BR><BR><BR><TABLE>");
    var price = 0.0;
    for(i=0; i<len; i++)
    {
        q = new Number(parent.purchasedQuantities[i]);
        if(q <= 0)
            continue;
        document.write("<TR><TD>" + parent.purchasedNames[i] + "</TD><TD>");
        document.write("<INPUT TYPE='text' NAME='ID_" + parent.purchasedIds[i]
            + "' SIZE='2' VALUE='" + parent.purchasedQuantities[i] + "'></TD>");
        if(belongsToRegularCart(parent.purchasedIds[i]))
        {
            document.write("<TD WIDTH='150' BGCOLOR='#CCFFCC'><INPUT TYPE=
'checkbox' NAME='regCart_" + parent.purchasedIds[i] + "' VALUE='Remove'><FONT
size='-2' face='Arial, Helvetical, San Serif'>Click to remove item from regular
cart</FONT></TD></TR>");
        }
        else
        {
            document.write("<TD WIDTH='150' BGCOLOR='#FFCCCC'>
                <INPUT TYPE='checkbox' NAME='regCart_" + parent.purchasedIds[i]
+ "' VALUE='Add'><FONT size='-2' face='Arial, Helvetical, San Serif'>
                Click to add item to regular cart</FONT></TD></TR>");
        }
        price = price + q*(new Number(parent.purchasedPrices[i]));
    }
    document.write("</TABLE>");
    prc = new String(price);
    indx = prc.indexOf(".");
    prc = prc.substring(0, indx + 3);
    document.write("Total Price: <INPUT TYPE='text' NAME = 'price' SIZE='5'
        VALUE='" + prc + "'> <INPUT TYPE='button' NAME='recalculate'
        VALUE='Recalculate Total Price'
```

```
onClick='calculateTotalPrice(this.form)'>");
    if(parent.newUser == false)
    {
        document.write("<BR>Make payment using:");
        document.write("<TABLE><TR><TD><INPUT TYPE='radio' NAME='paymentFrom'
            VALUE='regularCard' CHECKED></TD><TD>Regular Card</TD></TR>");
        document.write("<TR><TD><INPUT TYPE='radio' NAME='paymentFrom'
            VALUE='newCard'></TD><TD>Another Card</TD></TR></TABLE>");
        document.write("<INPUT TYPE='submit' NAME='submit' VALUE='Submit'>");
    }
    else
    {
        document.write("<INPUT TYPE='hidden' NAME='paymentFrom' VALUE='newCard'>");
        document.write("<INPUT TYPE='hidden' NAME='userType' VALUE='new'>");
        document.write("<BR><INPUT TYPE='submit' NAME='submit'
                VALUE='Get Credit Card Info'>");
    }
    document.write("<INPUT TYPE='hidden' NAME='calledFrom' VALUE='Checkout'>");

</SCRIPT>
</FORM>
</BODY>
</HTML>

mainOrdering.html

<HTML><HEAD></HEAD>
<SCRIPT>
    function verify(frm)
    {
        if(frm.username.value.length < 4)
        {
            alert('Username should be at least 4 characters');
            return false;
        }
        return true;
    }
</SCRIPT>
<BODY BGCOLOR='#FFFFFF'>
    <CENTER><H1><B>Welcome!</H1></B></CENTER>
<P>
This is an example of an internet based shopping site.<BR>
Blah blah blah!
In order to look at our catalog and to purchase items you must sign in. If you
have established a password with use previousl you may enter  your username and
```

password below.

If you are a first time user, choose a username and a password
easy for you to remember. First time users will have to enter their password
twice (for confirmation).You may also enter a hint word that would help you
remember your password in case you forget.

```
<BR>
 <FORM ACTION='/newZone/Ordering.SignIn' METHOD='POST' onSubmit='return
verify(this);'>
 <TABLE><TR><TD>
   <TABLE BORDER='2'>
     <TH BGCOLOR='#CCCCCC'>All users</TH>
     <TR><TD>
       <TABLE>
           <TR><TD>Username</TD><TD><INPUT TYPE='text' SIZE='8'
               NAME='username' VALUE=''></TD></TR>
           <TR><TD>Password</TD><TD><INPUT TYPE='password' SIZE='8'
               NAME='password' VALUE=''></TD></TR>
       </TABLE>
     </TD></TR>
   </TABLE>
   </TD><TD>
   <TABLE BORDER='2'>
     <TH BGCOLOR='#CCCCCC'>First time users</TH>
     <TR><TD>
       <TABLE>
           <TR><TD>Confirm Password</TD><TD><INPUT TYPE='password'
               SIZE='8' NAME='pw_confirm' VALUE=''></TD></TR>
       </TABLE>
     </TD></TR>
   </TABLE>
 </TD></TR>
 <TR><TD></TD><TD ALIGN='right'>
     <INPUT TYPE='submit' NAME='submit' VALUE='Ok'>
 </TD></TR>
 </TABLE>
 </FORM>
</BODY>
</HTML>

ordering.html

<HTML><HEAD></HEAD>
<SCRIPT>
    var newUser = false;
    var windowUp = false;
```

```javascript
var lastCount = 0;
regularCartIds = new Array();
regularCartQuantities = new Array();
regularCartNames = new Array();
regularCartPrices = new Array();

purchasedIds = new Array();
purchasedQuantities = new Array();
purchasedNames = new Array();
purchasedPrices = new Array();
var cw;
function showOrderHistory(frm)
{
     right.location.replace('/newZone/Ordering.SelectOrder');
     return false;
}
function search(frm)
{
     right.location.replace('/newZone/Ordering.SearchProducts?
                          searchList=' + frm.searchList.value);
     return false;
}
function cartRefresh()
{
     if(windowUp)
         cw.location.reload();
}
function getCategories()
{
     right.location.replace("/newZone/Ordering.GetCategories");
     return false;
}
function checkout()
{
     right.location.replace("checkout.html");
     return false;
}
function regularCart()
{
     right.location.replace("regularCart.html");
     return false;
}
function showCart()
{
```

```
                windowUp = true;
                cw = window.open("/showCart.html", "cartWindow", "toolbar=no,
                    directories=no,menubar=no,location=no,scrollbars=yes,
                    width=450,height=400");
        }
</SCRIPT>
    <FRAMESET COLS='180, *' BORDER='0'>
        <FRAME NAME='left' SRC='blank.html'>
        <FRAME NAME='right' SRC='mainOrdering.html'>
    </FRAMESET>
<BODY BGCOLOR='#FFFFFF'>
</BODY>
</HTML>


orderingMenu.html

<HTML><HEAD></HEAD>
<SCRIPT>
    function checkout()
    {
        parent.right.location.replace("blank.html");
        d = parent.right.document;
        d.write("<BODY BGCOLOR='#FFFFFF'>Testing</BODY>");
    }
</SCRIPT>
<BODY BGCOLOR='#6699CC'>
    <FORM>
        <INPUT TYPE='button' NAME='chkout'
          VALUE='Categories   ' onClick='return parent.getCategories();'><BR>
        <INPUT TYPE='button' NAME='showContents' VALUE='Cart Contents'
            onClick='parent.showCart();'><BR>
        <INPUT TYPE='button' NAME='chkout' VALUE='Checkout   
              ' onClick='return parent.checkout();'><BR>
<BR><BR>

        <INPUT TYPE='button' NAME='personalCart' VALUE='Personal Cart'
            onClick='return parent.regularCart();'><BR>
        <INPUT TYPE='button' NAME='orderHistory' VALUE='Order History'
            onClick='return parent.showOrderHistory();'><BR>
<BR><BR><BR><BR>
         <FONT size='-2' face='Arial, Helvetica, San Serif'>
        <INPUT TYPE='text' NAME='searchList' VALUE='' SIZE='9'>
        <INPUT TYPE='button' NAME='search' VALUE='Search'
            onClick='return parent.search(this.form);'>
         </FONT>
```

```
    </FORM>
</BODY>
</HTML>

regularCart.html

<META HTTP-EQUIV="Pragma" CONTENT="no-cache">
<HTML><HEAD></HEAD>
<SCRIPT>
    function addToCheckoutCart(frm)
    {
        len = frm.elements.length;
        for(i=0; i<(len-1); i++) // All the text fields, not the button
        {
            q = new Number(frm.elements[i].value);
            if(q <= 0)
                continue;
            add(frm.elements[i].name, q);
        }
        parent.cartRefresh();
    }
    function add(id, quantity)
    {
        purchasedLen = parent.purchasedIds.length;
        foundItem = false;
        for(m=0; m<purchasedLen; m++)
        {
            pId = parent.purchasedIds[m];
            if(pId == id)
            {
                foundItem = true;
                pQtty = new Number(parent.purchasedQuantities[m]);
                pQtty += quantity;
                parent.purchasedQuantities[m] = pQtty;
                break;
            }
        }
        if(foundItem == false)
        {
            parent.purchasedIds[purchasedLen] = id;
            parent.purchasedQuantities[purchasedLen] = quantity;
            var name="";
            var regCartLen = parent.regularCartIds.length;
            for(z=0; z<regCartLen; z++)
            {
```

```
                    if(parent.regularCartIds[z] == id)
                    {
                        name = parent.regularCartNames[z];
                    }
                }
            price = getProductPrice(id);
            parent.purchasedNames[purchasedLen] = name;
            parent.purchasedPrices[purchasedLen] = price;
            parent.lastCount++;
        }
    }
    function getProductPrice(id)
    {
        var regCartLen = parent.regularCartIds.length;
        for(z=0; z<regCartLen; z++)
        {
            if(parent.regularCartIds[z] == id)
            {
                return parent.regularCartPrices[z];
            }
        }
        return "UNDEFINED";
    }
</SCRIPT>
<BODY BGCOLOR='#FFFFCC'>
<FORM>
<SCRIPT>
    len = parent.regularCartIds.length;
    document.write("<H1>Regular Cart Items</H1><BR><BR>");
    document.write("<TABLE><TR><TD WIDTH='500'>These are the items in your regu-
lar cart.<BR>");
    document.write("If you want to buy these items you may add them to the
                    checkout cart by pressing the button below.<BR>");
    document.write("If you want to add only a few items from this list,
                    set the quantity of items you don't want to 0.<BR>");
    document.write("</TD></TR></TABLE>");
    document.write("<TABLE>");

    for(i=0; i<len; i++)
    {
        q = new Number(parent.regularCartQuantities[i]);
        if(q <= 0)
            continue;
        document.write("<TR><TD>" + parent.regularCartNames[i] + "</TD><TD>");
```

```
            document.write("<INPUT TYPE='text' NAME='" + parent.regularCartIds[i]
                + "' SIZE='2' VALUE='" + parent.regularCartQuantities[i] + "'>
                </TD><TD></TD></TR>");
        }
        document.write("</TABLE>");
        document.write("<INPUT TYPE='button' NAME='button'
            VALUE='Add to checkout cart' onClick='addToCheckoutCart(this.form)'>");

</SCRIPT>
</FORM>
</BODY>
</HTML>

showCart.html

<HTML><HEAD></HEAD>
<BODY BGCOLOR='#FFFFFF'>
<FORM>
        <TABLE><TR><TD><TABLE BORDER='0'>
<SCRIPT>
        for(i = 0; i<window.opener.purchasedIds.length; i++)
        {
            q = new Number(window.opener.purchasedQuantities[i]);
            if(q == 0)
                continue;
            document.write("<TR BGCOLOR='#FFFFCC'><TD>" +
                window.opener.purchasedNames[i] + "</TD>
                <TD>    Quantity: " +
                window.opener.purchasedQuantities[i]  + "</TD></TR>");
        }
</SCRIPT>
        </TABLE></TD></TR><TR><TD><INPUT TYPE='button' NAME='Ok'
         VALUE='Dismiss Window'
onClick='parent.windowUp=false;window.close();'></TABLE>
</FORM>
</BODY>
</HTML>
Other Html Files and Templates

getCategories.html

<HTML><HEAD></HEAD>
<BODY BGCOLOR='#FFFFFF'>
 <FORM>
  <TABLE><TR><TD>
   <TABLE>
```

```
<VAR_TABLE_ROWS>
    </TABLE>
      </TD></TR>
      <TR><TD ALIGN='left'>
          <INPUT TYPE='button' NAME='back' VALUE='Back' onClick='history.back();'>
      </TD></TR>
    </TABLE>
  </FORM>
</BODY>
</HTML>

getProducts.html

<HTML><HEAD></HEAD>
<SCRIPT>
    function addToCart(frm, cbName, id, name, price)
    {
        el = frm.elements;
        ln = el.length;
        checked = false;
        for(i=0; i<ln; i++)
        {
            if(el[i].name == cbName)
            {
                if(el[i].checked == true)
                {
                    checked = true;
                }
                break;
            }
        }
        checkboxPos = i;

        quantity = frm.quantity.value;
        if(checked == true) // Add operation
        {
            if(quantity.length == 0)
            {
                frm.elements[checkboxPos].checked = false;
                alert('You did not specify a quantity');
                return;
            }
            len = quantity.length;
            for(i=0; i<len; i++)
            {
```

```
                c = quantity.charAt(i);
                if(c > '9' || c < '0')
                {
                    frm.elements[checkboxPos].checked = false;
                    alert('Invalid quantity');
                    return;
                }
        }
        totalInCart = parent.purchasedIds.length;
        alreadyPresent = false;
        presentAtPos = 0;
        for(i=0; i<totalInCart; i++)
        {
                if(parent.purchasedIds[i] == id)
                {
                    presentAtPos = i;
                    alreadyPresent = true;
                    ret = confirm('You already have ' +
                        parent.purchasedQuantities[i] + ' items\nof this
                        type. Are you sure you want more?');
                    if(ret == false)
                    {
                        frm.elements[checkboxPos].checked = false;
                        return;
                    }
                    break;
                }
        }
        if(alreadyPresent)
        {
            parent.purchasedQuantities[presentAtPos] =
                new Number(parent.purchasedQuantities[presentAtPos]) +
                new Number(quantity);
        }
        else
        {
            parent.purchasedIds[parent.lastCount] = id;
            parent.purchasedQuantities[parent.lastCount] = frm.quantity.value;
            parent.purchasedNames[parent.lastCount] = name;
            parent.purchasedPrices[parent.lastCount] = price;
            parent.lastCount++;
        }
}
else // Remove operation
```

```
            {
                ret = confirm('Are you sure you want to\nremove this product from the
                    cart?');
                if(ret == false)
                {
                    frm.elements[checkboxPos].checked = true;
                    return;
                }
                totalInCart = parent.purchasedIds.length;
                for(i=0; i<totalInCart; i++)
                {
                    if(parent.purchasedIds[i] == id)
                    {
                        parent.purchasedQuantities[i] = 0;
                        break;
                    }
                }
            }
        parent.cartRefresh();
    }
</SCRIPT>
<BODY BGCOLOR='#FFFFFF'>
    <P>
    <TABLE><TR><TD>
        <TABLE>
<VAR_TABLE_ROWS>
        </TABLE>
        </TD></TR>
<FORM>
    <TR><TD ALIGN='left'>
        <INPUT TYPE='button' NAME='back' VALUE='Back' onClick='history.back();'>
    </TD></TR>
    </TABLE>
    </FORM>
</BODY>
</HTML>

orderDetails.html

<HTML><HEAD></HEAD>
<BODY BGCOLOR='#FFFFFF'>
<CENTER><H1>Order Id:
<VAR_ORDER_ID>
</H1></CENTER><P>
Total charges: $
```

```
<VAR_TOTAL_BILLED>
<BR>
<TABLE BORDER='2'>
    <TR><TD><B>Date Ordered</B></TD><TD>
<VAR_DATE_ORDERED>
    </TD><TD>
    <B>Date Shipped</B></TD><TD>
<VAR_DATE_SHIPPED>
    </TD></TR>
    <TR><TD><B>Shipment Method</B></TD><TD>
<VAR_SHIP_METHOD>
    </TD><TD><B>
    Status</B></TD><TD>
<VAR_STATUS>
    </TD></TR>
</TABLE>
<PRE>

<PRE>
<TABLE BORDER='2'>
  <TH>Item</TH><TH>Price</TH><TH>Quantity</TH>
<VAR_TABLE_ROWS>
</TABLE>
</BODY>
</HTML>

orderingError.html

<HTML><HEAD></HEAD>
<BODY BGCOLOR='#FFFFFF'>
<H1><CENTER><B>Error!</B></CENTER></H1>
<P>
The following error occured:
<P>
<ERROR_MSG>
<P>
</BODY>
</HTML>

orderingThankYou.html

<HTML><HEAD></HEAD>
<BODY BGCOLOR='#FFFFFF'>
<H1><B><CENTER>Thank you for giving us the business</H1></B></CENTER><P>
Dear
<VAR_USERNAME>
```

```
,<BR>
Your credit card has been billed for $
<VAR_PRICE>
<P>
For reference purposes, your order id is:
<VAR_ORDER_ID>
<P>
The following items have been purchased by you:<BR>
<TABLE>
<VAR_PURCHASE_LIST>
</TABLE>
</BODY>
</HTML>
```

selectOrder.html

```
<HTML><HEAD></HEAD>
<BODY BGCOLOR='#FFFFFF'>
<TABLE>
    <TR><TD WIDTH='450'>
If you have purchased products from this site before, the order ids along with
the date on which the order was placed are shown below. By clicking on the link
you can get detailed information about that order.
        </TD>
    </TR>
</TABLE>
<VAR_ORDER_OPTIONS>
</BODY>
</HTML>
```

signIn.html

```
<HTML><HEAD></HEAD>
<SCRIPT>
    function showMenuAndCart()
    {
        parent.left.location.replace('HTTP_VALUE/orderingMenu.html');
        parent.showCart();
    }
</SCRIPT>
<BODY BGCOLOR='#FFFFFF' onLoad='showMenuAndCart();'>
    <TABLE>
<VAR_TABLE_ROWS>
    </TABLE>
<SCRIPT>
```

```
<VAR_SET_NEW_USER>
<VAR_REGULAR_CART_VALUES>
</SCRIPT>
</BODY>
</HTML>
```

Profile Management System

Java Files

BaseProfile.java

```java
package Profile;

import java.util.*;
import java.io.*;
import java.sql.*;
import javax.servlet.*;
import javax.servlet.http.*;
import Utilities.*;

public class BaseProfile extends HttpServlet
{
    static String BasePath = "HTML_DIRECTORY";
    static boolean debugOn = true;

    public void showErrorPage(PrintWriter out, String pgName, String value)
    {
        PageUtil p = new PageUtil(pgName, out);
        p.setReplaceItem("<ERROR_MSG>", value);
        p.printPage();
    }

    public PrintStream initializeDebugFile(String s)
    {
        PrintStream pos = null;
        try
        {
            if(debugOn == false)
                return null;
            pos = new PrintStream(new FileOutputStream(new File(s)));
        }catch(Exception ex){}
        return pos;
    }
    public void debug(String s, PrintStream pos)
```

```
    {
        try
        {
            if(debugOn == false)
                return;
            pos.println(s);
        }catch(Exception ex){}
    }
}

ContactUs.java

package Profile;

import java.util.*;
import java.io.*;
import java.sql.*;
import javax.servlet.*;
import javax.servlet.http.*;
import Utilities.*;

public class ContactUs extends BaseProfile
{
    static String errorHtml = BasePath + "profileError.html";
    static String contactMailSentHtml = BasePath + "contactMailSent.html";

    public void doPost (HttpServletRequest req,
                        HttpServletResponse res)
    {
      try{
          HttpSession session;

          String username = "", email="", description="", category="";
          String[] mailCategories = {"registrationProblem",
                                     "orderingProblem",
                                     "generalQuestion"};
          String[] mailAddresses = {"helpReg@myCompany.com",
                                    "helpOrder@myCompany.com",
                                    "helpGeneral@myCompany.com"};

          Enumeration paramNames = req.getParameterNames();
          while(paramNames.hasMoreElements())
          {
              String nm = (String)paramNames.nextElement();
              String vl = req.getParameterValues(nm)[0];
              if(nm.equalsIgnoreCase("username"))
                  username = vl;
              if(nm.equalsIgnoreCase("email"))
```

```
                    email = vl;
            if(nm.equalsIgnoreCase("category"))
                category = vl;
            if(nm.equalsIgnoreCase("description"))
                description = vl;
        }
        PrintWriter out = res.getWriter();
        res.setContentType("text/html");

        int len = mailCategories.length;
        String mailTo = "";
        for(int i=0; i<len; i++)
        {
            if(mailCategories[i].equals(category))
            {
                mailTo = mailAddresses[i];
                break;
            }
        }
        sendMail(out, mailTo, email, username, description,
                contactMailSentHtml);
        out.close();
    }catch(IOException ex){}
    }
    public void sendMail(PrintWriter out, String mailTo, String email,
            String username, String description, String pgNm)
    {
        PageUtil p = new PageUtil(pgNm, out);
        p.setReplaceItem("<VAR_USERNAME>", username);
        p.setReplaceItem("<VAR_MAIL_TO>", mailTo);
        p.setReplaceItem("<VAR_EMAIL>", email);
        p.setReplaceItem("<VAR_DESCRIPTION>", description);
        p.printPage();
    }
}

GetNewCard.java

package Profile;

import java.util.*;
import java.io.*;
import java.sql.*;
import javax.servlet.*;
import javax.servlet.http.*;
import Utilities.*;
```

```java
public class GetNewCard extends BaseProfile
{
    ConnectionPool c = null;

    static String errorHtml = BasePath + "profileError.html";
    static String getNewCardHtml = BasePath + "getNewCard.html";

    public void doGet (HttpServletRequest req,
                       HttpServletResponse res)
    {
      try{
          HttpSession session;

          String username = "", calledFrom="";
          Enumeration paramNames = req.getParameterNames();
          while(paramNames.hasMoreElements())
          {
              String nm = (String)paramNames.nextElement();
              String vl = req.getParameterValues(nm)[0];
              if(nm.equalsIgnoreCase("username"))
                  username = vl;
              if(nm.equalsIgnoreCase("calledFrom"))
                  calledFrom = vl;
          }
          PrintWriter out = res.getWriter();
          res.setContentType("text/html");

          username = "<INPUT TYPE='hidden' NAME='username' VALUE='" + username + "'>";
          calledFrom = "<INPUT TYPE='hidden' NAME='calledFrom' VALUE='" + calledFrom + "'>";
          PageUtil p = new PageUtil(getNewCardHtml, out);
          p.setReplaceItem("<VAR_USERNAME>", username);
          p.setReplaceItem("<VAR_CALLED_FROM>", calledFrom);
          p.printPage();
          out.close();
      }catch(IOException ex){}
    }
}

PasswordFinder.java

package Profile;

import java.util.*;
import java.io.*;
import java.sql.*;
import javax.servlet.*;
import javax.servlet.http.*;
import Utilities.*;
```

```java
public class PasswordFinder extends BaseProfile
{
    ConnectionPool c = null;

    static String errorHtml = BasePath + "profileError.html";
    static String showPasswordHtml = BasePath + "showPassword.html";

    public void doPost (HttpServletRequest req,
                        HttpServletResponse res)
    {
      Connection conn = null;
      PrintWriter out = null;
      try{
          HttpSession session;

          String username = "", password="", email="", lastName="";
          if(c == null)
          {
              c = ConnectionPool.getInstance();
              c.initialize();
          }
          conn = c.getConnection();
          Enumeration paramNames = req.getParameterNames();
          while(paramNames.hasMoreElements())
          {
              String nm = (String)paramNames.nextElement();
              String vl = req.getParameterValues(nm)[0];
              if(nm.equalsIgnoreCase("username"))
                  username = vl;
              if(nm.equalsIgnoreCase("email"))
                  email = vl;
              if(nm.equalsIgnoreCase("lastName"))
                  lastName = vl;
          }
          out = res.getWriter();
          res.setContentType("text/html");
          showPasswordFinder(out, username, email, lastName,
                             showPasswordHtml, errorHtml, conn);
          c.putConnection(conn);
          out.close();
      }catch(Exception ex)
        {
              if(c != null && conn != null)
                  c.putConnection(conn);
              showErrorPage(out, errorHtml, ex.getMessage());
```

```
        }
    }

    public void showPasswordFinder(PrintWriter out, String username,
                    String email, String lastName,
                    String showPasswordHtml, String errorHtml,
                    Connection conn)
        throws Exception
{
    if(email.equals("") || lastName.equals(""))
    {
        showErrorPage(out, errorHtml, "Insufficient data");
        return;
    }
        Statement stmt = conn.createStatement();
        String querySQL = "";
        if(username.equals("") == false)
        {
            querySQL = "SELECT password FROM profiles WHERE
                NLS_UPPER(email) = '" + email.toUpperCase() + "' AND
                NLS_UPPER(last_name) = '" + lastName.toUpperCase() + "'
                AND username='" + username + "'";
            ResultSet rset = stmt.executeQuery(querySQL);
            String pwd = "";
            while(rset.next())
            {
                pwd = rset.getString(1);
            }
            if(pwd.equalsIgnoreCase(""))
            {
                showErrorPage(out, errorHtml, "No password found for the
username you supplied with matching email address and last name.");
                stmt.close();
                return;
            }
            else
            {
                PageUtil pu = new PageUtil(showPasswordHtml, out);
                pu.setReplaceItem("<VAR_PASSWORD>", pwd);
                pu.printPage();
            }
        }
        else
```

```
            {
                querySQL = "SELECT username, password FROM profiles WHERE
                    NLS_UPPER(email) = '" + email.toUpperCase() + "' AND
                    NLS_UPPER(last_name) = '" + lastName.toUpperCase() + "'";
                ResultSet rset = stmt.executeQuery(querySQL);
                String usrName = "", pwd = "";
                while(rset.next())
                {
                    usrName = rset.getString(1);
                    pwd = rset.getString(2);
                }
                if(pwd.equalsIgnoreCase("") || usrName.equalsIgnoreCase(""))
                {
                    showErrorPage(out, errorHtml, "No password found for the
email address and last name you supplied.");
                    stmt.close();
                    return;
                }
                else
                {
                    sendMail(usrName, pwd);
                    PageUtil pu = new PageUtil(showPasswordHtml, out);
                    pu.setReplaceItem("<VAR_PASSWORD>", "For security reasons
your password has been sent to the associated email address.<BR>If you want your
password displayed on screen you must enter the username as well.");
                    pu.printPage();
                }
            }
            stmt.close();
    }
    public void sendMail(String username, String password)
    {
    }
}

Register.java

package Profile;

import java.util.*;
import java.io.*;
import java.sql.*;
import javax.servlet.*;
import javax.servlet.http.*;
import Utilities.*;
```

```
public class Register extends BaseProfile
{
    ConnectionPool c = null;

    static String errorHtml = BasePath + "profileError.html";
    static String registeredHtml = BasePath + "registered.html";

    public void doPost (HttpServletRequest req,
                        HttpServletResponse res)
    {
        Connection conn = null;
        PrintWriter out = null;
        try{
            HttpSession session;

            String username = "", password="", pw_confirm="";
            String firstName = "", lastName="", phone="";
            String fax = "", email="";
            String shipLine1 = "", shipLine2="";
            String shipCity = "", shipState="", shipZip="";
            String billLine1 = "", billLine2="";
            String billCity = "", billState="", billZip="";
            String ccardNumber = "", ccardCompany="";
            String date="", month="", year="";
            String calledFrom = "";
            if(c == null)
            {
                c = ConnectionPool.getInstance();
                c.initialize();
            }
            conn = c.getConnection();
            Enumeration paramNames = req.getParameterNames();
            while(paramNames.hasMoreElements())
            {
                String nm = (String)paramNames.nextElement();
                String vl = req.getParameterValues(nm)[0];
                if(nm.equalsIgnoreCase("username"))
                    username = vl;
                if(nm.equalsIgnoreCase("password"))
                    password = vl;
                if(nm.equalsIgnoreCase("pw_confirm"))
                    pw_confirm = vl;
                if(nm.equalsIgnoreCase("firstName"))
                    firstName = vl;
                if(nm.equalsIgnoreCase("lastName"))
```

```
                    lastName = vl;
            if(nm.equalsIgnoreCase("phone"))
                phone = vl;
            if(nm.equalsIgnoreCase("fax"))
                fax = vl;
            if(nm.equalsIgnoreCase("email"))
                email = vl;
            if(nm.equalsIgnoreCase("shipLine1"))
                shipLine1 = vl;
            if(nm.equalsIgnoreCase("shipLine2"))
                shipLine2 = vl;
            if(nm.equalsIgnoreCase("shipCity"))
                shipCity = vl;
            if(nm.equalsIgnoreCase("shipState"))
                shipState = vl;
            if(nm.equalsIgnoreCase("shipZip"))
                shipZip = vl;
            if(nm.equalsIgnoreCase("billLine1"))
                billLine1 = vl;
            if(nm.equalsIgnoreCase("billLine2"))
                billLine2 = vl;
            if(nm.equalsIgnoreCase("billCity"))
                billCity = vl;
            if(nm.equalsIgnoreCase("billState"))
                billState = vl;
            if(nm.equalsIgnoreCase("billZip"))
                billZip = vl;
            if(nm.equalsIgnoreCase("ccardNumber"))
                ccardNumber = vl;
            if(nm.equalsIgnoreCase("ccardCompany"))
                ccardCompany = vl;
            if(nm.equalsIgnoreCase("date"))
                date = vl;
            if(nm.equalsIgnoreCase("month"))
                month = vl;
            if(nm.equalsIgnoreCase("year"))
                year = vl;
            if(nm.equalsIgnoreCase("calledFrom"))
                calledFrom = vl;
    }
    out = res.getWriter();
    res.setContentType("text/html");
    if( dataError(out,
            username,password, pw_confirm,
```

```
                        firstName, lastName, phone,
                        fax, email, shipLine1, shipLine2,
                        shipCity, shipState, shipZip,
                        billLine1, billLine2, billCity, billState, billZip,
                        ccardNumber, ccardCompany, date, month, year, calledFrom,
                        errorHtml
                        ) == true)
    {
            c.putConnection(conn);
            out.close();
            return;
    }


    registerUser(out, username,password, pw_confirm,
                firstName, lastName, phone,
                fax, email, shipLine1, shipLine2,
                shipCity, shipState, shipZip,
                billLine1, billLine2, billCity, billState, billZip,
                ccardNumber, ccardCompany, date, month, year, calledFrom,
                registeredHtml, errorHtml, conn);
    c.putConnection(conn);
    out.close();
  }catch(Exception ex)
    {
            if(c != null && conn != null)
                c.putConnection(conn);
            showErrorPage(out, errorHtml, ex.getMessage());
    }
}
public boolean dataError(PrintWriter out,
                String username, String password,  String pw_confirm,
                String firstName,  String lastName,  String phone,
                String fax,  String email,  String shipLine1,
                String shipLine2, String shipCity,  String shipState,
                String shipZip, String billLine1,  String billLine2,
                String billCity,  String billState,  String billZip,
                String ccardNumber,  String ccardCompany,  String date,
                String month,  String year,  String calledFrom,
                String pgName)
{
    boolean error = false;
    String errorMsg = "";
    if(username.length() < 4)
```

```
    {
        error = true;
        errorMsg += "<LI>Username should be at least 4 characters";
    }
    if(password.equals(pw_confirm) == false)
    {
        error = true;
        errorMsg += "<LI>Password does not match confirm";
    }
    if(firstName.length() == 0)
    {
        error = true;
        errorMsg += "<LI>First name not specified";
    }
    if(lastName.length() == 0)
    {
        error = true;
        errorMsg += "<LI>Last name not specified";
    }
    if(ccardNumber.length() == 0)
    {
        error = true;
        errorMsg += "<LI>Credit Card Number not specified";
    }
    int ln = ccardNumber.length();
    for(int i=0; i<ln; i++)
    {
        char c = ccardNumber.charAt(i);
        if(c < '0' || c > '9')
        {
            error = true;
            errorMsg += "<LI>Invalid Credit Card Number";
        }
    }
    if(error == true)
    {
        showErrorPage(out, pgName, errorMsg);
    }
    return error;
}

public void registerUser(PrintWriter out, String username,
            String password,  String pw_confirm,
```

```
                    String firstName,  String lastName,  String phone,
                    String fax,  String email,  String shipLine1,
                    String shipLine2, String shipCity,  String shipState,
                    String shipZip, String billLine1,  String billLine2,
                    String billCity,  String billState,  String billZip,
                    String ccardNumber,  String ccardCompany,  String date,
                    String month,  String year,  String calledFrom,
                    String pgName, String errorHtml, Connection conn)
           throws Exception
    {
      boolean error = false;
      String errorMsg = "";
      String storedPassword = "";
       try{
          conn.setAutoCommit(false);
          Statement stmt = conn.createStatement();
          String querySQL = "SELECT id,password FROM profiles
                  WHERE username='" + username + "'";
          ResultSet rset = stmt.executeQuery(querySQL);
          boolean foundRecord = false;
          String id = "";
          while(rset.next())
          {
              foundRecord = true;
              id = rset.getString(1);
              storedPassword = rset.getString(2);
          }

          if(foundRecord == false)
          {
              querySQL = "SELECT profiles_seq.NEXTVAL FROM dual";
              rset = stmt.executeQuery(querySQL);
              while(rset.next())
              {
                  id = rset.getString(1);
              }
              String insertSQL = "INSERT INTO profiles(id, username,
                      password, first_name, last_name, phone, fax, email,
                      ccard_num, ccard_exp_date, ccard_company, status)
                      VALUES (" + id + ",'" + username + "','" + password +
                        "','" + firstName + "','" + lastName + "','" +
                        phone + "','" + fax + "','" + email + "','" +
                        ccardNumber + "', TO_DATE('" + date + "-" + month
```

```
                            + "-" + year + "'", 'DD-MON-YYYY'), '" +
                        ccardCompany + "'", 'UPDATED_USER')";

            stmt.executeUpdate(insertSQL);
    }
    else
    {

            /* To prevent a person from calling this servlet thru
    a form containing somebody's userid and updating that person's
    information without knowing the person's password.
    For a new user this is not an issue. */

            if(storedPassword.equals(password) == false)
            {
                error = true;
                errorMsg = "Access Denied-Password does not match your
                    original password";
            }
            else
            {
                    String updateSQL = "UPDATE profiles SET
                        password='" + password + "'", first_name='" +
                        firstName + "'", last_name='" + lastName + "'",
                        phone='" + phone + "'", fax='" + fax + "'",
                        email='" + email + "'", ccard_num='" +
                        ccardNumber + "'", ccard_exp_date=TO_DATE('" +
                        date + "-" + month + "-" + year + "'",
                        'DD-MON-YYYY'), ccard_company='" + ccardCompany
                        + "'", status='UPDATED_USER' WHERE id = " + id;
                    stmt.executeUpdate(updateSQL);
            }
    }
    if(error == false)
    {
        querySQL = "SELECT addresses_seq.NEXTVAL FROM dual";
        String addId = "";
        rset = stmt.executeQuery(querySQL);
        while(rset.next())
        {
            addId = rset.getString(1);
        }
        String insertSQL = "INSERT INTO addresses(id, profile_id,
            type, line1, line2, city, state, zip)
```

```
                VALUES (" + addId + "," + id + ",'SHIPPING', '" +
                    shipLine1 + "', '" + shipLine2 + "', '" + shipCity +
                    "', '" + shipState + "','" + shipZip + "')";
            stmt.executeUpdate(insertSQL);

            addId = "";
            rset = stmt.executeQuery(querySQL);
            while(rset.next())
            {
                addId = rset.getString(1);
            }
            insertSQL = "INSERT INTO addresses(id, profile_id, type,
                line1, line2, city, state, zip)
                VALUES (" + addId + "," + id + ",'BILLING', '" +
                    billLine1 + "', '" + billLine2 + "', '" +
                    billCity + "', '" + billState + "','" + billZip + "')";
            stmt.executeUpdate(insertSQL);
        }
        conn.commit();
        stmt.close();
        conn.setAutoCommit(true);
    }catch(SQLException ex){error = true; errorMsg=ex.getMessage();}
    if(error)
    {
        showErrorPage(out, errorHtml, errorMsg);
    }
    else
    {
        PageUtil p = new PageUtil(pgName, out);
        String submit = "";
        if(calledFrom.equalsIgnoreCase("GetPayment"))
            submit = "<BR>You may now proceed your payment<BR><INPUT
TYPE='submit' NAME='submit' VALUE='Pay'>";

        p.setReplaceItem("<VAR_SUBMIT>", submit);
        p.printPage();
    }
  }
}

RegistrationPage.java

package Profile;

import java.util.*;
import java.io.*;
```

```java
import java.sql.*;
import javax.servlet.*;
import javax.servlet.http.*;
import Utilities.*;

public class RegistrationPage extends BaseProfile
{
    ConnectionPool c = null;

    static String errorHtml = BasePath + "profileError.html";
    static String registrationPageHtml = BasePath + "registrationPage.html";

    public void doGet (HttpServletRequest req,
                       HttpServletResponse res)
    {
      Connection conn = null;
      PrintWriter out = null;
      try{
          HttpSession session;
          String username = "", calledFrom="";
          if(c == null)
          {
              c = ConnectionPool.getInstance();
              c.initialize();
          }
          conn = c.getConnection();
          Enumeration paramNames = req.getParameterNames();
          while(paramNames.hasMoreElements())
          {
              String nm = (String)paramNames.nextElement();
              String vl = req.getParameterValues(nm)[0];
              if(nm.equalsIgnoreCase("username"))
                  username = vl;
              if(nm.equalsIgnoreCase("calledFrom"))
                  calledFrom = vl;
          }
          out = res.getWriter();
          res.setContentType("text/html");
          showRegistrationPage(out, username, calledFrom,
                            registrationPageHtml, errorHtml, conn);
          c.putConnection(conn);
          out.close();
      }catch(Exception ex)
        {
           if(c != null && conn != null)
```

```
                    c.putConnection(conn);
                showErrorPage(out, errorHtml, ex.getMessage());
            }
        }
    }


    public void showRegistrationPage(PrintWriter out, String username,
                                     String calledFrom, String pgName,
                                     String errorHtml, Connection conn)
        throws Exception
    {
        calledFrom = "<INPUT TYPE='hidden' NAME='calledFrom' VALUE='" + calledFrom + "'>";
        String usernameField = "<INPUT TYPE='text' NAME='username' SIZE='10'>";
        String newUser = "";
        if(username.equalsIgnoreCase("") == false)
        {
            String status = "";
            boolean existingUser = false;
            try{
                    Statement stmt = conn.createStatement();
                    String querySQL = "SELECT status FROM profiles
                            WHERE username = '" + username + "'";
                    ResultSet rset = stmt.executeQuery(querySQL);
                    while(rset.next())
                    {
                        status = rset.getString(1);
                        existingUser = true;
                    }
                    stmt.close();
            }catch(SQLException ex){}
            if(existingUser)
            {
                if(status.equalsIgnoreCase("NEW_USER") == false)
                {
                    PageUtil p = new PageUtil(errorHtml, out);
                    String errorMsg = "You are already a registered user. To update your
                        profile you need to visit the Update section";
                    p.setReplaceItem("<ERROR_MSG>", errorMsg);
                    p.printPage();
                    return;
                }
            }
            usernameField = username + "<INPUT TYPE='hidden'
                NAME='username' VALUE='" + username + "'>";
            newUser = "<INPUT TYPE='hidden' NAME='newUser' VALUE='true'>";
```

```
        }
        PageUtil p = new PageUtil(pgName, out);
        p.setReplaceItem("<VAR_USERNAME_FIELD>", usernameField);
        p.setReplaceItem("<VAR_NEW_USER>", newUser);
        p.setReplaceItem("<VAR_CALLED_FROM>", calledFrom);
        p.printPage();

    }
}

UpdatePage.java

package Profile;

import java.util.*;
import java.io.*;
import java.sql.*;
import javax.servlet.*;
import javax.servlet.http.*;
import Utilities.*;

public class UpdatePage extends BaseProfile
{
    ConnectionPool c = null;

    static String errorHtml = BasePath + "profileError.html";
    static String updatePageHtml = BasePath + "updatePage.html";

    public void doPost (HttpServletRequest req,
                        HttpServletResponse res)
    {
      Connection conn = null;
      PrintWriter out = null;
      try{
          HttpSession session;

          String username = "", password="", calledFrom="";
          if(c == null)
          {
              c = ConnectionPool.getInstance();
              c.initialize();
          }
          conn = c.getConnection();
          Enumeration paramNames = req.getParameterNames();
          while(paramNames.hasMoreElements())
          {
              String nm = (String)paramNames.nextElement();
              String vl = req.getParameterValues(nm)[0];
```

```
            if(nm.equalsIgnoreCase("username"))
                username = vl;
            if(nm.equalsIgnoreCase("password"))
                password = vl;
            if(nm.equalsIgnoreCase("calledFrom"))
                calledFrom = vl;
        }
        out = res.getWriter();
        res.setContentType("text/html");
        showUpdatePage(out, username, password, calledFrom,
                            updatePageHtml, errorHtml, conn);
        c.putConnection(conn);
        out.close();
    }catch(Exception ex)
        {
         if(c != null && conn != null)
            c.putConnection(conn);
         showErrorPage(out, errorHtml, ex.getMessage());
        }
}

public void showUpdatePage(PrintWriter out, String username,
                                String password,
                                String calledFrom, String pgName,
                                String errorHtml, Connection conn)
        throws Exception
{
    String origPassword = password;
    String ccardCompanies[] = {"Visa", "MasterCard"};
    String dates[] = {
        "01", "02", "03", "04", "05", "06", "07", "08", "09", "10",
        "11", "12", "13", "14", "15", "16", "17", "18", "19", "20",
        "21", "22", "23", "24", "25", "26", "27", "28", "29", "30",
        "31"
     };
    String months[] = {"Jan", "Feb", "Mar", "Apr", "May", "Jun",
        "Jul", "Aug", "Sep", "Oct", "Nov", "Dec"};
    String years[] = {"1999", "2000", "2001", "2002", "2003", "2004", "2005", "2006"};

    calledFrom = "<INPUT TYPE='hidden' NAME='calledFrom' VALUE='" + calledFrom + "'>";
    if(username.equalsIgnoreCase("")  || password.equalsIgnoreCase(""))
    {
        showErrorPage(out, errorHtml, "Invalid Username/Password");
        return;
    }
```

```
String id = "", dbPassword="";
String firstName = "", lastName="", phone="";
String fax = "", email="";
String shipLine1 = "", shipLine2="";
String shipCity = "", shipState="", shipZip="";
String billLine1 = "", billLine2="";
String billCity = "", billState="", billZip="";
String ccardNumber = "", ccardCompany="";
String expDate="", date="", month="", year="", status="";
try{
        Statement stmt = conn.createStatement();

        String querySQL = "SELECT id, password, first_name,
                last_name, phone, fax, email, ccard_num,
                TO_CHAR(ccard_exp_date, 'DD-MON-YYYY'), ccard_company,
                 status FROM profiles WHERE username = '" + username + "'";
        ResultSet rset = stmt.executeQuery(querySQL);
        while(rset.next())
        {
                id = rset.getString(1);
                dbPassword = rset.getString(2);
                firstName = rset.getString(3);
                lastName = rset.getString(4);
                phone = rset.getString(5);
                if(phone == null) phone = "";
                fax = rset.getString(6);
                if(fax == null) fax = "";
                email = rset.getString(7);
                if(email == null) email = "";
                ccardNumber = rset.getString(8);
                if(ccardNumber == null) ccardNumber = "";
                expDate = rset.getString(9);
                ccardCompany = rset.getString(10);
                if(ccardCompany == null) ccardCompany = "";
                status = rset.getString(11);
                if(status == null) status = "";
        }
        if(password.equals(dbPassword) == false)
        {
            showErrorPage(out, errorHtml, "Invalid Username/Password");
            return;
        }
        StringTokenizer st = new StringTokenizer(expDate, "-");
        date = st.nextToken();
```

```
                month = st.nextToken();
                year = st.nextToken();

                String baseQuerySQL = "SELECT line1, line2, city, state, zip
                    FROM addresses WHERE profile_id=" + id + " AND type='";
                querySQL = baseQuerySQL + "SHIPPING'";
                rset = stmt.executeQuery(querySQL);
                while(rset.next())
                {
                    shipLine1 = rset.getString(1);
                    if(shipLine1 == null) shipLine1 = "";
                    shipLine2 = rset.getString(2);
                    if(shipLine2 == null) shipLine2 = "";
                    shipCity = rset.getString(3);
                    if(shipCity == null) shipCity = "";
                    shipState = rset.getString(4);
                    if(shipState == null) shipState = "";
                    shipZip = rset.getString(5);
                    if(shipZip == null) shipZip = "";
                }
                querySQL = baseQuerySQL + "BILLING'";
                rset = stmt.executeQuery(querySQL);
                while(rset.next())
                {
                    billLine1 = rset.getString(1);
                    if(billLine1 == null) billLine1 = "";
                    billLine2 = rset.getString(2);
                    if(billLine2 == null) billLine2 = "";
                    billCity = rset.getString(3);
                    if(billCity == null) billCity = "";
                    billState = rset.getString(4);
                    if(billState == null) billState = "";
                    billZip = rset.getString(5);
                    if(billZip == null) billZip = "";
                }
                stmt.close();
        }catch(SQLException ex){}

        String inputText = "<INPUT TYPE='text' SIZE='";
        String inputPassword = "<INPUT TYPE='password' SIZE='";
        int size = 10;
        String pw_confirm = inputPassword + size + "' NAME='pw_confirm' VALUE='" + password + "'>";
        password = inputPassword + size + "' NAME='password' VALUE='" + password + "'>";
        size = 20;
        firstName = inputText + size + "' NAME='firstName' VALUE='" + firstName + "'>";
```

```
lastName = inputText + size + "' NAME='lastName' VALUE='" + lastName + "'>";
phone = inputText + size + "' NAME='phone' VALUE='" + phone + "'>";
fax = inputText + size + "' NAME='fax' VALUE='" + fax + "'>";
email = inputText + size + "' NAME='email' VALUE='" + email + "'>";
size = 30;
shipLine1 = inputText + size + "' NAME='shipLine1' VALUE='" + shipLine1 + "'>";
shipLine2 = inputText + size + "' NAME='shipLine2' VALUE='" + shipLine2 + "'>";
billLine1 = inputText + size + "' NAME='billLine1' VALUE='" + billLine1 + "'>";
billLine2 = inputText + size + "' NAME='billLine2' VALUE='" + billLine2 + "'>";
size = 12;
billCity = inputText + size + "' NAME='billCity' VALUE='" + billCity + "'>";
shipCity = inputText + size + "' NAME='shipCity' VALUE='" + shipCity + "'>";
size = 2;
billState = inputText + size + "' NAME='billState' VALUE='" + billState + "'>";
shipState = inputText + size + "' NAME='shipState' VALUE='" + shipState + "'>";
size = 5;
billZip = inputText + size + "' NAME='billZip' VALUE='" + billZip + "'>";
shipZip = inputText + size + "' NAME='shipZip' VALUE='" + shipZip + "'>";
size = 12;
ccardNumber = inputText + size + "' NAME='ccardNumber' VALUE='" + ccardNumber + "'>";
String company = "";
int len = ccardCompanies.length;
int k;
for(k=0; k<len; k++)
{
    if(ccardCompany.equals(ccardCompanies[k]))
        company += "<OPTION SELECTED>" + ccardCompanies[k];
    else
        company += "<OPTION>" + ccardCompanies[k];
}
String theDate = "";
len = dates.length;
for(k=0; k<len; k++)
{
    if(date.equals(dates[k]))
        theDate += "<OPTION SELECTED>" + dates[k];
    else
        theDate += "<OPTION>" + dates[k];
}
String theMonth = "";
len = months.length;
for(k=0; k<len; k++)
{
    if(month.equals(months[k]))
```

```
            theMonth += "<OPTION SELECTED>" + months[k];
        else
            theMonth += "<OPTION>" + months[k];
    }
    String theYear = "";
    len = years.length;
    for(k=0; k<len; k++)
    {
        if(year.equals(years[k]))
            theYear += "<OPTION SELECTED>" + years[k];
        else
            theYear += "<OPTION>" + years[k];
    }

    origPassword = "<INPUT TYPE='hidden' NAME='origPassword' VALUE='" +
        origPassword + "'>";
    String usernameField = username + "<INPUT TYPE='hidden' NAME='username'
        VALUE='" + username + "'>";

    PageUtil p = new PageUtil(pgName, out);
    p.setReplaceItem("<VAR_USERNAME_FIELD>", usernameField);
    p.setReplaceItem("<VAR_PASSWORD>", password);
    p.setReplaceItem("<VAR_CONFIRM_PASSWORD>", pw_confirm);
    p.setReplaceItem("<VAR_FIRST_NAME>", firstName);
    p.setReplaceItem("<VAR_LAST_NAME>", lastName);
    p.setReplaceItem("<VAR_PHONE>", phone);
    p.setReplaceItem("<VAR_FAX>", fax);
    p.setReplaceItem("<VAR_EMAIL>", email);
    p.setReplaceItem("<VAR_SHIP_LINE1>", shipLine1);
    p.setReplaceItem("<VAR_SHIP_LINE2>", shipLine2);
    p.setReplaceItem("<VAR_SHIP_CITY>", shipCity);
    p.setReplaceItem("<VAR_SHIP_STATE>", shipState);
    p.setReplaceItem("<VAR_SHIP_ZIP>", shipZip);

    p.setReplaceItem("<VAR_BILL_LINE1>", billLine1);
    p.setReplaceItem("<VAR_BILL_LINE2>", billLine2);
    p.setReplaceItem("<VAR_BILL_CITY>", billCity);
    p.setReplaceItem("<VAR_BILL_STATE>", billState);
    p.setReplaceItem("<VAR_BILL_ZIP>", billZip);
    p.setReplaceItem("<VAR_CCARD_NUMBER>", ccardNumber);
    p.setReplaceItem("<VAR_CCARD_COMPANY>", company);
    p.setReplaceItem("<VAR_DATE>", theDate);
    p.setReplaceItem("<VAR_MONTH>", theMonth);
    p.setReplaceItem("<VAR_YEAR>", theYear);
    p.setReplaceItem("<VAR_ORIG_PASSWORD>", origPassword);
```

```
            p.setReplaceItem("<VAR_CALLED_FROM>", calledFrom);
            p.printPage();

    }
}

UpdateProfile.java

package Profile;

import java.util.*;
import java.io.*;
import java.sql.*;
import javax.servlet.*;
import javax.servlet.http.*;
import Utilities.*;

public class UpdateProfile extends BaseProfile
{
    ConnectionPool c = null;

    static String errorHtml = BasePath + "profileError.html";
    static String updatedHtml = BasePath + "updated.html";

    public void doPost (HttpServletRequest req,
                        HttpServletResponse res)
    {
      Connection conn = null;
      PrintWriter out = null;
      try{
          HttpSession session;

          String username = "", password="", pw_confirm="";
          String firstName = "", lastName="", phone="";
          String fax = "", email="";
          String shipLine1 = "", shipLine2="";
          String shipCity = "", shipState="", shipZip="";
          String billLine1 = "", billLine2="";
          String billCity = "", billState="", billZip="";
          String ccardNumber = "", ccardCompany="";
          String date="", month="", year="";
          String calledFrom = "", origPassword="";
          if(c == null)
          {
              c = ConnectionPool.getInstance();
              c.initialize();
          }
          conn = c.getConnection();
```

```
Enumeration paramNames = req.getParameterNames();
while(paramNames.hasMoreElements())
{
      String nm = (String)paramNames.nextElement();
      String vl = req.getParameterValues(nm)[0];
      if(nm.equalsIgnoreCase("username"))
          username = vl;
      if(nm.equalsIgnoreCase("password"))
          password = vl;
      if(nm.equalsIgnoreCase("pw_confirm"))
          pw_confirm = vl;
      if(nm.equalsIgnoreCase("firstName"))
          firstName = vl;
      if(nm.equalsIgnoreCase("lastName"))
          lastName = vl;
      if(nm.equalsIgnoreCase("phone"))
          phone = vl;
      if(nm.equalsIgnoreCase("fax"))
          fax = vl;
      if(nm.equalsIgnoreCase("email"))
          email = vl;
      if(nm.equalsIgnoreCase("shipLine1"))
          shipLine1 = vl;
      if(nm.equalsIgnoreCase("shipLine2"))
          shipLine2 = vl;
      if(nm.equalsIgnoreCase("shipCity"))
          shipCity = vl;
      if(nm.equalsIgnoreCase("shipState"))
          shipState = vl;
      if(nm.equalsIgnoreCase("shipZip"))
          shipZip = vl;
      if(nm.equalsIgnoreCase("billLine1"))
          billLine1 = vl;
      if(nm.equalsIgnoreCase("billLine2"))
          billLine2 = vl;
      if(nm.equalsIgnoreCase("billCity"))
          billCity = vl;
      if(nm.equalsIgnoreCase("billState"))
          billState = vl;
      if(nm.equalsIgnoreCase("billZip"))
          billZip = vl;
      if(nm.equalsIgnoreCase("ccardNumber"))
          ccardNumber = vl;
      if(nm.equalsIgnoreCase("ccardCompany"))
```

```
                      ccardCompany = v1;
                if(nm.equalsIgnoreCase("date"))
                    date = v1;
                if(nm.equalsIgnoreCase("month"))
                    month = v1;
                if(nm.equalsIgnoreCase("year"))
                    year = v1;
                if(nm.equalsIgnoreCase("calledFrom"))
                    calledFrom = v1;
                if(nm.equalsIgnoreCase("origPassword"))
                    origPassword = v1;
        }
        out = res.getWriter();
        res.setContentType("text/html");
        if( dataError(out,
                username,password, pw_confirm,
                firstName, lastName, phone,
                fax, email, shipLine1, shipLine2,
                shipCity, shipState, shipZip,
                billLine1, billLine2, billCity, billState, billZip,
                ccardNumber, ccardCompany, date, month, year, calledFrom,
                errorHtml
                ) == true)
        {
            c.putConnection(conn);
            out.close();
            return;
        }


        updateUser(out, username,password, pw_confirm, origPassword,
                firstName, lastName, phone,
                fax, email, shipLine1, shipLine2,
                shipCity, shipState, shipZip,
                billLine1, billLine2, billCity, billState, billZip,
                ccardNumber, ccardCompany, date, month, year, calledFrom,
                updatedHtml, errorHtml, conn);
        c.putConnection(conn);
        out.close();
}catch(Exception ex)
 {
        if(c != null && conn != null)
            c.putConnection(conn);
        showErrorPage(out, errorHtml, ex.getMessage());
   }
```

```
        }
        public boolean dataError(PrintWriter out,
                      String username, String password,  String pw_confirm,
                      String firstName,  String lastName,  String phone,
                      String fax,  String email,  String shipLine1,
                      String shipLine2, String shipCity,  String shipState,
                      String shipZip, String billLine1,  String billLine2,
                      String billCity,  String billState,  String billZip,
                      String ccardNumber,  String ccardCompany,  String date,
                      String month,  String year,  String calledFrom,
                      String pgName)
        {
            boolean error = false;
            String errorMsg = "";
            if(username.length() < 4)
            {
                error = true;
                errorMsg += "<LI>Username should be at least 4 characters";
            }
            if(password.equals(pw_confirm) == false)
            {
                error = true;
                errorMsg += "<LI>Password does not match confirm";
            }
            if(firstName.length() == 0)
            {
                error = true;
                errorMsg += "<LI>First name not specified";
            }
            if(lastName.length() == 0)
            {
                error = true;
                errorMsg += "<LI>Last name not specified";
            }
            if(ccardNumber.length() == 0)
            {
                error = true;
                errorMsg += "<LI>Credit Card Number not specified";
            }
            int ln = ccardNumber.length();
            for(int i=0; i<ln; i++)
            {
                char c = ccardNumber.charAt(i);
                if(c < '0' || c > '9')
```

```java
            {
                error = true;
                errorMsg += "<LI>Invalid Credit Card Number";
            }
        }
        if(error == true)
        {
            PageUtil p = new PageUtil(pgName, out);
            p.setReplaceItem("<VAR_ERROR_MSG>", errorMsg);
        }
        return error;
    }

    public void updateUser(PrintWriter out, String username,
                String password,  String pw_confirm, String origPassword,
                String firstName,  String lastName,  String phone,
                String fax,  String email,  String shipLine1,
                String shipLine2, String shipCity,  String shipState,
                String shipZip, String billLine1,  String billLine2,
                String billCity,  String billState,  String billZip,
                String ccardNumber,  String ccardCompany,  String date,
                String month,  String year,  String calledFrom,
                String pgName, String errorHtml, Connection conn)
        throws Exception
    {
        boolean error = false;
        String errorMsg = "";
        String storedPassword = "";
        try
        {
            conn.setAutoCommit(false);
            Statement stmt = conn.createStatement();
            String querySQL = "SELECT id,password FROM profiles
                    WHERE username='" + username + "'";
            ResultSet rset = stmt.executeQuery(querySQL);
            boolean foundRecord = false;
            String id = "";
            while(rset.next())
            {
                foundRecord = true;
                id = rset.getString(1);
                storedPassword = rset.getString(2);
            }

            if(foundRecord == false)
```

```
        {
            error = true;
            errorMsg = "Username does not exist. Please go to registration
                page";
        }
        else
        {
            if(storedPassword.equals(password) == false)
            {
                error = true;
                errorMsg = "The password you entered does not match your
                    profile. Please go back and try again";
            }
            else
            {
                    String updateSQL = "UPDATE profiles SET
                        password='" + password + "', first_name='" +
                        firstName + "', last_name='" + lastName + "',
                        phone='" + phone + "', fax='" + fax + "',
                        email='" + email + "', ccard_num='" + ccardNumber
                            + "', ccard_exp_date=TO_DATE('" + date + "-" +
                        month + "-" + year + "', 'DD-MON-YYYY'),
                        ccard_company='" + ccardCompany + "',
                        status='UPDATED_USER' WHERE id = " + id;
                    stmt.executeUpdate(updateSQL);
            }
        }
        if(error == false)
        {
            String updateSQL = "UPDATE addresses SET line1='" +
                shipLine1 + "', line2='" + shipLine2  + "', city='" +
                shipCity + "', state='" + shipState + "', zip='" +
                shipZip + "'
                WHERE profile_id=" + id + " AND type='SHIPPING'";
            stmt.executeUpdate(updateSQL);

            updateSQL = "UPDATE addresses SET line1='" + billLine1 +
                "', line2='" + billLine2  + "', city='" + billCity +
                "', state='" + billState + "', zip='" + billZip + "'
                WHERE profile_id=" + id + " AND type='BILLING'";
            stmt.executeUpdate(updateSQL);

        }
        conn.commit();
        conn.setAutoCommit(true);
```

```
                stmt.close();
        }catch(SQLException ex){error = true; errorMsg=ex.getMessage();}
        if(error)
        {
            PageUtil p = new PageUtil(errorHtml, out);
            p.setReplaceItem("<VAR_ERROR_MSG>", errorMsg);
            p.printPage();
        }
        else
        {
            PageUtil p = new PageUtil(pgName, out);
            String submit = "";
            if(calledFrom.equalsIgnoreCase("GetPayment"))
                submit = "<BR>You may now proceed your payment<BR>
                    <INPUT TYPE='submit' NAME='submit' VALUE='Pay'>";

            p.setReplaceItem("<VAR_SUBMIT>", submit);
            p.printPage();
        }
    }
}
```

Document Root Html Files

contactUs.html

```
<HTML><HEAD></HEAD>
<BODY BGCOLOR='#FFFFFF'>
    <FORM ACTION='/newZone/Profile.ContactUs' METHOD='POST'>
    <TABLE>
    <TR><TD WIDTH='350'>
        You can use this form to send us your queries. But before you do so, it
might be a good idea to read our list of <BR><A HREF='/faq.html'>Frequently Asked
Questions</A>
    </TD></TR>
    <TR><TD>
        <TABLE>
            <TR><TD>Username</TD><TD><INPUT TYPE='text' SIZE='8' NAME='username'
VALUE=''></TD></TR>
            <TR><TD>Email</TD><TD><INPUT TYPE='text' SIZE='8' NAME='email'
VALUE=''></TD></TR>
            <TR><TD>Category</TD><TD>
                <SELECT NAME='category'>
                    <OPTION VALUE='registrationProblem'>Registration Problem
                    <OPTION VALUE='orderingProblem'>Ordering Problem
                    <OPTION VALUE='generalQuestion'>General Question
```

```
                        </SELECT>
                    </TD></TR>
            </TABLE>
        </TD></TR>
        <TR><TD
Brief description<BR>
<TEXTAREA NAME='description' ROWS='8' COLS='60'>
</TEXTAREA
        </TD></TR>
        <TR><TD ALIGN='right'>
            <INPUT TYPE='submit' NAME='submit' VALUE='Submit'>
        </TD></TR>
    </TABLE>
    </FORM>
</BODY>
</HTML>


ordering.html

<HTML><HEAD></HEAD>
<SCRIPT>
    var newUser = false;
    var windowUp = false;
    var lastCount = 0;
    regularCartIds = new Array();
    regularCartQuantities = new Array();
    regularCartNames = new Array();
    regularCartPrices = new Array();

    purchasedIds = new Array();
    purchasedQuantities = new Array();
    purchasedNames = new Array();
    purchasedPrices = new Array();
    var cw;
    function showOrderHistory(frm)
    {
        right.location.replace('/newZone/Ordering.SelectOrder');
        return false;
    }
    function search(frm)
    {
        right.location.replace(
         '/newZone/Ordering.SearchProducts?searchList=' + frm.searchList.value);
        return false;
```

```
}
function cartRefresh()
{
      if(windowUp)
          cw.location.reload();
}
function getCategories()
{
     right.location.replace("/newZone/Ordering.GetCategories");
     return false;
}
function showRegister()
{
     right.location.replace("HTTP_VALUE/newZone/Profile.RegistrationPage");
     return false;
}
function showUpdate()
{
     right.location.replace("HTTP_VALUE/updateProfile.html");
     return false;
}
function showContactUs()
{
     right.location.replace("HTTP_VALUE/contactUs.html");
     return false;
}
function showPasswordFinder()
{
     right.location.replace("HTTP_VALUE/passwordFinder.html");
     return false;
}

function showLogin()
{
     right.location.replace("mainOrdering.html");
     return false;
}
function checkout()
{
     right.location.replace("checkout.html");
     return false;
}
function regularCart()
```

```
    {
        right.location.replace("regularCart.html");
        return false;
    }
    function showCart()
    {
        windowUp = true;
        cw = window.open("/showCart.html", "cartWindow", "toolbar=no,

directories=no,menubar=no,location=no,scrollbars=yes,width=450,height=400");
    }
</SCRIPT>
    <FRAMESET ROWS='60,*' BORDER='0'>
        <FRAME NAME='top' SRC='profileOptions.html'>
        <FRAMESET COLS='180, *' BORDER='0'>
            <FRAME NAME='left' SRC='blank.html'>
            <FRAME NAME='right' SRC='mainOrdering.html'>
        </FRAMESET>
    </FRAMESET>
<BODY BGCOLOR='#FFFFFF'>
</BODY>
</HTML>

passwordFinder.html

<HTML><HEAD></HEAD>
<BODY BGCOLOR='#FFFFFF'>
  <FORM ACTION='/newZone/Profile.PasswordFinder' METHOD='POST'>
  <TABLE>
   <TR><TD WIDTH='450'>
        Using this utility you can find out your password. You will need to pro-
vide some basic information for this to work. This includes your username, email
address and last name. These are required to verify your validity.
     </TD></TR>
  </TABLE>
  <TABLE>
    <TR><TD>
      <TABLE>
        <TR><TD>Username</TD><TD><INPUT TYPE='text' NAME='username' SIZE='15'
VALUE=''></TD></TR>
        <TR><TD>Last Name</TD><TD><INPUT TYPE='text' NAME='lastName' SIZE='15'
VALUE=''></TD></TR>
        <TR><TD>Email</TD><TD><INPUT TYPE='text' NAME='email' SIZE='15'
VALUE=''></TD></TR>
```

```
            </TABLE>
        </TD></TR>
        <TR><TD ALIGN='right'>
            <INPUT TYPE='submit' NAME='submit' VALUE='Submit'>
        </TD></TR>
    </TABLE>
    </FORM>
</BODY>
</HTML>
```

profileOptions.html

```
<HTML><HEAD></HEAD>
<BODY BGCOLOR='#000000'>
  <FORM>
      <INPUT TYPE='button' NAME='login' VALUE='Login'
        onClick='parent.showLogin();'>    
      <INPUT TYPE='button' NAME='register' VALUE='Register'
         onClick='parent.showRegister();'>    
      <INPUT TYPE='button' NAME='update' VALUE='Update'
        onClick='parent.showUpdate();'>    
      <INPUT TYPE='button' NAME='contactUs' VALUE='Contact  Us'
        onClick='parent.showContactUs();'>    
      <INPUT TYPE='button' NAME='passwordFinder' VALUE='Password Finder'
        onClick='parent.showPasswordFinder();'>    
  </FORM>
</BODY></HTML>
```

updateProfile.html

```
<HTML><HEAD></HEAD>
<BODY BGCOLOR='#FFFFFF'>
    <FORM ACTION='/newZone/Profile.UpdatePage' METHOD='POST'>
    <TABLE>
        <TR><TD WIDTH='450'>
    Please enter your username and password.
        </TD></TR>
        <TR><TD> <INPUT TYPE='username' NAME='username' VALUE=''></TD></TR>
        <TR><TD> <INPUT TYPE='password' NAME='password' VALUE=''></TD></TR>
        <TR><TD ALIGN='right'> <INPUT TYPE='submit' NAME='submit' VALUE='SUBMIT'>
</TD></TR>
    </TABLE>
  </FORM>
</BODY>
</HTML>
```

Other Html Files and Templates

contactMailSent.html

```
<HTML><HEAD></HEAD>
<BODY BGCOLOR='#FFFFFF'>
  <TABLE>
     <TR><TD WIDTH='400'>
The following mail message has been sent from user
<B>
<VAR_USERNAME>
</B>
at email address <B>
<VAR_EMAIL>
</B> to <B>
<VAR_MAIL_TO>
</B>:
<PRE>

</PRE>
     <TABLE BGCOLOR='#CCCCCC'>
            <TR BGCOLOR='#CCCCCC'><TD>
<VAR_DESCRIPTION>
            </TD></TR>
     </TABLE>
<PRE>

</PRE>
Thanks for contacting us. We will try to get back to you at the earliest.
     </TD></TR>
  </TABLE>
</BODY>
</HTML>
```

getNewCard.html

```
<HTML><HEAD></HEAD>
<BODY BGCOLOR='#FFFFFF'>
   <FORM ACTION='Profile.UpdatePage' METHOD='POST'>
<VAR_USERNAME>
<VAR_CALLED_FROM>
   <TABLE>
     <TR><TD WIDTH='450'>
   Please enter your password. In the next page you will get to specify your new
card. You can also change other things in your profile in that page like your
shipping address.
        </TD><TD></TD></TR>
```

```
      <TR><TD> <INPUT TYPE='password' NAME='password' VALUE=''>
        </TD><TD> <INPUT TYPE='submit' NAME='submit' VALUE='SUBMIT'>
      </TD></TR>
  </TABLE>
 </FORM>
</BODY>
</HTML>
```

profileError.html

```
<HTML><HEAD></HEAD>
<BODY BGCOLOR='#FFFFFF'>
<H1><CENTER><B>Error!</B></CENTER></H1>
<P>
The following error occured:
<P>
<ERROR_MSG>
<P>
</BODY>
</HTML>
```

registered.html

```
<HTML><HEAD></HEAD>
<BODY BGCOLOR='#FFFFFF'>
    Thanks for registering!<BR>
<FORM ACTION='HTTP_VALUE/newZone/Ordering.GetPayment' METHOD='POST'>
<VAR_SUBMIT>
</FORM>
</BODY>
</HTML>
```

registrationPage.html

```
<HTML><HEAD></HEAD>
<SCRIPT>
function copyBillingAddress(frm)
{
    if(frm.copy.checked == true)
    {
            frm.billLine1.value = frm.shipLine1.value;
            frm.billLine2.value = frm.shipLine2.value;
            frm.billCity.value = frm.shipCity.value;
            frm.billState.value = frm.shipState.value;
            frm.billZip.value = frm.shipZip.value;
    }
}
```

```
function verify(frm)
{
    alertMsg = "";
    if(frm.password.value != frm.pw_confirm.value)
        alertMsg += "\nPassword and Confirm do not match";
    if(frm.username.value.length < 4)
        alertMsg += "\nUsername should be at least 4 characters";
    if(frm.firstName.value.length == 0)
        alertMsg += "\nPlease specify first name";
    if(frm.lastName.value.length == 0)
        alertMsg += "\nPlease specify last name";
    len = frm.ccardNumber.value.length;
    for(i=0; i<len; i++)
    {
        c = frm.ccardNumber.value.charAt(i);
        if(c < '0' || c > '9')
        {
            alertMsg += "\nInvalid Credit Card Number";
            break;
        }
    }
    if(alertMsg != "")
    {
        alertMsg = "The following errors occured:\n" + alertMsg;
        alert(alertMsg);
        return false;
    }
    else
        return true;
}

</SCRIPT>
<BODY BGCOLOR='#FFFFFF'>
<FORM ACTION='Profile.Register' METHOD='POST' onSubmit='return verify(this);'>
<VAR_CALLED_FROM>
<VAR_NEW_USER>
 <TABLE>
  <B>Profile Information</B>
  <TR><TD>
   <TABLE>
        <TR><TD ALIGN='right'>Username</TD><TD>
<VAR_USERNAME_FIELD>
        </TD><TD></TD><TD></TD></TR>
```

```
        <TR><TD ALIGN='right'>Password</TD><TD><INPUT TYPE='password' NAME='pass
            word' VALUE='' SIZE='10'>
        </TD><TD ALIGN='right'>Confirm Password</TD><TD><INPUT TYPE='password'
            NAME='pw_confirm' VALUE='' SIZE='10'>
        </TD></TR>
    </TABLE>
<HR>
<B>Contact Information</BBR>
<TABLE>
        <TR><TD ALIGN='right'>First Name</TD><TD><INPUT TYPE='text'
            NAME='firstName' VALUE='' SIZE='20'>
        </TD><TD ALIGN='right'>Last Name</TD><TD><INPUT TYPE='text'
            NAME='lastName' VALUE='' SIZE='20'>
        </TD></TR>
    <TR><TD>Phone</TD><TD><INPUT TYPE='text' NAME='phone' SIZE='20'></TD>
        <TD>Fax</TD><TD><INPUT TYPE='text' NAME='fax' SIZE='20'></TD></TR>
    <TR><TD>Email</TD><TD><INPUT TYPE='text' NAME='email' SIZE='20'></TD>
        <TD></TD></TR>
</TABLE>
<TABLE><TR><TD WIDTH='100'>Shipping Address</TD></TR>
    <TR><TD></TD><TD>Line 1</TD><TD COLSPAN='3'><INPUT TYPE='text'
        NAME='shipLine1' SIZE='30'></TD><TD></TD></TR>
    <TR><TD></TD><TD>Line 2</TD><TD COLSPAN='3'><INPUT TYPE='text'
        NAME='shipLine2' SIZE='30'></TD><TD></TD></TR>
    <TR><TD></TD><TD>City</TD><TD><INPUT TYPE='text' NAME='shipCity'
      SIZE='12'></TD><TD>State</TD><TD><INPUT TYPE='text'
      NAME='shipState' SIZE='2'></TD><TD>Zip</TD>
        <TD><INPUT TYPE='text' NAME='shipZip' SIZE='5'></TD></TR>
</TABLE>
<HR>
<B>Billing Information</BBR>
<TABLE><TR><TD WIDTH='100'>Billing Address</TD></TR>
<TR><TD></TD><TD COLSPAN='3'><INPUT TYPE='checkbox' NAME='copy'
      VALUE='' onClick='copyBillingAddress(this.form);'>
      Copy from Shipping Address</TD></TR>
    <TR><TD></TD><TD>Line 1</TD><TD COLSPAN='3'><INPUT TYPE='text'
        NAME='billLine1' SIZE='30'></TD><TD></TD></TR>
    <TR><TD></TD><TD>Line 2</TD><TD COLSPAN='3'><INPUT TYPE='text'
        NAME='billLine2' SIZE='30'></TD><TD></TD></TR>
    <TR><TD></TD><TD>City</TD><TD><INPUT TYPE='text'
        NAME='billCity' SIZE='12'></TD><TD>State</TD>
        <TD><INPUT TYPE='text' NAME='billState' SIZE='2'></TD>
        <TD>Zip</TD><TD><INPUT TYPE='text' NAME='billZip' SIZE='5'></TD></TR>
</TABLE>
```

```
<TABLE><TR><TD>Credit Card</TD></TR>
    <TR><TD></TD><TD>
        <TABLE>
            <TR><TD>Credit Card Number</TD><TD><INPUT TYPE='text'
            NAME='ccardNumber' SIZE='12'></TD><TD>Credit Card Company</TD><TD>
                <SELECT NAME='ccardCompany'>
                    <OPTION>Visa
                    <OPTION>MasterCard
                </SELECT>
                </TD></TR>
        </TABLE></TD></TR>
    <TR><TD></TD><TD>
        <TABLE>
                <TD>Expiration Date</TD>
                <TD>
                  <SELECT NAME='date'>
                    <OPTION>01<OPTION>02<OPTION>03<OPTION>04<OPTION>05
                    <OPTION>06<OPTION>07<OPTION>08<OPTION>09<OPTION>10
                    <OPTION>11<OPTION>12<OPTION>13<OPTION>14<OPTION>15
                    <OPTION>16<OPTION>17<OPTION>18<OPTION>19<OPTION>20
                    <OPTION>21<OPTION>22<OPTION>23<OPTION>24<OPTION>25
                    <OPTION>26<OPTION>27<OPTION>28<OPTION>29<OPTION>30
                    <OPTION>31
                  </SELECT>
                </TD>
                <TD>
                    <SELECT NAME='month'>
                        <OPTION>Jan<OPTION>Feb<OPTION>Mar<OPTION>Apr
                        <OPTION>May<OPTION>Jun<OPTION>Jul<OPTION>Aug
                        <OPTION>Sep<OPTION>Oct<OPTION>Nov<OPTION>Dec
                    </SELECT>.
                </TD>
                <TD>
                    <SELECT NAME='year'>
                        <OPTION>1999<OPTION>2000<OPTION>2001<OPTION>2002
                        <OPTION>2003<OPTION>2004<OPTION>2005<OPTION>2006
                    </SELECT>
        </TABLE>
    </TD></TR>
</TABLE>
</TD></TR>
<TR><TD ALIGN='right'><INPUT TYPE='submit' NAME='submit' VALUE='Submit'>
    </TD></TR>
</TABLE>
```

```
</FORM>
</BODY>
</HTML>
```

showPassword.html

```
<HTML><HEAD></HEAD>
<BODY BGCOLOR='#FFFFFF'>
    <CENTER><H1>Password Found!</H1></CENTER><BR>
Your password has been located in the database as:<BR>
<VAR_PASSWORD>
</BODY>
</HTML>
```

updatePage.html

```
<HTML><HEAD></HEAD>
<SCRIPT>
function copyBillingAddress(frm)
{
    if(frm.copy.checked == true)
    {
            frm.billLine1.value = frm.shipLine1.value;
            frm.billLine2.value = frm.shipLine2.value;
            frm.billCity.value = frm.shipCity.value;
            frm.billState.value = frm.shipState.value;
            frm.billZip.value = frm.shipZip.value;
    }
}
function verify(frm)
{
    alertMsg = "";
    if(frm.password.value != frm.pw_confirm.value)
        alertMsg += "\nPassword and Confirm do not match";
    if(frm.username.value.length < 4)
        alertMsg += "\nUsername should be at least 4 characters";
    if(frm.firstName.value.length == 0)
        alertMsg += "\nPlease specify first name";
    if(frm.lastName.value.length == 0)
        alertMsg += "\nPlease specify last name";
    len = frm.ccardNumber.value.length;
    for(i=0; i<len; i++)
    {
        c = frm.ccardNumber.value.charAt(i);
        if(c < '0' || c > '9')
        {
```

```
                    alertMsg += "\nInvalid Credit Card Number";
                    break;
            }
        }
        if(alertMsg != "")
        {
            alertMsg = "The following errors occured:\n" + alertMsg;
            alert(alertMsg);
            return false;
        }
        else
            return true;
}


</SCRIPT>
<BODY BGCOLOR='#FFFFFF'>
<FORM ACTION='Profile.UpdateProfile' METHOD='POST' onSubmit='return verify(this);'>
<VAR_CALLED_FROM>
<VAR_ORIG_PASSWORD>
 <TABLE>
  <B>Profile Information</B>
  <TR><TD>
   <TABLE>
        <TR><TD ALIGN='right'>Username</TD><TD>
<VAR_USERNAME_FIELD>
        </TD><TD></TD><TD></TD></TR>
        <TR><TD ALIGN='right'>Password</TD><TD>
<VAR_PASSWORD>
        </TD><TD ALIGN='right'>Confirm Password</TD><TD>
<VAR_CONFIRM_PASSWORD>
        </TD></TR>
    </TABLE>
  <HR>
  <B>Contact Information</BBR>
  <TABLE>
        <TR><TD ALIGN='right'>First Name</TD><TD>
<VAR_FIRST_NAME>
        </TD><TD ALIGN='right'>Last Name</TD><TD>
<VAR_LAST_NAME>
        </TD></TR>
        <TR><TD>Phone</TD><TD>
<VAR_PHONE>
        </TD><TD>Fax</TD><TD>
<VAR_FAX>
```

```
            </TD></TR>
            <TR><TD>Email</TD><TD>
<VAR_EMAIL>
           </TD><TD></TD></TR>
  </TABLE>
  <TABLE><TR><TD WIDTH='100'>Shipping Address</TD></TR>
        <TR><TD></TD><TD>Line 1</TD><TD COLSPAN='3'>
<VAR_SHIP_LINE1>
           </TD><TD></TD></TR>
        <TR><TD></TD><TD>Line 2</TD><TD COLSPAN='3'>
<VAR_SHIP_LINE2>
         </TD><TD></TD></TR>
        <TR><TD></TD><TD>City</TD><TD>
<VAR_SHIP_CITY>
          </TD><TD>State</TD><TD>
<VAR_SHIP_STATE>
          </TD><TD>Zip</TD><TD>
<VAR_SHIP_ZIP>
          </TD></TR>
  </TABLE>
  <HR>
  <B>Billing Information</BBR>
  <TABLE><TR><TD WIDTH='100'>Billing Address</TD></TR>
  <TR><TD></TD>
      <TD COLSPAN='3'><INPUT TYPE='checkbox' NAME='copy' VALUE=''
          onClick='copyBillingAddress(this.form);'>
          Copy from Shipping Address</TD></TR>
        <TR><TD></TD><TD>Line 1</TD><TD COLSPAN='3'>
<VAR_BILL_LINE1>
         </TD><TD></TD></TR>
        <TR><TD></TD><TD>Line 2</TD><TD COLSPAN='3'>
<VAR_BILL_LINE2>
         </TD><TD></TD></TR>
        <TR><TD></TD><TD>City</TD><TD>
<VAR_BILL_CITY>
         </TD><TD>State</TD><TD>
<VAR_BILL_STATE>
         </TD><TD>Zip</TD><TD>
<VAR_BILL_ZIP>
         </TD></TR>
  </TABLE>
  <TABLE><TR><TD>Credit Card</TD></TR>
      <TR><TD></TD><TD>
            <TABLE>
```

```
                <TR><TD>Credit Card Number</TD><TD>
<VAR_CCARD_NUMBER>
                </TD><TD>Credit Card Company</TD><TD>
                    <SELECT NAME='ccardCompany'>
<VAR_CCARD_COMPANY>
                    </SELECT>
                    </TD></TR>
            </TABLE></TD></TR>
        <TR><TD></TD><TD>
            <TABLE>
                    <TD>Expiration Date</TD>
                    <TD>
                        <SELECT NAME='date'>
<VAR_DATE>
                        </SELECT>
                    </TD>
                    <TD>
                        <SELECT NAME='month'>
<VAR_MONTH>
                        </SELECT>
                    </TD>
                    <TD>
                        <SELECT NAME='year'>
<VAR_YEAR>
                        </SELECT>
            </TABLE>
        </TD></TR>
    </TABLE>
    </TD></TR>
    <TR><TD ALIGN='right'><INPUT TYPE='submit' NAME='submit' VALUE='Submit'>
        </TD></TR>
</TABLE>
</FORM>
</BODY>
</HTML>

updated.html

<HTML><HEAD></HEAD>
<BODY BGCOLOR='#FFFFFF'>
    Thanks for updating your profile!<BR>
<FORM ACTION='HTTP_VALUE/newZone/Ordering.GetPayment' METHOD='POST'>
<VAR_SUBMIT>
</FORM>
```

```
</BODY>
</HTML>
```

Shipping Management System

Java Files

BaseShipping.java

```
package Shipping;

import java.util.*;
import java.io.*;
import java.sql.*;
import javax.servlet.*;
import javax.servlet.http.*;
import Utilities.*;

public class BaseShipping extends HttpServlet
{
    static String BasePath = "HTML_DIRECTORY";
    static boolean debugOn = true;

    public boolean validPassword(String username, String password,
                String errorHtml, ConnectionPool c, Connection conn,
                PrintWriter out)
    {
        boolean isValid = true;
        if(username == null || password == null)
            isValid = false;
        Authenticator a = new Authenticator();
        if(a.isValidAdmin(username, password, conn) == false)
            isValid = false;
        if(isValid == false)
        {
            c.putConnection(conn);
            showErrorPage(out, errorHtml, "Invalid Username/Password");
            return false;
        }
        else
            return true;
    }

    public void showErrorPage(PrintWriter out, String pgName, String value)
    {
```

```
            PageUtil p = new PageUtil(pgName, out);    .
            p.setReplaceItem("<ERROR_MSG>", value);
            p.printPage();
    }

    public PrintStream initializeDebugFile(String s)
    {
        PrintStream pos = null;
        try
        {
            if(debugOn == false)
                return null;
            pos = new PrintStream(new FileOutputStream(new File(s)));
        }catch(Exception ex){}
        return pos;
    }
    public void debug(String s, PrintStream pos)
    {
        try
        {
            if(debugOn == false)
                return;
            pos.println(s);
        }catch(Exception ex){}
    }
}

ModifyOrders.java

package Shipping;

import java.util.*;
import java.io.*;
import java.sql.*;
import javax.servlet.*;
import javax.servlet.http.*;
import Utilities.*;

public class ModifyOrders extends BaseShipping
{
    ConnectionPool c = null;

    static String errorHtml = BasePath + "shippingError.html";
    static String updatedHtml = BasePath + "shippingOrderUpdated.html";
    public void doPost (HttpServletRequest req,
                        HttpServletResponse res)
    {
```

```
Connection conn = null;
PrintWriter out = null;
try{
    HttpSession session;
    String shipMethod="", dateShipped="", status="";
    Vector orderIds = new Vector();
    if(c == null)
    {
        c = ConnectionPool.getInstance();
        c.initialize();
    }
    conn = c.getConnection();
    Enumeration paramNames = req.getParameterNames();
    while(paramNames.hasMoreElements())
    {
        String nm = (String)paramNames.nextElement();
        if(nm.equalsIgnoreCase("orderIds"))
        {
            String[] allVals = req.getParameterValues(nm);
            int len = allVals.length;
            for(int k=0; k<len; k++)
                orderIds.addElement(allVals[k]);
        }
        String v1 = req.getParameterValues(nm)[0];
        if(nm.equalsIgnoreCase("shipMethod"))
            shipMethod = v1;
        if(nm.equalsIgnoreCase("dateShipped"))
            dateShipped = v1;
        if(nm.equalsIgnoreCase("status"))
            status = v1;
    }
    out = res.getWriter();
    res.setContentType("text/html");
    session = req.getSession(false);
    if(session == null)
    {
        showErrorPage(out, errorHtml, "Invalid Session");
        return;
    }
    updateShipOrder(out, orderIds, dateShipped, shipMethod, status,
        updatedHtml, conn);
    c.putConnection(conn);
    out.close();
}catch(Exception ex)
```

```
            {
                if(c != null && conn != null)
                    c.putConnection(conn);
                showErrorPage(out, errorHtml, ex.getMessage());
            }
        }
        public void updateShipOrder(PrintWriter out, Vector orderIds,
                    String dateShipped, String shipMethod, String status,
                    String pgName, Connection conn)
            throws Exception
        {

            Statement stmt = conn.createStatement();
            String querySQLbase = "UPDATE orders SET date_shipped=
              TO_DATE('" + dateShipped + "', 'DD-MON-YYYY'),
              shipment_method='" + shipMethod + "', status='" + status +
              "' WHERE id=";
            int len = orderIds.size();
            String querySQL;
            for(int i=0; i<len; i++)
            {
                querySQL = querySQLbase + (String)orderIds.elementAt(i);
                stmt.executeUpdate(querySQL);
            }
            PageUtil pu = new PageUtil(pgName, out);
            pu.printPage();
        }
    }
}


ModifyShippingOrder.java

package Shipping;

import java.util.*;
import java.io.*;
import java.sql.*;
import javax.servlet.*;
import javax.servlet.http.*;
import Utilities.*;

public class ModifyShippingOrder extends BaseShipping
{
    ConnectionPool c = null;

    static String errorHtml = BasePath + "shippingError.html";
    static String updatedHtml = BasePath + "shippingOrderUpdated.html";
```

```java
public void doPost (HttpServletRequest req,
                    HttpServletResponse res)
{
  Connection conn = null;
  PrintWriter out = null;
  try{
      HttpSession session;
      String orderId = "", shipMethod="", dateShipped="", status="";
      if(c == null)
      {
          c = ConnectionPool.getInstance();
          c.initialize();
      }
      conn = c.getConnection();
      Enumeration paramNames = req.getParameterNames();
      while(paramNames.hasMoreElements())
      {
          String nm = (String)paramNames.nextElement();
          String v1 = req.getParameterValues(nm)[0];
          if(nm.equalsIgnoreCase("orderId"))
              orderId = v1;
          if(nm.equalsIgnoreCase("shipMethod"))
              shipMethod = v1;
          if(nm.equalsIgnoreCase("dateShipped"))
              dateShipped = v1;
          if(nm.equalsIgnoreCase("status"))
              status = v1;
      }
      out = res.getWriter();
      res.setContentType("text/html");
      session = req.getSession(false);
      if(session == null)
      {
          showErrorPage(out, errorHtml, "Invalid Session");
          return;
      }
      updateShipOrder(out, orderId, dateShipped, shipMethod, status,
          updatedHtml, conn);
      c.putConnection(conn);
      out.close();
  }catch(Exception ex)
      {
          if(c != null && conn != null)
```

```
                c.putConnection(conn);
            showErrorPage(out, errorHtml, ex.getMessage());
        }
    }
    public void updateShipOrder(PrintWriter out, String orderId,
                String dateShipped, String shipMethod, String status,
                String pgName, Connection conn)
        throws Exception
    {
        Statement stmt = conn.createStatement();
        String querySQL = "UPDATE orders SET date_shipped=
            TO_DATE('" + dateShipped + "', 'DD-MON-YYYY'),
            shipment_method='" + shipMethod + "', status='" + status +
            "' WHERE id=" + orderId;
        stmt.executeUpdate(querySQL);
        PageUtil pu = new PageUtil(pgName, out);
        pu.printPage();
    }
}

SelectShippingOrders.java

package Shipping;

import java.util.*;
import java.io.*;
import java.sql.*;
import javax.servlet.*;
import javax.servlet.http.*;
import Utilities.*;

public class SelectShippingOrders extends BaseShipping
{
    ConnectionPool c = null;

    static String errorHtml = BasePath + "orderingError.html";
    static String selectOrderPage = BasePath + "selectShippingOrders.html";

    public void doGet (HttpServletRequest req,
                       HttpServletResponse res)
    {
      Connection conn = null;
      PrintWriter out = null;
      try{
          HttpSession session;
          String  type="";
          if(c == null)
```

```
        {
            c = ConnectionPool.getInstance();
            c.initialize();
        }
        conn = c.getConnection();
        Enumeration paramNames = req.getParameterNames();
        while(paramNames.hasMoreElements())
        {
            String nm = (String)paramNames.nextElement();
            String vl = req.getParameterValues(nm)[0];
            if(nm.equalsIgnoreCase("type"))
                type = vl;
        }
        out = res.getWriter();
        res.setContentType("text/html");
        session = req.getSession(false);
        if(session == null)
        {
            showErrorPage(out, errorHtml, "Invalid Session");
            return;
        }
        showSelectShippingOrdersPage(selectOrderPage, type, conn, out);
        c.putConnection(conn);
        out.close();
    }catch(Exception ex)
        {
            if(c != null && conn != null)
                c.putConnection(conn);
            showErrorPage(out, errorHtml, ex.getMessage());
        }
}
public void showSelectShippingOrdersPage(String pgName, String type,
            Connection conn, PrintWriter out)
        throws Exception
{
        Statement stmt = conn.createStatement();
        String profileId = "";
        String querySQL = "SELECT id,
                TO_CHAR(date_ordered, 'DD-MON-YYYY') FROM orders";
        if(type.equalsIgnoreCase("unshipped"))
                querySQL = querySQL + " WHERE date_shipped IS NULL";
        ResultSet rset = stmt.executeQuery(querySQL);
        String orderIdOptions = "";
        while(rset.next())
```

```
        {
            String orderId = rset.getString(1);
            String date_ordered = rset.getString(2);
            orderIdOptions += "<OPTION VALUE='" + orderId + "'>" +
                orderId + " : " + date_ordered;
        }
        stmt.close();
        PageUtil pu = new PageUtil(pgName, out);
        pu.setReplaceItem("<VAR_ORDER_OPTIONS>", orderIdOptions);
        pu.printPage();

    }
}

ShippingLogin.java

package Shipping;

import java.util.*;
import java.io.*;
import java.sql.*;
import javax.servlet.*;
import javax.servlet.http.*;
import Utilities.*;

public class ShippingLogin extends BaseShipping
{
    ConnectionPool c = null;
    static String shippingOptionsHtml = BasePath + "shippingOptions.html";
    static String errorHtml = BasePath + "shippingError.html";

    public void doPost (HttpServletRequest req,
                        HttpServletResponse res)
    {
      Connection conn = null;
      PrintWriter out=null;
      try{
          HttpSession session;

          String username="", password="";
          if(c == null)
          {
              c = ConnectionPool.getInstance();
              c.initialize();
          }
          conn = c.getConnection();
          Enumeration paramNames = req.getParameterNames();
          while(paramNames.hasMoreElements())
```

```
            {
                String nm = (String)paramNames.nextElement();
                String vl = req.getParameterValues(nm)[0];
                if(nm.equalsIgnoreCase("username"))
                    username = vl;
                if(nm.equalsIgnoreCase("password"))
                    password = vl;
            }
            out = res.getWriter();
            res.setContentType("text/html");
            if(validPassword(username, password, errorHtml, c,
                        conn, out) == false)
                return;
            session = req.getSession(true);
            session.putValue("Shipping.username", username);
            session.putValue("Shipping.password", password);
            showShippingOptionsPage(out, shippingOptionsHtml);
            c.putConnection(conn);
            out.close();
        }catch(Exception ex){
                if(c != null && conn != null)
                {
                    c.putConnection(conn);
                    showErrorPage(out, errorHtml, ex.getMessage());
                }
            }
    }

    public void showShippingOptionsPage(PrintWriter out,
                                String pgName)
            throws Exception
    {
            PageUtil p = new PageUtil(pgName, out);
            p.printPage();
    }
}

ShippingOrderDetails.java

package Shipping;

import java.util.*;
import java.io.*;
import java.sql.*;
import javax.servlet.*;
import javax.servlet.http.*;
```

```java
import Utilities.*;

public class ShippingOrderDetails extends BaseShipping
{
    ConnectionPool c = null;

    static String errorHtml = BasePath + "shippingError.html";
    static String shippingOrderDetailsPage = BasePath + "shippingOrderDetails.html";
    public void doPost (HttpServletRequest req,
                        HttpServletResponse res)
    {
        Connection conn = null;
        PrintWriter out = null;
        try{
            HttpSession session;
            String orderId = "";
            if(c == null)
            {
                c = ConnectionPool.getInstance();
                c.initialize();
            }
            conn = c.getConnection();
            Enumeration paramNames = req.getParameterNames();
            while(paramNames.hasMoreElements())
            {
                String nm = (String)paramNames.nextElement();
                String vl = req.getParameterValues(nm)[0];
                if(nm.equalsIgnoreCase("orderId"))
                    orderId = vl;
            }
            out = res.getWriter();
            res.setContentType("text/html");
            session = req.getSession(false);
            if(session == null)
            {
                showErrorPage(out, errorHtml, "Invalid Session");
                return;
            }
            showShippingOrderDetailsPage(out, shippingOrderDetailsPage,
                        orderId, conn);
            c.putConnection(conn);
            out.close();
        }catch(Exception ex)
            {
```

```
            if(c != null && conn != null)
                c.putConnection(conn);
            showErrorPage(out, errorHtml, ex.getMessage());
        }
    }
}
public void showShippingOrderDetailsPage(PrintWriter out,
            String pgName, String orderId, Connection conn)
        throws Exception
{
        Statement stmt = conn.createStatement();
        String profileId = "", dateOrdered="", dateShipped="";
        String totalBilled = "", shipMethod="", status="";
        String querySQL = "SELECT profile_id, TO_CHAR(date_ordered,
                'DD-MON-YYYY'), TO_CHAR(date_shipped, 'DD-MON-YYYY'),
                total_billed, shipment_method, status
                FROM orders WHERE id=" + orderId;
        ResultSet rset = stmt.executeQuery(querySQL);
        while(rset.next())
        {
            profileId = rset.getString(1);
            dateOrdered = rset.getString(2);
            dateShipped = rset.getString(3);
            totalBilled = rset.getString(4);
            shipMethod = rset.getString(5);
            status = rset.getString(6);
        }
        if(dateShipped == null)
            dateShipped = "";
        if(shipMethod == null)
            shipMethod = "";
        Vector prodIds = new Vector();
        Vector prodNames = new Vector();
        Vector prodQuantities = new Vector();
        Vector prodPrices = new Vector();

        querySQL = "SELECT product_id, quantity, price FROM one_order
                    WHERE orders_id =" + orderId;
        rset = stmt.executeQuery(querySQL);
        while(rset.next())
        {
            prodIds.addElement(rset.getString(1));
            prodQuantities.addElement(rset.getString(2));
            prodPrices.addElement(rset.getString(3));
```

```
        }
        String baseQuerySQL = "SELECT name FROM products WHERE id=";
        int size = prodIds.size();
        for(int i=0; i<size; i++)
        {
            querySQL = baseQuerySQL + (String)prodIds.elementAt(i);
            rset = stmt.executeQuery(querySQL);
            while(rset.next())
            {
                prodNames.addElement(rset.getString(1));
            }
        }
        String tableRows = "";
        for(int i=0; i<size; i++)
        {
            String name = (String)prodNames.elementAt(i);
            String price = (String)prodPrices.elementAt(i);
            String qtty = (String)prodQuantities.elementAt(i);
            tableRows += "<TR><TD>" + name + "</TD><TD>" +price +
                "</TD><TD>" + qtty + "</TD></TR>";
        }
        stmt.close();

        dateShipped = "<INPUT TYPE='text' NAME='dateShipped' SIZE='14'
                    VALUE='" + dateShipped + "'>";
        shipMethod = "<INPUT TYPE='text' NAME='shipMethod' SIZE='14'
                    VALUE='" + shipMethod + "'>";
        status = "<INPUT TYPE='text' NAME='status' SIZE='14' VALUE='"
                + status + "'>";
        orderId = "<INPUT TYPE='hidden' NAME='orderId' VALUE='" +
                orderId + "'>";

        PageUtil pu = new PageUtil(pgName, out);
        pu.setReplaceItem("<VAR_TABLE_ROWS>", tableRows);
        pu.setReplaceItem("<VAR_TOTAL_BILLED>", totalBilled);
        pu.setReplaceItem("<VAR_DATE_ORDERED>", dateOrdered);
        pu.setReplaceItem("<VAR_DATE_SHIPPED>", dateShipped);
        pu.setReplaceItem("<VAR_ORDER_ID>", orderId);
        pu.setReplaceItem("<VAR_SHIP_METHOD>", shipMethod);
        pu.setReplaceItem("<VAR_STATUS>", status);
        pu.printPage();
    }
}
```

Document Root Html Files

shipping.html

```
<HTML>
<FRAMESET COLS='100, *' BORDER='0'>
    <FRAME NAME='left' SRC='blank.html'>
    <FRAME NAME='right' SRC='shippingLogin.html'>
</FRAMESET>
<BODY>
</BODY>
</HTML>
```

shippingLogin.html

```
<HTML>
<BODY BGCOLOR='#FFFFFF'>
  <FORM ACTION='/newZone/Shipping.ShippingLogin' METHOD='POST'>
      <TABLE>
          <TR><TD WIDTH='500'>
              This is the login screen of the shipping system. This system allows
you to look at and modify the shipping status of all orders placed by customers.
You need an administrative password to use this system.
          </TD></TR>
      </TABLE>
      <TABLE>
              <TR><TD>Login</TD><TD><INPUT TYPE='text' NAME='username'
                  SIZE='10'></TD></TR>
              <TR><TD>Password</TD><TD><INPUT TYPE='password' NAME='password'
                  SIZE='10'></TD></TR>
              <TR><TD></TD><TD ALIGN='right'><INPUT TYPE='submit' NAME='submit'
                  VALUE='Submit' SIZE='10'></TD></TR>
      </TABLE>
  </FORM>
</BODY>
</HTML>
```

shippingSignoff.html

```
<HTML><HEAD></HEAD>
<BODY BGCOLOR='#6699CC'>
    <FORM ACTION='/newZone/Shipping.SignOff'>
      <INPUT TYPE='submit' NAME='submit' VALUE='Logout'>
    </FORM>
</BODY>
</HTML>
```

Other Html Files and Templates

selectShippingOrders.html

```
<HTML><HEAD></HEAD>
<BODY BGCOLOR='#FFFFFF'>
<FORM ACTION='/newZone/Shipping.ModifyOrders' METHOD='POST'>
<TABLE>
    <TR><TD WIDTH='400'>
Using this form you can update multiple orders at a time. The values you suppply
below will be  applied to all products selected in the list below.
    </TD></TR>
</TABLE>

<TABLE>
    <TR><TD>Shipping Date</TD><TD><INPUT TYPE='text' NAME='dateShipped'
            SIZE='14' VALUE=''> [DD-MON-YYYY]</TD></TR>
    <TR><TD>Shipping Method</TD><TD><INPUT TYPE='text' NAME='shipMethod'
            SIZE='14' VALUE=''></TD></TR>
    <TR><TD>Status</TD><TD><INPUT TYPE='text' NAME='status' SIZE='14'
            VALUE='SHIPPED'></TD></TR>
</TABLE>

<CENTER>
<TABLE>
    <TR><TD WIDTH='450'>
Select one or more orders from the list below to apply the shipping date, method
and status specified above.
    </TD></TR>
</TABLE>
<BR>
<TABLE>
    <TR><TD>
            <SELECT NAME='orderIds' SIZE='8' MULTIPLE>
<VAR_ORDER_OPTIONS>
            </SELECT>
    </TD></TR>
    <TR><TD ALIGN='right'>
        <INPUT TYPE='submit' NAME='submit' VALUE='Submit'>
    </TD></TR>
</TABLE>
</CENTER>
</BODY>
</HTML>
```

shippingError.html

```
<HTML><HEAD></HEAD>
<BODY BGCOLOR='#FFFFFF'>
<H1><CENTER><B>Error!</B></CENTER></H1>
<P>
The following error occured:
<P>
<ERROR_MSG>
<P>
</BODY>
</HTML>
```

shippingOptions.html

```
<HTML><HEAD></HEAD>
<SCRIPT>
    function showSignOff()
    {
        parent.left.location.replace('HTTP_VALUE/shippingSignoff.html');
    }
</SCRIPT>
<BODY BGCOLOR='#FFFFFF' onLoad='showSignOff();'>
    <TABLE>
        <TR><TD WIDTH='400'>
            You can view/modify shipping orders using this form.
            If you want to modify one order at a time and know the id of the order
you can use the first option below.
            If you want to do batch updates you can use the next two options.
        </TD></TR>
    </TABLE>
<P>
    <FORM ACTION='/newZone/Shipping.ShippingOrderDetails' METHOD='POST'>
        Get by order id: <INPUT TYPE='text' NAME='orderId' VALUE='' SIZE='6'>
<INPUT TYPE='submit' NAME='submit' VALUE='Go'>
    </FORM>
    <BR>
    <A HREF='/newZone/Shipping.SelectShippingOrders?type=all'>Show all
orders</ABR>
    <A HREF='/newZone/Shipping.SelectShippingOrders?type=unshipped'>Show orders
not shipped so far</ABR>
</BODY>
</HTML>
```

shippingOrderDetails.html

```
<HTML><HEAD></HEAD>
<BODY BGCOLOR='#FFFFFF'>
    <FORM ACTION='/newZone/Shipping.ModifyShippingOrder' METHOD='POST'>
<VAR_ORDER_ID>
Total charges: $
<VAR_TOTAL_BILLED>
<BR>
<TABLE>
    <TR><TD>
        <TABLE>
            <TR><TD>Date Ordered: </TD><TD>
<VAR_DATE_ORDERED>
            </TD><TD>
            Date Shipped:</TD><TD>
<VAR_DATE_SHIPPED>
[DD-MON-YYYY]
            </TD></TR>
            <TR><TD>Shipment Method:</TD><TD>
<VAR_SHIP_METHOD>
            </TD><TD>
            Status:</TD><TD>
<VAR_STATUS>
            </TD></TR>
        </TABLE>
    </TD></TR>
    <TR><TD>
     <TABLE BORDER='2'>
        <TH>Item</TH><TH>Price</TH><TH>Quantity</TH>
<VAR_TABLE_ROWS>
     </TABLE>
    </TD></TR>
    <TR><TD ALIGN='right'>
            <INPUT TYPE='submit' NAME='submit' VALUE='Submit'>
    </TD></TR>
</TABLE>
</BODY>
</HTML>

shippingOrderUpdated.html

<HTML>
<BODY>
    Shipping order Updated!
</BODY>
</HTML>
```

Reporting System

Java Files

BaseReporting.java

```java
package Reporting;

import java.util.*;
import java.io.*;
import java.sql.*;
import javax.servlet.*;
import javax.servlet.http.*;
import Utilities.*;

public class BaseReporting extends HttpServlet
{
    static String BasePath = "HTML_DIRECTORY";
    static boolean debugOn = true;

    public boolean validPassword(String username, String password,
                String errorHtml, ConnectionPool c, Connection conn,
                PrintWriter out)
    {
        boolean isValid = true;
        if(username == null || password == null)
            isValid = false;
        Authenticator a = new Authenticator();
        if(a.isValidAdmin(username, password, conn) == false)
            isValid = false;
        if(isValid == false)
        {
            c.putConnection(conn);
            showErrorPage(out, errorHtml, "Invalid Username/Password");
            return false;
        }
        else
           return true;
    }

    public void showErrorPage(PrintWriter out, String pgName, String value)
    {
        PageUtil p = new PageUtil(pgName, out);
        p.setReplaceItem("<ERROR_MSG>", value);
        p.printPage();
```

```
        }

        public PrintStream initializeDebugFile(String s)
        {
            PrintStream pos = null;
            try
            {
                if(debugOn == false)
                    return null;
                pos = new PrintStream(new FileOutputStream(new File(s)));
            }catch(Exception ex){}
            return pos;
        }
        public void debug(String s, PrintStream pos)
        {
            try
            {
                if(debugOn == false)
                    return;
                pos.println(s);
            }catch(Exception ex){}
        }
    }

DistributionReporting.java

package Reporting;

import java.util.*;
import java.io.*;
import java.sql.*;
import javax.servlet.*;
import javax.servlet.http.*;
import Utilities.*;

public class DistributionReporting extends BaseReporting
{
    static String errorHtml = BasePath + "reportingError.html";
    static String userDistReportingPage = BasePath + "userDistReporting.html";
    static String salesDistReportingPage = BasePath + "salesDistReporting.html";

    public void doGet (HttpServletRequest req,
                       HttpServletResponse res)
    {
      PrintWriter out = null;
      try{
          HttpSession session;
```

```java
            String  type="";
            Enumeration paramNames = req.getParameterNames();
            while(paramNames.hasMoreElements())
            {
                    String nm = (String)paramNames.nextElement();
                    String vl = req.getParameterValues(nm)[0];
                    if(nm.equalsIgnoreCase("type"))
                        type = vl;
            }
            out = res.getWriter();
            res.setContentType("text/html");
            session = req.getSession(false);
            if(session == null)
            {
                    showErrorPage(out, errorHtml, "Invalid Session");
                    return;
            }
            showDistributionReportingPage(salesDistReportingPage,
                    userDistReportingPage, type,out);
            out.close();
        }catch(Exception ex)
        {
                showErrorPage(out, errorHtml, ex.getMessage());
        }
    }
    public void showDistributionReportingPage(String salesDistPage,
            String userDistPage,
            String type, PrintWriter out)
        throws Exception
    {
            String pgName="";
            if(type.equalsIgnoreCase("sales"))
                pgName = salesDistPage;
            if(type.equalsIgnoreCase("user"))
                pgName = userDistPage;
            PageUtil pu = new PageUtil(pgName, out);
            pu.printPage();
    }
}

FrequencyReporting.java

package Reporting;

import java.util.*;
```

```java
import java.io.*;
import java.sql.*;
import javax.servlet.*;
import javax.servlet.http.*;
import Utilities.*;

public class FrequencyReporting extends BaseReporting
{
    static String errorHtml = BasePath + "reportingError.html";
    static String userFreqReportingPage = BasePath + "userFreqReporting.html";
    static String salesFreqReportingPage = BasePath + "salesFreqReporting.html";

    public void doGet (HttpServletRequest req,
                       HttpServletResponse res)
    {
      PrintWriter out = null;
      try{
          HttpSession session;
          String  type="";
          Enumeration paramNames = req.getParameterNames();
          while(paramNames.hasMoreElements())
          {
                String nm = (String)paramNames.nextElement();
                String vl = req.getParameterValues(nm)[0];
                if(nm.equalsIgnoreCase("type"))
                    type = vl;
          }
          out = res.getWriter();
          res.setContentType("text/html");
          session = req.getSession(false);
          if(session == null)
          {
                showErrorPage(out, errorHtml, "Invalid Session");
                return;
          }
          showFrequencyReportingPage(salesFreqReportingPage,
                  userFreqReportingPage, type,out);
          out.close();
      }catch(Exception ex)
        {
              showErrorPage(out, errorHtml, ex.getMessage());
        }
    }
    public void showFrequencyReportingPage(String salesFreqPage,
            String userFreqPage,
```

```java
                      String type, PrintWriter out)
              throws Exception
      {

          String pgName="";
          if(type.equalsIgnoreCase("sales"))
              pgName = salesFreqPage;
          if(type.equalsIgnoreCase("user"))
              pgName = userFreqPage;
          PageUtil pu = new PageUtil(pgName, out);
          pu.printPage();

      }
}
```

ReportingLogin.java

```java
package Reporting;

import java.util.*;
import java.io.*;
import java.sql.*;
import javax.servlet.*;
import javax.servlet.http.*;
import Utilities.*;

public class ReportingLogin extends BaseReporting
{
    ConnectionPool c = null;
    static String reportingOptionsHtml = BasePath + "reportingOptions.html";
    static String errorHtml = BasePath + "reportingError.html";

    public void doPost (HttpServletRequest req,
                        HttpServletResponse res)
    {
      Connection conn = null;
      PrintWriter out=null;
      try{
          HttpSession session;

          String username="", password="";
          if(c == null)
          {
              c = ConnectionPool.getInstance();
              c.initialize();
          }
          conn = c.getConnection();
          Enumeration paramNames = req.getParameterNames();
          while(paramNames.hasMoreElements())
```

```
        {
                String nm = (String)paramNames.nextElement();
                String vl = req.getParameterValues(nm)[0];
                if(nm.equalsIgnoreCase("username"))
                    username = vl;
                if(nm.equalsIgnoreCase("password"))
                    password = vl;
        }
        out = res.getWriter();
        res.setContentType("text/html");
        if(validPassword(username, password, errorHtml, c,
                        conn, out) == false)
            return;
        session = req.getSession(true);
        session.putValue("Reporting.username", username);
        session.putValue("Reporting.password", password);
        showReportingOptionsPage(out, reportingOptionsHtml);
        c.putConnection(conn);
        out.close();
    }catch(Exception ex){
            if(c != null && conn != null)
            {
                c.putConnection(conn);
                showErrorPage(out, errorHtml, ex.getMessage());
            }
        }
    }

    public void showReportingOptionsPage(PrintWriter out,
                            String pgName)
        throws Exception
    {
        PageUtil p = new PageUtil(pgName, out);
        p.printPage();
    }
}

SalesDistribution.java

package Reporting;

import java.util.*;
import java.io.*;
import java.sql.*;
import javax.servlet.*;
import javax.servlet.http.*;
```

```java
import Utilities.*;

public class SalesDistribution extends BaseReporting
{
    ConnectionPool c = null;
    static String errorHtml = BasePath + "reportingError.html";
    static String salesDistributionPage = BasePath + "salesDistribution.html";

    public void doGet (HttpServletRequest req,
                       HttpServletResponse res)
    {
      Connection conn = null;
      PrintWriter out = null;
      try{
          HttpSession session;
          String  type="";
          String  from="";
          String  to="";
          if(c == null)
          {
              c = ConnectionPool.getInstance();
              c.initialize();
          }
          conn = c.getConnection();
          Enumeration paramNames = req.getParameterNames();
          while(paramNames.hasMoreElements())
          {
              String nm = (String)paramNames.nextElement();
              String vl = req.getParameterValues(nm)[0];
              if(nm.equalsIgnoreCase("type"))
                  type = vl;
              if(nm.equalsIgnoreCase("from"))
                  from = vl;
              if(nm.equalsIgnoreCase("to"))
                  to = vl;
          }
          out = res.getWriter();
          res.setContentType("text/html");
          session = req.getSession(false);
          if(session == null)
          {
              showErrorPage(out, errorHtml, "Invalid Session");
              return;
          }
          showSalesDistributionPage(salesDistributionPage, type,out,
```

```
                    from, to, conn);
          c.putConnection(conn);
          out.close();
      }catch(Exception ex)
        {
              if(c != null && conn != null)
                  c.putConnection(conn);
              showErrorPage(out, errorHtml, ex.getMessage());
        }
    }
public void showSalesDistributionPage(String pgName, String type,
            PrintWriter out,
            String from, String to, Connection conn)
        throws Exception
  {

        if(type.equalsIgnoreCase("product"))
            showProductSalesDistributionPage(salesDistributionPage,
                type,out, from, to, conn);
        else
            showCategorySalesDistributionPage(salesDistributionPage,
                type,out, from, to, conn);
    }
public void showCategorySalesDistributionPage(String pgName, String type,
            PrintWriter out,
            String from, String to, Connection conn)
        throws Exception
  {

      /* This code is similar to the one for product sales distribution -
          you can implement it based on the kind of category reporting you
          are most interested in—each top level categories or categories
          at lower levels */
    }
public void showProductSalesDistributionPage(String pgName, String type,
            PrintWriter out,
            String from, String to, Connection conn)
        throws Exception
  {

        Statement stmt = conn.createStatement();
        ResultSet rset;
        String querySQL = "";

        Hashtable productNames = new Hashtable();
        Hashtable productQuantities = new Hashtable();
        Hashtable productRevenues = new Hashtable();
```

```
querySQL = "SELECT id, name FROM products";
rset = stmt.executeQuery(querySQL);
while(rset.next())
{
    productNames.put(rset.getString(1), rset.getString(2));
}


Vector orderIds = new Vector();
querySQL = "SELECT id FROM orders WHERE date_ordered BETWEEN
  TO_DATE('" + from + "', 'DD-MON-YYYY') AND
  TO_DATE('" + to + "', 'DD-MON-YYYY')";
rset = stmt.executeQuery(querySQL);
while(rset.next())
{
    orderIds.addElement(rset.getString(1));
}
int size = orderIds.size();
for(int i=0; i<size; i++)
{
    String orderId = (String)orderIds.elementAt(i);
    querySQL = "SELECT product_id, quantity, price FROM one_order
        WHERE orders_id=" + orderId;
    rset = stmt.executeQuery(querySQL);
    while(rset.next())
    {
        String prodId = rset.getString(1);
        int q = rset.getInt(2);
        double p = rset.getDouble(3);
        Integer pq = (Integer)productQuantities.get(prodId);
        if(pq == null)
                pq = new Integer(q);
        else
                pq = new Integer(q + pq.intValue());
        productQuantities.put(prodId, pq);
        Double pr = (Double)productRevenues.get(prodId);
        if(pr == null)
            pr = new Double(p*q);
        else
            pr = new Double(p*q + pr.doubleValue());
        productRevenues.put(prodId, pr);
    }
}
stmt.close();
String tableRows = "<TH>Product Id</TH><TH>Product Name</TH>
```

```
                    <TH>Quantity</TH><TH>Revenue</TH>";
        Enumeration e = productNames.keys();
        while(e.hasMoreElements())
        {
            String key = (String)e.nextElement();
            String name = (String)productNames.get(key);
            Double r = (Double)productRevenues.get(key);
            if(r == null)
                r = new Double(0.0);
            String revenue = r.toString();
            Integer q = (Integer)productQuantities.get(key);
            if(q == null)
                q = new Integer(0);
            String quantity = q.toString();
            tableRows += "<TR><TD>" + key + "</TD><TD>" + name + "</TD><TD>"
                + quantity + "</TD><TD ALIGN='right'>$" + revenue + "</TD></TR>";
        }

        stmt.close();
        PageUtil pu = new PageUtil(pgName, out);
        pu.setReplaceItem("<VAR_TABLE_ROWS>", tableRows);
        pu.printPage();
    }
}


SalesFrequency.java

package Reporting;

import java.util.*;
import java.io.*;
import java.sql.*;
import javax.servlet.*;
import javax.servlet.http.*;
import Utilities.*;

public class SalesFrequency extends BaseReporting
{
    ConnectionPool c = null;
    static String errorHtml = BasePath + "reportingError.html";
    static String salesFrequencyPage = BasePath + "salesFrequency.html";
    static String[] allMonths = {"JAN", "FEB", "MAR", "APR", "MAY",
            "JUN", "JUL", "AUG", "SEP", "OCT", "NOV", "DEC"};

    public void doGet (HttpServletRequest req,
                    HttpServletResponse res)
    {
```

```java
    Connection conn = null;
    PrintWriter out = null;
    try{
        HttpSession session;
        String  type="";
        String  from="";
        String  to="";
        if(c == null)
        {
            c = ConnectionPool.getInstance();
            c.initialize();
        }
        conn = c.getConnection();
        Enumeration paramNames = req.getParameterNames();
        while(paramNames.hasMoreElements())
        {
            String nm = (String)paramNames.nextElement();
            String vl = req.getParameterValues(nm)[0];
            if(nm.equalsIgnoreCase("type"))
                type = vl;
            if(nm.equalsIgnoreCase("from"))
                from = vl;
            if(nm.equalsIgnoreCase("to"))
                to = vl;
        }
        out = res.getWriter();
        res.setContentType("text/html");
        session = req.getSession(false);
        if(session == null)
        {
            showErrorPage(out, errorHtml, "Invalid Session");
            return;
        }
        showSalesFrequencyPage(salesFrequencyPage, type,from, to, out, conn);
        c.putConnection(conn);
        out.close();
    }catch(Exception ex)
        {
            if(c != null && conn != null)
                c.putConnection(conn);
            showErrorPage(out, errorHtml, ex.getMessage());
        }
}
public void showSalesFrequencyPage(String pgName, String type, String from,
```

```
              String to, PrintWriter out, Connection conn)
        throws Exception
{
    java.util.Date startDate;
    java.util.Date endDate;
    java.util.Date curDate;
    java.util.Date nextDate;

    startDate = getDate(from);
    endDate = getDate(to);
    curDate = startDate;
    nextDate = startDate;

    String tableRows = "<TH>From</TH><TH>To</TH><TH>Revenue</TH>";
    while(nextDate.before(endDate))
    {
        nextDate = getNextDate(curDate, type);
        int month = curDate.getMonth();
        int date = curDate.getDate();
        int year = curDate.getYear() + 1900;
        int nextMonth = nextDate.getMonth();
        int nextDt = nextDate.getDate();
        int nextYear = nextDate.getYear() + 1900;

        String fromDate = getDate(date, month, year);
        String toDate = getDate(nextDt, nextMonth, nextYear);
        double count = getFrequency(fromDate, toDate, conn);
        curDate = nextDate;
        tableRows += "<TR><TD>" + fromDate + "</TD><TD>" + toDate +
            "</TD><TD ALIGN='right'>$" + count + "</TD></TR>";
    }
    PageUtil pu = new PageUtil(pgName, out);
    pu.setReplaceItem("<VAR_TABLE_ROWS>", tableRows);
    pu.printPage();
}
public double getFrequency(String from, String to, Connection conn)
    throws Exception
{
    Statement stmt = conn.createStatement();
    ResultSet rset;
    String querySQL = "";
    querySQL = "SELECT SUM(total_billed) FROM orders WHERE date_ordered
        BETWEEN TO_DATE('" + from + "', 'DD-MON-YYYY') AND
        TO_DATE('" + to + "','DD-MON-YYYY')";
    rset = stmt.executeQuery(querySQL);
```

```
              rset.next();
              double count = rset.getDouble(1);
              stmt.close();
              return count;
}
    public java.util.Date getNextDate(java.util.Date curDate, String type)
    {
          int month = curDate.getMonth();
          int date = curDate.getDate();
          int year = curDate.getYear() + 1900;
          Calendar cal;
          cal = new GregorianCalendar(year, month, date, 0, 0, 0);
          if(type.equalsIgnoreCase("daily"))
             cal.add(Calendar.DATE, 1);
          if(type.equalsIgnoreCase("weekly"))
             cal.add(Calendar.DATE, 7);
          if(type.equalsIgnoreCase("monthly"))
             cal.add(Calendar.MONTH, 1);
          if(type.equalsIgnoreCase("yearly"))
             cal.add(Calendar.YEAR, 1);

          month = cal.get(Calendar.MONTH);
          date = cal.get(Calendar.DATE);
          year = cal.get(Calendar.YEAR)-1900;
          java.util.Date toRet = new  java.util.Date(year, month, date);
          return toRet;
    }
public String getDate(int date, int month, int year)
     throws Exception
{
    String retDate = "";
    retDate += (new Integer(date)).toString() + "-";
    retDate += getMonth(month) + "-";
    retDate += (new Integer(year)).toString();
    return retDate;
}
public java.util.Date getDate(String theDate)
     throws Exception
{
    StringTokenizer st = new StringTokenizer(theDate, "-");
    int dt = (new Integer(st.nextToken())).intValue();
    int mon = getMonth(st.nextToken());
    int yr = (new Integer(st.nextToken())).intValue()-1900;
    java.util.Date retDate = new java.util.Date(yr, mon, dt);
```

```
                return retDate;
        }
        public String getMonth(int i)
        {
                return allMonths[i];
        }
        public int getMonth(String s)
        {
                int len = allMonths.length;
                int mon = -1;
                for(int i=0; i<len; i++)
                {
                        if(s.equalsIgnoreCase(allMonths[i]))
                        {
                                mon = i;
                                break;
                        }
                }
                return mon;
        }
}
```

UserDistribution.java

```
package Reporting;

import java.util.*;
import java.io.*;
import java.sql.*;
import javax.servlet.*;
import javax.servlet.http.*;
import Utilities.*;

public class UserDistribution extends BaseReporting
{
    ConnectionPool c = null;
    static String errorHtml = BasePath + "reportingError.html";
    static String userDistributionPage = BasePath + "userDistribution.html";

    public void doGet (HttpServletRequest req,
                        HttpServletResponse res)
    {
      Connection conn = null;
      PrintWriter out = null;
      try{
          HttpSession session;
```

```
            String   type="";
            String   from="";
            String   to="";
            if(c == null)
            {
                c = ConnectionPool.getInstance();
                c.initialize();
            }
            conn = c.getConnection();
            Enumeration paramNames = req.getParameterNames();
            while(paramNames.hasMoreElements())
            {
                String nm = (String)paramNames.nextElement();
                String vl = req.getParameterValues(nm)[0];
                if(nm.equalsIgnoreCase("type"))
                    type = vl;
                if(nm.equalsIgnoreCase("from"))
                    from = vl;
                if(nm.equalsIgnoreCase("to"))
                    to = vl;
            }
            out = res.getWriter();
            res.setContentType("text/html");
            session = req.getSession(false);
            if(session == null)
            {
                showErrorPage(out, errorHtml, "Invalid Session");
                return;
            }
            showUserDistributionPage(userDistributionPage,
                    type,out, from, to, conn);
            c.putConnection(conn);
            out.close();
        }catch(Exception ex)
        {
            if(c != null && conn != null)
                c.putConnection(conn);
            showErrorPage(out, errorHtml, ex.getMessage());
        }
    }
public void showUserDistributionPage(String pgName,
            String type, PrintWriter out,
            String from, String to, Connection conn)
        throws Exception
```

```
{
    Statement stmt = conn.createStatement();
    ResultSet rset;
    String querySQL = "";
    String tableRows = "<TH>" + type + "</TH><TH>Total Users</TH>";
    Hashtable allIds = new Hashtable();
    Hashtable ht = new Hashtable();
    Vector typeValues = new Vector();

    querySQL = "SELECT id FROM profiles WHERE registration_date
        BETWEEN TO_DATE('" + from + "', 'DD-MON-YYYY') AND
        TO_DATE('" + to + "','DD-MON-YYYY')";
    rset = stmt.executeQuery(querySQL);
    while(rset.next())
    {
        allIds.put(rset.getString(1), "NO_VAL");
    }
    querySQL = "SELECT profile_id, " + type + " FROM addresses
                WHERE type='SHIPPING'";
    rset = stmt.executeQuery(querySQL);
    while(rset.next())
    {
        String profId = rset.getString(1);
        String stateOrZip = rset.getString(2);
        /* If profileId is not in list of people who registered between given
           dates, don't count it. */
        if(allIds.get(profId) == null)
            continue;

        Integer total = (Integer)ht.get(stateOrZip);
        if(total == null)
            total = new Integer(1);
        else
            total = new Integer(total.intValue() + 1);
        ht.put(stateOrZip, total);
    }
    //Now it contains all stateOrZip names and total users in that state/zip

    Enumeration e = ht.keys();
    while(e.hasMoreElements())
    {
        String key = (String)e.nextElement();
        Integer val = (Integer)ht.get(key);
        tableRows += "<TR><TD>" + key + "</TD><TD ALIGN='right'>" +
            val + "</TD></TR>";
```

```
            }
            stmt.close();
            PageUtil pu = new PageUtil(pgName, out);
            pu.setReplaceItem("<VAR_TABLE_ROWS>", tableRows);
            pu.printPage();
        }
    }

UserFrequency.java

package Reporting;

import java.util.*;
import java.io.*;
import java.sql.*;
import javax.servlet.*;
import javax.servlet.http.*;
import Utilities.*;

public class UserFrequency extends BaseReporting
{
    ConnectionPool c = null;
    static String errorHtml = BasePath + "reportingError.html";
    static String userFrequencyPage = BasePath + "userFrequency.html";
    static String[] allMonths = {"JAN", "FEB", "MAR", "APR", "MAY", "JUN", "JUL", "AUG",
                                 "SEP", "OCT", "NOV", "DEC"};

    public void doGet (HttpServletRequest req,
                       HttpServletResponse res)
    {
      Connection conn = null;
      PrintWriter out = null;
      try{
          HttpSession session;
          String  type="";
          String  from="";
          String  to="";
          if(c == null)
          {
              c = ConnectionPool.getInstance();
              c.initialize();
          }
          conn = c.getConnection();
          Enumeration paramNames = req.getParameterNames();
          while(paramNames.hasMoreElements())
          {
```

```java
                String nm = (String)paramNames.nextElement();
                String vl = req.getParameterValues(nm)[0];
                if(nm.equalsIgnoreCase("type"))
                    type = vl;
                if(nm.equalsIgnoreCase("from"))
                    from = vl;
                if(nm.equalsIgnoreCase("to"))
                    to = vl;
            }
        out = res.getWriter();
        res.setContentType("text/html");
        session = req.getSession(false);
        if(session == null)
        {
            showErrorPage(out, errorHtml, "Invalid Session");
            return;
        }
        showUserFrequencyPage(userFrequencyPage, type,from, to, out, conn);
        c.putConnection(conn);
        out.close();
    }catch(Exception ex)
        {
            if(c != null && conn != null)
                c.putConnection(conn);
            showErrorPage(out, errorHtml, ex.getMessage());
        }
    }
    public void showUserFrequencyPage(String pgName, String type, String from,
                String to, PrintWriter out, Connection conn)
        throws Exception
    {
        java.util.Date startDate;
        java.util.Date endDate;
        java.util.Date curDate;
        java.util.Date nextDate;

        startDate = getDate(from);
        endDate = getDate(to);
        curDate = startDate;
        nextDate = startDate;

        String tableRows = "<TH>From</TH><TH>To</TH><TH>Total
Registrations</TH>";
        while(nextDate.before(endDate))
        {
```

```java
                nextDate = getNextDate(curDate, type);
                int month = curDate.getMonth();
                int date = curDate.getDate();
                int year = curDate.getYear() + 1900;
                int nextMonth = nextDate.getMonth();
                int nextDt = nextDate.getDate();
                int nextYear = nextDate.getYear() + 1900;

                String fromDate = getDate(date, month, year);
                String toDate = getDate(nextDt, nextMonth, nextYear);
                int count = getFrequency(fromDate, toDate, conn);
                curDate = nextDate;
                tableRows += "<TR><TD>" + fromDate + "</TD><TD>" + toDate +
                    "</TD><TD ALIGN='right'>" + count + "</TD></TR>";
        }
        PageUtil pu = new PageUtil(pgName, out);
        pu.setReplaceItem("<VAR_TABLE_ROWS>", tableRows);
        pu.printPage();
}
public int getFrequency(String from, String to, Connection conn)
        throws Exception
{
        Statement stmt = conn.createStatement();
        ResultSet rset;
        String querySQL = "";
        querySQL = "SELECT count(*) FROM profiles WHERE registration_date
            BETWEEN TO_DATE('" + from + "', 'DD-MON-YYYY') AND
            TO_DATE('" + to + "','DD-MON-YYYY')";
        rset = stmt.executeQuery(querySQL);
        rset.next();
        int count = rset.getInt(1);
        stmt.close();
        return count;
}
    public java.util.Date getNextDate(java.util.Date curDate, String type)
    {
        int month = curDate.getMonth();
        int date = curDate.getDate();
        int year = curDate.getYear() + 1900;
        Calendar cal;
        cal = new GregorianCalendar(year, month, date, 0, 0, 0);
        if(type.equalsIgnoreCase("daily"))
           cal.add(Calendar.DATE, 1);
        if(type.equalsIgnoreCase("weekly"))
```

```
                  cal.add(Calendar.DATE, 7);
              if(type.equalsIgnoreCase("monthly"))
                  cal.add(Calendar.MONTH, 1);
              if(type.equalsIgnoreCase("yearly"))
                  cal.add(Calendar.YEAR, 1);

              month = cal.get(Calendar.MONTH);
              date = cal.get(Calendar.DATE);
              year = cal.get(Calendar.YEAR)-1900;
              java.util.Date toRet = new  java.util.Date(year, month, date);
              return toRet;
      }

public String getDate(int date, int month, int year)
      throws Exception
{
    String retDate = "";
    retDate += (new Integer(date)).toString() + "-";
    retDate += getMonth(month) + "-";
    retDate += (new Integer(year)).toString();
    return retDate;
}

public java.util.Date getDate(String theDate)
      throws Exception
{
    StringTokenizer st = new StringTokenizer(theDate, "-");
    int dt = (new Integer(st.nextToken())).intValue();
    int mon = getMonth(st.nextToken());
    int yr = (new Integer(st.nextToken())).intValue()-1900;
    java.util.Date retDate = new java.util.Date(yr, mon, dt);
    return retDate;
}
public String getMonth(int i)
{
    return allMonths[i];
}
public int getMonth(String s)
{
    int len = allMonths.length;
    int mon = -1;
    for(int i=0; i<len; i++)
    {
            if(s.equalsIgnoreCase(allMonths[i]))
```

```
            {
                    mon = i;
                    break;
            }
        }
        return mon;
    }
}
```

Document Root Html Files

reporting.html

```
<HTML>
<FRAMESET COLS='100, *' BORDER='0'>
    <FRAME NAME='left' SRC='blank.html'>
    <FRAME NAME='right' SRC='reportingLogin.html'>
</FRAMESET>
<BODY>
</BODY>
</HTML>
```

reportingLogin.html

```
<HTML>
<BODY BGCOLOR='#FFFFFF'>
  <FORM ACTION='/newZone/Reporting.ReportingLogin' METHOD='POST'>
      <TABLE>
          <TR><TD WIDTH='500'>
          This is the login screen of the reporting system. This system allows
you to analyze your user base and monitor sales of your products. You need an
administrative account to use this system.
          </TD></TR>
      </TABLE>
      <TABLE>
          <TR><TD>Login</TD><TD><INPUT TYPE='text' NAME='username'
              SIZE='10'></TD></TR>
          <TR><TD>Password</TD><TD><INPUT TYPE='password' NAME='password'
              SIZE='10'></TD></TR>
          <TR><TD></TD><TD ALIGN='right'><INPUT TYPE='submit' NAME='submit'
              VALUE='Submit' SIZE='10'></TD></TR>
      </TABLE>
  </FORM>
</BODY>
</HTML>
```

reportingSignoff.html

```
<HTML><HEAD></HEAD>
<BODY BGCOLOR='#6699CC'>
    <FORM ACTION='/newZone/Reporting.SignOff'>
      <INPUT TYPE='submit' NAME='submit' VALUE='Logout'>
    </FORM>
</BODY>
</HTML>
```

Other Html Files and Templates

reportingError.html

```
<HTML><HEAD></HEAD>
<BODY BGCOLOR='#FFFFFF'>
<H1><CENTER><B>Error!</B></CENTER></H1>
<P>
The following error occured:
<P>
<ERROR_MSG>
<P>
</BODY>
</HTML>
```

reportingOptions.html

```
<HTML><HEAD></HEAD>
<SCRIPT>
    function showSignOff()
    {
        parent.left.location.replace('HTTP_VALUE/reportingSignoff.html');
    }
</SCRIPT>
<BODY BGCOLOR='#FFFFFF' onLoad='showSignOff();'>
<TABLE>
    <TR><TD>
          Distribution analysis
        </TD><TD></TD></TR>
    <TR><TD></TD><TD>
    <TABLE>
      <TR><TD><A HREF=
        '/newZone/Reporting.DistributionReporting?type=user'>User
            base</A></TD><TD></TD></TR>
      <TR><TD></TD><TD WIDTH='350'>
      This report allows you to see the distribution of your customers by geographical
```

location. You can see how many customers have registered in each state or zip between given dates.
```
        </TD></TR>
        <TR><TD><A HREF=

'/newZone/Reporting.DistributionReporting?type=sales'>Sales</A></TD><TD></TD></TR>
        <TR><TD></TD><TD WIDTH='350'>
```
This report allows you to see the distribution of your sales by products/categries. You can see total sales from each product or category between given dates.
```
        </TD></TR>
      </TABLE>
    </TD></TR>
    <TR><TD>
          Time/Frequency analysis
        </TD><TD></TD></TR>
    <TR><TD></TD><TD>
    <TABLE>
      <TR><TD><A HREF=
          '/newZone/Reporting.FrequencyReporting?type=user'>User
Registrations</A></TD><TD></TD></TR>
        <TR><TD></TD><TD WIDTH='350'>
```
This report allows you to see the total number of registrations each week, each day, each month or each year between given dates.
```
        </TD></TR>
        <TR><TD><A HREF=
          '/newZone/Reporting.FrequencyReporting?type=sales'>Sales</A></TD><TD></TD></TR>
        <TR><TD></TD><TD WIDTH='350'>
```
This report allows you to see the total sales each week, each day, each month or each year between given dates.
```
        </TD></TR>
      </TABLE>
    </TD></TR>
</TABLE>
</BODY>
</HTML>

salesDistReporting.html

<HTML><HEAD></HEAD>
<BODY BGCOLOR='#FFFFFF'>

<FORM ACTION='/newZone/Reporting.SalesDistribution'>
  <TABLE>
      <TR><TD WIDTH='450'>
```

This form allows you to analyze your products/categories and see where most sales are concentrated. You can get total quantities sold and revenue generated for each product or category. You can also specify that you want to see only those products/categories that were sold between 2 given dates.

```
      </TD></TR>
    </TABLE>
    Select whether you want to see distribution by product or by category:<BR>
    <INPUT TYPE='radio' NAME='type' VALUE='product'> By Product<BR>
    <INPUT TYPE='radio' NAME='type' VALUE='category'> By Category<BR>
    From: <INPUT TYPE='text' NAME='from' VALUE='20-AUG-1999' SIZE='11'
          MAXLENGTH='11'> To: <INPUT TYPE='text' NAME='to' VALUE='31-AUG-1999'
          SIZE='11' MAXLENGTH='11'><BR>
<INPUT TYPE='submit' NAME='submit' VALUE='Submit'>
</FORM>

</BODY>
</HTML>
```

salesDistribution.html

```
<HTML><HEAD></HEAD>
<BODY BGCOLOR='#FFFFFF'>
<CENTER>
Sales distribution<BR><BR><BR>
   <TABLE BORDER='2'>
<VAR_TABLE_ROWS>
   </TABLE>
</CENTER>
</BODY>
</HTML>
```

salesFreqReporting.html

```
<HTML><HEAD></HEAD>
<BODY BGCOLOR='#FFFFFF'>

<FORM ACTION='/newZone/Reporting.SalesFrequency'>
   <TABLE>
      <TR><TD WIDTH='450'>
```

This form allows you to analyze the pattern of sales. You can see how much revenue was generated on your site each day, week, month or year between 2 given dates.</TD></TR>

```
   </TABLE>
   Select the frequency:<BR>
   <INPUT TYPE='radio' NAME='type' VALUE='daily'> Daily<BR>
   <INPUT TYPE='radio' NAME='type' VALUE='weekly'> Weekly<BR>
   <INPUT TYPE='radio' NAME='type' VALUE='monthly'> Monthly<BR>
```

```
    <INPUT TYPE='radio' NAME='type' VALUE='yearly'> Yearly<BR>
    From: <INPUT TYPE='text' NAME='from' VALUE='20-AUG-1999' SIZE='11'
        MAXLENGTH='11'>
    To: <INPUT TYPE='text' NAME='to' VALUE='31-AUG-1999' SIZE='11'
        MAXLENGTH='11'><BR>
<INPUT TYPE='submit' NAME='submit' VALUE='Submit'>
</FORM>

</BODY>
</HTML>

salesFrequency.html

<HTML><HEAD></HEAD>
<BODY BGCOLOR='#FFFFFF'>
<CENTER>
Sales Frequency<BR><BR><BR>
    <TABLE BORDER='2'>
<VAR_TABLE_ROWS>
    </TABLE>
</CENTER>
</BODY>
</HTML>

userDistReporting.html

<HTML><HEAD></HEAD>
<BODY BGCOLOR='#FFFFFF'>

<FORM ACTION='/newZone/Reporting.UserDistribution'>
    <TABLE>
        <TR><TD WIDTH='450'>
    This form allows you to analyze your user base and see where most are concen-
trated. You can get total number of users for each state or each zip code. You can
also specify that you want to see only those users who registered between 2 given
dates.
        </TD></TR>
    </TABLE>
    Select whether you want to see distribution by state or by zip:<BR>
    <INPUT TYPE='radio' NAME='type' VALUE='state'> By State<BR>
    <INPUT TYPE='radio' NAME='type' VALUE='zip'> By Zip<BR>
    From: <INPUT TYPE='text' NAME='from' VALUE='20-AUG-1999' SIZE='11' MAXLENGTH='11'>
    To: <INPUT TYPE='text' NAME='to' VALUE='31-AUG-1999' SIZE='11' MAXLENGTH='11'><BR>
<INPUT TYPE='submit' NAME='submit' VALUE='Submit'>
</FORM>

</BODY>
```

```
</HTML>
```

userDistribution.html

```
<HTML><HEAD></HEAD>
<BODY BGCOLOR='#FFFFFF'>
<CENTER>
User distribution<BR><BR><BR>
    <TABLE BORDER='2'>
<VAR_TABLE_ROWS>
    </TABLE>
</CENTER>
</BODY>
</HTML>
```

userFreqReporting.html

```
<HTML><HEAD></HEAD>
<BODY BGCOLOR='#FFFFFF'>

<FORM ACTION='/newZone/Reporting.UserFrequency'>
    <TABLE>
        <TR><TD WIDTH='450'>
        This form allows you to analyze the pattern of user registrations. You can
see how many users registered on your site each day, week, month or year between
2 given dates.</TD></TR>
    </TABLE>
    Select the frequency:<BR>
    <INPUT TYPE='radio' NAME='type' VALUE='daily'> Daily<BR>
    <INPUT TYPE='radio' NAME='type' VALUE='weekly'> Weekly<BR>
    <INPUT TYPE='radio' NAME='type' VALUE='monthly'> Monthly<BR>
    <INPUT TYPE='radio' NAME='type' VALUE='yearly'> Yearly<BR>
    From: <INPUT TYPE='text' NAME='from' VALUE='20-AUG-1999' SIZE='11'
MAXLENGTH='11'>
    To: <INPUT TYPE='text' NAME='to' VALUE='31-AUG-1999' SIZE='11'
MAXLENGTH='11'><BR>
<INPUT TYPE='submit' NAME='submit' VALUE='Submit'>
</FORM>

</BODY>
</HTML>
```

userFrequency.html

```
<HTML><HEAD></HEAD>
<BODY BGCOLOR='#FFFFFF'>
<CENTER>
User frequency<BR><BR><BR>
```

```
    <TABLE BORDER='2'>
<VAR_TABLE_ROWS>
    </TABLE>
</CENTER>
</BODY>
</HTML>
```

Utilities

Java Files

Authenticator.java

```
/** Authenticator.java
  * Centralized class for checking validity of usernames/passwords
  *
 **/
package Utilities;

import java.sql.*;
public class Authenticator
{
     public static int NEW_USER = 1;
     public static int INVALID_PASSWORD = 2;
     public static int VALID_PASSWORD = 3;
     public static int NEW_USER_COMING_AGAIN = 4;
      /* User who signed in but did not do checkout (hence information
         about C.card etc. was not captured-has to be treated like
         a new user, though not quite */
     public int verifyPassword(String username, String password,
                  Connection conn)
     {
         try{
                Statement stmt = conn.createStatement();
                String querySQL = "SELECT password, status FROM profiles
                     WHERE username='" + username + "'";
                ResultSet rset = stmt.executeQuery(querySQL);
                boolean foundUser = false;
                String dbPassword = "";
                String status = "";
                while(rset.next())
```

```
                        {
                            foundUser = true;
                            dbPassword = rset.getString(1);
                            status = rset.getString(2);
                        }
                        if(foundUser == false)
                            return NEW_USER;
                        if(password.equals(dbPassword))
                        {
                            if(status.equalsIgnoreCase("NEW_USER"))
                                return NEW_USER_COMING_AGAIN;
                            else
                                return VALID_PASSWORD;
                        }
                        return INVALID_PASSWORD;
                }catch(SQLException ex){}
                return INVALID_PASSWORD;
        }
        public boolean isValidAdmin(String username, String password,
                    Connection conn)
        {
            boolean isValid = false;
            try
            {
                Statement stmt = conn.createStatement();
                String toExec = "SELECT password FROM admins
                        WHERE username='" + username + "'";
                ResultSet rset = stmt.executeQuery(toExec);
                rset.next();
                String pwd = rset.getString(1);
                if(pwd.equalsIgnoreCase(password))
                    isValid = true;
            }catch(Exception ex){}
            return isValid;
        }
    }
}


ConnectionPool.java

package Utilities;

import java.io.*;
import java.sql.*;
import java.util.*;
public class ConnectionPool
```

```
{
    static final int MAX_CONNECTIONS = 10;
    static Vector connections = null;
    String hostName = "HOST";
    String login = "LOGIN", password="PASSWORD", sidName="SID", port="PORT";
    String connectString = "jdbc:oracle:thin:@" + hostName +
                                ":" + port + ":" + sidName;

    static ConnectionPool instance = null;
    public synchronized void removeAllConnections()
    {
        try{
            if(connections == null)
                return;
            int sz = connections.size();
            for(int i=0; i<sz; i++)
            {
                Connection c = (Connection)connections.elementAt(i);
                c.close();
            }
            connections.removeAllElements();
            connections = null;
        }catch(SQLException sqlE){}
    }
    public static synchronized ConnectionPool getInstance()
    {
        if(instance == null)
            instance = new ConnectionPool();
        return instance;
    }
    public synchronized void initialize()
    {
        if(connections == null)
        {
            try
            {
                DriverManager.registerDriver(new oracle.jdbc.driver.Ora-
cleDriver());

                connections = new Vector();
                int count = 0;
                while(count < MAX_CONNECTIONS)
                {
                    Connection c =
                        DriverManager.getConnection (
```

```
                                                    connectString,
                                                    login, password);
                                connections.addElement(c);
                                count++;
                        }
                }catch(SQLException sqlE){}
            }
        }
        public synchronized Connection getConnection()
        {
            Connection c = null;
            if(connections == null)
                return null;
            if(connections.size() > 0)
            {
                    c = (Connection)connections.elementAt(0);
                    connections.removeElementAt(0);
            }
            return c;
        }
        public synchronized void putConnection(Connection c)
        {
            connections.addElement(c);
            notifyAll();
        }
}


MailSender.java

package Utilities;

import java.io.*;
import java.net.InetAddress;
import java.util.Properties;
import java.util.Date;

import javax.mail.*;
import javax.mail.internet.*;
import javax.activation.*;

public class MailSender
{
    static String smtphost = "SMTPHOST";
    public void send(String from, String to, String mailHeader, String mailBody)
        throws Exception
    {
```

```
            Properties props = new Properties();
            props.put("mail.smtp.host", smtphost);
            Session session = Session.getDefaultInstance(props, null);
            Message msg = new MimeMessage(session);
            msg.setFrom(new InternetAddress(from));
            InternetAddress[] address = {new InternetAddress(to)};
            msg.setRecipients(Message.RecipientType.TO, address);
            msg.setSubject(mailHeader);
            msg.setSentDate(new Date());
            msg.setText(mailBody);
            Transport.send(msg);
        }
}


PageUtil.java

package Utilities;

import java.util.*;
import java.io.*;
public class PageUtil
{
    public String fName;
    public Hashtable replaceItems = null;
    public PrintWriter out;
    public PageUtil(String fileName, PrintWriter o)
    {
        fName = fileName;
        replaceItems = new Hashtable();
        out = o;
    }
    public void printPage()
    {
        try
        {
            File f = new File(fName);
            FileReader fr = new FileReader(f);
            BufferedReader bis = new BufferedReader(fr);
            String inpu;
            while((inpu = bis.readLine()) != null)
            {
                String repVal;
                repVal = (String)replaceItems.get(inpu);
                if(repVal == null)
                        out.println(inpu);
```

```
                else
                        out.println(repVal);
                }
                bis.close();
        }catch(Exception e){
            out.println("<HTML><HEAD></HEAD><BODY>");
            e.printStackTrace();
            out.println("</BODY></HTML>");
        }
    }
    public void setReplaceItem(String tag, String replaceWith)
    {
        replaceItems.put(tag, replaceWith);
    }
}
```

SQL for Creating Tables and Sequences

```
CREATE TABLE admins
    (id              NUMBER,
    name            VARCHAR2(40),
    email           VARCHAR2(40),
    username        VARCHAR2(20),
    password        VARCHAR2(20));

CREATE SEQUENCE admins_seq START WITH 1;
```

Sample Data:

```
INSERT INTO admins (id, name, email, username, password)
    VALUES(1, 'Vivek Sharma', 'vivek_sharma_99@yahoo.com', 'vsharma', 'cuSoon');

CREATE TABLE categories
    (id                 NUMBER PRIMARY KEY,
    category_id        NUMBER CONSTRAINT cat_cat_fkey REFERENCES categories,
                            - eg. Cans belong to Food which belongs to Grocery
                            - Cans would have Garbanzo beans as product
                            - Top levels have id = 0
    has_sub_categories NUMBER, - 0 if it contains products, 1 if sub_categories
    name               VARCHAR2(100),
    description_url    VARCHAR2(100),
    description        VARCHAR2(1000),
    search_keywords    VARCHAR2(200),
    last_modified_by   VARCHAR2(100),
```

```
    last_modification_date DATE
    );

INSERT INTO categories(id, category_id, has_sub_categories, name,
description_url, description, search_keywords, last_modified_by, last_modifica-
tion_date) VALUES (0, NULL, NULL, 'TOP LEVEL', NULL, NULL, NULL, NULL, NULL);

CREATE SEQUENCE categories_seq START WITH 1;

CREATE TABLE products
    (id                 NUMBER PRIMARY KEY,
    category_id         NUMBER CONSTRAINT cat_fkey REFERENCES categories,
    name                VARCHAR2(100),
    description_url     VARCHAR2(100),
    email               VARCHAR2(50), - email address for reporting problems
    price               NUMBER(10, 2),
    display_price       VARCHAR2(20),
    quantity_in_stock   NUMBER,
    danger_level        NUMBER, - percentage of quantity_in_stock
    description         VARCHAR2(1000),
    search_keywords     VARCHAR2(200),
    last_modified_by    VARCHAR2(100),
    last_modification_date DATE
    );

CREATE SEQUENCE products_seq START WITH 1;

CREATE TABLE profiles
    (id                 NUMBER PRIMARY KEY,
    username            VARCHAR2(20) CONSTRAINT  uq_user UNIQUE,
    password            VARCHAR2(20),
    registration_date DATE,
    first_name          VARCHAR2(30),
    last_name           VARCHAR2(30),
    phone               VARCHAR2(30),
    fax                 VARCHAR2(30),
    email               VARCHAR2(30),
    ccard_num           VARCHAR2(20),
    ccard_exp_date DATE,
    ccard_company   VARCHAR2(20), - Visa,Mastercard etc.
    status              VARCHAR2(20)  - NEW_USER
    );

CREATE SEQUENCE profiles_seq START WITH 1;

CREATE TABLE addresses
    (id                 NUMBER PRIMARY KEY,
```

```
    profile_id     NUMBER CONSTRAINT profile_fkey REFERENCES profiles,
    type           VARCHAR2(10),
    line1          VARCHAR2(100),
    line2          VARCHAR2(100),
    city           VARCHAR2(100),
    state          VARCHAR2(20),
    zip            VARCHAR2(20)
    );
CREATE SEQUENCE addresses_seq START WITH 1;

CREATE TABLE orders
  (id              NUMBER PRIMARY KEY,
   profile_id      NUMBER CONSTRAINT prof_key REFERENCES profiles,
   date_ordered    DATE,
   date_shipped    DATE,
   shipment_method VARCHAR2(20),
   status          VARCHAR2(30), - WITH_SHIPPING_DEPARTMENT, SHIPPED, INCOR-
RECT_ADDRESS
   payment_received NUMBER,
   total_billed    NUMBER(10, 2)
  );
CREATE SEQUENCE orders_seq START WITH 1;


CREATE TABLE one_order  - order is a reserved word
  (id              NUMBER PRIMARY KEY,
   orders_id       NUMBER CONSTRAINT ord_fkey REFERENCES orders,
   product_id      NUMBER CONSTRAINT prod_fkey REFERENCES products,
   quantity        NUMBER,
   price           NUMBER(10, 2));
CREATE SEQUENCE one_order_seq START WITH 1;

CREATE TABLE regular_cart
  (id              NUMBER PRIMARY KEY,
   profile_id      NUMBER CONSTRAINT prf_fkey REFERENCES profiles,
   product_id      NUMBER CONSTRAINT prd_fkey REFERENCES products,
   quantity        NUMBER
   );
CREATE SEQUENCE regular_cart_seq START WITH 1;
```

Index

CD-ROM Warranty

Addison-Wesley warrants the enclosed disc to be free of defects in materials and faulty workmanship under normal use for a period of ninety days after purchase. If a defect is discovered in the disc during this warranty period, a replacement disc can be obtained at no charge by sending the defective disc, postage prepaid, with proof of purchase to:

Editorial Department
Addison-Wesley Professional
Pearson Technology Group
75 Arlington Street, Suite 300
Boston, MA 02116
email: AWPro@awl.com

Addison-Wesley and Vivek Sharma and Rajiv Sharma make no warranty or representation, either expressed or implied, with respect to this software, its quality, performance, merchantability, or fitness for a particular purpose. In no event will Vivek Sharma and Rajiv Sharma or Addison-Wesley, its distributors, or dealers be liable for direct, indirect, special, incidental, or consequential damages arising out of the use or inability to use the software. The exclusion of implied royalties is not permitted in some states. Therefore, the above exclusion may not apply to you. This warranty provides you with specific legal rights. There may be other rights that you may have that vary from state to state. The contents of this CD-ROM are intended for non-commercial use only.

More information and updates are available at:
http://www.awl.com/cseng/titles/0-201-65764-3

Addison-Wesley Professional

How to Register Your Book

Register this Book

Visit: **http://www.aw.com/cseng/register**

Enter the ISBN*

Then you will receive:

- Notices and reminders about upcoming author appearances, tradeshows, and online chats with special guests
- Advanced notice of forthcoming editions of your book
- Book recommendations
- Notification about special contests and promotions throughout the year

*The ISBN can be found on the copyright page of the book

Visit our Web site

http://www.aw.com/cseng

When you think you've read enough, there's always more content for you at Addison-Wesley's web site. Our web site contains a directory of complete product information including:

- Chapters
- Exclusive author interviews
- Links to authors' pages
- Tables of contents
- Source code

You can also discover what tradeshows and conferences Addison-Wesley will be attending, read what others are saying about our titles, and find out where and when you can meet our authors and have them sign your book.

We encourage you to patronize the many fine retailers who stock Addison-Wesley titles. Visit our online directory to find stores near you.

Contact Us via Email

cepubprof@awl.com

Ask general questions about our books.
Sign up for our electronic mailing lists.
Submit corrections for our web site.

cepubeditors@awl.com

Submit a book proposal.
Send errata for a book.

cepubpublicity@awl.com

Request a review copy for a member of the media interested in reviewing new titles.

registration@awl.com

Request information about book registration.

Addison-Wesley Professional
One Jacob Way, Reading, Massachusetts 01867 USA
TEL 781-944-3700 • FAX 781-942-3076

Learning Resources
Centre